Crisis and order in English towns
1500–1700

Crisis and order in English towns
1500-1700
Essays in urban history

Edited by

Peter Clark
Fellow of Magdalen College, Oxford

and

Paul Slack
Lecturer in History, University of York

Routledge & Kegan Paul

First published 1972
by Routledge & Kegan Paul Ltd
Broadway House, 68–74 Carter Lane,
London EC4V5EL
Printed in Great Britain by
Butler & Tanner Ltd
Frome and London

ISBN 0 7100 7140 X

Foreword

W. G. Hoskins

I welcome this volume of essays in English urban history, covering as it does a variety of important towns and a variety of important problems over a period of some two centuries. Moreover, they are two centuries which Professor F. J. Fisher, in his stimulating inaugural lecture in 1956, called into question as The Dark Ages in English Economic History. It is natural for all historians to think that their own special field of study is particularly dark with unsolved problems; and as one who has specialized in the same period I would naturally agree that we know far too little about the sixteenth and seventeenth centuries. This book adds greatly to our knowledge of the social and economic history of the period, but it does more than that: it will provoke further studies of other towns and other urban problems, not least because it suggests new methods of approach besides merely adding to our information.

In *Writings on British Urban History 1934–57*, published by Dr W. H. Chaloner in *Vierteljahrschrift für Sozial und Wirtschaftge-schichte* (vol. 45, 1958) he was kind enough to say of my own first-born work—*Industry, Trade, and People in Exeter 1688–1800*, published as long ago as 1935—that it was 'a pioneer study ... which may be said to have started the modern spate of urban studies'. Be that as it may, we have certainly seen a revolution in urban historiography in this country in the last twenty years or so. Long neglected by historians, or treated simply from a legalistic and constitutional standpoint which left so many fields of enquiry untouched, it is now one of the major growing-points of English history.

As I look back at my own first attempt at tackling the social and economic history of an English city, opening up in a limited way new questions or putting well-known records to new uses, I see now how simplistic was my approach. It was useful at the time and served a purpose; but reading this new collection of essays thirty-five years later I observe with pleasure how techniques have been refined by the succeeding generation, and entirely new fields of urban history opened up. It would be invidious for me, even were I competent to do so, to comment on the individual studies that follow; but when I speak of new ways of looking at historical problems I think especially of the remarkable and provocative essay by Charles Phythian-Adams on what he calls 'the communal year' at Coventry between the mid-fifteenth century and the mid-sixteenth.

I notice another thing about these essays also, and that is the pre-occupation (though not to the exclusion of other problems) with the poor as a class, the most difficult of all social classes to write about historically. In *Howard's End*, published in 1910, E. M. Forster opens his sixth chapter with the words: 'We are not concerned with the very poor. They are unthinkable, and only to be approached by the statistician or the poet.' But now the historian is also learning how to think about the unthinkable. At least three of the eight essays here are concerned primarily with the poor—in the Kentish towns, in Salisbury, and in East London—and they make their appearance to some extent in some of the other essays. It is not that the poor have no annals, as used to be said: their annals may almost be said on the contrary to be interminable, for they have always formed the great majority of our urban populations. As far back as Domesday Book there are indications that they formed a large class, if not the largest single class, in the bigger towns at least. Now we are slowly beginning to write their distinctive history. I am not saying they are important merely because they are so numerous, but a history which ignores a half or three-quarters of the human race at any given time can scarcely be called History.

Another of the many uncharted fields of urban history until recent years was how towns actually grew as physical organisms. We talk of populations growing, but who built the houses (especially the working-class houses) and who planned or laid out the streets and lanes in a growing town? The study of housing in East London in this volume, of its expansion street by street, the plans of individual houses, and who built them, is so far as I know a pioneer study of urban history in this period along what may be called topographical lines. It has been said that 'towns do not grow: they are built'. But who built the needed houses, laid out the streets, financed the work, is still largely a mystery before the nineteenth century, above all in our provincial towns. Here we are getting down to real detail, to the nails and plaster if not the brass tacks.

These studies show, in their varied ways, the growing use of the microscope in the service of what we may call national history for want of a better term. Anyone can generalize and be called 'brilliant' but I recall once again some words of William Blake which I have quoted elsewhere: 'To Generalize is to be an Idiot. To Particularize is the Alone Distinction of Merit.' Not all the contributors to this volume would subscribe wholeheartedly to this aphorism, and indeed there are serious historical reservations we could all make to it: but it is well worth keeping in mind at all times. Microscopic studies such as we have in this book are a valuable corrective to the easy generalizations that infest so many historical works on a grander scale: they show us how changes really come about at the *cell* level, as it were; how great events and even epochs are slowly and often unknowingly generated out of local communities in fumbling action and thought. Conversely they show, too, how local communities reacted in their own way to great events at the centre, at the national level.

There are, of course, favourite themes of my own which are left untouched in this volume. One important and almost untilled field of urban study is that of the personnel of the governing class in different towns, the *potentiores* as they were called at Lynn in the fifteenth century. Were they oligarchies (indeed, are they still in some county boroughs behind a façade of democracy?) and if so how were they recruited? Was it relatively easy to make the grade in one's own town, or was it intimidatingly difficult? What kind of people 'got on' in this special sense and how did they do it? Agrarian historians have long been familiar with the concept of 'open villages' and 'closed villages' and their profound influence upon local social and economic history. But were there 'open towns' and 'closed towns' also? If so, why the difference from place to place?

The readers of this volume will doubtless all have their own ideas about adding to its range, but there is plenty of meat in it already. There could have been more towns and other problems: the editors are conscious of that possible criticism, but there must be an end to the best of things.

Preface

Interest in English urban problems has grown largely in the last decade, and with it has come an increase in the number of historians in the field. This collection originated in the enthusiasms and warm debates of a group of friends, first at Oxford in the mid-1960s, later extended to London. It has always been a co-operative venture. We have benefited considerably from discussion and mutual criticism; it also goes without saying that the arguments continue.

We have all depended on the patient assistance of local Archivists and their staff, particularly those at Coventry, York, Maidstone, Canterbury, Salisbury, Chester, Norwich and the Guildhall, London. The editors are grateful to the Master and Fellows of Balliol College and to the President and Fellows of Magdalen College, Oxford, for electing them to Research Fellowships which provided the opportunity for preparing this volume. We are also indebted for advice and encouragement to C. S. L. Davies, Dr R. B. Dobson, Christopher Hill, Dr A. Macintyre and P. J. Waller, and in particular to Professor W. G. Hoskins, who has guided the research of many of us and generously contributed a foreword to this book. Finally, our thanks go to Jill Slack, who, in addition to helping with the proofs and the index, has cheerfully tolerated the crises associated with English towns and their historians.

Oxford and York
P.A. C
P.A.S.

ix

Contents

Contents

Illustrations

Abbreviations

Agric. Hist. Rev.	*Agricultural History Review*
AO	Archives Office
APC	*Acts of the Privy Council*
B.I.H.R.	*Bulletin of the Institute of Historical Research*
Bodl.	Bodleian Library, Oxford
BM	British Museum
C	Proceedings in the Court of Chancery, Public Record Office
CPR	*Calendar of Patent Rolls*
CSPD	*Calendar of State Papers, Domestic*
E	Exchequer Records, Public Record Office
Ec.H.R.	*Economic History Review*
E.H.R.	*English Historical Review*
GL	Guildhall Library, London
GLCRO	Greater London Record Office
HMC	*Historical Manuscripts Commission*
LP	*Letters and Papers of Henry VIII*
P. & P.	*Past and Present*
PRO	Public Record Office, London
RO	Record Office
SP	State Papers Domestic, Public Record Office

St Ch	Star Chamber Records, Public Record Office
Trans. Roy. Hist. Soc.	*Transactions of the Royal Historical Society*
Univ. Birmingham Hist. J.	*University of Birmingham Historical Journal*
VCH	*Victoria County Histories*

Place of publication of books referred to is London unless otherwise indicated.

In dates, the Old Style has been retained except that the year has been taken to begin on 1 January.

I

Introduction

Peter Clark and Paul Slack

The chronology of urban historiography in England has been erratic.[1]
The so-called 'Historical Revolution' of the late sixteenth and seventeenth centuries stimulated an enhanced awareness of the local community and its history, producing a crescendo of county surveys and
descriptions; but, although there were a number of important publications, concern with the peculiar urban phenomenon never had the same
impetus.[2] If a trickle of town histories nourished urban antiquarianism
in the first part of the eighteenth century only the last decades witnessed
any surge of writing, a movement which swept into the early years of
the nineteenth century precipitated by radical demands for franchise
reform and an allied desire to investigate the origin of corporate
privileges.[3] With the achievement of reform in the 1830s the level of
urban historiography fell away; to be revived again by the High
Victorians. However, the academic world of late nineteenth-century
England was dominated by medievalists, their interest often confined
to early burghal institutions. Their instrument, the Historical Manuscripts Commission, during its early perambulations of town archives
calendared medieval deeds and charters *in extenso* but too often passed
over the accumulations of later centuries. Under this influence local
antiquarian societies with their charabancs of clergy and gentlefolk
pursued the grail of democracy in the history of the medieval town.[4]
The sixteenth- and seventeenth-century town was put on one side. It
was equally outflanked by the other wing of Victorian urban historiography, a manifestation of the civic self-confidence of the great
industrial cities. Unfortunately, few of these centres were important

before the last years of the seventeenth century and the detection of
the industrial city in the shade of the pre-industrial township tells us
comparatively little about early modern urban society.[5] Paradoxically,
the Victorian interest in urban history did some positive disservice to
historical writing. Town records left to slumber were now exposed
to the rigours of antiquarian zeal: collections were jumbled and documents rifled; parchment deeds were turned into glue or sometimes
incinerated. The influence of Maitland had led to the valuable publication of municipal records by some towns, but the momentum of the
last years of the century lasted for little more than a decade.[6]

In recent years, however, English historians have turned once more
to the study of urban problems.[7] Towns of the sixteenth and seventeenth centuries are being explored seriously for the first time, most
notably in the pioneering work of Professor W. G. Hoskins.[8] However, English urban historiography for this period has yet to reach the
age of academic majority so clearly attained by the French with their
massive urban theses.[9] There are some analyses of trade structure,
political organization and demographic change in individual towns; but
with a handful of exceptions we lack both studies of the urban community in all its interrelated functions and surveys of towns in direct
comparison one with another.[10] Our image of the English town
between 1500 and 1700 is fragmentary and the promise of English
urban studies remains as yet unfulfilled.

The orthodox excuses for publication come in two varieties: either
there is too much or too little material already in print. Clearly the
argument for this collection must fall into the second category. But
if the immaturity of urban historiography for this period affords an
excuse for this volume, it likewise imposes serious restraints on its
content. Omissions are patent: coastal shipping, the growth of Puritanism, education, the image of the town in contemporary literature,
for themes; Bristol, Manchester, Newcastle, the market towns, for
towns. Any hope of providing a more comprehensive survey of urban
development from 1500 to 1700 is limited by the present state of
research. Nevertheless, the papers in this volume, discussing as they
do some of the most significant problems of urban society, including
the erosion of civic ritual, poverty, housing and political conflict, may
help to re-draw the outline of the early modern town; they suggest
that in the sixteenth and seventeenth centuries it experienced a major
reorientation of its role.

*   *   *

Any attempt to write an introductory survey of English towns in the sixteenth and seventeenth centuries is beset by an army of problems. There are the source difficulties we have already mentioned: too often we are at the mercy of a random scattering of information about a town, too rarely do we learn of more than a handful of its contemporaneous characteristics. More problems are created by the necessity to relate structure and the dynamics of change. It is arguable that in the following account urban dynamics are given undue prominence, that there is insufficient portrayal of the quality of urban life. But there is perhaps some justification for an approach which lays less stress on the static image. Firstly, the continuities of urban institutions and attitudes are described in some of the detailed papers elsewhere in this volume. Secondly, general discussion by historians has tended to concentrate on structural problems and consequently the theme of urban transformation has been neglected. Such problems dictate the character of this introduction: it must be seen at most as a model for discussion, an attempt to set in a new framework the work so far completed on the English town in the years 1500 to 1700.

The historian is also confronted with another problem: one of definition. What does he mean by a 'town'? For the modern industrial community we have the conceptual tools of Park and Burgess, and others.[11] However, sometimes these are hardly relevant to the pre-industrial town and demand quantitative information rarely at the disposal of the historian of the early modern period. G. Sjoberg in *The Preindustrial City* describes from the viewpoint of the sociologist the basic characteristics of this sort of community, relying on examples from a wide range of societies. His outline of urban characteristics—with its emphasis on demographic structure, social and kinship organization, economic function, political structure, religion and education—is more valuable than the selective evidence with which he seeks to support them.[12] Part of the confusion springs from the kaleidoscopic quality of urban society in England. The complexity of corporate types alone defeated the Webbs. It is not surprising that sixteenth- and seventeenth-century commentators were themselves overwhelmed. William Harrison was reduced to drawing a rough demographic divide between a market town with two thousand communicants and villages with two or three hundred. John Hooker of Exeter described a 'civitas' baldly as a 'multitude of people assembled and collected to the end to continue and live together in a common society yielding dutiful obedience unto their superiors and mutual love to [one] another'.[13] Information is only superficially more illuminating at the end of the seventeenth century: the vagueness of John Adams and the fluctuating tables of Gregory King do not evince much confidence in their categorization of urban society.[14]

The problems here are obviously enormous but we can perhaps suggest that there were four characteristics of the pre-industrial town: a specialist economic function, a peculiar concentration of population, a sophisticated political superstructure, and a community function and impact beyond the immediate limits of the town and its inhabitants. This is not to say that every community which we might describe as 'urban' in the sixteenth and seventeenth centuries possessed all the elements of this definition. The wealth of urban types comprehending the proto-modern enormity of London and the still manorial and partially rural Manchester and Birmingham make this an unreal possibility. But we can use this definition as a starting point for a rough categorization of urban phenomena, an attempt to relate to a recognizable framework the disparate multiplicity of communities which contemporaries called cities and market towns.

There were three tiers of urban society in England from 1500 to 1700. On the most simple level were communities which revealed three (sometimes only two) characteristics of urbanism, as well as having strong rural overtones. In this group were decaying, small corporate towns, the developing market centre and the incipient industrial agglomeration: New Romney or Winchelsea, Ashford or Lough-borough, Halifax or Birmingham. One of the few common denominators was low population size or density. When Gregory King sought to classify towns by size of population in 1696 he believed that of his 794 towns outside London 650 had between 150 and 200 houses; many were probably to be found amongst this group of 'simple towns'. Even where population size was considerably greater, as amongst the new industrial centres, density remained fairly low.[15] Another feature shared by a number of these towns was the absence of a sophisticated political superstructure: the political organization of the small corporate town was barely more elaborate than the sub-political institutions of the ordinary market town.

The middle tier of urban society is distinguished by towns which exhibit all the elements of the urban definition described earlier. By 1700 they may have numbered about 120 and were all incorporated. Sidney and Beatrice Webb found about 200 municipal corporations in existence in 1689 but not all these showed the other characteristics of a complete urban community. There was also a quantitative difference between these chartered towns and the 'simple towns'. In general, they correspond with the 130 towns listed by King as having between 300 and 500 houses each, although a number had substantially more inhabitants.[16] Population density was also greater. Other characteristics included a more elaborate community organization framed by gilds and civic ceremonial, a more sophisticated economic function combining industry, trade and specialist service activity, and (potentially) a more extensive urban impact. Towns belonging to this middle sector of urban society included many of the smaller cathedral cities such as Canterbury, Chichester, Gloucester, Lincoln and Rochester.

In the first division of the urban league table were seven or eight major cities; by the end of the seventeenth century they included Bristol, Exeter, York, Norwich, Newcastle-upon-Tyne, perhaps Hull, certainly London. London in the years 1500 to 1700 established a metropolitan hegemony unrivalled in Western Europe embracing almost all aspects of national life. As early as 1588 the political theorist Giovanni Botero declared, 'in England, London excepted, although the country do abound in plenty of all good things, yet there is not a city in it that deserves to be called great'.[17] However, Botero exaggerated: on a less exalted level Bristol, Exeter and York all played the important role of quasi-metropolitan centres with their own large areas of influence for most of this period. All the cities in this group exhibited the four elements of urbanism defined earlier but, unlike our middle tier of chartered towns, they may also have reached the take-off point of urban viability, able to absorb at least short-term crises. By 1700 they all had populations in excess of 8,000 though only Bristol and Norwich apart from London had more than 20,000 inhabitants. For most of these two centuries they parade a highly developed economic function, the full paraphernalia, civic and political, of the great city (some have county jurisdiction) and a dominating influence over urban and rural society in an extensive area about them. If London claims the lead of the national league of urban society, the major cities are in turn champions of the regional hierarchies.[18]

Any categorization of urban phenomena in this period is to some extent vitiated by the size and complexity of the change which urban society was undergoing. The rise of the London colossus from about 60,000 inhabitants in 1520 to approximately 575,000 in 1700 (or about 10 per cent of the total population of England), its merchants coming to

dominate most aspects of English trade, its fashions becoming synonymous with national taste, was itself momentous enough to restructure
English urban society.[19] *Prima facie* evidence of other change is found
in the development of new centres of growth—the spa towns like
Tunbridge Wells or Harrogate, the industrial centres like Halifax or
Leeds, and the naval towns of Chatham, Plymouth and Portsmouth.
On the somewhat precise level of legal technicality these two centuries
saw the incorporation of more than sixty new boroughs:[20] in the real
terms of political, economic, social and demographic change urban
society suffered critical transformation.

As we said earlier, this analysis of urban society in England from
1500 to 1700 will concentrate more on the dynamics of change than on
structure. Clearly, however, there were strong elements of continuity
and stability in town life at this time. Firstly, the proportion of the
English population resident in towns remained small: in 1500 perhaps
rather more than one-tenth lived in towns of more than 1,000 inhabitants; by 1700 the figure was about one-fifth.[21] This increase,
however, was primarily the consequence of the great metropolitan
expansion; England remained overwhelmingly a rural society. The
urban community was permeated by the countryside: gardens and
orchards, oast-houses, pigs and poultry flourished within the limits of
the largest towns, while the countryside crept to the back-door of
houses on the High Street of the smaller centre. Townsmen were often
farmers or labourers in the surrounding fields and if their main occupation was a town craft they might yet find time to go harvesting in
the summer months. Many townsfolk were rural immigrants or their
offspring and many families after two or three generations in a town
moved back to village society. Even London wore something of a
rural smock: although the area within the city walls was densely
populated the newly colonized suburbs were still more country than
town; the great squares to the west were open and increasingly tree-
lined, and the royal parks and common fields hedged the urban
sprawl.[22] Finally, for all men and women, countryfolk and town-
dwellers alike, the harvest was the vital factor in economic life.

Another chain of continuity is also obvious: that of topography.
Although the physical image of towns often changed considerably in
these two centuries the ground plan did not. There were accretions,
but the topographical heartland of towns remained the same in 1700 as
it had been in 1500. This was equally true of the declining city of
Coventry whose medieval lay-out persisted into the mid-eighteenth

century as of an expanding centre like Liverpool where the framework of streets laid out in the reign of King John contained the town until the last years of the seventeenth century. Almost as stable was the national topography of urban society. In 1700 the heaviest concentration of towns was still in the south and east; if growth tended now to be in the highland areas of the north and west, urban society as a whole continued to exemplify the medieval pattern of lowland settlement.[23]

There was also a considerable degree of institutional continuity. Population, industry and trade might all decay but towns self-consciously clung to their particular image. They schemed to preserve the peculiar style of their officials, and protracted legal battles were waged to maintain rights of way or negligible rents decreed by medieval precedent. Most corporate towns struggled to sustain the fabric of civic ceremonial, even if it were now focused exclusively on the mayor and aldermanic bench. The more precipitate the decline of a town the more it fought to parade the civic formalities of the past. It is more than a coincidence that the most carefully kept town archives are often those of the embattled small community.[24]

The continuity in urban society serves to frame the scenario of change. Most change, as we shall see, was the consequence of long-term factors. Nevertheless specific incidents, an accident or natural disaster, might well play an important role in affecting the future of an individual town. Fire was one of the most important. The Great Fire of London in 1666 was only the most spectacular example of this kind of civic disaster; Chester was devastated in 1564 and Banbury in 1628, a fire at Bury St Edmunds in 1608 destroyed 160 dwelling-houses and 400 outhouses at a cost of £60,000, and 'the spacious, compact and glorious town' of Northampton was largely laid waste by fire in 1675.[25] Plague, another act of God, might have equally calamitous consequences for an individual town. In 1579 Norwich lost almost a third of its population during an epidemic and the mortality in Newcastle in 1636 may have been as great. In Exeter in 1625 the mayor elect refused to serve because of an outbreak of plague, and the City was said to be 'in a most miserable condition, and through the exceeding poverty of multitudes in danger to fall into distemper and mutiny'.[26] Another natural calamity which most towns proved themselves incapable of withstanding was the silting up of their harbours. The havens of Rye, New Romney, Sandwich, Boston and Chester were all eventually strangled by shingle banks.[27] The falling water-level of the Stour, Fossdyke and Exe threatened the economic arteries of

Canterbury, Lincoln and Exeter, but the fatality rate here was determined less by the perverse sentence of the deity than by political and other mundane forces affecting urban society as a whole; it is these we must now consider.[28]

Any attempt to describe urban development in the sixteenth and seventeenth centuries demands an understanding of the problems of the late medieval, particularly fifteenth-century, town. Although this century is the Dark Age of English urban historiography,[29] in which all generalizations are controversial, it is possible to construct a tentative model of the major characteristics of the urban community at that time, relying on the definition of urbanism described earlier.

In most cases urban communities were economically self-sufficient. Although we should be wary of accepting all the conclusions presented by A. R. Bridbury in *Economic Growth: England in the Later Middle Ages* (1962) it does seem clear that there were as many growth centres as there were pockets of urban decay. As Professor Carus-Wilson has said, 'If English towns with the possible exceptions of London, Bristol and Southampton were declining in the fourteenth and fifteenth centuries, what are we to make of Coventry and Salisbury, or of York in the fourteenth century? If the outports were being strangled by the London colossus, how was it that Newcastle enjoyed a period of unprecedented prosperity in the fifteenth century?' Towns retained their basic industries; manufacturing as well as marketing cloth played a crucial part in the life of some of the largest provincial centres. Good examples were York, Bristol, Norwich, Coventry and Salisbury. Southampton, Exeter and other West Country towns grew fat on the profits of cloth exports in the fifteenth century.[30] By 1500 some marketing centres, like Lincoln or Stamford or Canterbury, were in decay but generally towns continued as important foci of internal trade.[31] In the long run, however, it may be true that the economic tide had already set by the end of the fifteenth century against certain well-established towns, with industry following merchant investment in land into the countryside and wealth increasingly concentrated in the hands of a few urban magnates.[32]

The fifteenth century appears to have been a period of extended demographic stagnation although, as J. C. Russell comments, our information about the population of English boroughs 'is rather meagre'. A few centres experience some growth in numbers of inhabitants (including London and Exeter) but even Bridbury accepts the fact of overall demographic decline. A factor here may have been the absence of large-scale immigration from the countryside caused by the comparative increase in rural prosperity. There is little evidence of large numbers of poor vagrants coming to town, nor indeed of many urban paupers at all.[33]

The ceremony and ritual of the self-contained, self-conscious community dominated the political life of the majority of town-dwellers in the late fifteenth century. The paper by C. V. Phythian-Adams demonstrates how at Coventry the social tensions inherent within a hierarchical society which excluded at least one-fifth of its adult males and the majority of its women from participation in political life were released through customary channels of civic ceremonial. The most distinctive feature of the ceremonies of the late medieval urban community was their emphasis on preserving and enhancing the wholeness of the social order, the subordination of the parts to the whole, and the pervasive role of the pre-Reformation Church. Not all towns of course had a calendar of civic ritual as complicated as that of the great city of Coventry. Nor can we argue that divisiveness was thereby eradicated from city life. But gilds and mayoral ritual, miracle plays and religious processions performed a central part in preserving the proscenium arch of the integrated community: conflict was contained.

Ceremony also cemented together the disparate elements of city or town government with its multiplicity of communal organizations. Of these the most active was the vertical chain of corporate government from mayor, aldermen and council down to the parish meeting by way of ward leets. But in the larger towns this was complemented by the horizontal chain of craft bodies—microcosms of the body politic. In addition, the authority of town government might be limited by the independence of civil and ecclesiastical liberties. Ceremony then supported the corporate government's attempts to provide centralized magistracy. To conclude, the administrative back of town government was broad and the demands made upon it fairly constant: the quality of government seems to have been stained with only occasional corruption; and the political landscape is one of relative flexibility and openness.[34]

How much political independence and influence towns with parliamentary representation enjoyed in this period remains uncertain. Gentry already served as burgesses in Parliament by the mid-fifteenth century, but this in itself proves little: representation by a respectable gentleman might well increase the effective volume of the urban voice. On the other hand, civic pride preferred to elect citizen M.P.s. Either way the large prosperous community stood a greater chance of getting its opinion noticed than the declining centre. In the field of national politics, as far as we can see from the little evidence at our disposal, towns endeavoured to preserve their neutrality amidst the sporadic violence of fifteenth-century civil war. Thus we are told that a striking feature of Coventry's history in this period 'is the lack of political partisanship in the town . . . there is little sign that the local disputes were ever caught up into the national'.[35] Neutralism may have been determined less by calculated self-interest than by the limited awareness in urban society of national political issues.

Finally, what was the impact of the town on late medieval society? Through the splendour of civic building many towns continued to display the self-confident sense of community we have already described. By the mid-fifteenth century Coventry had rebuilt its two great parish churches and constructed a colossal circuit of city walls. At York, city pride manifested itself in a new Guildhall, the completion of the town walls, St Anthony's Hall, St William's College and the rebuilding of a number of important parish churches. In the small towns of the southwest there was equally vigorous public building. The peasant tramping to the larger town was still impressed by this physical act of faith in the urban way of life.[36] Civic and religious ceremonial, pageants, plays and processions likewise inspired the wonder of countryfolk.[37]

In conclusion, we can say that even though High Medieval towns were on the wane by the late fifteenth century they still fulfilled a peculiar urban role in society, having an impact transcending the narrow limits of civic liberties. It was the role primarily of the moderate sized, probably incorporate, town: London had yet to overshadow urban society and the new growth centres amongst the 'simple towns' were still awaiting their important phase of expansion. It was in this second tier of urban society that post-medieval change was to be most critical, affecting almost every facet of community life.

The economic function of almost all English towns was transformed from 1500 to 1700. Towns like Norwich or Bath, Colchester or Buckingham only discovered a new economic role after some period of uncertainty. Others found their new function involved a major reduction of their importance, and amongst the casualties were Coventry and Southampton—two of the most prosperous towns of late medieval England.[38]

From the end of the fifteenth century the decay of basic industries was increasingly obvious in certain towns. The contraction of York clothmaking infected other trades such as leather and metal-work; in Kent the main centre for clothing was no longer at Canterbury but in the Wealden market towns. Industrial migration into the countryside, particularly of clothing, was common.[39] It followed the path of merchant investment in rural property (itself a comment on declining confidence in urban investment), the slow spread of the Tudor peace, and, paradoxically, the steady decline of rural living standards during the sixteenth century. The latter prompted small farmers to take up by-employments like clothmaking, and their lower wage-rates offered the incentive for capital to drift from high-cost urban production centres. Part of the heavy overheads of town industry was the price of the elaborateness of civic life, but a major charge was created by the regulations of craft bodies concerned less with the maximization of profits than with the maintenance of social and civic harmony. In 1534 Parliament enacted a statute for the preservation of the City of Worcester and the towns of Evesham, Droitwich, Kidderminster and Bromsgrove from competition by rural clothiers which threatened 'their great decay, depopulation and ruin', and this was extended by a general statute in 1554. However, industrial competition was also suburban-based which would suggest that the disincentive of existing urban controls was a more important factor than the positive incentives of the rural economy. Whether the rise of new industrial centres such as Leeds, Halifax and Birmingham had a causal connexion with the decay of York, Beverley and Coventry is unproven, but the coincidence of chronology is suspicious. The new towns afforded little or no regulation and lower costs: the mayor of York complained in 1561,

the cause of the decay of the weavers etc. . . . is the lack of clothmaking in the said city as was in old time accustomed, which is now increased . . . in the town of Halifax, Leeds and Wakefield for that not only the commodity of the water mills is there nigh at hand but also the poor folk as spinners, carders and other necessary work folks . . . have kine, fire and other relief good and cheap which is in this city very dear and wanting.[40]

Another source of economic disruption may have been the Reformation, although its impact on the urban economy has never been carefully examined. Almost certainly capital inflow was curtailed, for not only were the profits of the pilgrim trade forfeit (these were probably negligible in any case by 1500), but the dispersal of monastic and later episcopal lands meant that the rents once transferred to urban treasuries were lost to the coffers of the Crown and country gentry. This may well have damaged the markets and viability of urban industry.[41]

By no means all towns suffered the erosion of their old industry without finding another. Leicester after the contraction of its old textile industry in the early sixteenth century grew prosperous in the next century from its new trade of hosiery. The making of worsted, serges, lace and thread inserted by Flemish and French refugees into the economies of Norwich, Colchester, Canterbury and Southampton helped to revitalize their failing textile industries in the second half of the sixteenth century. But most towns shifted their economic emphasis from industry to the development of trade and the expansion of their social facilities.[42]

Expansion into foreign trade was never a very real option for more than a few towns in these years, even if they were ports. The obsessive importance of the woollen cloth trade for the sixteenth and early part of the seventeenth centuries, and the severity of trade depressions in that period laid the foundations for the mercantile hegemony of the all-resourceful London. A 'Discourse of Corporations', written in the 1580s, complained that 'the only trade of merchants is now to London, which has eaten up all the rest of the towns and havens of England, because there they find speedy vent and speedy freight again'. In addition, the foreign trade of lesser ports was adversely affected by the loss of Calais (for South Coast havens) and the growth of Dutch competition. Indeed in 1598 Lord Burghley could speak of the decay of Newcastle, Hull, Boston, Lynn, Southampton, Poole, Weymouth, Bristol and Chester. In the early years of James I's reign conflict between London and the provincial ports exploded in the Free Trade controversy. London won; so that by the time of the great expansion of late seventeenth-century trade only a few outports were strong enough to grasp a share of it.[43]

The abdication by some provincial towns of their interest in foreign trade was perhaps as much deliberate as through force of circumstance: towns were attracted by the expansion of internal trade, where yields were more certain and the unit of investment smaller. There has been little recent work on coastal and river shipping but its significance cannot be underestimated in an economy which experienced a large-scale development of local trade without a comparable improvement in land communication. Fortunately more is known about marketing mechanisms, especially in relation to towns.[44] The sixteenth century was the great age of the fair and market, of the enhanced complexity of commercial exchange, of broggers, badgers, drovers and pedlars. It was a phenomenon which benefited most towns. Among its determinants was a growth of agricultural specialization, the rising standard of living among the middling sort of men, and ultimately, the development of London. As London trebled its population in the sixteenth century, its merchants spread widely across the countryside buying basic commodities and in return supplying finished, sometimes luxury goods. In the first phase of this penetration London merchants operated in market towns. At Chelmsford in the 1630s the town complained that 'the chandlers of London haunt all the markets near unto London and sweep the market of all the corn that comes'. The prosperity of Elizabethan Faversham, a port on the North Kent coast, depended on its function as one of London's principal suppliers of grain and as a market through which Londoners moved cart-loads of merchandise into the Kentish hinterland. But once the trade link had been welded Londoners abandoned the urban market place and engaged in direct buying and (to a lesser extent) retailing. At Faversham while the volume of port traffic with the capital increased steadily throughout these two centuries the number of local merchants trading with London declined in the later Stuart period. England by the early years of the eighteenth century, dominated as it was by London trade, had little room for the independent role of the provincial town in local commerce.[45]

Conflict with London merchants, a spreading sore in late sixteenth- and seventeenth-century internal trade, was only one cause of the comparative decline of town markets and fairs by 1700. Already in the reign of Elizabeth there was some attempt to erode civic trade control. In 1595 at Chester a complaint was made that 'wares do not come to the common hall of this city according to the former orders' but are 'privily laid in men's houses within the said city to the great decay of the revenues of this city'. But the sharpest fall in the level of public marketing in comparison with the overall expansion of internal trade came in the last part of the seventeenth century. At Boston the annual town income from stalls in the market place fell by about

40 per cent from 1651 to 1700. The now respectable middleman travelling the countryside, the town shop and the provincial inn overshadowed the market and reduced the town fair to little more than an opportunity for social jollification.[46]

The later Stuart town demonstrated an economic dependence on its role as a social centre for the county community. This function was not new but it came to predominate. The most orthodox aspect was the provision of specialist services of which the most significant were medical and legal. If fashionable doctors of the sixteenth and seventeenth centuries had town houses their practices extended well into the countryside. Such a man was John Symcotts of Huntingdon who had patients amongst the Cromwell and St John families in the county.[47] The lawyer, another social phenomenon of this period, also had a peculiar urban identity. Partly this was because the probate business of the ecclesiastical courts was conducted in the cathedral cities, partly because lawyers who were not London barristers were often town clerks or attorneys in civic courts, and partly because the county courts of Quarter Session and the Assizes were held in towns. Prominent lawyers lived on their outskirts and served as Stewards or Recorders—powerful figures in urban politics. Countryfolk, gentry, yeomen and peasantry, rode or walked to town to testify or consult a lawyer or instruct an attorney. Towns not only benefited from the inflow of capital in the form of fees and the employment of a significant number of inhabitants in these specialist services, but profited from the money spent on food, drink and lodgings by clients.[48]

Victualling and hostelry were the obvious growth sectors of the Stuart town. It was as a hostelry centre that Chelmsford became the principal town in Essex next to Colchester, overshadowing the old clothing communities. Innkeepers and victuallers were numerous and influential: at the market town of Abingdon in 1696 there were sixty-four traders engaged in victualling and after 1660 the Leicester mayoralty was frequently filled by innkeepers. If specialist services brought some business the main impetus to expansion of hostelry came from the growth of local trade; back parlours of inns served as informal markets where contracts were exchanged and goods stored. The close connexion of victuallers with local trade is illustrated by their activity in issuing tokens for it: of all token issuers at High Wycombe from 1648 to 1672 a third were innkeepers. Victuallers also grew fat from the evolution of larger towns as social centres. Meetings of country administrators—at Assizes, Quarter Sessions, Petty Sessions and

Sessions for the Sewers—had been held customarily in towns, but they were now the occasion for social gatherings of country gentlemen, their wives, children and retinues.[49]

The attraction of the town as a social centre was not limited in impact to the upper classes. John Bodle came from Hailsham in Sussex to Southampton in 1639; he said he had inherited an income of ten pounds per annum and was a bricklayer but 'that he does not use to work at his profession in the winter time, but does use to go abroad to see fashions'. Nevertheless, of those drawn to town the most significant economically were the lesser gentry for whom a season in the capital was impossible for financial reasons but who hoped to find in their county town a cheaper mirror of fashionable London. At Norwich the mayoral inauguration aped the festivities of the Lord Mayor's Show in the metropolis; in Buckingham in about 1670 Henry Robinson built a large assembly room in Castle Street, called the Trolley House, Castle Hill was laid out as a bowling green, and Buckingham became a recognized resort for local gentry; Coventry initiated Lady Godiva's procession in 1678 in a crude appeal to the neighbouring countryside; Preston by the early eighteenth century had transformed its Guild Merchant ceremony into a social pantomime for the benefit of Lancashire respectability; and the city of Lincoln grossed profits in the reign of Charles II and after from the horse-racing arranged in the neighbourhood by the county aristocracy. By 1700 many towns had a considerable, in some cases overwhelming, number of gentry living there for at least part of the year, some renting, others owning town houses. After an extensive fire in 1694 Warwick endeavoured to encourage the settlement of gentle and professional men by the careful provision of salubrious housing.[50]

The development of a town as a social centre at best stabilized an urban economy. It opened up few avenues for long-term expansion and meant that the prosperity of a town depended on the prosperity of the county society for which it served as a meeting point. Moreover, the rise of urban social centres was selective since only one or two communities in each county benefited: smaller towns that had once served as informal meeting places for the squirarchy were no longer fashionable.

Urban society in England from 1500 to 1700 was confronted with critical economic problems which it showed itself too often unable or unwilling to solve. Constructive remedial action was often initiated by outsiders. Thus county projectors were largely responsible for navigating the Ouse as far as Bedford, and a county magnate, Sir Richard Weston, opened the river Wey from Guildford to the Thames in 1650.[51] Towns themselves, it is often argued, tended to concentrate on restriction and regulation. At Newark the largest group of town ordinances from 1604 to 1642, apart from those concerned with the structure of the corporation and the exclusion of poor strangers, represented 'efforts on well-established lines to enforce the freemen's monopoly of trade'. D. M. Palliser in his paper on the trade gilds of York cites evidence to refute the argument of S. Kramer and T. H. Marshall that the gild was the ordinary instrument of restriction for remedying economic decay and that its controls exacerbated contraction: rather at York elaboration of gild controls was the fruit of prosperity, the city having previously combated the decay of its textile industry by the relaxation of craft requirements. Certainly magistrates had more than one economic option: Lincoln on one occasion, as well as York, hoped that liberalization of controls would restore trade prosperity. But in practice, governing bodies in a good number of towns including Abingdon, Canterbury, Coventry, Rye and in general Lincoln itself followed the path of elaborating and reorganizing craft regulations as the only defence against industrial or trade competition. Here at least a vicious circle of recession was set in motion and by the mid-seventeenth century gilds were often starting to disintegrate. At Lincoln most of the gilds disappeared, at Gloucester they required radical reorganization, and in St Albans only two of the earlier four companies survived at the Restoration. Too often they had been shipwrecked by the continued fall of urban industrial activity and the increasing informality of trade.[52]

All that we can say definitely about urban demography in the sixteenth and seventeenth centuries is that our figures founder in uncertainty.[53] If a town has only one parish church the register is unlikely to be comprehensive—leakages of registrations to neighbouring churches will occur, especially in times of heavy mortality, as for instance during a plague epidemic. If it has more than one church the chances that compatible registers survive are not good, and if, as in the case of the older cities, there are ten or more parishes the possibility of ever establishing a complete picture is slight. In addition, we have the unreliability of individual registers and the significant distortions caused from time to time by large-scale migration.

.rvey of population trends in towns between
speculative. It seems probable, however, that
.w a substantial growth of urban populations.
ortant demographic crises—on a local level, as
.os; on a national scale, as a consequence of the
influen.. / the 1550s or the protracted incidence of harvest
distress and plague in the last years of Elizabeth—but the general
trend reaching into the early part of the seventeenth century was
upward. The number of York inhabitants rose from about 8,000 in
the mid-sixteenth century to approximately 12,000 in the early
seventeenth century, while Warwick's population increased by perhaps 50 per cent in the Tudor period and that of Leicester by the rather
smaller figure of 16 per cent from 1509 to 1600. Even in the grievously
decayed city of Coventry there were about 800 more inhabitants in
1587 than there had been in 1523.[54]

Population increase in the sixteenth century had two main sources.
The first was the growth of some sections of the indigenous urban
population about which we know almost nothing. Whether it was a
long-term consequence of prosperous *per capita* economic conditions in
the fifteenth century or of housing improvements and a real if selective bettering of living standards in the sixteenth century remains in
doubt.[55] But for the larger towns where mortality was always high,
the second source of growth—immigration—was probably more important. P. Clark in his paper on migration into Kentish towns from
1580 to 1640 argues that those years saw a massive influx of long-
distance, *subsistence* migrants superimposed on local or *betterment*
migration (a constant feature of rural/urban contacts), that migration
was the rule and not the exception, and the tramping pauper a demographic commonplace. A core of migrants entered through the orthodox channel of apprenticeship: at Southampton for much of the period
from 1500 to 1700 60 per cent of apprentices came from outside the
town but the catchment area was localized—'most came from Hampshire and most seem to have come, at least in the early decades, from
rural places rather than from corporate or market towns'; a high
percentage were the sons of the rural better-off. At Norwich apprentices
were drawn predominantly from Norfolk, each agricultural class having a connexion with an urban craft. But by the middle years of the
sixteenth century paupers came to overshadow the immigrant traffic.
As early as 1518 Coventry denounced 'these big beggars that will not
work well to get their living but lie in the fields and break hedges'.[56]

Any expansion of urban population at a time when town
were often suffering radical functional change, when the price o
stuffs was soaring and real wages falling could only precipitate mas.
social problems, especially as part of the demographic increase took
the form of an inrush of paupers. At Tiverton, according to Stow,
the destitute were 'daily seen to perish in the streets of that town for
lack of relief'. Vagrants lived in sheds or sometimes in cellars; at
Southampton they colonized the small towers of the town walls. Others
were boxed like bugs in single rooms: Thomas Warrington, a carpenter, erected a hovel in Petty France, Westminster, and took into
one room 'six masterless persons, both men and women, to lie and
dwell there . . . being newly come out of the country'. But the destitute
were only the spectacular tip of a vast iceberg of impoverishment.
P. Slack in his paper on poverty in Salisbury shows that in years of
prolonged economic distress a much greater number of normally self-
supporting poor might be reduced to subsistence level. Often the
greatest concentration of poor was in the suburbs: at Leicester outside
Southgate and along Belgrave Gate, and in Canterbury in Westgate.
Finally, the polarization of wealthy and poverty stricken areas in a
town implied a demographic polarization, for poor parishes and suburbs tended to have a lower average size of household and higher
mortality rates than did prosperous parishes.[57]

It is not clear how far migration into towns accentuated a slow down
of national population growth in the seventeenth century. London,
with its constant excess of deaths over births, represented a demographic drain of considerable depth but there is little evidence of the
impact of other urban communities through an excessive level of
mortality. On the other hand, by the mid-seventeenth century a
number of towns like York, Coventry, Southampton and some West
Riding clothing centres are exhibiting signs of population stagnation.
This may have reflected a country-wide stagnation, a phenomenon
which not only reduced indigenous urban expansion but also immigration. Other factors were also at work: the decline of all but the very
local element in apprentice registrations evident at Southampton may
indicate the lessened attraction of certain urban economies for countryfolk by the later Stuart era; and immigration by vagrants may have
been affected by the growth of town regulations culminating in the
Settlement Act of 1662.[58]

*   *   *

Urban society was faced with a large-scale administrative problem for most of this period, that of poverty. Slack shows the difficulties experienced at Salisbury in categorizing the poor when confronted by the fluctuating spectrum of the needy and the exigencies of particular economic crises—in the 1590s or 1620s. Here the administrative dilemma was exacerbated by the political. Town authorities could never forget that lurking in the field of social distress was the monster of political disorder. Thus Clark argues that the hostility of magistrates to cheap alehouses was inflamed by their fear of an institution which acted as the only medium of communication for the lowest classes. In 1547 and 1553 the Coventry magistrates tried to prevent small craftsmen and labourers from resorting to inns and alehouses, and in years of distress there was a universal hunting and suppression of victuallers.[59] Possibly authorities exaggerated the danger represented by the destitute or perhaps their vigilance was rewarded. There were few serious outbreaks of popular disturbance in provincial towns in this period. At Gloucester in 1586 'great numbers of weavers, tuckers and other persons most poor, and many wealthy assembled themselves at Severn side and there stopped a boat laden with grain', but significantly leadership came from the upper classes. At Southampton in 1608 respectable approval took the guise of the town crier who 'animated the women in their disorderly rising about the corn'. Only at Bristol in 1660 when the city was taken over for a week by an apprentices' riot is there evidence of a significant disruption of urban government. Certainly the years after 1660 see only sporadic urban violence.[60]

Yet the problem of poverty had serious repercussions for town government. On one level, certain basic assumptions of the civic community were questioned: that it was a self-sustaining, integral organism; that it could solve community problems through neighbourliness; and that its problems could in fact be overcome. In the early Tudor era towns endeavoured to preserve the façade of these assumptions by providing their own poor with badges to beg and driving 'foreign' paupers out of town. But this nice distinction was erased by the friction of overwhelming poverty. The problem could not be contained within the existing framework of almsgiving and neighbourliness, even less could it be ignored. From the 1540s eastern towns instituted compulsory rating for poor relief: London in 1547, Norwich in 1549, Ipswich and Colchester in 1557.[61] With Crown sanction many towns followed their example during Elizabeth's reign. Food stocks and workhouses were only variations on the same theme: the reduction of a community function to an administrative problem. Attempts at Salisbury and elsewhere to resurrect some element of community responsibility through the establishment of a municipal brewhouse failed.

Hostility to urban schemes for the poor was generated not merely by their formality and by their increasing tendency to operate under the sanction of extra-community controls, but by their cost. Financially the poor imposed a serious strain on town governments: at Tiverton for instance the cost of poor relief rose from £120 per annum in 1612 to over £300 in 1656 and £410 in 1699. To some extent, charitable endowments for the poor took part of the strain off public relief. We know the names of some distinguished philanthropists like Henry Tooley of Ipswich or Roger Manwood of Canterbury; Professor W. K. Jordan has provided some statistics for the volume of bequests to the poor before 1660. But the seventeenth-century Chancery inquisitions into charitable trusts comment eloquently on the prevalent abuse of charities. As Samuel Bird, minister at St Peter's, Ipswich, preached in 1598: 'For let men give never so large legacies, yet if there be failing in the execution all comes to nothing.'[62] Ultimately, the responsibility and cost lay with the town government.

Poverty threw up a massive financial burden at a time when town finances were often strained. The decay or disruption of urban industries, the falling yield in the late seventeenth century of fair and market revenues, together with the inflationary spiral of costs were not consistent with financial solvency. Towns were also mulcted heavily by both sides in the Civil War. While the corporation finances of York were unsound by 1700 we find earlier indebtedness at Devizes, Kingston-on-Thames, St Albans, Southampton, Totnes and Winchester.[63]

This questioning of the assumptions and even solvency of the town community coincided with a narrowing of the political framework of urban society. The decades after the Reformation saw the elimination of most community ritual. In 1536 there is evidence of decay at Guildford where young men objected to serving in the pageant as 'summer kings, princes and swordbearers'. The 1540s saw the abolition of religious gilds including the Trinity and Corpus Christi gilds at Coventry, and even when craft-companies survived to stage pageants these had by 1600 little more than antiquarian significance: Chester, for instance, had a contractor manage its plays in the early seventeenth century.[64] The new, restrictive regulations of craft bodies underlined their disappearance as a unifying element in the urban community, complementary to that of the corporate mechanism.

The political community by the late sixteenth century was both short-sighted and inward-looking. As Phythian-Adams indicates, community ritual was driven off the streets, and town halls, the seat of the magisterial oligarchy, are frequently the only instances of civic building. At Hastings in 1603 to avoid great inconveniences, it was said, by reason of the election of the mayor in the public view of the multitude in the open Hundred place, all future elections were ordered to be held in the Court Hall as a place more decent, apt and secret. One of the clearest institutions of oligarchy came with an Act of 1489 which appointed Councils of Forty-Eight at Leicester and Northampton. Thereafter the disease reached epidemic proportions. The two hundred or so borough charters issued during the Tudor and early Stuart regimes reduced the democratic element in town government, and town magistrates orchestrated their own variations on the same theme; as we find at Abingdon, Gloucester, Nottingham, Rye and Great Yarmouth.[65] Conciliar membership was now small and intermarriage common: at Basingstoke in 1641 the new charter established a magistracy composed of a mayor, seven aldermen and seven burgesses; 'it was not only a close corporation but in the course of time became a family party, all its members being allied to one another either by kinship or marriage'. Entry into craft companies became more difficult and the price of entry into civic freedom often extortionate. Thus Lincoln raised its freeman's fine (by purchase) from £1 to £5 during the reign of Elizabeth and in 1670 Rye closed the civic door to future freemen by right.[66]

The growth of oligarchy was encouraged by a complex of factors. One was a fear of social disorder made articulate by the Recorder of Nottingham who wrote in 1512: 'If you shall suffer the commons to rule and follow their appetite and desire, farewell all good order'; he also repeated the reference of a courtier to 'the inconveniences that have ensued upon the calling of the commons together in the City of London, and in other cities and boroughs'.[67] Another determinant was the accumulating administrative pressure on the corporate mechanism which not only demanded the operation of a standing committee system but discouraged men from serving in town government. The growing economic and financial difficulties of towns constituted a further influence; office-holders were expected to subsidize town administration at a time when wealth was being concentrated in the hands of a few urban magnates—adding further to the unwillingness to serve, which is a common phenomenon by the end of the seventeenth century.[68] Moreover, the concentration of political power itself reflected an overall polarization within urban society affecting not only economic but demographic and social structures. All these factors arise from urban tensions. But the most important cause was exogenous: the Crown was obsessed in the years before 1640 with the need for small knots of reliable men in every town and promoted this policy by the grant or revision of charters, and through widespread conciliar intervention.[69]

The administrative problems which coincided with the tightening of the political base of urban communities did not make for good or strong government. Charges of corruption were frequent. John Elwell of Devizes denounced the corporation there in 1575 because they are 'partial and not indifferent and that he could not have justice for that they were so partial', and the Council of Nottingham was attacked in 1606 because they leased the best land 'to the richest men and let poor men have nothing'.[70] It would be wrong to ascribe abuses in the running of town finances and estates to a declining sense of community responsibility; rather they were the rewards necessary for magistrates who spent progressively more time and money in the maintenance of town government. It is not surprising, however, that these abuses were seized upon and denounced by the anti-oligarchical forces in town politics which developed in the later years of Elizabeth's reign. Before the Revolution political conflict disfigured the communities of Abingdon, Devizes, Dorchester, Nottingham, St Albans, Rye and Winchelsea, and disputes between town oligarchies and their commons were exploited by anti-government candidates at Parliamentary elections from the 1620s.[71]

Not only was there political conflict within towns at this time but also disputes with outside agencies. One of the most aggressive intruders was the central government. The Crown through charters and legislation enlarged the scope of corporation power within the community so that town governments came to monopolize responsibility for moral and social disciplines, previously shared with ecclesiastical and gild authorities.[72] But if town government was thereby consolidated, the Crown was further concerned with asserting its own control, indirectly through the creation of subservient oligarchies and directly by blows at particular privileges. This last attack reached its climax in the Elizabethan war at the end of the sixteenth century; under the guise of improved efficiency town liberties were overridden by county administrators. When towns drew back from the increasing financial and administrative impositions the Crown retaliated by threatening to annul their charters. Lincoln was warned by the Privy Council in 1596: 'You are to consider that in a time of such necessity as this, it is unfit to stand curiously and precisely upon advantages of privileges, when it is much more fit for every man to put his helping hand to supply the common want'—a concept the medieval townsman would have found it difficult to understand.[73] The exigencies of the end of Elizabeth's reign recurred in the 1620s and in the 1640s with the same damaging disruption of town administration. During the Civil War both parties demonstrated a systematic indifference to the pretensions of corporate privileges. A. M. Johnson in his paper on the city of Chester in the two decades of the Revolution stresses how civic government played in a minor key compared with the major chord of the military regime, whether Royalist or Parliamentarian. This uneasy concert was rehearsed in a number of towns.[74] Overall, there was a blurring of county and town jurisdictions. But we should not exaggerate the effect of the Revolution: it was the period after 1660 that was to see the most vicious onslaught on urban political life.

The purge of magistracy which followed the Corporation Act of 1661 was more wide-sweeping than anything experienced before. While only 4 out of 30 magistrates were excluded in New Windsor, at Gloucester 30 lost their places out of 47, at Shrewsbury 49 out of 73, at Oxford 31 out of 114 and at Leicester 40 out of 72. It is true that sometimes those excluded formally continued to serve, as at Leicester; it is also true that at Chester this purge did not silence the city's vociferous opposition to outside intervention.[75] But in the long run systematic deprivation could only be harmful at a time when in any case fewer men were forthcoming to take up the responsibilities of public office. Moreover, the Restoration upheavals were only a prelude to the *Quo Warranto* attacks which culminated in those of James II's reign; these precipitated political and administrative disorganization in municipal corporations. For instance, Northampton in 1688 witnessed the dismissal first of the mayor, three aldermen, eight bailiffs and twelve burgesses, then of three more aldermen, two bailiffs and eleven burgesses; a further alderman and six bailiffs rapidly followed and the game of corporate musical chairs concluded with the sacking of two acting-bailiffs and the mayor-elect. In some towns the early years of William III's reign were spent in unravelling the confusion of magistrates, charters, leases and accounts; in Chester the troubles endured on and off for a century leading to three law cases between 1786 and 1790. Others like Wilton were left in complete disarray. The disorders prior to 1688 may explain the separation of certain administrative functions from magisterial control into the less vulnerable hands of trustees, a phenomenon common in the early eighteenth century.[76]

Another invasion was mounted by the local gentry. The last years of the seventeenth century saw their final penetration of town politics as parliamentary conflict between county Whig and county Tory was fought out in urban elections. But this was only the last phase of an old and influential experience. Already in the fifteenth century towns had elected gentlemen as burgesses, and after the Reformation with the purchase by gentry families of religious property, another arena for influence and dispute was opened. In the sixteenth-century scramble for land, town estates were attractive plunder to the prospecting gentleman; urban property in the countryside was especially vulnerable to predatory despoilment but even common lands encircling the town were not inviolate.[77] As the central government extended its influence in town politics, its agents (often country gentry) were the ultimate beneficiaries. C. G. Parsloe observes that if the flood of Crown charters freed townsmen from formal subordination to county authorities 'they could not afford protection from the private pressure of county magnates and privy councillors'.[78] As the economic and political balance tipped against a town the favour of a Court or County aristocrat became indispensable for survival: a patron procured a new charter or fair and warded off the most extortionate demands of Whitehall. Only a few towns like prosperous Exeter and Liverpool were able to dispense with their patrons in these years, although most saw the fatal logic. A Leicester man summed up the value of Lord Stamford as patron in 1632: 'He never had done good nor ever would do for he had undone two or three towns'.[79]

The phenomenon of gentlemen burgesses was, as we have said, neither new in 1500 nor absolute by 1700. The picture is uneven. Some towns held out strongly against electing any foreigner, a few succeeded, and others capitulated without more than a token struggle. None the less, these two centuries saw a general takeover of borough seats by country gentlemen. Sir John Neale points out that the numerous creation of parliamentary boroughs in the reign of Elizabeth was at the demand of the country gentry. The contractual element remained strong into the seventeenth century; if the gentleman gained status in county society the town gained, or thought it had gained, an effective spokesman in Parliament. But by the later years of the seventeenth century many small boroughs and some larger towns had been locked up by patrons with no concern for their interests, parliamentary or otherwise. At Aylesbury the Lord of the Manor, Sir Thomas Pakington, managed to nullify the town charter in 1664; and at Chichester politics, both parliamentary and municipal, were increasingly dictated from Petworth, the country mansion of the Earl of Northumberland.[80]

To conclude, the continuous growth of oligarchic magistracy is the most obvious theme in English urban history from 1500 to 1700. Despite the strength of anti-oligarchic agitation in the decades before 1640 and the incidence of purges during the Revolution there is no evidence that the Civil War and Interregnum led to any broadening of town government. Johnson's paper on Chester shows the absence of significant change in the social background of men elected to city government at this time; nor were there any important reforms of administration. At Newcastle one clique of town politicians replaced another and political alteration in Barnstaple, Bristol, Durham, Exeter, Leicester and Rye was as undramatic. Only in London, Bedford and Wells is there the example of more radical town politics. Certainly Cromwellian corporations were as oligarchic as their Royalist forerunners.[81] This persistence of the order of government by clique is an indicator less of internal stability and quietism than of civic friability: few members of the respectable classes dared, in the last analysis, tolerate any major disruption.

How far the fragility of the urban structure dictated the comparative inactivity of towns during the English Revolution is difficult to assess. It may be that towns had always sought to evade involvement in national political issues, that the local community was its own political nation. But in an age of developing political consciousness and communication, in the new world of ideological combat, it is surprising that so few urban centres took anything that might be construed as a positive role from 1640 to 1660: London, Gloucester, Coventry and Birmingham are isolated instances of political involvement with the common denominator of vigorous Puritan leadership.[82] Elsewhere, as at Chester, expediency and pragmatism were the sole urban touchstones in the chemistry of revolutionary politics.

*　　*　　*

As far as the political role of the town in the wider community is concerned it is probably more meaningful by 1700 to talk of the function of county politics in the town than of the town's function in the county. We need finally to examine three other roles of the town beyond its boundaries: the impact of its physical image, the religious role, and the educational or cultural influence.

In 1500 the most important element of urban society's impact on the wider community was the physical appearance of the medium-sized or larger town. By 1700 a medieval countryman might sometimes have needed to examine the skeletal street-plan to recognize the same community. The dissolution of religious houses in the 1530s and 1540s undoubtedly did most to disfigure the image of the medieval town. At Coventry wholesale destruction succeeded the surrender of St Mary's Priory in 1539, its fabric transformed into a quarry for building stone, while at Faversham the splendid abbey founded by King Stephen was so completely obliterated within a few years of its dissolution that only recent archaeology has rescued it from architectural oblivion. Where religious houses were not demolished their fabric was often mutilated on their conversion into the houses of merchants and gentlemen. Such was the fate of the White Friars, Coventry, which became the residence of the Edwardian politician John Hales and was later demolished. Parish churches also fell victim to demolition for many were surplus and semi-derelict before the Reformation: York lost 16 churches after 1547, Lincoln a number in the 1550s, but at Dover destruction was delayed until the last years of James I's reign.[83] Town walls frequently fell into decay and at Coventry the destruction of the fortifications in 1662 came as a reprisal for the city's harbouring of rebels after the Restoration. The Civil War itself did considerable damage: Lancaster in 1684 had still not recovered from the assault of 1643, and Leicester alone lost 120 houses as a consequence of Fairfax's preparations for its defence.[84]

There was little new public building except for the town halls and market-crosses which exemplified the two growth sectors of urban life, oligarchy and local trade. At Coventry the new cross erected in 1541 was partly built with stone from the dissolved city priory. New meeting houses for magistrates were constructed at Abingdon, Aylesbury, Gravesend, Guildford and many other towns. But civic building was overshadowed by the great rebuilding of private housing—the mansions of merchants and lawyers, the town houses of country gentry

and the shacks of the suburban poor. Alteration and improvement
were even more noticeable: the glass windows, fire-places and ornate
porticoes that fashion dictated should be the memorial of even mild
prosperity.[85] Towards the end of the seventeenth century there was
public recognition of the town's importance as a social centre for the
county in the building of Assembly Rooms.

Another function of the medieval town in county society was religious. Not only did quasi-religious pageants and plays attract
countryfolk into towns but the urban church with its more sophisticated ritual was a focus of ecclesiastical life in the surrounding parishes.
The Reformation partially eliminated both these urban activities but
towns continued to perform a significant religious role: they played a
major, if fluctuating, part in the propagation of Protestant and then
Puritan truths. Religious radicalism in older towns may reflect the
widespread friction between civic and ecclesiastical (mainly monastic)
jurisdictions that smouldered throughout the later Middle Ages and
was to some extent perpetuated after the Reformation in disputes
between Cathedrals and their host cities; it was also a response to the
poverty of the urban establishment of parish clergy. In a few towns
like Bristol and Canterbury there was an active Protestant party from
the 1530s, but other towns followed more cautiously. The experience
of Mary's reign showed how susceptible towns were to Crown
pressure, and only with the second decade of Elizabeth's reign do we
find vigorous urban Protestantism denouncing crypto-Catholic
magistrates. Professor Collinson has described how the town-based
prophesying movement of the late 1560s led the way in Puritan
progress.[86] Northampton in 1571 had 'a weekly assembly every
Thursday, after the lecture, by the mayor and his brethren assisted
with the preacher, minister and other gentlemen . . . in commission of
peace', where if the immediate purpose was to reform town discipline,
the greater impact was on the county as a whole; by the next decade
Northampton was the focus of an increasingly Puritan county. Banbury, that Geneva of English provincial towns, had its principal
Puritan impetus in the decade of the Spanish Armada and there were
growing Puritan elements in towns like Barnstaple, Lincoln, Southampton, Warwick and Great Yarmouth by 1603.[87] If some towns had small
groups of Presbyterian extremists, men for instance who printed the
Marprelate tracts, the main emphasis of urban Puritanism was moderate
and Sabbatarian into the reign of James I. Its instruments were the
market-day lecturer and the Godly sermon, its manifestation the

punctilious moderation of the merchant and the deritualized community. At Dorchester, Exeter, Manchester and Salisbury Puritan ministers and magistrates earned approval not merely for their theological superiority but for their greater sense of civic service and responsibility.[88] However, the Arminian regime demonstrated the vulnerability of urban Puritanism to Crown interference. Most towns were compelled to make serious concessions to Laudian ritual in the 1630s, and, as a consequence, the middle ground of moderate Puritanism was lost: congregational cells active since the early years of the century attracted increasing support. If Laudian persecution strengthened the radicalism of urban religion, fragmentation was the fruit of the Civil War and Interregnum. While the Presbyterian Classical organization, which formalized the urban focus of religious activity, had only partial success in England, the most successful religious movement of the Interregnum was Quakerism, drawing its early following as much from the rural areas of the north and west as from the towns.[89]

It would be premature to exaggerate the weakness of the urban voice of Dissent after 1660. The Corporation, Coventicle and Five Mile Acts which sought to silence it through persecution also helped to retard fragmentation. Dissent remained an important force in the politics of Bristol, Chichester, Coventry, Hull and York in the reigns of Charles II and James II.[90] On the other hand, the Toleration Act of 1689 and the Occasional Conformity Act of 1711 weakened its evangelical appeal. Thereafter urban Dissent was less a movement than a vested interest.

Finally, the educational role of towns in the wider community expanded in the sixteenth century only to contract in the seventeenth. Apart from the University towns, the Inns of Court and the small monastic schools located in towns (together with a handful of civic foundations), education was not an especially urban phenomenon in 1500. Gentlemen sent their sons to be trained in aristocratic households and the yeoman's son had to be content with the parish priest or chantry clerk as a teacher. But the early sixteenth century brought the foundation of a large number of schools, often in towns. Town schools were seen now as divine instruments for disseminating both knowledge and true religion in the countryside. It was with the former that Hugh Oldham, Bishop of Exeter, was concerned when he founded Manchester Grammar School in 1525, 'for the good mind which he had and bore to the country of Lancashire, considering the bringing up in learning virtue and good manners of children in the same country should be the key and ground to have good people there'. But Professor W. K. Jordan has demonstrated that a considerable proportion of charitable investment in education in the Tudor and early Stuart period was dedicated by merchants for radical religious improvement. The progress of grammar schools in the market towns of Leicestershire, attended by town and country, gentle and plebeian, has been described in detail by Mrs Simon. A petition at Leicester in the reign of Charles I proclaimed that schoolmasters are 'one of the best jewels and most necessary men . . . which the commonwealth can have to profit and polish with his hand, the best jewels which God gives us [and] our children'. On the lowest level innumerable petty schools flourished in the spirit of educational improvement, providing elementary instruction for the child about to go to grammar school or enter his father's business.[91] But by the third decade of the seventeenth century the provincial town grammar school was losing its comprehensive appeal. Gentlemen preferred to employ a household tutor and then send their sons to a distinguished or fashionable school, to Winchester or Tonbridge or one of the smart North London establishments. After 1660 there was also some competition from dissenting academies. Smaller town schools survived with diminished influence, servicing the neighbourhood with little more than tuition in English grammar. Significantly, control over town schools often passed into the hands of local gentry: thus at Clitheroe in Lancashire and King Edward's School, Birmingham.[92]

A more stable element in the educational function of towns derived from the establishment of town libraries including those at Bristol, Norwich, Colchester and King's Lynn.[93] Unfortunately we know little about the people who made use of their books, whether they came from countryside as well as town. Newspapers were as yet unimportant: although they appear at the very end of our period (some slight compensation for the disappearance of the early Tudor provincial printing presses), they were printed in only the largest provincial centres and were as yet 'mere parasites upon the London press'.[94]

In literature the provincial town had little impact between 1500 and 1700. The mayoral annals which survive from medieval historiography barely continue into the Stuart era while the quasi-religious play that had once determined the reputation of a town in country society had likewise played its last scene. As we mentioned earlier, outside London urban examples of the new fascination with local history are less common than county ones. When Nicholas Bacon came to write the *Annalls of Ipswich* (1654) he did so less out of pride in his community than because of the decay of its government: 'I did perceive few or none of the inhabitants of this town were acquainted with the true nature of the government, and therefore could not so exactly conform themselves to the ancient rules.' England's literary art was increasingly that of London alone and it exhibited the fact: as Lucia, a lady of wit, beauty and fortune in Shadwell's *Epsom Wells*, declares, 'Why people do really live no where else; they breathe and move, and have a kind of insipid being: but there is no life but in London.'[95]

The argument presented so far has been that many English towns between 1500 and 1700 underwent major changes which transformed and to some extent vitiated traditional urban life, affecting not only their economic and demographic structure but their political and cultural make-up. However, it is clear there were exceptions to this thesis inasmuch as certain towns appear to enjoy a substantial demographic and economic expansion in the years up to 1700. These towns fall into two main groups: the new towns of the seventeenth century—the future industrial centres (mostly in the north), the spas, and the naval or dockyard towns; and a number of expanding old communities including Norwich, Newcastle, Bristol, Hull, Exeter and London.

In the case of the industrial towns, Manchester, Birmingham, Leeds, Sheffield and Halifax were by the end of this period large urban centres, something barely conceivable in the sixteenth century. Sheffield, according to Daniel Defoe (1724), was 'very populous and large, the streets narrow, and the houses dark and black, occasioned by the continued smoke of the forges, which are always at work'. As early as 1650 Manchester was described as having a trade 'not inferior to that of many cities in the kingdom' and a parish population in excess of 27,000 communicants. While the prosperity of Sheffield and Birmingham was founded on the metal industry, that of Manchester was worked on cotton, linen and fustian, and the Yorkshire towns grew rich on the sales of cheaper cloths like kersies and, later, worsteds.[96]

Together with the new industrial agglomerations the last part of the seventeenth century saw the arrival of the spa-town. Although as late as 1646 'dogs, cats, pigs and even human creatures' were still being hurled into its waters the spa at Bath was definitely established by 1700.

Bath, of course, was not a new town but it developed a novel style of urban life which was imitated at Tunbridge Wells, Epsom and Harrogate. These were becoming not so much health farms as holiday camps for the magnates of the kingdom, microcosms of London fashion planted in the countryside.[97]

Despite Defoe's comment that 'the war has brought a flux of business and people, and consequently of wealth, to several places, as well as to Portsmouth, Chatham, Plymouth, Falmouth and others', naval and dockyard centres have been the least studied of all the new towns. Probably they constitute the most spectacular cases of urban expansion. Plymouth's boom was a consequence of the Elizabethan wars but most development of these towns occurred in the next century. Philipot described Deptford in 1659 as 'so greatly increased in small tenements ... for number of inhabitants and communicants it may compare with divers counties in the kingdom', and D. C. Coleman argues that 'in shape and appearance, in social and economic structure, as well as in their dependence on a single heavy industry these dockyard towns approximated to the type of industrial town which the nineteenth century made familiar'. Chatham was booming in the 1620s, Portsmouth and the North Kent ports from the decade of the Cromwellian wars, while Falmouth was incorporated in 1660. Economically, these towns had an extensive impact on the countryside through the employment of direct labour at the yards and the demand for large quantities of supplies, especially timber. As Defoe remarks, their development reached its climax in this period with the wars of William III and Anne.[98]

Compared with the new expanding centres it is much more difficult to categorize our older growth towns. Defoe's general comment on urban development is especially relevant: 'And if it be ... some other towns ... are lately increased in trade and navigation, wealth and people, while their neighbours decay, it is because they have some particular trade or accident to trade, which is a kind of nostrum to them.' Thus Norwich by 1693 had a population approaching 29,000 after two decades of considerable demographic progress which P. Corfield argues was sustained through the specialist exploitation of home demand for woollen textiles. Newcastle was the principal port for coal in the country, exporting for domestic consumption in the south, especially London, and to Northern Europe; by 1665 it had a population of over 13,000. Exeter had a more broadly based prosperity being 'a city famous for two things which we seldom find united in the same town, (viz.) that 'tis full of gentry and good company, and yet full of trade and manufactures also'; but its main source of prosperity sprang from expanding exports of west country cloth to the Netherlands, and from coastal shipping; in 1676 it had about 13,000 inhabitants. Bristol concentrated on exploitation of the American, West Indian and Mediterranean trades with a strong base of coastal shipping, and this supported a population which rose from about 12,000 to about 20,000 during the seventeenth century. Another expanding centre in the seventeenth century was Hull, whose exports of Yorkshire cloth rose from £109,000 worth in 1609 to £340,000 worth at the end of the century, but whose strength again lay with its dual function as seaport and head of a network of river and coastal trade; by 1695 8,000 or so people lived there.[99] While Hull served as the port for Yorkshire industry Liverpool expanded as an outlet for the textile production of the Lancashire hinterland, using as a springboard for its American and West Indian commerce a strong interest in Anglo-Irish trade and control over the Cheshire salt trade; in 1700 it had a population in excess of 5,000.[100] The greatness of London has recurred throughout this introduction and we shall analyse its importance more closely in the last section.

The explanation of the exception is always more interesting than its description. How do we account for the growth of these centres? The common feature of the industrial, spa and dockyard towns is their newness. Some were villages, others in our category of 'simple towns' in 1500. Expansion occurred without the traditional controls of the urban community. Even when industrial centres like Leeds (1626) or Sheffield (1554) achieved corporate status and in some cases acquired gilds they remained comparatively free communities. The distinguished provincial journalist J. T. Bunce who published a *History of the Corporation of Birmingham* under the auspices of Joseph Chamberlain may have been infected by free trade Liberalism but he was probably right when he wrote: 'The great glory of Birmingham, the source of its strength and the cause of its rapid advance in prosperity and population was that it was a free town. Neither personal nor corporate hindrances existed in it.'[101] These new industrial towns were freed from the heavy overheads coincident with sophisticated civic machinery. The absence of urban regulation was less significant for the development of spa or dockyard towns, but the rapidity of their advance might have been slowed by the harassment of civic restraint: it is not without significance that the ancient city of Rochester was defeated by the open towns of Chatham and Gillingham as the principal dockyard centre on the Medway estuary.

The growth points of seventeenth-century urban expansion are to be found mostly among 'simple towns', as we have seen, and the largest old centres. With the exception of Liverpool and perhaps Hull all our expanding older centres had been important in 1500. One possible explanation is that these towns had reached the stage of becoming self-sustaining urban economies, less liable to sudden decay, strong enough to weather depression, and more able to exploit with accumulating success favourable economic opportunities. Another common feature is also significant: with the exception of Norwich all were ports. Since foreign trade was probably the most dynamic element in the later Stuart economy it is not surprising that towns with good port facilities came to expand. But this does not terminate the argument. Why did certain ports fail so signally to share in this prosperity? Was it simply a function of size? Undoubtedly the scale of shipping engaged in foreign trade increased in the seventeenth century demanding better harbour facilities, but the success of certain ports depended less on this than on their control of local shipping, both river and coastal (although the two phenomena are not entirely unrelated). Bristol in the Stuart period engrossed the trade of the Bristol Channel havens such as Bideford, Barnstaple and Minehead, exploiting its geographical position at the junction of the Bristol Channel and the Severn and Wye network of rivers and canals; Exeter may have built up the same kind of hegemony on the south-west coast.[102]

Finally, growth appears to have been encouraged by the absence of stringent community control. At Bristol the impetus for trade expansion derived from the Company of Merchants Adventurers, an outward looking, comparatively open organization which was responsible for the building of dock facilities and attempts to control piracy, while Exeter's advance coincided with the decay of the monopoly organization of merchants engaged in the French trade and the growth of free commerce with the Netherlands. Norwich company regulations lapsed in the late seventeenth century and the Newcastle cartel of Hostmen had a diminished importance in the exploitation of coal about the town in the early eighteenth century.[103] Thus where there was major long-term economic expansion in urban society from 1500 to 1700 it tended to occur either in the absence of some of those political, economic and social structures which we identify with medieval urban communities (the case with the new urban centres) or through economic initiative external to the traditional community (as with the expanding old towns).

Apart then from their continued economic and demographic expansion, how far did these exceptional towns differ from the urban norm? The answer must be: not very much. The price of population rise remained high. Late Stuart Liverpool and Manchester were inundated with a tide of immigrant poverty and squalor: Liverpool complained in 1678 that 'a great concourse of people have of late time resorted hither and have been concealed in design to gain settlement', and the levy for poor relief rose from £40 (1681) to £520 (1719). Norwich relief cost over £149 in 1621 but by 1711 it had soared to more than £602. After the middle of the seventeenth century the magistrates of Sheffield were constantly preoccupied with poverty problems. The topography of poverty was the same as elsewhere; the greatest concentration being in the suburbs, for instance, the suburb of St Sidwell, Exeter, was the most impoverished in the city.[104]

The tensions within the political community were often as acute in expanding as declining towns. There were oligarchies in Leeds, Sheffield, Bristol, Exeter, Liverpool, Newcastle and Norwich.[105] In most cases the parliamentary boroughs suffered from the same affliction of party conflict in the late seventeenth century. By 1700 the traditional civic organization of the old cities was showing signs of its inadequacy: the magistrates of Bristol handed over their responsibility for the poor to a Corporation originated by a non-magistrate in 1696; in this they were followed by Exeter and Norwich.[106] Most chartered towns had recoiled under the force of the *Quo Warranto* proceedings instituted by Charles II and James II. As far as county influence is concerned the smaller, especially new, towns were vulnerable to gentry meddling in their politics and pillaging their property but it is less clear how far the greater communities suffered from the same intrusion.[107] In a way the problem may have ceased to exist for them because at least in the cases of Bristol, Norwich and perhaps Exeter their magnates were themselves quasi-gentry following the dictates of county and London society. Indeed, even in the larger cities oligarchies no longer governed as municipal officials but as justices of the peace, like their counterparts in the countryside.[108]

To conclude, we return to the urban image in the wider community. Few of these expanding centres undertook expensive civic building: Liverpool had a new Exchange in the reign of Charles II and Manchester a court building about 1656, but construction was dominated by private housing. In religion there is some evidence to suggest a number of the larger communities survived as important havens for radical religion in the last part of the seventeenth century, but there is little to prove they continued their proselytizing importance in the national community.[109] Similarly in their educational chronology these towns conform to the urban pattern described earlier: after massive early expansion town schools contracted from the Restoration. Thus at Hull the principal phase of school growth had apparently terminated by 1680 and Bristol Grammar School became steadily more exclusive in the seventeenth century.[110]

If the France of Louis XIV orbited on the axis of the Court of the Sun-King at Versailles and the counting houses of Amsterdam instructed the taste and policy of the Dutch for most of the seventeenth century, England by 1700 focused its admiration not on the Palace of Whitehall, nor on the political and mercantile cartels of the City but rather on the greater metropolis that embraced them both. How far does London exemplify the urban reorientation and disorganization which, as we have seen, was widespread in the sixteenth and seventeenth centuries?

The most dynamic elements in London's growth from 1500 to 1700 were demographic and economic. Some recent work has begun to analyse the structure and processes of these developments, but here we are primarily concerned with their impact.[111] As might be expected, neither of these growth sectors could be contained within the medieval framework of the capital. M. Power in his paper on housing in seventeenth-century London shows that by 1600 large numbers of newcomers were settling in the parishes to the east of the City. Over the river in Southwark congregated more poor folk, whereas the area to the west of Temple Bar was inhabited by prosperous Londoners. Although the population of metropolitan London nearly trebled in the seventeenth century, that of the parishes within the City walls fell from about 103,000 to 99,000 in the years 1659 to 1694, a decline probably accentuated by the Great Fire. A substantial part of the metropolitan population was poor, often recruited from the countryside. Perhaps as many as one in six of the adult national population had visited the capital by the end of this period, but little is known of how they lived. The turnover rate was high; many of those who survived endemic disease soon left for the provinces and London was the graveyard of pauper England. It was this which motivated the enormous contribution of London merchants to the charitable relief of the poor; that necessitated London's institution of one of the earliest schemes of civic relief in England; and which made London notorious for popular unrest in the sixteenth century and political radicalism in the seventeenth.[112]

If London's inhabitants migrated increasingly outside the constraints of the medieval city so did its economic impetus. Again the shift was partially geographical as industry moved to the suburbs. Thus in 1632 the City magistrates complained that the 'freedom of London, which was heretofore of very great esteem is grown to be little worth by reason of the extraordinary enlargement of the suburbs where great numbers of traders and handicraftsmen do enjoy without charge equal benefit with the freemen and citizens of London'. The incentives for migration were the same as elsewhere: less civic regulation, lower overheads and cheaper labour—together with the new demand of a booming suburban population.[113] The flight of industry was turned into a stampede by the Great Fire of 1666: as T. F. Reddaway observed, 'with four-fifths of its area burnt, it [the City] had to watch its citizens acquiring leases of suburban properties, setting up shops in the Strand, or moving down the river to the havens of Wapping'. Others fled further, some to Liverpool, encouraged by the King's proclamation opening all towns to refugees from the Fire. Not only industry but markets tended to slide out of City jurisdiction: sixteen new markets were established in the suburbs in the seventeenth century, most of them after 1650.[114]

But the changing economic emphasis of London was not simply a matter of topography. The rise of the East India Company, the joint-stock companies and the Bank of England in the later Stuart period, institutions having a London location yet with considerable numbers of extra-City investors and obeying exigencies usually unrelated to City interest, further threatened the traditional economic structure of the City. When in 1712 City magistrates abandoned any further attempt to enforce its freedom upon wholesalers and merchants trading overseas they recognized the writing on the wall: the City's diminishing relevance for the great mercantile interests of the capital. Already the events of the 1690s had proven that exogenous factors determined the calculations of the London business community. As D. W. Jones shows in his paper on the London merchants and the crisis of that decade, London businessmen diverted capital from the wine trade into the Bank of England and then the New East India Company under the economic pressures caused by Continental war: international not civic forces were in command.

Naturally, the causes and, to some extent, the consequences of this demographic and economic expansion were largely beyond the control of the City magistrates. But whenever the latter did have an opportunity to assert their authority they failed, conspicuously, to seize it. The City consistently refused to take responsibility for administering the suburban conglomerations. As a consequence, local government in the metropolis remained chaotic.[115] Fundamentally, City magistrates were terrified lest by enlarging civic jurisdiction they weaken an oligarchy erected on the tight circle of City gild and ward elections.

The fact that 'the primary significance of the Corporation was not as a body to govern London but as an assembly of the traditional companies' explains not only its failure to deal with these problems but its ultimate decline. While City merchants rode across the countryside articulating a decisive voice in local trade, the great City companies were under siege, harassed partly from within by dissident small masters, traders and workmen, partly by suburban competition, and partly by the rivalry of incipient industrial centres such as Birmingham or Sheffield. Companies in retaliation tended to be restrictive, recruitment stagnated, and they lost contact with the economic realities of the capital.[116] City government was undermined both by the spreading paralysis of gild institutions and by internal weaknesses. Although oligarchy had been in effective control since the fifteenth century the City exhibited the national bias towards more rigid and inflexible rule by clique in the early seventeenth century, a regime broadened only intermittently during the English Revolution. Consequent political conflict was aggravated by the approaching insolvency of City finances. The extortion of government loans during and after the Civil War only speeded the deterioration and the Great Fire came as a climax to years of further financial disorder. In 1666 the City's liabilities exceeded £300,000 and its assets had been reduced to £200,000: expenditure ran at twice the level of income. Final disintegration was postponed in 1672 at the price of appropriating coal dues approved by Parliament for specific rebuilding schemes and by plundering the funds of the Orphans' Court, but the cost of opposing the *Quo Warranto* proceedings of Charles II and James II precipitated the onrush of bankruptcy and in 1694 City credit and finance collapsed. Crown lawsuits against corporation and gild charters also created administrative dislocation which propelled both towards that rarefied world of social magnificence and administrative impotence they inhabited in the next century.[117]

That radicalism survived in London from the seventeenth into the eighteenth century as a political virus is a footnote to the dichotomy between accumulating metropolitan wealth, population and social problems on the one hand, and the decline of the City machine on the other. There is an optimum size for a radical urban centre: too extensive for there to be good government or for the instruments of repression to be effective, small enough for the existence of a coherent community of opposition. London alone in pre-industrial England had the correct dimensions for effective radicalism. The radical focus was to be found in the confrontation of great mercantile oligarchs and smaller merchants and tradesmen differing from provincial agitations only in its scale. However, this is an explanation less of London's importance as a radical centre, erupting sporadically into the world of national politics, than of radical survival in the doldrum years between such crises. London radicalism depended for its importance on factors external to City or metropolitan politics. After 1640 the extraordinary success of agitation in the City was only made possible by the support of parliamentary and army malcontents; while party conflict in the 1670s smouldered on the issue of civic finance the political explosion of 1678–81 was ignited by the fusion of City radicalism with external political forces, especially Westminster politicians. Already by the early eighteenth century City politics constituted an arena for the confrontation of national politicians on national issues, an outlet for the frustration of oligarchic manipulations at Westminster: the qualification was finally one of proximity.[118]

The incipient divorce of City and metropolis was most obvious in the physical sense. Rows of houses pushed the urban sprawl eastwards, with the highest density in 1664 in East Smithfield and St Katharine's. If, as Power argues, East London building became more orderly in the course of the seventeenth century, it remains true that even the better houses were often jerry-built, short-lived and expensive to rent; and beyond the verge of respectability, of the self-supporting poor, crouched the utterly destitute, drifting in a third world of crime and disease. But to the west of London speculators like Dr Nicholas Barbon, Colonel Thomas Panton and Sir Thomas Bond were constructing a different architectural landscape, of splendid mansions and spacious squares, which form the backcloth to eighteenth-century political society. Definitively the social heartland of the capital had left the walled City. The latter, of course, continued to contribute something to the physical image of London: the cool elegance of the new parish churches after the Fire is a splendid testimonial to the respectability and moderation of London merchants. Even so, the City's lack of money and imagination prevented the execution of other schemes for large-scale public building.[119]

Another crucial element of London's role in the national community was religion. It would be inconceivable to discuss the ecclesiastical history of England without reference to London. Perhaps for this very reason, that the strands of metropolitan and national religious pre-occupations are so inextricably confused, there is no recent historian of London's importance as a religious centre. We know something of the fervour of London's anti-clericalism before 1529; of the importance of foreign Protestant communities there; of the sectarian preference for the London liberties and suburbs; of the importance of London merchants in planting Puritan lectureships in provincial towns, and of the highly sophisticated Puritan apparatus, based on London, for evading episcopal supervision of clergy.[120] On the other hand, our ignorance is virtually absolute as far as the multi-generational experience of religious radicalism within the capital and the relation of religion to London's changing economic and social problems are concerned.

If London was England's Rome for most of this period, it also had a strong claim to be regarded as the nation's educator, especially in the years up to the Civil War. The humanist innovations of St Paul's School founded in 1509 influenced generations of English intellectual and educational thought; London mercantile wealth was invested in the endowments of many country grammar schools; the Inns of Court, the third university of the kingdom, introduced the sons of gentlemen to the costly fascination of the law; and the Scientific Revolution may have been unveiled to a wider audience in the lectures given at Gresham's College, Surgeons' Hall and the College of Physicians. But after the Restoration educational facilities in the capital reflect the growing separation of the City and the aristocratic metropolis: the generality of grammar schools decayed or disappeared, and educational advance was restricted to fashionable schools like Westminster, dissenting academies like that of Charles Morton at Newington Green, and smart establishments such as Thomas Swadlin's school at Paddington; many of these new institutions were located in the northern or western suburbs to provide for the aristocracy and gentry living there.[121]

London in the seventeenth century became for the nation what every county town aspired to become for its own locality: a centre for conspicuous consumption by the upper classes. In the early eighteenth century London was the seat of national oligarchy, both social and political. What we do not know is how far the aristocracy was influenced by its urban situation. Probably little. That aristocratic duet, Young Bellair and Harriet, in Etherege's *The Man of Mode* (1676), might from the window of London society dismiss provincial England as 'Hampshire':

Young Bellair Are you in love?
Harriet Yes, with this dear town, to that degree, I can scarce indure the country in landscapes and in hangings.
Young Bellair What a dreadful thing 'twould be to be hurried back to Hampshire!

But they knew little and cared less about the problems of the capital.[122] In fact it is arguable that in the growth points which affected the metropolitan community there is little to distinguish a London characteristic from a national one. London was already on its way to losing its peculiar identity.

The argument put forward in this introduction has been that English urban society from 1500 to 1700 witnessed a major collision of continuity and change. Within the apparently ordered framework of pre-industrial society many communities underwent a severe reorientation affecting all sectors of urban life. Even towns which exhibit signs of continuous economic as well as demographic expansion may have been affected by this decay of the sense of urban community. London itself suffered a reverse takeover by the national community. However, it is true to add that the most critical change in this period occurred within the medium-size, municipal centres—the second tier of urban society. Indeed, these years demonstrate the changing balance of English urbanism.[123] Whereas towns in this second tier, like Salisbury or Canterbury or Boston, had supplied the predominant image of the urban community in fifteenth-century England, the most striking and dynamic centres in the eighteenth century are, on the one hand, new agglomerations like Birmingham or Manchester, which had developed from our lowest tier of the urban hierarchy, and, on the other, the great ancient cities of Bristol and Norwich themselves aping the urban modernity of London.

Notes

1 For a general survey of urban historiography, see H. J. Dyos, ed., *The Study of Urban History* (1968), pp. 19–43. C. Gross, *A Bibliography of British Municipal History* (reprinted with a preface by G. H. Martin, Leicester, 1966) lists publications to 1897; Dr Martin is preparing supplementary volumes.

2 Cf. F. S. Fussner, *The Historical Revolution* (1962), pp. 179–82, and W. G. Hoskins, *Local History in England* (1959), pp. 15–24, for a discussion of the beginnings of local history. Among the more important town histories were W. Somner, *The Antiquities of Canterbury* (1640); J. Stow, *Survey of London* (1598); and Richard Butcher, *The Survey and Antiquitie of the Towne of Stamford* (1646). Significantly, John Hooker's late Elizabethan *Description of the Citie of Excester* and Henry Manship's Jacobean *History of Great Yarmouth* were not published in full until 1919 and 1854 respectively.

3 The best town histories published in the eighteenth century include F. Drake, *Eboracum or the History and Antiquities of the City of York* (1736); W. Hutton, *The History of Birmingham* (Birmingham, 1781); J. Milner, *The History and Survey of the Antiquities of Winchester* (Winchester, 1798). The influence of franchise reform is obvious from the title of W. R. James, *The Charters and other documents relating to the King's Town and Parish of Maidstone . . . clearly shewing the right of election of members of Parliament to be in the inhabitant householders* (1825). The early histories of Worcester were published in 1790, 1796, 1808 and 1820, those of Bristol in 1789, 1794, 1816 and 1821.

4 For instance, the obsession with gilds can be seen from Gross, *op. cit.*, pp. 83–8. The Historical Manuscripts Commission first reported in 1870. The *Victoria County Histories*, begun in 1899, still bear the birth marks of conception by medievalists.

5 Cf. J. T. Bunce, *History of the Corporation of Birmingham* (Birmingham, 1878–85); J. A. Picton, *Memorials of Liverpool* (1875) (heavily nineteenth-century); J. Reilly, *The History of Manchester* (1861); W. E. A. Axon, *The Annals of Manchester* (1886).

6 For example, M. Bateson, ed., *Records of the Borough of Leicester* (3 vols, Cambridge, 1899–1905). A further valuable contribution to early modern urban studies was made by the foundation of the Southampton Record Society in 1905, and the Bristol Record Society in 1930. There was of course increasing analysis of industrialization and this shed some light on town development: Dyos, *op. cit.*, p. 24n.

7 The scale of interest is apparent in the long lists of work in progress published by the *Urban History Newsletter* (Leicester, 1963–), itself symptomatic of the new movement.

8 Particularly, W. G. Hoskins, *Provincial England* (1963), chaps iv, v; 'The Elizabethan Merchants of Exeter', in S. T. Bindoff, J. Hurstfield, C. H. Williams, eds, *Elizabethan Government and Society* (1961), pp. 163–212; and for the later period, *Industry, Trade and People in Exeter 1688–1800* (2nd edn, Exeter, 1968).

9 Cf. P. Deyon, *Amiens, capitale provinciale* (Paris, 1967), and B. Bennassar, *Valladolid au siècle d'or* (Paris, 1967).

10 Including A. D. Dyer, 'The Economy of Tudor Worcester', *Univ. Birmingham Hist. J.*, X (1966), 117–36; J. F. Pound, 'The Social and Trade Structure of Norwich 1525–1575', *P. & P.*, no. 34 (1966), 49–69; R. Howell, *Newcastle-upon-Tyne and the Puritan Revolution* (Oxford, 1967); V. Pearl, *London and the Outbreak of the Puritan Revolution* (Oxford, 1961); P. E. Jones and A. V. Judges, 'London Population in the late Seventeenth Century', *Ec.H.R.*, VI (1935), 45–63. Among the exceptions are the histories of Coventry, Warwick, Hull and York in the recent volumes of the *VCH*; W. T. MacCaffrey, *Exeter 1540–1640* (Cambridge, Mass., 1958); J. Cornwall, 'English Country Towns in the Fifteen-Twenties', *Ec.H.R.*, 2nd Series, XV (1962–3), 54–69; Hoskins, *Provincial England*, chap. iv. There is an excellent comparative description of market towns by A. M. Everitt in J. Thirsk, ed., *The Agrarian History of England and Wales: IV* (Cambridge, 1967), pp. 467–90. An old-fashioned synthesis almost entirely concerned with structural problems is J. H. Thomas, *Town Government in the Sixteenth Century* (1933).

11 R. E. Park, W. W. Burgess and R. D. McKenzie, *The City* (Chicago, 1925). For a general survey of recent conceptual work, see P. M. Hauser and L. F. Schnore, eds, *The Study of Urbanization* (1965), chap. v.

12 *The Preindustrial City* (Chicago, 1960), esp. chaps iv–x.

13 S. and B. Webb, *English Local Government from the Revolution to the Municipal Corporations Act: the Manor and the Borough* (1924); W. Harrison, *Description of England* (ed. F. J. Furnivall, New Shakespeare Soc., 1877–1908), part i, p. 259; Hooker is quoted in MacCaffrey, *op. cit.*, p. 275.

14 J. Adams, *Index Villaris or An Alphabetical Table of All the Cities, Market-Towns, Parishes, Villages and Private Seats in England and Wales* (1st edn, 1680, 2nd edn, 1690); D. V. Glass, 'Two Papers on Gregory King', in D. V. Glass and D. E. C. Eversley, eds, *Population in History* (1965), pp. 159–220.

15 Glass, *op. cit.*, pp. 186–7; cf. the description of Halifax in D. Defoe, *A Tour Through the Whole Island of Great Britain* (Dent, 1962), II, 193.

16 Webbs, *op. cit.*, I, 202, Glass, *loc. cit.*

17 G. Botero, *The Reason of State and the Greatness of Cities* (ed. P. J. and D. P. Waley, 1956), p. 235. For a recent discussion of London, see E. A. Wrigley, 'A Simple Model of London's Importance in Changing English Society and Economy 1650–1750', *P. & P.*, no. 37 (1967), 44–70.

18 E.g., Bristol: W. E. Minchinton, 'Bristol—Metropolis of the West in the Eighteenth Century', *Trans. Roy. Hist. Soc.*, 5th Series, IV (1954), 70–85; Exeter: Hoskins, *Industry, Trade and People in Exeter 1688–1800*, pp. 18–19; York: *VCH York*, pp. 198–9. For cities with county jurisdiction, see Webbs, *op. cit.*, I, 330 and n.

19 Hoskins, *Provincial England*, p. 72; Wrigley, *op. cit.*, pp. 44 *et seq.*

20 M. Weinbaum, ed., *British Borough Charters 1307–1660* (Cambridge, 1943).

21 These estimates, inevitably tentative, are based on King (*vide* Glass, *op. cit.*, pp. 186–7, 201–4), supplemented by Professor Hoskins's suggestions for specific towns (*Provincial England*, p. 72); but more work is needed on local populations of the kind begun by J. Cornwall: cf. his 'English Country Towns in the Fifteen-Twenties', and 'English Population in the Early Sixteenth Century', *Ec.H.R.*, 2nd Series, XXIII (1970), 32–44.

22 Cf. N. G. Brett-James, *The Growth of Stuart London* (1935), esp. chap. xviii.

23 *VCH Warwicks*, VIII, 8; G. Chandler, *Liverpool under Charles I* (Liverpool, 1965), p. 33; Hoskins, *Provincial England*, p. 71. The topography of the pre-industrial town is being drawn in the series of plans of *Historic Towns*, edited by M. D. Lobel (1969–).

24 E.g., the corporation records of New Romney kept at the Kent Archives Office, Maidstone.

25 R. H. Morris, *Chester in the Plantagenet and Tudor Reigns* (Chester, 1893), p. 74; A. Beesley, *The History of Banbury* (1841), p. 278; *HMC* 14th Report, App. VIII, p. 141; *A True and Faithful Relation of the late Dreadful Fire at Northampton* (1675), p. 2.

26 W. H. Hudson and J. C. Tingey, eds, *The Records of the City of Norwich*, *II* (1910), pp. cxxvi–cxxvii; Howell, *op. cit.*, pp. 7–8; *APC 1625–6*, pp. 217–18, 312.

27 K. M. E. Murray, *The Constitutional History of the Cinque Ports* (Manchester, 1935), p. 209; P. Thompson, *The History and Antiquities of Boston* (1856), p. 72; Morris, *op. cit.*, pp. 459–62; W. B. Stephens, 'The Overseas Trade of Chester in the Early Seventeenth Century', *Trans. Hist. Soc. of Lancs. and Cheshire*, CXX (1968), 23 *et seq.*

28 Somner, *op. cit.*, pp. 39–41; J. W. F. Hill, *Tudor and Stuart Lincoln* (Cambridge, 1956), p. 131; MacCaffrey, *op. cit.*, pp. 127 *et seq.*

29 S. L. Thrupp, *The Merchant Class of Medieval London 1300–1500* (Chicago, 1948), is a major exception, but there has been less work on provincial urban society; the urban section of A. R. Myers, ed., *English Historical Documents: IV 1327–1485* (1969) (hereafter cited as *E.H.D.*) does only a little to lighten the gloom.

30 E. M. Carus-Wilson, *The Expansion of Exeter at the Close of the Middle Ages* (Harte Memorial Lecture, Exeter, 1963), pp. 4–5 *et passim*; A. R. Bridbury, *Economic Growth* (1962), pp. 48–51.

31 A. Rogers, ed., *The Making of Stamford* (Leicester, 1965), pp. 58–9; Canterbury, *ex inform.* Mr A. Butcher.

32 E.g., *VCH York*, p. 113; Hoskins, *Provincial England*, pp. 73–4, 83–5.

33 J. C. Russell, *British Medieval Population* (Albuquerque, 1948), p. 294; Carus-Wilson, *op. cit.*, p. 31; Bridbury, *op. cit.*, p. 74; for declining immigration at York: *VCH York*, p. 108. The thesis of population stagnation posited by M. Postan in 'Some Economic Evidence of Declining Population in the Later Middle Ages', *Ec.H.R.*, 2nd Series, II (1950), 221–46, has been attacked by J. M. W. Bean, 'Plague, Population and Economic Decline in England in the later Middle Ages', *Ec.H.R.*, 2nd Series, XV (1963), 423–37, but Bean concedes that towns were more vulnerable to demographic crisis (p. 435). For the urban poor, see F. Graus, 'The Late Medieval Poor in Town and Countryside', in S. Thrupp, ed., *Change in Medieval Society* (1965), p. 317.

34 Cf. Bridbury, *op. cit.*, p. 61. Accounts of gild plays at Beverley, and town processions and pageants at Norwich are printed in *E.H.D.*, IV, 1064–6, 1095–6. On the complex gild structure at York, see the paper of D. M. Palliser, below.

35 J. S. Roskell, *The Commons in the Parliament of 1422* (Manchester, 1954), p. 59; C. Gill, *Studies in Midland History* (Oxford, 1930), p. 32. Cf. *E.H.D.*, IV, 1104–6, for Canterbury's efforts to buy off both Yorkist and Lancastrian forces in turn in 1469–70.

36 *VCH Warwicks*, VIII, 209; *VCH York*, p. 107; Carus-Wilson, *op. cit.*, p. 21. Leland was always impressed by town walls: E. Moir, *The Discovery of Britain* (1964), pp. 18–19.

37 Town and country were not only united in the audience at a play: at Lincoln the garments for the pageants of St Anne's gild were borrowed every year from the gentry of the shire: *HMC*, 14th Report, App. VIII, p. 25.

38 Pound, *op. cit.*, pp. 58 *et seq.*; A. J. King and B. H. Watts, *Cavaliers and Roundheads, a Chapter in the History of Bath* (1887), pp. 3–4; G. H. Martin, *The Story of Colchester* (Colchester, 1959), pp. 48 *et seq.*; *VCH Bucks*, III, 471–2; *VCH Warwicks*, VIII, 162–3 (although

Coventry became important again in the mid-eighteenth century: J. M. Prest, *The Industrial Revolution in Coventry* (1960), pp. 44–5); A. Ruddock, 'London Capitalists and the Decline of Southampton in the Early Tudor Period', *Ec.H.R.*, 2nd Series, II (1949–50), 137–51.

39 *VCH York*, pp. 89–90; *VCH Kent*, III, 406. Cf. J. Thirsk, 'Industries in the Countryside', in F. J. Fisher, ed., *Essays in the Economic and Social History of Tudor and Stuart England in honour of R. H. Tawney* (Cambridge, 1961), pp. 70–88.

40 R. H. Tawney and E. Power, *Tudor Economic Documents* (1924), I, 173–5, 119–21; *VCH Leics*, IV, 107; A. Raine, ed., *York Civic Records*, VI (Yorks. Arch. Soc., Record Series, CXII, 1946), p. 17.

41 On the decay of pilgrimage profits, see C. E. Woodruff, 'The Financial Aspect of the Cult of St Thomas of Canterbury', *Archaeologia Cantiana*, XLIV (1932), 13–32. Abingdon was one of a number of towns seriously affected by the Reformation: *VCH Berks*, IV, 439.

42 H. Stocks, ed., *Records of the Borough of Leicester*, IV, xliii; W. Cunningham, *Alien Immigrants to England* (1897), chap. iv. Nottingham in the late seventeenth century acquired both an expanding framework-knitting industry and enhanced social importance: J. D. Chambers, 'Population Change in a Provincial Town: Nottingham 1700–1800, in L. S. Pressnell, ed., *Studies in the Industrial Revolution* (1960), p. 103.

43 Tawney and Power, *op. cit.*, III, 274; R. P. Cruden, *The History of the Town of Gravesend* (1843), pp. 189–90, R. W. K. Hinton, ed., *The Port Books of Boston 1601–40* (Lincoln Record Soc., L, 1956), p. xl; *CSPD 1598–1601*, p. 2. For the Free Trade dispute see R. Ashton, 'The Parliamentary Agitation for Free Trade in the Opening Years of the reign of James I', *P. & P.*, no. 38 (1967), 40–55, in combat with T. K. Rabb, 'Free Trade and the Gentry in the Parliament of 1604', *P. & P.*, no. 40 (1968), 165–73; B. Supple, *Commercial Crisis and Change in England 1600–1642* (Cambridge, 1959), pp. 30–1. P. McGrath in *Records Relating to the Society of Merchant Adventurers of the City of Bristol in the Seventeenth Century* (Bristol Record Soc., XVII, 1952), pp. xxxviii–xxxix, suggests that this controversy involved as much fratricide among the outports as warfare between them and London.

44 T. S. Willan published *The English Coasting Trade 1600–1750* (Manchester) in 1938 (reprinted 1967); see also Willan, *River Navigation in England* (Oxford, 1936); A. M. Everitt, 'The Marketing of Agricultural Produce' in J. Thirsk, ed., *The Agrarian History of England and Wales IV*, pp. 466–592; F. J. Fisher, 'The Development of the London Food Market 1540–1640', *Ec.H.R.*, V (2) (1934–5), 46–64; P. V. McGrath, 'The Marketing of Food, Fodder and Livestock in the London Area in the Seventeenth Century with some reference to the sources of supply' (unpublished M.A. thesis, London University, 1948).

45 M. R. Innes, 'Chelmsford: the Evolution of a County Town' (unpublished M.A. thesis, London University, 1951), p. 243; C. W. Chalklin, *Seventeenth Century Kent* (1965), pp. 173–4; J. H. Andrews, 'The Trade of the Port of Faversham 1650–1750', *Archaeologia Cantiana*, LXIX (1955), 125–31; D. C. Coleman, 'The Economy of Kent under the later Stuarts' (unpublished Ph.D. thesis, London University, 1951), p. 128 (we are grateful to Dr Coleman for permission to quote from his thesis); Fisher, 'The Development of the London Food Market', pp. 63–4. Towns further from London retained a relatively independent role for rather longer: Shrewsbury acted as an entrepôt between London and the Welsh woollen area: T. C. Mendenhall, *The Shrewsbury Drapers and the Welsh Wool Trade in the XVI and XVII Centuries* (1953), pp. 214–15.

46 Morris, *op. cit.*, p. 400; Thompson, *op. cit.*, p. 346. Cf. Everitt, 'Social Mobility in Early Modern England,' *P. & P.*, no. 33 (1966), 56–73, and R. B. Westerfield, *Middlemen in English Business* (New Haven, 1915). For provincial disputes with London traders, see W. B. Stephens, *Seventeenth-Century Exeter* (Exeter, 1958), pp. 141–2; Mendenhall, *op. cit.*, pp. 147 *et seq.*; Tawney and Power, *op. cit.*, II, 49–50.

47 F. N. L. Poynter and W. J. Bishop, eds, *A Seventeenth Century Doctor and his Patients: John Symcotts 1592–1662* (Beds. Hist. Record Soc., XXXI, 1951), *passim*. On the medical profession in provincial towns in this period, see J. H. Raach, *A Directory of English Country Physicians 1603–43* (1962), esp. p. 14; R. S. Roberts, 'The Personnel and Practice of Medicine in Tudor and Stuart England: Part I The Provinces', *Medical History*, VI (1962), 363–82.

48 There is a dearth of published material on provincial law and lawyers at this time. On lawyers in the church courts at York, see R. A. Marchant, *The Church under the Law* (Cambridge, 1969), pp. 41–60; the importance of attorneys in Lincoln is mentioned by Hill, *op. cit.*, pp. 92–3.

49 Innes, *op. cit.*, pp. 363–4; information on Abingdon from Mr J. A. Chartres; *VCH Leics*, IV, 180; C. H. Mayo, ed., *The Municipal Records of the Borough of Dorchester* (Exeter, 1908), p. 502; G. Berry, 'New Light on the Seventeenth Century Token Issuers of Chepping Wycombe', *Records of Bucks.*, XVIII (1967), 151. Cf. Everitt, 'Social Mobility', pp. 69–72.

50 R. C. Anderson, ed., *Book of Examinations and Depositions IV* (Southampton Record Soc., 1936), p. 1; P. Corfield, below, p. 292; *VCH Bucks*, III, 472; *VCH Warwicks*, VIII, 219; A. Hewitson, *History of Preston* (Preston, 1883), pp. 94–5; *HMC*, 14th Report, App. VIII, p. 106; *VCH Warwicks*, VIII, 512.

51 T. S. Willan, ed., *The Navigation of the Great Ouse* (Beds. Hist. Rec.

Soc., XXIV, 1946), p. 5; J. Russell, *The History of Guildford* (1801), p. 9.

52 C. G. Parsloe, 'The Growth of a Borough Constitution: Newark-on-Trent 1549–1688', *Trans. Roy. Hist. Soc.*, 4th Series, XXII (1940), 189; *HMC*, 14th Report, App. VIII, p. 48; *VCH Berks*, IV, 440; Canterbury Cathedral Library, Woodruffe List 54; *VCH Warwicks*, VIII, 158, 164; R. F. Dell, ed., *The Records of Rye Corporation* (Lewes, 1962), p. 35; Hill, *op. cit.*, pp. 79 *et seq.*, 31–2; W. Bazeley, 'The Guilds of Gloucester', *Trans. Bristol and Glouc. Arch. Soc.*, XIII (1888–9), 264; *VCH Herts*, II, 482. There was similar decay at Beverley and Carlisle: J. Dennet, ed., *Beverley Borough Records 1575–1821* (Yorks. Arch. Soc. Records Series, LXXXIV, 1932), p. ix; R. S. Ferguson and W. Nanson, 'Some Municipal Records of the City of Carlisle', *Trans. Cumb. and Westmorland Antiq. and Arch. Soc.*, Extra Series, IV (1887), 31–2. There were, of course, exceptions: in Chester, as York, the craft company retained some importance into the eighteenth century: M. J. Groombridge, 'City Gilds of Chester', *Journal of the Chester and N. Wales Architect., Archaeol. and Hist. Soc.*, XXXIX (1952), 101.

53 For an example of the limitations to detailed demographic analysis of towns, see U. M. Cowgill, 'Life and Death in the Sixteenth Century in the City of York', *Population Studies*, XXI (1967), 53–62, and L. Henry's criticism, *ibid.*, XXII (1968), 165–70.

54 *VCH Warwicks*, VIII, 4–5; F. J. Fisher, 'Influenza and Inflation in Tudor England', *Ec.H.R.*, 2nd Series, XVIII (1965), 125–9; M. Drake, 'An Elementary Exercise in Parish Register Demography', *Ec.H.R.*, 2nd Series, XIV (1961–2), 432; Palliser, below, p. 87; *VCH Warwicks*, VIII, 418; *VCH Leics*, IV, 76; *VCH Warwicks*, VIII, 4–5.

55 There is some theorizing on the rate of national population increase for this period in G. S. L. Tucker, 'English Pre-industrial Population Trends', *Ec.H.R.*, 2nd Series, XVI (1963–4), 208–12; M. Drake, *op. cit.*, pp. 427–37; J. Cornwall, 'English Population in the Early Sixteenth Century', *Ec.H.R.*, 2nd Series, XXIII (1970), 32–44. But there has been little discussion of causation.

56 A. J. Willis and A. L. Merson, eds, *A Calendar of Southampton Apprenticeship Registers 1609–1740* (Southampton Record Soc., 1968), pp. xxx–xxxi; B. H. Allen, 'The Administrative and Social History of the Norwich Merchant Class 1485–1660' (unpublished Ph.D. thesis, Harvard Univ., 1951), pp. 61–9; M. D. Harris, ed., *The Coventry Leet Book*, *Part III* (Early English Text Soc., Original Series, CXXXVIII, 1909), p. 658.

57 Lt. Col. Harding, *The History of Tiverton* (1845), I, 40; F. J. C. and D. M. Hearnshaw, eds, *Southampton Court Leet Records I* (Southampton Record Soc., 1905), p. 312; W. H. Manchee, *The Westminster City*

Fathers (1924), p. 94; Hoskins, *Provincial England*, p. 92; Clark, below, p. 142.

58 Wrigley, *op. cit.*, pp. 45–8; *VCH York*, p. 162; *VCH Warwicks*, VIII, 5; A. L. Merson, 'Southampton in the Sixteenth and Seventeenth Century', in F. J. Monkhouse, ed., *A Survey of Southampton and its Region* (Southampton, 1964), p. 223; Drake, *op. cit.*, p. 437; Willis and Merson, *op. cit.*, p. xxx; P. Styles, 'The Evolution of the Law of Settlement', *Univ. Birmingham Hist. J.*, IX (1963), 33–63.

59 *VCH Warwicks*, VIII, 216; Thomas, *op. cit.*, pp. 86–93.

60 *HMC*, 12th Report, App. IX, p. 459; J. W. Horrocks, ed., *The Assembly Books of Southampton I: 1602–8* (Southampton Record Soc., 1917), p. 63; J. F. Nicholls and J. Taylor, *Bristol, Past and Present* (Bristol, 1881–2), III, 44; M. Beloff, *Public Order and Popular Disturbances 1660–1714* (Oxford, 1938), *passim*. For a recent survey of popular revolts, see C. S. L. Davies, 'Les Revoltes populaires en Angleterre 1500–1700', *Annales E.S.C.*, 24 (1969), 24–60.

61 Thomas, *op. cit.*, pp. 114 *et seq.*; Martin, *op. cit.*, p. 48.

62 Harding, *op. cit.*, I, 45n.; J. Webb, ed., *Poor Relief in Elizabethan Ipswich* (Suffolk Records Soc., IX, 1966), pp. 11, 18; W. K. Jordan, 'Social Institutions in Kent 1480–1660', *Archaeologia Cantiana*, LXXV (1961), 42–3; Jordan, *Philanthropy in England 1480–1660* (1959), *passim*; PRO C93 series; G. Jones, *History of the Law of Charity 1532–1827* (Cambridge, 1969), pp. 52–6; quoted by J. Webb, *op. cit.*, p. 20.

63 *VCH York*, p. 186; B. H. Cunnington, ed., *Some Annals of the Borough of Devizes 1555–1791* (Devizes, 1925), I, 101–2, 122; J. Whitter, 'A Survey of the Economic and Administrative Life of Kingston-upon-Thames' (unpublished M.Sc. (Econ.) thesis, University of London, 1932–3), pp. 116, 119; A. E. Gibbs, ed., *The Corporation Records of St Albans* (St Albans, 1890), p.52; J. S. Davies, *A History of Southampton* (1883), p. 160; P. Russell, *The Good Town of Totnes* (Torquay, 1965), p. 55; T. Atkinson, *Elizabethan Winchester* (1963), pp. 118–20.

64 E. M. Dance, ed., *Guildford Borough Records 1514–1546* (Surrey Record Soc., XXIV, 1958), p. 33; Phythian-Adams, below, p. 79; *History of the City of Chester* (Chester, 1815), pp. 284–6.

65 *HMC*, 15th Report, App. IV, pp. 358–9; J. D. Cox, ed., *The Records of the Borough of Northampton* (1898), II, 17; Weinbaum, *British Borough Charters*; B. Challenor, ed., *Selections from the Municipal Chronicles of the Borough of Abingdon* (Abingdon, 1898), App. XI; W. H. Stevenson, *Gloucester Corporation Records* (Gloucester, 1893), pp. 40–5; W. H. Stevenson, ed., *Records of the Borough of Nottingham* (Nottingham, 1882–9), IV, xvi; *HMC*, 13th Report, App. IV, pp. 44–5; C. J. Palmer, *The History of Great Yarmouth* (1856), p. 53.

66 F. J. Baigent and J. E. Millard, *A History of the Ancient Town and Manor of Basingstoke* (1889), p. 461; Hill, *op. cit.*, pp. 87–8; W. Holloway, *The History and Antiquities of Rye* (1847), p. 221.

67 *Records of Nottingham*, III, 341–2.

68 For instance, refusals to serve are found in growing numbers at Bristol (R. C. Latham, ed., *Bristol Charters 1509–1899* (Bristol Record Soc., XII, 1947), p. 58); Leicester (*Leicester Records*, IV, lvi); and York (*VCH York*, pp. 176–7). For a good description of the administrative burden on the Aldermen of Norwich see the introduction to W. L. Sachse, ed., *Minutes of the Norwich Court of Mayoralty 1630–1* (Norfolk Record Soc., XV, 1942).

69 Cf. M. Weinbaum, *op. cit.*, pp. xvii–xviii; M. Weinbaum, *The Incorporation of Boroughs* (Manchester, 1937), pp. 92, 99 *et seq.* The Crown's policy of developing greater uniformity of local government through the device of incorporation was not accepted without question. A 'Discourse of Corporations', written *c.* 1587–9, disputes the value of municipal charters, asserting 'It is the site and place where every town or city is builded which is the chief cause of the flourishing of the same, or else some special trade and traffic appropriate to the same, and not the incorporation thereof': Tawney and Power, *op. cit.*, III, 273–4.

70 Cunnington, *op. cit.*, I, 55; *Records of Nottingham*, IV, 282. Other instances of corruption include Kingston-on-Thames (Whitter, *op. cit.*, p. 116), Lincoln (Hill, *op. cit.*, p. 36) and Southampton (Horrocks, *op. cit.*, I, 26 *et seq.*).

71 Challenor, *op. cit.*, App. X; Cunnington, *op. cit.*, I, 42 *et seq.*; C. H. Mayo, *op. cit.*, pp. 401–2; *Records of Nottingham*, IV, xiii *et seq.*; A. E. Gibbs, *op. cit.*, p. 50 *et seq.*; *HMC*, 13th Report, App. IV, p. 164; R. F. Dell, *op. cit.*, p. 2. The agitation for a wider franchise is discussed in R. L. Bushman, 'English Franchise Reform in the Seventeenth Century', *Journal of British Studies*, III (1963), 36–53.

72 The intervention of town government in the fields of street improvement, water-supply, sanitation as well as poor relief is discussed in some detail by J. H. Thomas, *op. cit.*, chaps v–xviii.

73 Quoted in Hill, *op. cit.*, p. 77. Hill also provides instances of similar conflict at Bristol and Coventry.

74 E.g. conciliar purges at Beverley (Dennet, *op. cit.*, pp. 48–9), Newcastle (Howell, *op. cit.*, chap. v) and York (B. M. Wilson, 'The Corporation of York 1580–1660' (unpublished M.Phil. thesis, University of York, 1967), pp. 275, 277).

75 S. Bond, ed., *The First Hall Book of the Borough of New Windsor 1653–1725* (Windsor Borough Historical Records Publications, I, 1968), p. xiv; *Leicester Records*, IV, lv; J. H. Sacret, 'The Restoration

Government and Municipal Corporations', *E.H.R.*, XLV (1930), 232–59.

76 Cox, *op. cit.*, pp. 476–7; *VCH Wilts*, VI, 22; Webbs, *op. cit.*, I, 393 *et seq.* For a discussion of *Quo Warranto* proceedings against London in 1683, see J. Levin, *The Charter Controversy in the City of London 1660–1688 and its Consequences* (1969).

77 For an account of party feeling in boroughs at the end of our period see W. A. Speck, *Tory and Whig* (1970), chap. 4; at Maidstone there was persistent guerrilla warfare between the town and county families residing in the former Archbishop's Palace (cf. *Maidstone Records* (Maidstone, 1926), pp. 87 *et seq.*). For disputes with gentry over town lands, see *VCH Warwicks*, VIII, 204 (Coventry); *HMC*, 13th Report, App. IV, p. 328 (Hereford); *HMC*, 14th Report, App. VIII, p. 88 (Lincoln); Davies, *op. cit.*, pp. 42–3 (Southampton).

78 Parsloe, *op. cit.*, p. 184. Sir Edward Moore, erstwhile patron of Liverpool, noted the contractual element in the relationship when he wrote to his son: 'So long as the town and you hold closely together, your interest [is] as a gentleman, to countenance them [the town corporation] before the King, Privy Council, or in any place or court of England, their purse discreetly managed, to back you . . . [otherwise] it is the ready way to undo you both'; although elsewhere he counsels, 'Trust them not . . . for such a nest of rogues was never educated in one town of that bigness'; E. Moore, *Liverpool in King Charles the Second's Time* (Liverpool, 1899), pp. 111, 11.

79 MacCaffrey, *op. cit.*, p. 216; T. Baines, *History of the Commerce and Town of Liverpool* (1852), pp. 332–4; *Leicester Records*, IV, 267. Some towns saw that the advantages of corporate independence were delusory: the bailiff of Great Grimsby declared in 1564 that 'It were a good deed and very necessary that the borough of Great Grimsby were ordered by the wise justices of the county, and the liberty taken clean from us' (*HMC*, 14th Report, App. VIII, p. 280).

80 J. E. Neale, *The Elizabethan House of Commons* (1949), p. 146; *ibid.*, chaps vii–xiii for a survey of Elizabethan borough elections; *VCH Bucks*, III, 9–10; *VCH Sussex*, III, 99. Newark and the Buckinghamshire boroughs afford examples of the overwhelming gentry domination at Parliamentary elections: C. Brown, *Annals of Newark-upon-Trent* (1879), pp. 191–4; J. L. Stern, 'Worthies of Buckinghamshire . . .', *Records of Bucks*, XVII (1961–5), 4; at St Albans the mayors were often gentry from outside (Gibbs, *op. cit.*, p. 7).

81 Summarized in Howell, *op. cit.*, pp. 340–3; B. L. K. Henderson, 'The Commonwealth Charters', *Trans. Roy. Hist. Soc.*, 3rd Series, VI (1912), 129–55. J. H. Plumb has recently argued for the continuance (and success) of the movement for a wider Parliamentary franchise into the

late Stuart period, in 'The Growth of the Electorate in England from 1600 to 1715', *P. & P.*, no. 45 (1969), 90–116, but there is little evidence that its impact extended to the opening up of municipal government.

82 Pearl, *op. cit., passim.*; J. K. G. Taylor, 'The Civil Government of Gloucester 1640–6', *Trans. Bristol and Glouc. Arch. Soc.*, LXVII (1946–8), 59–118; T. W. Whitley, *The Parliamentary Representation of the City of Coventry* (Coventry, 1894), p. 82.

83 *VCH Warwicks*, VIII, 125–7, 132; B. Philp, *Excavations at Faversham* (Bromley, 1965); *VCH York*, p. 117; *HMC*, 14th Report, App. VIII, pp. 44–5; J. B. Jones, *Annals of Dover* (Dover, 1916), p. 187.

84 *VCH Warwicks*, VIII, 23; K. H. Docton, 'Lancashire 1684', *Trans. Hist. Soc. of Lancs. and Cheshire*, CIX (1957), 129; *Leicester Records*, IV, 349. Cf. *VCH York*, p. 160.

85 *VCH Warwicks*, VIII, 143; *VCH Berks*, IV, 432; *VCH Bucks*, III, 3; Cruden, *op. cit.*, p. 198; Russell, *History of Guildford*, p. 135. The 'rebuilding of rural England' at this time is described by Professor Hoskins in *Provincial England*, chap. vii; many of his comments are apposite here.

86 S. Seyer, *Memoirs Historical and Topographical of Bristol* (Bristol, 1821–3), II, 216–23; *LP*, XVIII(2), 1543, pp. 291 *et seq.*; P. Collinson, *The Elizabethan Puritan Movement* (1967), pp. 168 *et seq.*

87 Cox, *op. cit.*, II, 387; Beesley, *op. cit.*, pp. 238 *et seq.*; J. R. Chanter and T. Wainwright, *Reprint of the Barnstaple Records* (Barnstaple, 1900), II, 13, 99; Hill, *op. cit.*, pp. 101 *et seq.*; J. S. Davies, *op. cit.*, p. 358; *VCH Warwicks*, VIII, 496; Palmer, *op. cit.*, p. 151.

88 Whitley, *op. cit.*, p. 62; T. Agnew, *History of the Foundations in Manchester of Christ's College, Cheetham's Hospital and the Free Grammar School* (Manchester, 1830), I, 124; *VCH Dorset*, II, 35–6; MacCaffrey, *op. cit.*, p. 273; J. P. Earwaker, *The Constables Accounts of the Manor of Manchester* (Manchester, 1891–2), II, 155; Slack, below, pp. 184–6.

89 Agnew, *op. cit.*, I, 124, 254 *et seq.*; H. Barbour, *The Quakers in Puritan England* (New Haven, 1964), chap. iii, and cf. R. T. Vann, 'Quakerism and the Social Structure in the Interregnum', *P. & P.*, no. 43 (1969), esp. p. 90.

90 Latham, *op. cit.*, pp. 42–7; *VCH Sussex*, III, 88; *VCH Warwicks*, VIII, 250–1; *VCH Yorks: East Riding*, I, 111, 114; *VCH York*, p. 205.

91 J. Simon, *Education and Society in Tudor England* (Cambridge, 1966), pp. 165–268 *passim*; Agnew, *op. cit.*, III, 21; Jordan, *Philanthropy*, pp. 279–97; J. Simon, 'Town Estates and Schools in the Sixteenth and Early Seventeenth Centuries', in B. Simon, ed., *Education in Leicestershire 1540–1940* (Leicester, 1968), pp. 3–26; *Leicester Records*, IV, 231; L. Stone, 'The Educational Revolution in England 1560–1640', *P. & P.*, no. 28 (1964), 42–7.

92 W. A. L. Vincent, *The Grammar Schools: Their Continuing Tradition 1660–1714* (1969), chap. ix; J. Simon, 'Post-Restoration Developments', in B. Simon, *op. cit.*, pp. 39, 49; C. W. Stokes, *Queen Mary's Grammar School Clitheroe* (Chetham Soc., New Series, XCII, 1934), p. 130; W. F. Carter, ed., *The Records of King Edward's School, Birmingham II* (Dugdale Soc., VII, 1928), p. xix. For examples of later Stuart decay in grammar schools, see: Baigent and Millard, *op. cit.*, pp. 149–50 (Basingstoke); *King Henry VIII School, Coventry* (Coventry, 1945), p. 21; A. W. Thomas, *A History of Nottingham High School 1513–1957* (Nottingham, 1957), p. 50; *VCH Berks*, II, 269–70 (Abingdon).

93 Nicholls and Taylor, *op. cit.*, I, 277, III, 40; Hudson and Tingey, *op. cit.*, II, cxlvi–cxlvii; T. Cromwell, *History and Description of the Ancient Town and Borough of Colchester* (1825), p. 343; W. Taylor, *The Antiquities of King's Lynn* (1844), p. 57.

94 C. Blagden, *The Stationers' Company, A History 1403–1959* (1960), p. 28; G. A. Cranfield, *The Development of the Provincial Newspaper 1700–1760* (Oxford, 1962), pp. 16, 28–9.

95 N. Bacon, *The Annalls of Ipswich* (ed. W. H. Richardson, Ipswich, 1880), p. ii; T. Shadwell, *Epsom Wells* (1673), p. 19.

96 D. Defoe, *Tour*, II, 183; W. E. A. Axon, *The Annals of Manchester* (1886), p. 59; W. H. B. Court, *The Rise of the Midland Industries* (Oxford, 1953), *passim*; A. P. Wadsworth and J. De L. Mann, *The Cotton Trade and Industrial Lancashire 1660–1780* (Manchester, 1931), pp. 111 *et seq.*; H. Heaton, *The Yorkshire Woollen and Worsted Industries* (2nd edn, Oxford, 1965), esp. pp. 258 *et seq.* For a full discussion of the early growth of Halifax, see M. E. François, 'The Social and Economic Development of Halifax 1558–1640', *Procs. of the Leeds Philosophical and Literary Soc. (Lit. and Hist. Section)*, XI (1964–6), 217–80.

97 A. J. King and B. H. Watts, *The Municipal Records of Bath 1189–1604* (1885), pp. 34 *et seq.*; M. Barton, *Tunbridge Wells* (1937), chaps i–viii; E. Hargrove, *The History of . . . Knaresbrough with Harrogate* (Knaresborough, 1809), pp. 108–9. There is a short description of the early spa towns in E. W. Gilbert, 'The Growth of Inland and Seaside Health Resorts in England', *Scottish Geographical Magazine*, LV (1939), 22 *et seq.* See also C. F. Mullett, 'Public Baths and Health in England', *Supplement to the Bulletin of the History of Medicine*, 5 (1946); T. Shadwell, *Epsom Wells* (1673).

98 Defoe, *Tour*, I, 43; W. G. Hoskins, *Devon* (1954), p. 455; D. C. Coleman, 'The Economy of Kent under the later Stuarts', pp. 16–17, 269; H. Rees, 'The Medway Towns, their Settlement, Growth and Economic Development' (unpublished Ph.D. thesis, University of London, 1955), pp. 92 *et seq.*; F. N. G. Thomas, 'Portsmouth and Gosport: A Study

in the Historical Geography of a Naval Port' (unpublished M.Sc. (Econ.) thesis, University of London, 1961), pp. 32–3; R. Thomas, *History . . . of Falmouth* (Falmouth, 1828), p. 58; D. C. Coleman, 'Naval Dockyards under the Later Stuarts', *Ec.H.R.*, 2nd Series, VI (1953–4), 134–55.

99 Defoe, *Tour*, I, 43; there is no adequate general account of Newcastle in the later 17th century, but see J. U. Nef, *The Rise of the British Coal Industry* (1932), *passim*; R. Howell, *op. cit.*, p. 9; Defoe, *Tour*, I, 222; W. B. Stephens, *Seventeenth Century Exeter*, pp. 103, 105, 146; Hoskins, *Industry, Trade and People in Exeter 1688–1800*, pp. 12–19; P. McGrath, *Merchants and Merchandise in Seventeenth Century Bristol* (Bristol Record Soc., XIX, 1955), pp. 18 *et seq.*; W. E. Minchinton, 'Bristol— Metropolis of the West in the Eighteenth Century', *passim*; *VCH Yorks: East Riding*, I, 139–41, 152, 158.

100 Wadsworth and Mann, *op. cit.*, pp. 71–2; F. J. Routledge, 'History of Liverpool to 1700', in W. Smith, ed., *A Scientific Survey of Merseyside* (Liverpool, 1953), pp. 104–5; T. C. Barker, 'Lancashire Coal, Cheshire Salt and the Rise of Liverpool', *Trans. Hist. Soc. of Lancs. and Cheshire*, CIII (1951), 83–101; J. A. Picton, *Memorials of Liverpool* (Liverpool, 1903), I, 147.

101 J. T. Bunce, *History of Birmingham*, I, 36. The Elizabethan author of a 'Discourse of Corporations' had similar ideas on the cost of corporate incumbrances: Tawney and Power, *op. cit.*, III, 265–76. On Leeds, see G. C. F. Forster's chapter in M. W. Beresford and G. R. J. Jones, eds, *Leeds and its Region* (Leeds, 1967), pp. 131–45.

102 Minchinton, *op. cit.*, pp. 70–1; cf. also Bristol's influence on Cardiff: M. I. Williams, 'Cardiff—its People and its Trade 1660–1720', *Trans. Glamorgan Local History Soc.*, VII (1963), 97; W. B. Stephens, *op. cit.*, pp. 142, 162–3.

103 P. McGrath, ed., *Records Relating to the Society of Merchant Venturers of Bristol*, pp. xli–xliv; Stephens, *op. cit.*, p. 65; P. Corfield, below, p. 273; E. Hughes, *North Country Life in the Eighteenth Century* (Oxford, 1952), p. 11.

104 J. A. Picton, *Selections from the Municipal Archives and Records* (Liverpool, 1883), p. 314; H. Peet, ed., *Liverpool Vestry Books 1681–1834* (Liverpool, 1912), I, xxviii; J. F., *An Exact Account of the Charge for Supporting the Poor of the City of Norwich* (1720), p. 31; J. D. Leader, ed., *The Records of the Burgery of Sheffield* (1897), pp. 128 *et seq.*; Hoskins, *Industry, Trade and People in Exeter*, p. 120. In 1648 Liverpool shipped numbers of young children and beggars to the Barbados (Chandler, *op. cit.*, pp. 411–12). For examples of poverty in Manchester, see J. P. Earwaker, ed., *The Court Leet Records of the Manor of Manchester* (Manchester, 1884–90), III, 122, 268 *et seq.*

105 Heaton, *op. cit.*, pp. 223 *et seq.*; Leader, *op. cit.*, p. xlix; Latham, *op. cit.*, pp. 3 *et seq.*; MacCaffrey, *op. cit.*, pp. 16–17; Baines, *op. cit.*, p. 339; Howell, *op. cit.*, pp. 45 *et seq.*; *ex inform.* P. Corfield.

106 Webbs, *op. cit.*, II, 458–60, 555; Hoskins, *Industry, Trade and People in Exeter*, p. 142.

107 E.g. at Manchester: Earwaker, *Court Leet Records*, II, 328 *et seq.*

108 Cf. R. W. Greaves, *The Corporation of Leicester 1689–1836* (Oxford, 1939), pp. 20–3.

109 Routledge, *op. cit.*, p. 105; Earwaker, *Court Leet Records*, IV, 321; there were important Dissenting groups at Bristol (Nicholls and Taylor, *op. cit.*, III, 68–9, 101), and Exeter (A. Brockett, *Nonconformity in Exeter 1650–1875* (Manchester, 1962), pp. 23 *et seq.*).

110 J. Lawson, *A Town Grammar School through Six Centuries* (Oxford, 1963), pp. 97–8, 101; G. Pryce, *A Popular History of Bristol* (Bristol, 1861), pp. 159–60. Although the foundation deed of 1523 appointed that the feoffees of Manchester Grammar School should be parishioners, the bulk of them after 1660 were landed gentry living outside the parish: J. A. Graham and B. A. Phythian, eds, *The Manchester Grammar School 1515–1965* (Manchester, 1965), p. 12.

111 See Wrigley, 'A Simple Model of London's Importance'; F. J. Fisher, 'London's Export Trade in the early Seventeenth Century', *Ec.H.R.*, 2nd Series, III (1950), 151–61; F. J. Fisher, 'The Development of London as a Centre for Conspicuous Consumption in the Sixteenth and Seventeenth Centuries', *Trans. Roy. Hist. Soc.*, 4th Series, XXX (1948), 37–50; R. Grassby, 'English Merchant Capitalism in the Late Seventeenth Century: The Composition of Business Fortunes', *P. & P.*, no. 46 (1970), 87–107; D. V. Glass, 'Notes on the Demography of London at the end of the Seventeenth Century', *Daedalus*, spring 1968, pp. 581–92.

112 Brett-James, *op. cit.*, *passim*; J. R. Kellett, 'The Causes and Progress of the Financial Decline of the Corporation of London 1660–1694' (unpublished Ph.D. thesis, University of London, 1958), pp. 6–7 (we are grateful to Dr Kellett for permission to use information in his thesis); Wrigley, *op. cit.*, p. 49; W. K. Jordan, *The Charities of London 1480–1660* (1960), pp. 86 *et seq.*

113 Quoted in T. F. Reddaway, *The Rebuilding of London after the Great Fire* (1940), pp. 42–3; luxury trades like that of the goldsmiths followed their customers westwards: Reddaway, 'Elizabethan London: Goldsmith's Row in Cheapside 1558–1645', *Guildhall Miscellany*, II (5) (1963), 189–90.

114 Reddaway, *The Rebuilding*, p. 47; Picton, *Memorials*, I, 145–6; P. V. McGrath, 'The Marketing of Food, Fodder and Livestock in the London Area in the Seventeenth Century', p. 77. See also A. B. Robert-

son, 'The Suburban Food Markets of Eighteenth Century London', *East London Papers*, II (1959), 21–6.

115 Reddaway, *The Rebuilding*, pp. 44–5; see Webbs, *op. cit.*, II, 572n., for the City's dog-in-the-manger attitude towards the government of Southwark.

116 Kellett, *op. cit.*, p. 19; Kellett, 'The Breakdown of Gild and Corporation Control over the Handicraft and Retail Trade in London', *Ec.H.R.*, 2nd Series, X (1957–8), 381–94. For a sample of the decline of London companies, see R. Champness, *The Worshipful Company of Turners of London* (1886), esp. p. 76; J. Steven Watson, *A History of the Salters' Company* (Oxford, 1963), pp. 60, 86; B. W. E. Alford and T. C. Barker, *A History of the Carpenters' Company* (1968), chap. vi.

117 V. Pearl, *op. cit.*, chaps i–iv; M. James, *Social Problems and Policy during the Puritan Revolution* (1930), chap. v; J. E. Farnell, 'The Usurpation of Honest London Householders: Barebones' Parliament', *E.H.R.*, LXXXII (1967), 24–46; Reddaway, *The Rebuilding*, pp. 174–9, 188–9.

118 Pearl, *op. cit.*, pp. 37 *et seq.*; J. R. Jones, *The First Whigs* (1961), is inadequate on the London background to Exclusion, but see O. W. Furley, 'The Pope Burning Processions of the late Seventeenth Century', *History*, XLIV (1955), 16–23; L. Sutherland, 'The City of London in Eighteenth Century Politics', in R. Pares and A. J. P. Taylor, eds, *Essays presented to Sir L. Namier* (1956), pp. 49 *et seq.*

119 Brett-James, *op. cit.*, pp. 324 *et seq.*

120 See for example, A. Ogle, *The Tragedy of the Lollard's Tower* (1949), pp. 11–87; P. Collinson, 'The Elizabethan Puritans and the Foreign Reformed Churches in London', *Procs. of the Huguenot Soc. of London*, XX (1958–64), 528–55; D. A. Williams 'London Puritanism: the Parish of St Botolph without Aldgate', *Guildhall Miscellany*, II (1) (1960), pp. 24–38; H. G. Owen, 'The Liberty of the Minories', *East London Papers*, VIII (1965), 81–97; Jordan, *The Charities of London*, pp. 284–92; C. Hill, *Economic Problems of the Church* (Oxford, 1956), chap. xi; V. Pearl, 'London Puritans and Scotch Fifth Columnists: A Mid-Seventeenth Century Phenomenon', in A. E. J. Hollaender and W. Kellaway, eds, *Studies in London History presented to P. E. Jones* (1969), pp. 318–31.

121 J. Simon, *Education and Society in Tudor England*, pp. 73–80; Jordan, *The Charities of London*, pp. 223 *et seq.*, 310–11; W. Prest, 'Legal Education of the Gentry at the Inns of Court 1560-1640', *P. & P.* no. 38 (1967), 20–39; C. Hill, *Intellectual Origins of the English Revolution* (Oxford, 1965), pp. 37–63; S. M. Wide and J. A. Morris, 'The Episcopal Licensing of Schoolmasters in the Diocese of London 1627–1685', *Guildhall Miscellany*, II (9) (1967), 405; *VCH Middlesex*, I, 242–3, 251.

122 G. Salgado, ed., *Three Restoration Comedies* (Penguin, 1968), pp. 80–1; for a similar use of 'Hampshire' as a generic epithet for the provinces see Wycherley's *The Country Wife* (1675), *ibid.*, p. 166.
123 The changing balance had its most immediate impact in schemes for parliamentary reapportionment: V. F. Snow, 'Parliamentary Reapportionment Proposals in the Puritan Revolution', *E.H.R.*, LXXIV (1959), 409–42.

2

Ceremony and the citizen:
The communal year at Coventry
1450–1550

Charles Phythian-Adams

For urban communities in particular, the middle and later years of the sixteenth century represented a more abrupt break with the past than any period since the era of the Black Death or before the age of industrialization. Not only were specific customs and institutions brusquely changed or abolished, but a whole, vigorous and variegated popular culture, the matrix of everyday life, was eroded and began to perish. At the very heart of social activity, before these changes were effected, lay the repetitive annual pattern of ceremonies and cognate observances peculiar to each local community. An enquiry into the contemporary relevance of such practices as a whole for a particular urban society may, therefore, help to promote a wider acknowledgment of the magnitude of the subsequent shift in the social and cultural environment.

Accordingly, this exploratory analysis will seek first to demonstrate some simple congruities between Coventry's late medieval social structure (that relatively enduring but adaptable framework of institutionalized positions and connective relationships) and its ceremonial or ritualized expression in action, in time—with respect to the local calendar—and on the ground. It will then become possible, secondly, to establish the extent and nature (rather than the social effects) of the subsequent change by briefly charting the rapid disintegration of what had once evidently formed a coherent ceremonial pattern.

Methodologically, such an approach is only possible if the evidence for unquestionably perennial customs may be extracted from a wide period. Here, however, in that minority of cases where the documentation is not contemporary, the evidence of survivals has not been trusted after 1640, and earlier justification for its use has always been sought where possible. While this reconstruction seems broadly appropriate to the century from 1450 to 1550, known structural modifications therein have had to be sacrificed at the altar of brevity. The picture probably remains truest for the generation living between 1490 and 1520 when the surviving evidence is peculiarly rich, and before the tempo of social change had been accelerated by the final collapse of the city's medieval economy.[1]

Since the citizens of Coventry themselves were convinced that ceremonial proceedings like the Corpus Christi procession and plays contributed to 'the welth & worship of the hole body', it is first necessary to establish the composition of this entity whose welfare and dignity were thus promoted. That it included only those persons who shared the expense of attaining these ends, the members of craft fellowships, is put beyond dispute by the same and similar contexts. At this period, only the crafts had the power to admit those who would later be called Freemen; the city could merely register new apprentices and swear them to the franchise. Hence 'to be discomyned oute of this Cite' involved *inter alia* estrangement from a man's craft. Exclusion from the fellowships of building workers or journeymen dyers automatically meant the stigma of inferior status as 'only comen laborers' or mere servants. When all masters and journeymen annually processed in their respective companies at Corpus Christi-tide and on the eves of Midsummer and St Peter, therefore, the community in its entirety was literally defining itself for all to see.[2]

There can be little doubt that practically every ceremony hereinafter to be discussed related to this restricted communal membership. In a total population of between 8,000 and 9,000 in 1500, all unqualified adult males, possibly 20 per cent of all householders to judge from extrapolating craft records, were excluded. So too, in effect, were all single females under forty. For all such women, whether or not they had served an apprenticeship, were specifically debarred from keeping house by themselves; in-service evidently being felt to be preferable even to their possession of a chamber, let alone a shop. Surviving lists of journeymen, moreover, contain no women's names. Marriage thus remained the only realistic avenue of admission to the community for females. It was therefore no accident that the wedding ceremonies of masters or journeymen were compulsorily attended by the groom's particular fellowship. In the case of the tanners, indeed, the journeymen were accustomed to attend the marriages of masters. But communal recognition clearly did not mean immediate occupational privileges even for a newly married woman. These probably had to await her (first) husband's demise—a fact which, no doubt, added a further level of meaning to the craft's attendance at his funeral.[3]

Ceremonial occasions repeatedly underlined this peripheral status of wives. Men or boys played the female parts in the Corpus Christi plays and there is some evidence, at least from 1565, that the women sat separately in St Michael's, the larger of the two parish churches. Certainly it was unusual for them to be present at either gild or craft banquets with their menfolk. Master Cappers' wives rarely attended craft meetings until they were widows. Even 'the Mairasse & hir Sisters', the other civic officers' wives, dined apart from their husbands when the Queen sent a present of venison in 1474. An early seventeenth-century description of the mayoral inauguration, which evidently fossilized traditional practice, moreover, makes it clear that these ladies did not even attend the civic oath-taking. Instead, 'Old Mistress Maioris', the other officers' wives and the town sergeant, separately escorted the new Mayoress to the church where they awaited the arrival of their husbands after the ceremony was over.[4]

To all those outside or on the edge of the community, therefore, ceremonies must have been a constant reminder of its discrete and predominantly masculine identity. For those inside it, on the other hand, they were the visible means of relating individuals to the social structure. The sequence of oath-taking ceremonies, in particular, regularly punctuated the life cycle of the successful citizen from the moment he pledged himself to his city, his craft or his gild, to that later period in life when similar *rites de passage* admitted him to the authority which was the reward of advanced years. Initiation to the annually held senior craft office, some thirteen or fourteen years after joining, in the case of the Cappers for example, had a special significance in this last respect. For by the mid-sixteenth century, ex-officers were being termed 'the Auncente' or 'the moost auncient persones' of a craft—designations that implied more than official seniority when 60 per cent of the members of even a prosperous craft like the Cappers do not seem to have survived twenty years of membership, and at a period in which 'the best age' was considered over at forty. The civic sequence of office, furthermore, usually seems to have succeeded that of the craft except in the cases of the richest companies like the Drapers whose head masters appear to have been at least ex-sheriffs. Even though potential civic office holders often reached the top of their fellowships more rapidly than normal, it still took a further seventeen years on average to reach the appropriately designated position of 'alderman' from junior civic office.[5]

The relevance of age to the oath-taking ceremonies, which accompanied every step on this ladder, was emphasized by the apparent timing of the citizen's progress through the two religious and social gilds of Corpus Christi and Holy Trinity. Usually within four years or so of being sworn to their fellowships, potential office-holders from the middling to wealthy crafts were pledging themselves to the junior gild of Corpus Christi. The composition of this fraternity seems to have been strongly biased to the less aged office-holders, a characteristic which was underlined by the admission of dependent young offspring of the city's élite. Despite the destruction of the Trinity Gild's register, there are indications that in mid-career, the successful citizen transferred from the junior to the senior fraternity. Certainly regular attendance at the former seems to have ceased at about the time a man assumed the shrievalty. Out of fifteen cappers, moreover, who had held craft office prior to 1520, only six were still attending Corpus Christi gild banquets in or after that year, though all were yet alive. Since both fraternities were ostensibly focused on eternity, it seems reasonable to suggest that in such cases the same need was being met by the only alternative organization available, the Trinity Gild. There remains, therefore, the strong implication that the senior fraternity was dominated by the ageing élite of the city—certainly the aldermen and probably the more elderly ancients of at least the wealthiest crafts.[6]

The importance of this broad but basic age categorization was brought out in inaugural ceremonies. In many crafts, authority was clearly conferred on new officers by the most senior members on behalf of the whole, the choice being made as with the Smiths by 'xij of the Eldest & discretest of the feliship'. In a rather more complex manner, the mayor and junior civic officers were secretly elected and sounded in mid-January by the aldermen, whose choice was formally rubber-stamped on the 25th at a purely ceremonial meeting of twenty-four men. Here, however, in those cases where it can be checked, attendance was divided between a contingent of more junior civic officers, particularly ex-sheriffs, headed by the Master of the Corpus Christi Gild who would himself be about to undertake the mayoralty within a year or two; and the ex-mayors, preceded by the Master of the Trinity Gild, who, by the early sixteenth century, was assuming his office immediately after relinquishing the mayoralty. When the civic oath-taking itself took place a week later, the ceremony heavily underlined the accountability of the new mayor to his senior colleagues. The incoming officers processed into St Mary's Hall where the retiring officers and aldermen were already symbolically in possession. At the culmination of the ceremony the new mayor was obliged to doff his hat, in the presence of the people, as a public gesture of deference to the old mayor and aldermen, 'intreating their loves and assistances'. Of the sheriffs and the coroner, on the other hand, he simply entreated assistance, while the junior civic officers and the rest were more tersely 'required' to do their duties.[7]

Oath-taking ceremonies were thus of wider significance than purely technical exercises which related only to the specific institutions concerned; by following an established sequence, they also helped each time to transfer the initiate to another broad social age category. In a number of further ways, too, they invested office with solemn and social attributes over and above the practical demands of annual executive position. A corporate act of worship by all the participants, for example, seems to have been the normal custom at both craft and civic levels. In the early fifteenth century, the Tilers were accustomed to offer at High Mass in the White Friars before their election. The Mercers, on the other hand, were 'after election, to bringe the new Maister to churche' in Elizabeth's reign. The mayoral oath-taking ceremony, by the seventeenth century, was actually sandwiched between the first lesson and the sermon during morning prayer at the adjacent parish church of St Michael.[8]

Such observances were not irrelevant in view of the officers' obligations. Medieval head masters of the Weavers were sworn, indeed, not only to be good and true to their craft but also to its chapel of St James the apostle. The Mayor and his retinue were expected to attend church daily before the Reformation. As in other societies, furthermore, office was hedged with taboos. If even the job of town gaoler could be put at risk because its holder succumbed to the temptations of fornication, senior civic officers were specifically debarred in 1492 from adultery and usury as well. Regular worship and theoretically high standards of morality thus helped to legitimate authority in ways which transcended the group concerned.[9]

Another seemingly supernumerary facet of inauguration ceremonies was the Choice Dinner. Either before the election as in the case of the

Drapers, or after, like the Weavers and the Dyers (who in fact held a breakfast), it was customary for the old and/or new masters to bear at least a substantial proportion of the cost of a dinner for their company. After his oath-taking on Candlemas day, the Mayor likewise had to throw a huge banquet at his own very considerable expense. Whether it was largely furnished by the incoming or the outgoing office-holder such an occasion was either the first or last formal exercise of his position. Despite subsidization, however, it was also clearly meant to be an act of 'hospitality' and as such was an expression more of social than of official obligation and status.[10]

The culminating procedure of inaugural ceremonies ensured that the citizen's new official status was unquestionably established outside the confines of his specific group in his own home neighbourhood. Most crafts probably observed the same custom as the Mercers who processed with the new masters 'from churche to the head-maisteres' houses'. Certainly the same effect was achieved when the master Dyers obeyed the order to fetch their under-master before the marching of the watch on Midsummer and St Peter's eves 'at hys howse, And from thence to goe to the head master's howse'. Likewise after the Mayor's inaugural banquet, the civic body was accustomed to attend on the new and old Mayors; first to the former's home, where the civic insignia, the sword and the mace, were symbolically deposited, and thence for the last time to the house of the retiring Mayor. By making an officer's home a focus for his group, a man's social status outside it was also inevitably enhanced.[11]

And indeed it was by the spectacular advertisement of specific status in general contexts that ceremony made its most vital contribution to the viability of the city's late medieval social structure. For office was otherwise unremunerative. Unpaid or underpaid and greedy of time, it was unpopular and hence compulsory on pain of fine for those elected. Apart from the possibility of future promotion and the actuality of present influence, therefore, the exaggerated social precedence of ceremonial occasions was an office-holder's basic reward. 'In every procession and all other Congregacions for Worschipp of the Citte and Welth of the seyd Crafte,' the Weavers ordained in 1452–3, 'every man shall goo & sytt in order as he hath byn put in Rule of the seyd crafte.' Significantly, the worst punishment that could befall a contumacious ex-mayor after fine and imprisonment, was to be 'utterly abiect from the Counsell of the Citee & the Company of theym in all theire comen processions, ffestes, and all other assembles & from weryng of his cloke or skerlet in theire companyes'. In magnifying and publicizing the importance of annually held offices, ceremony completed the transformation of wealth ownership into class standing for the upper levels of society.[12]

It is therefore notable that the order of march laid down in 1445 for the massive processions at Corpus Christi and Midsummer was based not on a system of precedence reflecting some *economic* class division of society (which might, for example, have allotted an inferior position to the handicraftsmen), but on occupational groupings whose order was determined apparently by the contribution of each to civic office-holding. Leaving aside two misfits in this scheme—the combined fellowship of pinners, tilers and wrights, and the craft of weavers, who may have been the occasion of the ordinance—the order of precedence was simple. It began, in the junior position, with the victuallers, all of whom, despite their wealth, were theoretically banned by parliamentary statute (even after 1512 at Coventry) from holding civic offices unless they suspended their occupations. Next came the leather and metal trades (though the identity of the latter grouping was somewhat blurred by the amalgamation of miscellaneous crafts with the fellowship of Cardmakers), neither of which were overly conspicuous for their tenure of offices. Last were the wool and textile occupations on which the prosperity of the city depended, culminating in the places of honour with the Dyers, Drapers and Mercers in that order. Not only were these the wealthiest companies in the city; they also furnished a disproportionate quota of its officers.[13]

Civic office consequently lent prestige even to the crafts whose representatives held it, and though the order of march did not apparently vary with the occupation of the mayor, his own fellowship would often find a means of advertising its temporary prominence. As from 1533 the parvenu craft of Cappers aped a custom of the London companies by bearing a carnival-type giant, with illuminated eyes, through the dusky streets at Midsummer and St Peter's, on the increasingly numerous years in which their fellowship could boast any civic officer or Master of the Trinity Gild. Not to be outdone, the established company of Drapers in later years provided this titan with a spouse, though 'when Master Norton was mere' in 1554, they blasted off 12 lb. of gunpowder.[14]

Thus although ceremony obviously helped to transform the formal constitution of the city into some sort of social reality, conversely it was also a valued instrument through which the basic divisions of humanity, by sex, age and wealth, could be related to the structure of the community. In addition, ceremonial occasions often provided at least the opportunities for bringing together in celebratory circumstances those who might otherwise be opposed or separated in their respective spheres.

In this connexion, little needs to be added to the preceding discussion of those almost wholly ceremonious institutions, the two gilds, whose formal non-charitable activities were restricted to the observance of obits and religious festivals, public processions, civic or gild inaugurations and regular sumptuous banquets. For the office-holding class, their membership cut horizontally, as it were, across those major vertical subdivisions of the community, the individual crafts, since there was no restriction by occupation. Even the seeming division into broad social age categories was significantly blurred within the junior fraternity. Only a minority of officers from the humbler crafts could afford to join it—between 1515 and 1524, for example, there were only five carpenters as members—and fewer still could have found the £5 admission fine to the Trinity Gild. As a result, elderly ancients, like the carpenter Robert Hammond, were to be found rubbing shoulders with the adolescent sons of aldermen at the proceedings of the Corpus Christi Gild.[15]

The gulf between the senior civic officers and the current craft officers, whether or not they were gild members, was bridged at least twice during the year. It would seem that prior to 1545, the mayor at Midsummer and the two sheriffs at St Peter's were respectively accustomed to entertain at least the officers of the crafts after the marchings of the watch. The composition of the guests at these established 'drynkynges' is suggested in the craft accounts by gifts from the Mayor of money for wine and cakes 'that we shold have had at Medssomer nyght' as from about that date: 'my wyn' as the head master of the Weavers once described it. There is, however, the further interesting possibility that whole fellowships were the beneficiaries of this largesse. The quantity of drink—three gallons or its equivalent cost was usual for the Weavers—would seem somewhat excessive even when, as in this instance, there may have been two rent-gatherers as well as the two keepers to help consume it. In fifteenth-century Bristol, all those 'persones of Craftes' who had actually attended the watch were to 'send ther own servantes and ther own pottes for the seide wyn', which was issued in quantities varying from two to ten gallons. Since some face-to-face contact does seem to be implied at

Coventry, however, it is possible that the craft officers attended in person on their civic hosts in order to supervise the transfer of the bulk of the liquor for their members to imbibe elsewhere.[16]

Evidence for structurally integrative commensality lower down the social scale is inevitably harder to find. But it is not impossible that other crafts practised the same custom as the Weavers, whose masters partook of a communal meal and drinking with their journeymen once a year in the early fifteenth century. Both Dyers and Smiths at least provided ale or wine for their journeymen at Corpus Christi, Midsummer and St Peter's.[17]

On certain fixed occasions, however, commensality did express those topographical arrangements of the population which cut across formal social groups or groupings. For while in 1522–4 there was no mistaking the geographical concentration of some occupations in certain quarters of the city, even in the most extreme cases, the butchers and the cappers, there was considerable overlapping into different areas. To judge from ranking the wards by mean household sizes, other neighbourhoods, especially near the heart of the city, were similarly biased towards the wealthier levels of society, though none was totally exclusive. Taken as a whole, the social topography of Coventry was remarkable chiefly for the evident intermixture of all types of person.[18]

It was this which gave significance to the social activities of the two huge parishes into which the city was divided. As elsewhere, the Holy Cake, for example, was consumed together in church by the parishioners after the celebration of Mass even in times of famine. On other occasions, in accordance with the instructions laid down for him in 1462, the first deacon of Holy Trinity was to serve the parishioners with 'bred & alle, and other thengs', at Mylborne's, Meynley's and other *diriges* 'made of the churche cost'. This is to say nothing of Whitsun ales and wakes at the feasts of dedication for which local evidence has yet to come to light.[19]

A rather different kind of observance was the informal gathering around each of the bonfires that are known to have blazed on the streets during Midsummer and St Peter's nights. These occasions were widely acknowledged celebrations of neighbourliness. 'At Baptis-day with Ale and cakes bout bon-fires neighbours stood' carolled William Warner in his *Albion's England*, while at nearby Warwick, money was specifically bequeathed to the 'neyhboures of the other thre bonfyres' within a ward 'to make merry withall'. Stow stated quite categorically that in London, 'These were called Bone-fires, as well of amity amongst neighbours, that being before at controversie, were there by the labour of others reconciled, and made of bitter enemies, loving friends'. Topographical groupings when expressed in such convivial ways must have helped at least to encourage cross-cutting ties within the social structure.[20]

Just as customary commensality served to promote cohesion within the community, so tensions stemming from rigidities within the social structure seem to have been provided with institutionalized outlets. The most clear-cut example of what amounted to periodic relaxations of the social order was the Coventry Hock Tuesday play. The structural implications of this are perhaps best revealed by comparison with the practices of May Day, since these two occasions involved distinctly contrasted social age categories. May Day everywhere was, of course, primarily a festival of unmarried young people, the 'Maides and their Makes', as Ben Jonson characterized the Coventry participants; while Hock Tuesday concerned the women or the wives. In view of the markedly inferior status with regard to the opposite sex which females incurred as a consequence of the oath-taking ceremony of marriage, it is hardly surprising that the contrast between these two traditional observances was complete.[21]

On May Day the relationship was one of equality expressed in friendly dance. The preoccupation with courtship and love-making hardly needs emphasizing, but it is worth drawing attention to an aspect of popular symbolism which lay at the core of that seasonal rite. This was the widespread custom whereby yearning maidens on May Day in particular, and at other relevant moments in their lives, sported articles of clothing conspicuously embroidered with blue thread, for blue was the universal symbol of constant love. This simple practice, to which Coventry's dyeing industry traditionally catered and lent the term 'Coventry blue' because of its appropriate permanence, underlines what was probably a basic feature of May Day: the deliberate pairing-off by couples for the holiday as opposed to the unselective promiscuity implied in the more fevered castigations of certain Puritans.[22]

By contrast, the Hock Tuesday play used the anonymity of a *generalized* division of the sexes to reverse temporarily the *in*equalities existing between married men and women through the medium of conflict. This play-cum-mock-battle, in celebrating the putative historic overthrow of the Danish yoke by the citizens of Coventry in particular, culminated in a much diluted dramatization (with no doubt

66

a reduced number of participants) of the rural custom by which the wives of the parish were accustomed to bind and/or heave the menfolk before releasing them on payment of a ransom. At Coventry, after the men had fought out the battle, the play harped on 'how valiantly our English women for loove of their cuntree behaved themselvez', and how the Danish warriors having been beaten down 'many [were] led captive for triumph by our English weemen'. For once there is no doubt that women did take part; references to feminine costume hire amongst the expenses of special performances of this play before Queen Elizabeth are conspicuously absent.[23]

If relationships between the sexes concerned everyone in the community at an informal level, the position of mayor was the keystone in the formal structure of office-holding. It is, therefore, notable that at Christmas-time the mayoral dignity probably fell victim to institutionalized ridicule. Coventry then seems to have emulated that annual custom of a Lord of Misrule which was also to be found at Court, in great households, university colleges and the Inns of Court.[24]

Now it may be that this personage represented or came eventually to represent no other function than that of 'Master of Merry Disports' or superintendent of the revels, a purely prestigious adjunct to the seasonal festivities and hence to the standing of the host. Yet there are a number of pointers which suggest that there may have been more to it than this. The very title, for example, indicates that he was Lord not of *un*ruliness and licence, though this may have been and indeed possibly was a consequence of his activities, but of *mis*-rule or misgovernment. Early commentators like Polydore Vergil and Selden, moreover, were emphatic that Christmas was a season when the master of the house abdicated his position in order to obey or wait upon his own servants, one of whom would act as the Christmas Lord during the festivities. In the restricted context of a great man's home, some connexion between misrule at Christmas and the normal sway of the household head (whether in a public or private capacity) during the rest of the year could hardly have been avoided.[25]

It is in these circumstances that the urban version of this custom must be judged. For it is evident that Lords of Misrule pertained only to civic governors and not to other rich merchants or tradesmen. At Coventry and Chester they were associated with the mayor; at London with both the mayor and the sheriffs. It may also be significant that at Coventry in 1517 the Lord himself was one of the civic sergeants. Since mayors' sergeants were to be found at this time in the Corpus

Christi Gild they clearly belonged to the office-holding class, and so may have been considered suitably dependable candidates for the festive post. Alternatively, there may even have been some form of deliberate status elevation within the body of civic officers for the duration of the holiday. Either way, the indications are that within the confines of his household or even elsewhere, the civic ruler had to be seen or known to put temporarily aside his formal status, in order to become, instead, the subject of satirical government: hence perhaps in part, the open house kept by the mayor for the whole twelve days at Coventry, at least in 1517, and the public processions of the London sheriffs with their respective Lords of Misrule through the streets of the capital.[26]

The only other time of the year at which the social barriers were lowered was the period of early summer. In this instance it was the classic antipathy between town and country which was expressed, the sanctity of private property that was annually violated and the privileged immunity of the local land-owning class which was breached. For the festivities of Midsummer, St Peter's and probably May Day required the lavish decoration of houses, halls and streets with birch boughs and blossoms, quite apart from Maypoles, all of which were most conveniently procured without permission or payment from nearby estates. Thus, when in 1480 the Prior of Coventry complained that every summer his underwood was being taken, the mayor had to invoke a widespread custom in answering the charge, 'remembryng that the people of every gret Cite, as London & other Citeez, yerely in somur doon harme to divers lordes & gentyles havyng wodes & Groves nygh to such Citees be takyng of boughes & treez, and yit the lordes & gentils suffren sych dedes ofte tymes of theire goode will'. In like manner the citizens of Leicester hacked down timber for use on May Day in the woods of Sir Henry Hastings in 1603, while the gardens of the gentry in the neighbourhood of Nottingham were being ransacked for flowers at Midsummer up to the reign of Charles I. It seems that at such times everyday rules did not apply, while the privileged class, whose interests normally ensured their preservation, was expected to acquiesce passively in their flagrant transgression.[27]

The significance of all these practices lay not in the ways in which social tensions were haphazardly released but in the methods by which they were controlled. In the first place, such observances appear to have been the means of canalizing traditional periods of licence—a process which seems to have been completed at Coventry during the fifteenth century. The Hock Tuesday play, created in 1416, for example, was clearly a deliberate urban rationalization of contemporary bawdy practice in the rural Midlands generally. Accordingly Hock Monday, when the men usually bound the women in the country, withered away completely in an urban environment to become merely the Monday before Hock Tuesday. Local evidence for Christmas licence does not survive, but it is worth noting in passing that if Lords of Misrule did not originate during the fifteenth century, they only seem to have become generally popular towards its end. Midsummer and St Peter's were, however, indubitably times of extreme disorder and even riot. It was as a necessary response to this that the Prior of Coventry and other worried ecclesiastical dignitaries had suggested the inception of a special watch in 1421 to control 'the grett multytude of peopull' and to avoid the 'grett debate and man-slaughter and othure perels and synnes that myght fall, and late have fallen'. There is no evidence before 1445, however, that their recommendations were accepted.[28]

These customs, secondly, had built into them, as it were, certain safeguards for the preservation of the structure. In all cases those in subordinate roles encroached in some way only on certain *attributes* of socially superior positions. At Hocktide representatives of the women overcame the menfolk in their unaccustomed masculine role as warriors and not as husbands or householders. In summertime the townspeople did not specifically attack the gentry class: they merely appropriated its property. Even at Christmas, the Lord of Misrule seems to have been a bad ruler rather than a 'mock mayor' or 'mayor of misrule'. If such customs deliberately distorted certain aspects of the social order, there was no question of altering the whole: in disfiguring the structure temporarily, the participants were in fact accepting the *status quo* in the long run.[29]

And it was perhaps this emphasis on preserving and enhancing the wholeness of the social order which most distinguished the ceremonies of this late medieval urban community. In a close-knit structure composed of overlapping groups or groupings, where a change of status in one sphere so often could affect standing in another, ceremony performed a crucial clarifying role. It was a societal mechanism ensuring continuity within the structure, promoting cohesion and controlling some of its inherent conflicts, which was not only valued as contributing to the 'worship' of the city, but also enjoyed by contemporaries. Even in times of crisis the plays were performed and the watches marched. If anything, before 1545 the tendency was not to cut back on over-costly trappings but to preserve and elaborate them. A reforming mayor in the 1530s was quite unable to stop accustomed drinkings even when craftsmen were being ruined by the expense. Feelings in favour of the Hock Tuesday and Corpus Christi plays, or some substitute for them, survived their formal abolition, and some way of observing Midsummer and St Peter's evidently outlived the watches. But the real significance which contemporaries attached to such practices may be better gauged by turning now to the cultural, temporal and spatial contexts in which they took place.[30]

The citizen's year was marked by rather different seasonal quarterings to those which, according to Homans, characterized the open-field husbandman's calendar. At Coventry, the beginning of the year seems to have been determined by the long-standing tradition by which the city's Lammas pastures reverted to private hands on 2 February, the date at which the mayoral inauguration had also come to take place and from which the mayoral year accordingly began. It is more than probable that, as elsewhere, May Day was accepted as the start of summer, and the re-opening of the Lammas lands to common pasturing on 1 August as the beginning of autumn. Judging from lighting regulations, winter was thought to lie between 1 November and 2 February. It seems indeed to have been a function of the city waits to emphasize this seasonal and predominantly pastoral framework. With the exception of the first quarter when they played from the first week in Clean Lent through to Easter, the waits performed nightly during the first part of each of these quarters, up to Midsummer, Michaelmas and Christmas respectively.[31]

Cutting clean through this seasonal sectionalization of the calendar, however, was another division of the year. In this instance, subdivision was by halves: a bisection made possible by that evident unity of the six months between 24–5 December and 24 June inclusively ($182\frac{1}{2}$ days), which stemmed from an oft-noted coincidence of Christian and archaic native practice. In the case of the church, the outcome was to cram all the major observances connected with the birth, life, death and resurrection of Christ into these six months, the unity of which is still roughly expressed when reference is made to Christmas, Easter and Whitsun in preference to a strictly calendrical ordering. Even the movable feasts were tied in a way to Christmas: Lent could begin as early as 4 February, only two days after the feast of the Purification, logically the last rite of Christmas. Similarly, at the latter end of the moiety when Easter fell at its latest, the feast of Corpus Christi, the culminating festival of the cycle, coincided with Midsummer Day. Whatever the date of Easter, it seems reasonable to suggest that the very movability of the greatest feasts of the Church, and the universal custom of relational dating thereto, helped to invest the whole of this period with an appreciable quality of its own.[32]

Through their origins and practice, moreover, native popular observances served to emphasize this unity. The widespread acceptance of the end of December as pertaining more logically to the succeeding than to the current year, for example, had its origins in remote antiquity: according to Bede, the heathen year, which also broke down into two halves, had begun on 25 December. In later times, the twelve days, of course, remained inseparable from Christmas itself and so acted as the connecting link with the following year. Events on each of these days were commonly seen as predictive of the weather or fortunes of the succeeding twelve months.[33]

Such popular attitudes served also to bridge the gap between Christian observances. At Norwich, Lent was ushered in by the King of Christmas on Shrove Tuesday 'in the last ende of Cristemesse', 'as hath ben accustomed in ony Cite or Burgh thrugh al this reame'. In like fashion did native customs span the interval, when there was one, between the end of the movable Church cycle and Midsummer. There are indications, for example, that May games were played in London up to 24 June (though a command performance was once held on the following day before Queen Elizabeth). It may be significant in this connexion that at the Coventry Midsummer watch in the 1550s, the Dyers' contingent was attended by a herdsman blowing his horn and someone 'carrying the tree before the hartt'—probably a reference to a 'company' of morris dancers with a maypole and other props. A relevant confusion in popular thought was also criticized by one puritan preacher who claimed that 'What offences soever happened from that tyme [Rogation] to Midsommer, the fumes of the fiers dedicated to John, Peter, and [though uncelebrated at Coventry] Thomas Becket the traytor, consumed them.' Any attempt at analysing popular culture has to take into consideration the ways in which religious and vulgar symbolism thus complemented each other and often merged into one.[34]

Particularly notable in this respect was the manner in which the contrasted symbols of fire and vegetation were accepted in Coventry, as elsewhere, by both Church and layman alike during this temporal moiety. If at Christmas time, Holy Trinity church was ablaze with extra candles, the Smiths' craft also specifically employed 'iij tapers at Crystmas & a candle ageynst xij day', while both Church and craft sported the obvious evergreens, holly and ivy. There is no need to dwell on the relevance of Candlemas, the ritualized burning of 'palm' leaves on Ash Wednesday, the bearing of 'palms' on Palm Sunday, nor on the hallowing of fire in church at Easter. The use of fresh foliage to decorate the city at the summer feasts has already been indicated as have the Midsummer bonfires. It is worth emphasizing, however, that half the point of the marching watch seems to have been literally to carry fire through the streets. Each craft had its own special cresset bearers for this purpose, probably an urban echo of that rural custom of rolling burning wheels down hills to mark the summer solstice.[35]

Also to be found in these six months were the extremes of sacred and profane drama with their common themes of birth, death and re-birth, and their corollary sexual relationships. Though Christmas mummers are not evidenced, the parish churches dramatized Palm Sunday with the unveiling of the Rood and Easter Day with the resurrection from the Easter sepulchre, while the crafts performed their plays at Corpus Christi. The inter-sex dramas or ritualized games of Hocktide and May Day have already been discussed, but as at nearby Leicester and Stratford-upon-Avon, it is likely that the procession which marked St George's Day (23 April) was also enlivened by some representation of the traditional fight with the dragon. A courtly version of what would probably have been stock practice was the highlight of Prince Edward's visit to Coventry on 28 April 1474 to observe a late St George's feast. This showed a King and a Queen 'beholdyng seint George savyng theire doughter from the dragon', a very similar tableau being presented before Prince Arthur in 1498.[36]

This temporal unit was further characterized by pronounced polarities in everyday activities and behaviour. On the one hand were the long period of Lenten diet, the accompanying civic enforcement of personal morality—the aldermen were specifically ordered to punish 'bawdry' during Clean Lent—and, more often than not, the eight-day Corpus Christi fair, that annual apogee of the city's economic endeavour. On the other were the traditional periods of licence and the only major extended holidays in the year. An obviously pre-Reformation ruling in a later sixteenth-century recension of the Cardmakers' ordinances was probably representative in permitting neither

> Cutinge, prickyng, doublyng, Crooking, nor Settinge, within
> the xij dayes at Christmas neyther at any Satterday, at after noone,
> after one of the clock, neyther on any Vygill Even after the
> same houre, . . . neyther shall they woork at any of the poynts
> above specyfyed in Easter weeke, neither in Whitsune week . . .[37]

The contrast with the six months between 25 June and about midday on the vigil of Christmas (182½ days) was absolute. In this period there was no religious or popular symbolic coherence, there were no institutionalized extremes of behaviour and there were no extended holidays. Essentially this was a time for uninterrupted, normal economic activities, some of which, even in a city the size of Coventry, were still dependent on rural rhythms. The Lammas pastures could only have been free for use on 1 August if, as elsewhere, the hay harvest began at Midsummer, while the grain harvest made the few Michaelmas lands similarly available. More germane were the completion of sheep shearing by mid-June and the wool sales which followed: new supplies may have been reaching the army of wool and textile workers soon after Midsummer. Similarly, if somewhat later in the year there was no early winter slaughtering in the locality to bring supplies of meat into the city, there were, very probably, sales of surplus stock well before Christmas. The importance of this generally drier season for travel, finally, emphasizes the conspicuous number of fairs which at least the merchants might have wanted to attend. Coventry seems to have belonged to a minority in holding its own fair before Midsummer in nearly all years.[38]

It is thus difficult to doubt the existence of a marked pre-Reformation dichotomy of the year, the two halves of which it is surely no exaggeration to denominate for convenience as respectively 'ritualistic' and 'secular'. It must be stressed, however, that this is to suggest not that the former necessarily saw a general slowing down of economic activity, but rather that the same routines continued to be carried out against an abnormal background. When ceremonies occurred in this half, they did so in a heightened context which was wholly absent in the secular moiety. It is therefore relevant to enquire into what sorts of ceremonies were most usually associated with each, leaving aside those largely administrative occasions which recurred half yearly or quarterly like the ordinary meetings of crafts or the court leet, and arbitrarily fixed events like obits.

With this obvious proviso it is an interesting comment on the value attached to the ideal of local community, that the ritualistic half embraced every major public ceremony (St Peter's eve excepted) which formally interrelated separate whole groups or groupings of the social structure. Even as late as the seventeenth century, all the festival days on which the aldermen were to wear their scarlet fell in this period with the only exceptions of two post-medieval additions, 1 November and 5 November.[39]

This emphasis on the ritualistic half was further brought out by the frequency of processions and occasions which, in so far as sepate ceremonies pertained to similar structural relationships, seem to have been concentrated into sometimes overlapping temporal blocs. The half began by expressing the relation of the civic body to the community. If the retiring mayor was burlesqued over Christmas, his successor and junior colleagues were chosen and then approved in January prior to their inauguration before the citizens at Candlemas in, appropriately, St Mary's Hall. On the morrow of Lenten mortification, it was the turn of those socially cohesive topographical groupings, the parishes, which, from as early as the Palm Sunday processions through the entire Easter celebrations, seem to have been the unrivalled foci of ceremonial activity. It is even conceivable that the two sides in the Hock Tuesday play (ten days after Easter) originally represented the two parishes which, in any case, came into their own again with the normal Rogationtide processions. Hock Tuesday, however, could fall on any day between 6 April and 3 May, only two days after that other celebration of inter-sex relationships, May Day itself.[40]

At this juncture the gilds and probably the civic body began to dominate the scene. There is some evidence to suggest that both gilds processed with their cross-bearers on St George's Day (23 April), Ascension (which fell between 30 April and 3 June), and Whit Sunday (10 May to 13 June). It is more than probable that the mayor and his brethren were associated with the first and, certainly in company with the commonalty, the last, which was indeed still an official festival day for aldermen in 1640. Not that the parishes were excluded—Holy Trinity, at least, also fielded its cross, banner and streamers on all three days.[41]

The ceremonial activities of this ritualistic half reached a spectacular climax with four processions: on Corpus Christi day (21 May to 24

June), the following day—Fair Friday, Midsummer eve, and (for the sake of analytical continuity, though it belonged strictly to the secular half) five days later on St Peter's eve. In all of these, of course, the civic body was accompanied by the craft fellowships or, in the case of Fair Friday alone, two or three accoutred representatives.[42]

In a very real sense the community thus ceremonialized itself *vis-à-vis* all its major activities, with a changing emphasis on worship, work and particularly authority. The ritualistic half may have begun with a parody of government, but it ended with the mayor processing as the king's representative backed by a token armed force provided by each company. In more general fashion the frequent ultra-formalization of group interrelationships throughout this half was conspicuously balanced by the structurally distortive customs of Christmas, Hocktide and Midsummer, which fell broadly at the beginning, middle and end of the period in question. It is thus tempting to see such practices as representing in this instance, not the exact opposite of everyday life, as has been suggested on general grounds by Dr Leach, but rather of communal ceremonialization. For *both* ceremony *and* structural distortion operated on an exaggerated plane which was quite distinct from normality: the former idealized and the latter inverted social norms. Conceptually they complemented each other.[43]

Whereas during the ritualistic half the component groups of the community were ceremonially interrelated in public, throughout the secular period the parts, on the whole, ceremonialized themselves in private. Perhaps to avoid the interruption of the next ceremonial 'season', this half was primarily concerned with the election of those officers who, unlike the mayor, could not be regarded as symbols of the community as a whole. Both gilds, for example, then elected their masters; the Trinity Gild on 18 October and the Corpus Christi Gild on 8 December. Ten out of the fourteen fellowships for which information survives or can be inferred, furthermore, also elected their officers in the secular half. There even remains, in some cases, traces of an occupational pattern. The elections of the 'textile' crafts, for instance, seem to have been fairly closely bunched. The Cappers who began in 1496 with 26 July, later changed to 7 August in 1520, while both the Weavers and apparently the Fullers favoured 25 July. The accounts of the latter were usually rendered on 23 November, a popular date for this, and the same day as the Dyers, the date of whose elections may thus be broadly inferred. By contrast, the Cordwainers and Tanners elected on or near 9 October and 16 October respectively, while the new master of the Butchers held his inaugural dinner on the 18th of the same month.[44]

All the four fellowships whose elections overlapped into the ritualistic half chose their officers between Christmas and New Year's Day. The Tilers, who elected on 26 December (although the St Stephen's Day in question could conceivably have been 2 August), represent the only serious aberration in an otherwise remarkable overall pattern. The leet ordinance on the hybrid character of the fellowship of Cardmakers, Saddlers, Masons and Painters probably explains their date (29 December) during the holiday period when either disputes might in theory, perhaps, have been more easily avoided, or a mutually convenient date on which to meet, most readily found. Clearly the Mercers and Drapers, on the other hand, whose dates fell on 27 December and 31 December, had to fall in line with the elections to civic office which were due to take place during the succeeding month.[45]

Differences between the two halves of the year were not restricted to the varying ceremonialization of social structure, however; there were also significant contrasts in the actual territory over which open-air ceremonies took place. This was partly due to the peculiar topography of Coventry. For, firstly, at its heart lay what was virtually a single vast churchyard containing not only the two parish churches, but also the Cathedral priory. Flanking it were the Bishop's palace, and halls for priests, as well as the major civic administrative buildings like St Mary's Hall and the gaol, and finally the huge covered cloth-market, the Drapery. Since the approach to the Cathedral and the circuits around the parish churches were mostly if not all known as 'procession ways', it is clear that this whole consecrated area constituted a ritual centre for the city. It is therefore noteworthy that the ceremonies in the earlier part of the ritualistic period were mainly confined to it. The mayoral inauguration was focused on St Michael's Church and St Mary's Hall, while the parochial processions around the churchyard on Palm Sunday, the Easter celebrations and quite possibly rather more elaborate occasions, as at Whitsuntide, were likewise restricted.[46]

The city, secondly, was triangulated by gild chapels: the chapel of St Nicholas which belonged to the Corpus Christi Gild lay just outside Bishop Gate to the north-west; that of the Trinity Gild, St John Bablake, was situated just inside the Spon Gate at the western end of the city; and the unique craft-cum-gild chapel of St George which pertained to the Shermen and Tailors was attached to Gosford Gate itself, on the eastern side. Most probably, each of these was the departure

point or destination of a major procession in the latter part of the ritualistic half. That at Corpus Christi must have started from St Nicholas
chapel, where the host would have been consecrated, before proceed-
ing through the streets until it reached what seems to have been the
first pageant station at Gosford Gate where the plays were to begin.
Since the Feast of the Nativity of St John the Baptist was the dedication day of the Trinity Gild chapel, and since the mayor who presided
over the procession was accustomed to visit Bablake 'overnight' for
dirige, 'dyvers consideracions & other great busynes', it is very possible
that the riding on Midsummer's eve began there. (It will be recalled
that following the watch, which evidently did not start until after dark,
he was engaged in entertaining at least the craft officers.) More probably still, the St George's Day procession, after leaving Bailey Lane
which skirted the churchyard centre, would have included a visit to
the only chapel dedicated to that saint in the city and to an area
customarily connected, at second-hand, with the chivalrous slaughter
of monsters. A bone of the fabulous boar slain by Guy of Warwick
hung at Gosford Gate, while a few hundred yards up the hill outside
was a chapel dedicated to yet another dragon dispatcher, whose fame
was locally celebrated, St Margaret.[47]

During the ritualistic half, therefore, there seems to have been a
movement of formal ceremony from the centre outwards to the limits
of the city but no further. Nearly every other observance during this
moiety was similarly confined. Hocktide games took place 'in' the city
and not on adjacent waste ground; maypoles stood over the streets;
bonfires burnt on them; 'pageants' trundled through them. The one
part-exception would have been the Rogationtide processions which
traced the parish boundaries outside as well as within the city. Such
practices are not only a reminder that medieval streets were as important
for recreation and marketing as for communication; rites and processions, like the carriage through the streets of the Corpus Christi
host or the Midsummer fire, periodically added a mystical dimension
to this utilitarian valuation of the immediate topographical context.
While doing so, they underlined further the physical inescapability of
communal involvement.[48]

Though somewhat mitigated by the fewness of the occasions, a
contrast was provided, once again, by the secular half. Here the
emphasis was on the surrounding countryside, the city's fields and the
County of Coventry. Communal participation, moreover, was atten-
uated. Attendance on the Chamberlains' annual Lammas ride (1

August), to oversee the renewal of common access to pasture land, for example, was restricted as from 1474 to those appointed, and after 1495 to representatives from each ward. What theoretically became a triennial activity as from 1469, the riding of the metes and bounds of the County of Coventry, also seems to have taken place in the secular half. If the intention to ride before the Michaelmas leet was sometimes announced at its Easter predecessor, the only surviving exact dates indicate that the execution was left to the last possible moment: 4 October in 1509 and 26–7 September in 1581. On the latter occasion, the party included not only a number of aldermen, sheriffs, other civic officers, and 'yonge men appoynted', no doubt as guardians of the future, but also 'dyvers others of everie Townshipp sommune within the forrens'.[49]

The correlation between town and country, which seems to have been associated with this moiety, was emphasized in another way. For to accommodate the demands of the Exchequer year, the sheriffs for the county were sworn and so designated at the Michaelmas Leet in the secular half. When the same men appeared at the following Easter Leet in the ritualistic half, however, they did so only in their *civic* capacities as 'bailiffs'. It may not be too far-fetched to suggest, therefore, that the marching of the watch on St Peter's eve in the first week of the secular half may have had an extra-urban bias. It was conducted by the sheriffs and not by the mayor; fines for non-attendance by craftsmen were, at least in one instance, less severe than at Midsummer; the city Weavers do not even seem to have participated; and there appears to have been no formally defined order of march by crafts. It is thus just possible either that there may have been some progression from township to township or, more likely, that county representatives joined the civic procession. Such an explanation might help to account for the overlap of this ritualistic activity into the secular half of the year.[50]

Taken as a whole, however, Coventry's calendar seems to betray a conspicuous correspondence between social structure and its ceremonialization in time and space. That observances occasionally overlapped their temporal contexts cannot be denied, but by and large the intricate regularity of the pattern is remarkably clear. Reconstructed, it bears mute witness both to the communal quality of a late medieval urban society, particularly the evident subordination of the parts to the working of the whole, and to the pervasive role of the pre-Reformation Church and its practices in that community. Such a reconstitution also highlights the extent of the subsequent change: the destructive impact of the events of the mid-sixteenth century and the consequent obliteration of the established rhythm of life itself.

The modernization of this late medieval framework was characterized by the triumph of the secular half over its ritualistic counterpart as, one after another, the principal ceremonies vanished. The important processions of St George's Day, Ascension, Whitsun and Corpus Christi were either unrecognizably altered or later abolished by the amalgamation of the Corpus Christi Gild in 1535 with the Trinity Gild, and their subsequent dissolution in 1547. At the same time, St George's chapel was probably abandoned though the Shermen and Tailors survived as a craft fellowship. Like London and Bristol, Coventry then also secured some respite from the summer watches, officially relinquishing that on St Peter's in 1549, though the last riding at Midsummer does not seem to have taken place until some fourteen or fifteen years later. Meanwhile, in 1552, a new October fair had been granted, and during the very year that the Queen had foisted a Catholic mayor on the city (1556), the mayoral inauguration had been moved from Candlemas to 1 November, a date with fewer papistical overtones. A first attempt at abolishing the Hock Tuesday play seems to date from 1561, but the insistence of the citizenry ensured its spasmodic resurrection thereafter. Thirty years later it was finally moved out of context to St Peter's eve, when its performance was theoretically to be restricted by confinement to the stages of the Corpus Christi 'pageants'. The sacred plays, for which these theatrical waggons had originally been designed, were last acted in 1579. For a few years, however, they were replaced by a safe Protestant substitute which, in 1591 at least, seems to have been performed at Midsummer. With the removal, finally, of all maypoles from the city in the same year, the ritualistic half no longer existed as a recognizable unit for both church and society.[51]

The changing venue of ceremony was itself indicative of the nature of this momentous alteration in the yearly round. The only open-air ceremonies to survive, for example, were now justifiable on technical grounds alone: to proclaim the fair or to perpetuate the boundaries, of parish, field or county. With the emasculation of popular practices at May Day, Hock Tuesday or Midsummer, profane rites and even a recreation, like football in 1595, were banished from the streets. The

Queen's highway was left to its purely materialistic functions. If the opportunity for popular participation in public rituals was consequently largely removed, that especial meaning which sacred ceremonies and popular rites had periodically conferred on the citizens' tangible environment also fell victim to the new 'secular' order. Ceremony and religion together withdrew indoors from the vulgar gaze. The formalization of social structure was now passively restricted accordingly to the hierarchical seating arrangements within the parish churches. As a result, that unknown proportion of the population which bothered to attend them was automatically divided.[52]

For, most significantly, formal communal processions had totally disappeared. The nearest the later sixteenth century could come to former practices was the Fair Friday display with its minimal craft representation. Indeed, until the days of the later Godiva procession (which in origin bore all the hallmarks of an advertising stunt), formal communal involvement of any sort was restricted to the annual mayoral inauguration, a largely indoor affair. The civic body may have ceremonially observed certain church festivals, but there is no evidence that anyone else took part.[53]

The leading representatives of that simultaneously adjusting social structure, who had helped to bring about all these changes, may have belonged to a wider cultural and economic environment than their predecessors, but at least in one respect their societal horizons were narrower. By the seventeenth century the claims of the community, at this level, were yielding first place to class loyalties. With this development, the annihilation of what had evolved into a ceremonial system in the late medieval period, was closely connected. It was no accident that the elaborate official inaugurations which had characterized the old secular moiety alone survived untarnished, in the post-Reformation world, to dominate the altered and abbreviated ceremonial calendar of the Coventry citizen.

Notes

1 I am particularly grateful to Professor W. G. Hoskins under whose sympathetic aegis this investigation was begun while the author was Research Fellow in English Local History at the University of Leicester between 1966 and 1968; to Messrs A. A. Dibben, D. J. H. Smith and colleagues for multifarious assistance far in excess of their statutory

duties; and to the Company of Cappers and Feltmakers of Coventry for permission to study their earliest account book. A full-scale study of Coventry society between 1480 and 1660 on social anthropological lines, which will amplify matters only touched on here, is currently in preparation. Unless otherwise specified all MS. references relate to the Coventry Record Office.

2 M. D. Harris, ed., *The Coventry Leet Book* (*LB*) (Early English Text Society, 1907–13), p. 556; *ibid.*, p. 558; *ibid.*, pp. 655, 560; *ibid.*, p. 294; *ibid.*, pp. 653, 694; *ibid.*, p. 417; T. Sharp, *A Dissertation on the Pageants or Dramatic Mysteries Anciently Performed at Coventry* (*Dissertation*) (Coventry, 1825), pp. 22, 79–80, 161, n.f, 182–3; accession 241, original fols 2v., 4; cf. p. 78, below.

3 See my forthcoming *Coventry in Crisis 1518–1525* (Department of English Local History Occasional Papers, second series, Leicester); accession 100: Weavers 11 (unfol.), quarterage payments and journeymen's groats 1523–1537; A5, fols 152r., 164r., 173r.; Cappers and Feltmakers' Company MSS, first account book (Cappers' accs), fols 67v., 68r., 70v., 71r.; *LB*, pp. 568, 545; *ibid.*, p. 249; Cappers' accs fols 68r., 71r.; A5, *loc. cit.*; Weavers 2a, fol. 2v.; Weavers 2c, journeymen's orders; A99, fol. 2r.; accession 241, original fols 2v.–3r.; Weavers 2a, fol. 4r.; A5, fol. 1r.; cf. L. Fox, 'The Coventry Guilds and Trading Companies with Special Reference to the Position of Women', in *Essays in Honour of Philip B. Chatwin* (Oxford, 1962), pp. 13–26.

4 Accession 100: Weavers 11, 1524; A166 (with acknowledgment to Professor R. W. Ingram), extracts from S. Michael's vestry book; cf. A98, 'For comyng to the Churche'; A6, *passim*; A5, *passim*; Cappers' accs *passim*; *LB*, pp. 405–6; A34, fol. 269r.

5 *LB*, p. 560; Bodl. MS. Top Warwick c. 7 (Reader), fol. 118r.; A5, fol. 2r.; G. Templeman, ed., *The Records of the Guild of the Holy Trinity, St. Mary, St. John the Baptist and St. Katherine of Coventry* (Dugdale Society, XIX, 1944), p. 31. Calculations from Cappers' accs have been made on the basis of 'New Brethren' up to 1513. Weavers 2a, fol. 6r.; A98, rules 6 and 3; A110, rules 11, 13, 28; *LB*, p. 792; Reader 92v.; Bodl. MS. Top Warwick d. 4, fol. 19v.; accession 154, *passim*; Cappers' accs, *passim*; *LB*, calculated from all those serving as warden or chamberlain between 1490 and 1520. Coventry's gerontocracy will be fully discussed in the larger work mentioned in n. 1.

6 Calculated for all cappers in A6 between 1515 and 1524; Cappers' accs *passim*; A6, fols 206r. *et seq.* A microscopic examination of gild membership has yet to be completed.

7 *LB*, p. 743; *LP*, XII, 108; *e.g. LB*, pp. 604–5; A6, fol. 148r.; A34, fol. 269r.

8 Reader, fol. 217r.; A99, fol. 16v.; A34, fol. 269r.; cf. Reader, fol. 100r.

9 Weavers 2a, fol. 7v.; *LB*, p. 662; *ibid.*, pp. 279, 544; M. Fortes, 'Ritual and Office in Tribal Society', in M. Gluckman, ed., *Essays on the Ritual of Social Relations* (Manchester, 1962), pp. 82-3.

10 Phrase used in 1615, A98 (unfol.); Reader, fol. 92r.; Weavers 2a, fols 5v., 6; Reader, fol. 117r.; *LP*, XIV (1), 77; cf. Reader, fol. 100.

11 A99, fol. 16v.; Sharp, *op. cit.*, p. 183; A34, fol. 269v.

12 *LB*, p. 107; Templeman, *op. cit.*, p. 173; *LB*, pp. 619-21, 676-7; Weavers 2a, fol. 2v.; *LB*, pp. 670, 743; Weavers 2a, fol. 3v.; *LB*, p. 648.

13 *LB*, p. 220; *Statutes of the Realm*, 3 Hen. VIII c. 8; *LB*, p. 533; Templeman, *op. cit.*, p. 6, n. 5, the Mercers' Craft included Grocers, Merchants and perhaps Vintners.

14 G. Unwin, *The Gilds and Companies of London* (fourth edition, 1963), p. 269; Cappers' accs fols 45v. *et seq.*; *LB*, *passim*, and A7(a), *passim*— in a minority of years the junior civic officers cannot be ascertained; Sharp, *op. cit.*, pp. 203-5; accession 154, p. 34; the Drapers' possession of a male giant cannot be proved.

15 Templeman, *op. cit.*, pp. 152-9, 179-84; A6 and A5, *passim*; Templeman, *op. cit.*, p. 178; A6, fols 226r., 225r.; A5, fols 38v., 60r., 106v.

16 *LB*, p. 779; accession 100: Weavers 11 (unfol.) 1544, 1550, 1557; A5, fol. 140r.; E. W. W. Veale, ed., *The Great Red Book of Bristol* (Bristol Record Society, 1933), I, 125-6.

17 *LB*, p. 94; Sharp, *op. cit.*, p. 181, n.p.

18 A96; E 179/192/125; 1523 census; Phythian-Adams, *op. cit.*

19 J. C. Cox, *Churchwardens' Accounts* (1913), p. 58; *LB*, p. 669; T. Sharp, *Illustrative Papers on the History and Antiquities of the City of Coventry* (*Antiquities*) (corrected by W. G. Fretton, Birmingham, 1871), p. 123.

20 *LB*, p. 233; G. C. Homans, *English Villagers of the Thirteenth Century* (New York, 1960), p. 375; Sharp, *Dissertation*, pp. 175-6.

21 B. C. H. H. Percy and E. Simpson, eds, *Ben Jonson* (Oxford, 1941), VII, 785; Cox, *op. cit.*, pp. 64-5, 261-3.

22 Percy and Simpson, *op. cit.*, p. 785; J. Brand, *Observations on the Popular Antiquities of Great Britain* (1841), II, 69, 59, 75, 80; B. Poole, *Coventry—its History and Antiquities* (Coventry, 1870), p. 358; Brand, *op. cit.* (1859 edition), I, 213.

23 E. K. Chambers, *The Mediaeval Stage* (Oxford, 1903), I, 155; Poole, *op. cit.*, pp. 51-2; Sharp, *Dissertation*, p. 128.

24 Chambers, *op. cit.*, pp. 403, 407, 418.

25 *Ibid.*, p. 403; Thomas Langley, *An Abridgemente of the Notable Worke of Polidore Virgile* (?1570), fol. Cr.; Sir F. Pollock, ed., *Table Talk of John Selden* (1927), p. 28.

26 BM. Harl. MS. 6388, fol. 28v.; Chambers, *op. cit.*, p. 418; A6, fols 216r., 217v., 218r., 221v., 223r.; J. G. Nichols, ed., *The Diary of Henry Machyn* (Camden Society, XLII, 1848), pp. 28, 274.

27 *LB*, p. 233; Sharp, *Dissertation*, pp. 179–80; *LB*, p. 455; W. Kelly, *Notices Illustrative of the Drama and other Popular Amusements chiefly in the Sixteenth and Seventeenth Centuries, . . . Extracted from . . . Manuscripts of the Borough of Leicester* (1865), pp. 102, 72, 99; C. Deering, *Nottinghamia Vetus et Nova* (Nottingham, 1751), p. 124.

28 F. Bliss Burbidge, *Old Coventry and Lady Godiva* (Birmingham, n.d.), p. 218; n. 23, above; Brand, *op. cit.*, pp. 184–91; Cappers' accs fol. 68v.; cf. J. Latimer, *Sixteenth Century Bristol* (Bristol, 1908), p. 10 and Brand, *op. cit.*, p. 377; most early references to Lords of Misrule are sixteenth century: Chambers, *op. cit.*, pp. 403–18, cf. p. 173; *LB*, pp. 35, 220.

29 M. Gluckman, *Order and Rebellion in Tribal Africa* (1963), chap. III; E. Norbeck, 'African Rituals of Conflict', *American Anthropologist*, LXV (1963), 1254–75; P. Rigby, 'Some Gogo Rituals of "Purification"—an Essay on Social and Moral Categories', in E. R. Leach, ed., *Dialectic in Practical Religion* (Cambridge, 1968), pp. 153–78; V. W. Turner, *The Ritual Process* (1969), pp. 170–8, 183–5.

30 Phythian-Adams, *op. cit.*; Cappers' accs fols 24r., 26v., 29v.; accession 100: Weavers 11, 1523; cf. Cappers' accs fols 24r. and 94r.; *LP*, XIV, 1, 77; A14(a), p. 216.

31 Homans, *op. cit.*, p. 354; E. O. James, *Seasonal Feasts and Festivals* (1961), p. 309; *LB*, p. 777; Sharp, *Dissertation*, p. 211.

32 James, *op. cit.*, pp. 291, 230, 225–6, 207–25.

33 M. P. Nilsson, *Primitive Time-Reckoning* (Lund, 1920), pp. 294–5; Chambers, *op. cit.*, pp. 247 n. 3, 269; Brand, *op. cit.*, pp. 478–80.

34 W. Hudson and J. C. Tingey, eds, *The Records of the City of Norwich* (1906), I, p. 345, n. 2, and unconvincing assertions, p. xc; Nichols, *op. cit.*, pp. 20, 89, 137, 201; cf. J. Godber, *History of Bedfordshire* (Luton, 1969), p. 170; Sharp, *Dissertation*, pp. 200–1; Brand, *op. cit.*, p. 308.

35 Sharp, *Antiquities*, pp. 123–4; Reader, fol. 84r.; accession 154, p. 41; cf. Brand, *op. cit.*, p. 305; Sharp, *Dissertation*, p. 184; Homans, *op. cit.*, pp. 369–70.

36 James, *op. cit.*, p. 272; cf. *LB*, p. lii, n. 12; Sharp, *Antiquities*, pp. 122, 124; Kelly, *op. cit.*, p. 47; E. I. Fripp, ed., *Minutes and Accounts of the Corporation of Stratford-upon-Avon* (Dugdale Society, I, 1921), p. xix; *LB*, pp. 393, 590–1.

37 *LP*, IV(3), Appendix I; J. C. Jeaffreson, *Coventry Charters and Manuscripts* (Coventry, 1896), B48; Reader, fol. 95v.

38 Homans, *op. cit.*, p. 370; P. J. Bowden, *The Wool Trade in Tudor and Stuart England* (1962), p. 22 and cf. pp. 86–7, 91; P. J. Bowden, 'Agricultural Prices, Farm Profits, and Rents', in J. Thirsk, ed., *The Agrarian History of England and Wales* (Cambridge, 1967), p. 621; Alan Everitt, 'The Marketing of Agricultural Produce', *ibid.*, p. 533; F. Emery, 'The Farming Regions of Wales', *ibid.*, p. 121; H. P. R. Finberg, 'The Genesis

of the Gloucestershire Towns', in H. P. R. Finberg, ed., *Gloucestershire Studies* (Leicester, 1957), pp. 86–8.

39 A14(b), p. 6.

40 Above, pp. 60–1, 67–8; Sharp, *Antiquities*, pp. 120, 122–3; cf. James, *op. cit.*, pp. 300–4.

41 Sharp, *Dissertation*, p. 161; Templeman, *op. cit.*, p. 158; Poole, *op. cit.*, p. 211; A6, fol. 322r.; *LB*, pp. 588–9, 299–300; A14(b), p. 6; Sharp, *Antiquities*, p. 120. The evidence seems to be against a number of separate processions on each day. At Whitsun, for example, the gilds would hardly have segregated themselves from the Mayor's procession which contained their two Masters.

42 Above, p. 63; Reader, fol. 33. The Corpus Christi Gild may have processed as a separate entity on its major feast day, but no provision was made for this in Craft ordinances (e.g. accession 241, original fol. 2v.). There is evidence for processional activity by the Gild on the vigil: A6, fol. 325r.

43 Sharp, *Dissertation*, pp. 182–3, 192–5; Turner, *op. cit.*, pp. 168–9, 176–7; E. R. Leach, *Rethinking Anthropology* (1966), p. 135; E. R. Leach, *Political Systems of Highland Burma* (Boston, 1965), p. 286. The logical opposite of everyday behaviour in Dr Leach's schema should surely be disguise or masquerade—even holiday as opposed to work.

44 Cf. Templeman, *op. cit.*, p. 157; *ibid.*, pp. 159, 152; A6, fols 332v., 347v.; *LB*, pp. 573, 670; Weavers 2a, fol. 6 and cf. fol. 5v. and accession 100: Weavers 11 (unfol.) 1523 expenses; accession 30, pp. 10, 17; Reader, fol. 117r.; A98, rule 3; accession 241, original fol. 4r.; Reader, fol. 100r.; *LB*, p. 743; A110, rules 22 and 20; A5, fol. 21r.

45 Reader, fol. 217r.; *LB*, p. 205; A99, fol. 2r.; Reader, fol. 92r.

46 *LP*, XIII (2), 674; *VCH*, *Warwickshire*, VIII, 329; J. Speed, *Theatre o, the Empire of Great Britaine* (1611), fols 49v.–50; Poole, *op. cit.*, p. 203; A24, pp. 33, 32, 29; *LB*, pp. 460–1, 264, 299, 588; Sharp, *Antiquities*, pp. 122, 120; Cox, *op. cit.*, pp. 253–8; *LB*, p. 299.

47 Hardin Craig, ed., *Two Coventry Corpus Christi Plays* (Early English Text Society, E.S. 87, 1957), pp. xiii–xiv, 84–5; *LB*, p. 558: significantly, a number of 'pageant houses' were conveniently sited nearby, e.g. *ibid.*, p. xiii, n. 2, A24, p. 8; Poole, *op. cit.*, p. 211; above, p. 64; *LB*, p. 589; Speed, *op. cit.*, fol. 49r.; *LB*, pp. 738, 291–2.

48 Poole, *op. cit.*, p. 90; A14(a), p. 216; *LB*, p. 233.

49 *LB*, pp. 843, 565; *ibid.*, pp. 348, 571, 622, 628, 821—a special survey.

50 *Ibid.*, pp. 271–2 *passim*; *ibid.*, p. 791; Sharp, *Dissertation*, p. 182; accession 100: Weavers 11, Expenses 1523, *passim*; *LB*, p. 220; cf. Brand, *op. cit.*, pp. 337–8.

51 *LB*, pp. 722–3; cf. A99, fol. 2 (pre-1551: *ibid.*, fol. 2v.); *VCH*, *op. cit.*, p. 332; *APC*, New Series, I, pp. 447, 422, and cf. Cappers' accs fol. 72;

LB, p. 791; Sharp, *Dissertation*, p. 201 and cf. accession 100: Weavers 11, fols 53 *et seq.*; A5, fols 185r., 187r.; *CPR, Edward VI*, IV, 380; *APC*, New Series, V, p. 218; Bodl. MS. Top Warwick d. 4, fol. 20; Craig, *op. cit.*, pp. xxi–xxii; A14(a), p. 216; *VCH, Warwickshire*, VIII, 218.

52 A3(b), p. 13; Bodl. MS. Top Warwick d. 4, fol. 36; A98 (unfol.) 'For comynge to the Churche'; Poole, *op. cit.*, p. 157.

53 Cf. accession 100: Weavers 9 (unfol.), 1622; Bliss Burbidge, *op. cit.*, p. 256; Cappers' accs fol. 208v.; A14(b), p. 6.

3

The trade gilds of Tudor York

D. M. Palliser

'The history of English [craft] Gilds is yet to be written,' wrote Charles Gross eighty years ago, 'though materials in abundance . . . are to be found in town archives and in printed local histories.'[1] For most English towns that is still true, so no excuse is needed for this study of the gilds of one important city over a single century, especially as the sixteenth century has received little attention at York compared with the fourteenth or fifteenth.[2]

And it is a particularly interesting century to consider. For in the Tudor and Stuart periods the volume of trade was increasing, many towns were specializing in particular products and selling them over wider areas, and the craft gilds of the corporate towns are often seen as anachronisms which were in decline in the prospering towns, and which dragged down those towns unwise enough to leave the system intact. Stella Kramer sees the age as one of rapid amalgamation of gilds in the face of external competition which was infringing their monopoly powers more often and more seriously.[3] Yet there is no evidence that the York gild system changed greatly in the Tudor period, nor is it easy to argue that the retention of the medieval system proved an economic liability. It is worth looking at the gilds in some detail with these suggestions in mind.

The Tudor age is not a wholly arbitrary unit for this study, since it corresponds roughly to a period of ebb in York's economic fortunes. A comparison of varying types of evidence suggests that the peak of its medieval prosperity, based on a combination of textile crafts and overseas trading, coincided with the century after the Black Death. A decline set in between about 1450 and 1550 as textiles shifted out of York and overseas trade dwindled. Thereafter there was a gradual recovery, based partly on the growth of travel and of York's social importance for the county gentry and partly on the business generated by the King's Council in the North and the Ecclesiastical Commission for the Northern Province, both of which were located there between 1561 and 1641. This pattern is corroborated by taxation returns and by available population estimates, though neither are altogether satisfactory. York's place among provincial towns in terms of taxable wealth was second in 1334, fourteenth in 1523–7, and second again in 1662. Its population was perhaps over 12,000 in the early fifteenth century, 8,000 in the mid-sixteenth, and nearly 12,000 again in the early seventeenth.[4]

This population—the largest in northern England after Newcastle—lived mainly by handicrafts, distribution and services; and the dominant class, both economically and politically, were the freemen—in other words the master craftsmen, shopkeepers and traders. Anyone wishing to run his own business had first to become free of the city, by apprenticeship, inheritance, purchase or (occasionally) by gift of the corporation. (Some, of course, tried to evade this rule, and since we learn only of those who were caught, there is no means of knowing how many they were.) The freeman class provided the framework within which the trade gilds operated, for only freemen were eligible to join them. They enjoyed a trading monopoly in York, and a 'foreigner' or non-freeman could buy no goods there except from a freeman, nor could he sell there except to one. The custom of 'foreign bought and sold', by which the city confiscated all goods sold directly from one non-freeman to another, was jealously guarded. A 'foreigner' could just as easily be someone living in York as not: in 1579 there was a dispute between the free butchers, who lived in the Shambles, and the 'strainge' butchers living in Micklegate Ward, who had to sell in markets because they did not enjoy the freemen's privilege of shopkeeping.[5] Significantly, the terms 'citizen' and 'freeman', originally meaning those with political and economic rights respectively, had by now become interchangeable. However, we should not think of the freemen as being few, because they were a privileged class. There were some 1,200 freemen alive in 1548, nearly half the adult male population.[6]

The freemen's trading monopoly was limited in one important way, for those living in the 'liberties' or immunities within the city boundaries had no need to take up freedom. These liberties accounted before the

Reformation for a dozen areas of varying sizes and importance: the royal castle, the jurisdiction of the cathedral dean and chapter, nine religious houses, and the anachronistic Davy Hall, the former mansion of the larderers of a nearby royal forest. The most important was probably the dean and chapter's liberty, the home of some wealthy professional men, especially notaries and stationers. It took in not only the Minster Garth (the cathedral close) but also parts of the busy trading streets of Petergate and Stonegate. In 1584 the city's M.P.s sued in vain for the right of the city gilds to 'have searche of suche artificers as do dwell within the close'.[7] Even the quarter-acre Davy Hall became a real nuisance to the freemen, as shoemakers and other poor craftsmen set up shop there. As the craft searchers could not enter these immunities, two of the gilds involved in putting out work to subordinate craftsmen ordered that no work should be given to dwellers in those areas (cappers 1482, glovers 1482–3), though the former rescinded their ban in 1524.[8] Another such craft, the weavers, came to terms with the problem by taking annual payments from workers dwelling in the Minster Garth and Marygate, presumably in lieu of gild membership.

With these exceptions every master craftsman had to be enfranchised, and that meant taking the freeman's oath and being bound to obey the city by-laws, including those on trading matters. Immediately afterwards he had then to join the appropriate craft gild, if one existed.[9] There were two main kinds of gild, with differing degrees of organization. The larger ones were as a rule formally sanctioned by the city corporation, and given the right to elect officers and to make their own craft regulations, subject to corporation approval. An example is the brewers and tipplers (sellers) of ale and beer, who in 1600 were permitted to 'be all united into one companie or fellowshipp as other trades misteries or occupacions' were. Such grants are sometimes described as acts of incorporation, a term used by the city corporation itself, though it is strictly incorrect, as the Crown alone had the power to incorporate.[10] Hence only those two crafts with royal charters were legal corporations, and when the tailors made a third in 1662 their charter properly described them as 'being not incorporated' previously, although 'they have bin an ancient and great Company in the said Citty'.[11] Other York crafts had not even the formal organization provided by the city, yet banded together in some sort of unofficial way for common purposes. The mariners, for instance, are not known to have been organized by the corporation, or to have had craft regulations, but they united before the Reformation to perform one of the

Corpus Christi plays, and afterwards are known to have held meetings in St Anthony's Hall and to have contributed to its upkeep.

It is worth settling another problem of definitions at the outset. I have chosen to speak of 'gilds', this being the usual term employed in York histories, but at the time the craft organizations were called interchangeably misteries, crafts, trades or occupations. 'Gild' was sometimes used before the Reformation, while 'company' became fashionable under Elizabeth. But there is really no significance in the terminology, and certainly no evidence that the shift from 'gild' to 'company' represents a change from handicraft unions in an age of town economies to trader-dominated groups in an age of developing national economy, as Unwin believed.[12] 'Gild' probably disappeared because confusion with religious gilds would put the crafts in danger of state confiscation, and the innovation 'company' may have been simply a following of London fashion.

Let us first try to estimate how many gilds there were in all. Taking as gilds those incorporated by the Crown or sanctioned by the city corporation, and accepting as evidence any known regulations or provision for electing officials, there were at least 51 in 1485, besides 19 or more with no evidence of formal organization. Of the 51, the drapers and tailors united soon afterwards, while several others seem later to have disappeared (e.g. the bowyers and fletchers), though it is more difficult to establish the disappearance of a gild than its existence. On the other hand, new gilds were sanctioned by the corporation— the hatmakers in 1494 (reorganized under the haberdashers in 1591), the minstrels in 1561, the free labourers by 1578, the cobblers by 1582, the embroiderers in 1590 and the brewers in 1600—so that the numbers of gilds by the end of the period probably equalled that at the beginning. A list of crafts drawn up in 1579 totals 64, though not all need have been formally constituted.[13] This is a remarkably large number, though by no means incredible in the light of figures from cities of a comparable size.

Adopting Dr Kramer's classification, we can divide these numerous gilds into two types, trading or mercantile, and handicraft. Of these, the first exhibit a simple pattern according fairly well with her general picture. The most important at York was that designated in successive royal charters as the mistery of mercers (1430) or Society of Merchants Adventurers (1581), but which in fact was an amalgamated gild of mercers, merchants, grocers, spicers and apothecaries.[14] Alongside it grew up two further trading amalgamations. The drapers and tailors united in 1551-2 and were shortly afterwards joined by the hosiers; and in 1591 the haberdashers, feltmakers and cappers were united, at their own request, by the corporation. York fits neatly into a category of larger towns where the traders were grouped into two or three gilds of this type, contrasting on the one hand with London, with its twelve great merchant companies, and on the other with smaller towns with a single mercantile organization.

Kramer suggests that these gilds were formed by the merchants as a means of mutual protection after the collapse of the gild merchant, the early medieval association comprising all traders and craftsmen in the town. This may be so, though her picture of a gradual snowballing of the traders needs the modification required by most generalizations. For at York, where trading rather than manufacture was the mainstay of the economy, the reverse process was in operation; the haberdashers' union of 1591 does not represent a new union so much as a hiving off of the haberdashers from the general merchants' gild.[15] In any case the line between trade and handicraft gilds was never a sharp one. The mercers' and merchants' gild was purely a trading group, but the draper—tailor—hosier and haberdasher—feltmaker—capper unions each represented a fusion of a trading gild with two handicraft gilds of overlapping interests.

The merchants' and tailors' gilds were larger than any of the purely handicraft gilds. Between 1500 and 1600, 627 drapers, tailors and hosiers were made freemen of York, and 617 merchants and associated traders, each gild comprising just over 10 per cent of all freemen admitted.[16] The merchants also enjoyed the privileges of a royal charter, unlike any other gild except the once proud weavers. A first charter of 1430 made them a mistery of mercers, and a second in 1581, reconstituting them as the Society of Merchants Adventurers, gave them a monopoly of the sale of all overseas goods brought to York except fish and salt, thus putting them on the same footing as the merchants of other large provincial towns like Chester and Exeter. And even before the 1581 grant, they were wealthy and powerful out of all proportion to their size. As well as having their own hall, they made the largest contribution of any gild to St Anthony's, the smaller gilds' hall, with 5s a year (the next largest contributions were 4s each from the drapers, butchers, tanners and innholders, who by this date, 1623, will have been the wealthiest crafts next to the merchants).[17] More strikingly, the merchants really dominated city government, occupying the mayoralty for exactly half of the sixteenth century. Most of the merchants who became Lord Mayor also had a spell as governor of their own gild, and in eleven years between 1500 and 1600 the same man was simultaneously mayor and governor. So there was no danger of much divergence of interests between corporation and merchants, and indeed the former was thought of largely as an institution for the merchants' benefit. In 1528 the corporation asked the King to support their liberties and customs 'so that they may contynue and have . . . fredom for the relyeff and succour of poore merchaunt men of your said City', though here 'merchant' may be used in its older sense to mean any independent tradesman.[18]

The York merchants' gild excluded craftsmen, but they made no attempt, as did their fellow-merchants at Bristol and Chester, to keep out all retailers and become a society of wholesalers only. Indeed it is clear that in 1560, when the national Merchant Adventurers were considering excluding retailers, all the York merchants, even the most important, kept shops; and although the national company did ban retailers in 1564, Hull and York were certainly exempted.[19] This raises the question of how the York merchants related to the national company, for alone among York's trade gilds they were linked with several wider organizations. At the beginning of the period some were still connected with the Staplers, the national wool-exporting monopoly, and Sir Richard York (d. 1498) was the last of several Yorkers to be Mayor of the Staple at Calais. In the sixteenth century it was instead the Adventurers, the national cloth exporters to the Low Countries, whom the richer York merchants joined. Of the other exporting monopolies chartered in the latter half of the sixteenth century, the Muscovy and Eastland Companies certainly enrolled York members, while in the early seventeenth branches of the Eastland Company and of the national Merchant Adventurers were opened in the city. But the involvement of York men with these national companies remained small compared with that of the Londoners. At the only date for which we have a figure, the number of York merchants among the national Merchant Adventurers was only seven.[20]

The drapers and tailors, the other large merchant gild of York, came second only to the merchants proper, but second by a long way. They too had their own gildhall, and their share of wealth and power, symbolized by the fact that their members were mayors more often than any others except the merchants. But whereas the merchants enjoyed that office for fifty years of the sixteenth century, the drapers and tailors held it for only eleven and a half. Nor did they have the protection of a royal charter as the merchants did. Even so, the corporation handled such a powerful body more gently than the craft gilds. When, for instance, some refractory drapers were imprisoned in 1563, it was in a fairly easy confinement in their own hall rather than in one of the notorious city prisons.[21] And after the union of drapers, tailors and hosiers their combined membership, and probably their power and influence, grew, until in 1662 they too achieved the coveted distinction of a royal charter.[22]

The pattern of handicraft gilds was much more complex than that of the mercantile unions. They are generally less well documented, and it is often impossible to decide when or why they amalgamated, separated or disappeared. Fortunately there is no need to trace here the individual histories of all; it will be enough to look briefly at each group of crafts in turn, considering what relationships can be seen between the size and wealth of crafts and the pattern of their gild organization. An appropriate point to start is with textiles, which together with long-distance trading had been one of the twin bases of York's earlier prosperity. They were now facing the bleak wind of West Riding competition, and the results can be seen in the plight of the once powerful weavers' gild, which had been important enough to secure a royal charter from Henry II, in the days when the gild merchant was still a reality and when separate craft gilds had been frowned on. Now they were merely one of the lesser crafts on the city's common council; a rash separation of the gild into two, for linen and woollen weavers, had to be abrogated in 1549; and in 1561 the corporation told the government that only ten weavers were left in the city, all of them poor.[23] A modest amount of linen weaving just kept the gild alive, but some of the other textile gilds fared even worse. The walkers' and cardmakers' gilds vanished some time after 1529, though a few individuals continued to be made free of those trades for a little while longer.[24] The pinners and wiredrawers maintained themselves only by uniting in 1482–3. The dyers, and the tapiters or coverlet weavers, alone of the textile gilds, continued to flourish. Both included a few rich members, while the dyers provided the only three mayors drawn from the textile crafts, and the more numerous tapiters benefited from an act of 1543 granting them a monopoly of coverlet weaving in Yorkshire.

But if York ceased to be a textile town of importance, it remained a regional centre for the sale of cloth and for making up clothing both from cloth and leather. The largest clothing craft gild, as we have seen, was the tailors, who amalgamated with the drapers and hosiers to form a powerful mercantile gild. Likewise, the declining cappers and the rising hatters joined forces with the haberdashers in a similar union.[25]

York was also one of those towns, situated in mixed agricultural areas, where 'the leather crafts assumed a large importance in the absence of any other dominant industrial activity'.[26] All of them flourished, both the workers in raw material (skinners, curriers, tanners) and those making it into clothing and other articles (cordwainers, glovers, saddlers), so it is not surprising that all six had their own organized gilds throughout the period. The glovers did particularly well in Elizabeth's reign, when they rose to be one of the eight largest crafts, with an intake of two new freemen a year. Altogether, these six crafts accounted for 15 per cent of freemen admissions between 1550 and 1600.

The victualling crafts kept steady at about a fifth of the total number of freemen. The largest, the bakers and butchers, numbered respectively 4 and $3\frac{1}{2}$ per cent of freemen's admissions. Their gilds, though wealthy and powerful, were more strictly supervised than most by the corporation, as was the smaller millers' gild: after all, these were crafts of vital importance to all townsmen. As in other towns, victuallers seem to have been deliberately kept from high civic office, although there are no rules surviving making this explicit.[27] Fishmongers, fishers, coopers and vintners also had their own gilds, as did the small but fairly wealthy group of cooks who ran public eating houses. The innholders, who also had a gild, increased greatly in numbers after about 1560, probably because of a growing number of visitors to York, and also became the only victualling craft to provide any members of the aldermanic bench.[28] Finally, this group of trades provides an example of essential services outside the gild framework. Occasional references establish the existence of a group of 'burnleders' or 'waterleders', who fulfilled the vital function of carrying water to those with no access to wells or the rivers. This important group of men, probably very poor, had no gild at all, and furnished only a single freeman in the whole century.

The building and furnishing crafts provided more fluctuations than most groups. Domestic building was almost entirely timbered, and the masons, who concentrated on the city walls and on church building, were hard hit by the Reformation, and had definitely disappeared by 1561. The alabasterers and carvers, responsible for church furnishings, also disappeared, and the glaziers too nearly died out; what saved them was the increasing use of domestic window glass, which revived their numbers in Elizabeth's reign. The carpenters, who built almost all private houses, and the plasterers and tilers, who covered and roofed them, were large and important gilds throughout the century. The carpenters were involved in some ineffective unions with the joiners and others, which led to much squabbling, and they were clearly trying to gain a privileged position over all the woodworking crafts. They were perhaps spurred on as timber ceased to be the only available building material, for the use of brick was increasing, and it is symptomatic that by 1592 the brickmakers were trying to break away from the tilers' gild.[29]

The other York gilds included the small but wealthy craft of goldsmiths, who worked in silver as well as gold, and a number of other metal-working gilds whose identity and amalgamations are not easy to disentangle. There is no need to catalogue the remaining and very varied gilds, but it is worth remarking on one or two changes. The waxchandlers were falling in numbers as tallow became commoner, until in 1606 the tallowchandlers formed their own gild. The scriveners' craft was in understandable difficulty, and amalgamated in 1579 with the prosperous stationers, though interestingly the parchment makers preserved a working gild throughout the period.

The gilds so far reviewed have been mostly the normal kind of Tudor craft gilds, autonomous but definitely subordinate to the city corporation. But just as the merchants and weavers enjoyed a more privileged status by virtue of their royal charters, so there were gilds at the other end of the scale which were less privileged than most. Such were, for instance, the brewers and tipplers who made a gild in 1600 and whose craft needed special supervision not only because of its importance to the whole town but also because its labour force was part-time.[30] Other trades in this category were the free labourers, who loaded and unloaded boats at King's Staith, the city quay, and the porters, who carried goods between the staith and the merchants' premises. With such gilds the corporation felt that a tight rein was needed. Whereas most gilds elected their own officials who had to appear before the mayor only to take their oaths of office, the subordinate gilds were given only the right to make nominations from whom the corporation made a final choice (labourers 1578, brewers

1600). The porters were not allowed to stop anywhere while carrying goods, except to rest in the open street (1587), and the labourers were forbidden to drink or play cards as long as there was any work to be done at the staith (1593). On the other hand, if these unskilled workers, gilds were more restricted than most, they were also more protected. The corporation in 1593 ordered parish constables to stop boat-owners from employing labourers who had been 'blacked' by the labourers' searchers.

Leaving aside these gilds with restricted powers, how did the others function? We can deduce a fair amount from the large number of surviving craft ordinances, which reveal a pattern common to nearly all. Each gild would hold annual meetings, and often quarterly ones also, or others called *ad hoc*. All masters practising the craft concerned were not only entitled but expected to attend all these meetings on pain of fine, so that the wish not to lose working time was probably a factor in keeping the number of meetings to the necessary minimum. Often the youngest 'brother' (member) was expected to summon all the others, and full attendance was checked by reading out a 'call roll', kept up to date, which listed all members in order of seniority. That the meetings could be disorderly is clear from the penalties laid down for brawling and bad language, such as fines for those calling their colleagues 'knave, slave, villayne or anye evill words' (marshals and smiths 1574).

The purpose of the gild meetings, according to a description of city customs in 1530, was for the craftsmen to 'lovyngly . . . entre communicacon and counsaill together of such thyngs as they thynke best to be usyd within theyr occupacon bothe to the laude and prayse of God and profett for theym selffs and also the helpyng forward of yong men [in] tyme to cum'.[31] The stress on pleasing God (which echoes the motto of the merchant of Prato, 'In the name of God and of profit') finds expression in the bakers' ordinary (1596), where paintings of the various stages in baking are accompanied by suitable jingles. Above a scene of measuring flour, for instance, is

> 'He that giveth measure,
> God blessethe with treasure.'[32]

The wish to please God was perhaps sincere and not merely a matter of buying rewards; and it chimes in with a similar emphasis on the public good. Many ordinances expressly stated that they were for the benefit of all citizens and not of the craft only, and one made provision that the proceedings of its meetings were to remain confidential only if the secrets involved were 'not hurtful to the common wealth' (plasterers 1590). We shall see how forceful the city corporation could be when they felt that a gild was betraying this public trust.

One purpose of the gilds' business meetings was to agree on draft regulations or ordinances for their government and protection, which they then submitted to the corporation. The corporation would, if they approved, ratify them with or without amendment, and enter a copy into their own records, while giving another to the gild, who entered it into their own 'ordinary' or 'ordinal', a book in which all their earlier regulations had been accumulated. These ordinances were intended to be confidential to the corporation and the gild concerned, and a cordwainer who 'made Copies of ther saide ordinary . . . and published them abroade' was ordered to hand them in to the town clerk on pain of imprisonment.[33] The ordinances once agreed remained, in theory, in force until revoked, which might be anything up to two centuries later; and this created problems, especially if the ordinances were in Latin or French, or even in obsolete English. This tenacious conservatism meant that some orders had been negated by economic or religious change long before they were repealed, and it would be rash to assume that any set of ordinances fully represented current practice for very long.

Four of the larger gilds, merchants, tailors, butchers and cordwainers, had their own halls, and a fifth was built for the haberdashers at the end of the period. It is not clear where any other gilds met before the Reformation, but afterwards the corporation decided to provide a common hall for them all, and in 1554 handed over to them St Anthony's Hall, the former meeting place of a large religious fraternity.

Every gild, in addition to its normal meeting for discussions and legislation, held an annual assembly at which new officers were elected and the outgoing ones presented their financial accounts for scrutiny. We need not explore the widely varying numbers and types of gild officer: it suffices that nearly all fall into one or other of two systems, with the searcher common to both. All gilds had two or more searchers, whose main job was to inspect the output of members to ensure quality control and conformity with the craft rules. They were empowered to enter members' premises, and even in certain cases the premises of non-members. Until 1519 they also had power to punish for breaches of rules or for faulty goods, and their justice could be summary. About 1492, for instance, the vintners' searchers unearthed unfit wine in a Stonegate house and elsewhere, and struck off the heads of the bottles 'openly in syght of the people'.[34] After 1519, however, the searchers were required instead to report offences to the city corporation for action. They swore before the mayor to disclose all offences against the ordinances, and could be fined for perjury if they concealed any.

In some gilds the searchers were the effective rulers of the craft for their year of office, but in others, especially in the larger ones, it was too onerous for the same men to administer and to search in person, and a senior officer (variously named governor, master or warden) was placed over the searchers. In addition, many crafts had one or two pageant masters, whose principal duty was to organize the craft plays on Corpus Christi Day, and to levy 'pageant money' to uphold them. In some gilds the pageant masters long outlived the plays, and became subordinate treasurers. All of these gild offices were unpaid, and could be burdensome, to judge from the repeated provisions for fining members refusing to take them up.

These officers were, of course, responsible only to the other master craftsmen, who alone participated in gild meetings. It is easy to forget the others, the journeymen, apprentices and servants, who worked for the masters. The 'servants' are the most obscure; the term sometimes embraces apprentices and journeymen, but may have included others, unskilled and lowly-paid. Apprentices were youths indentured for a term of years to serve a master in return for board, lodging and instruction, while journeymen were those ex-apprentices without enough capital to set up as masters on their own, who had perforce to work for wages under the more fortunate. Since masters were usually ex-apprentices, it is not surprising that the gild ordinaries have much to say on regulating apprenticeship and on restricting entry to it. Too wide an intake of apprentices would weaken their position.

The first restriction imposed was a minimum term for apprenticeship. Already in the fifteenth century seven years was commonly required, though a few allowed six, and one four, perhaps because of the relatively low skill needed (stringers 1420–1). The last ordinances to permit less than seven years were passed in 1503 (smiths and marshals), and by 1530 it was a general rule in York that no craftsman should take on any apprentices for less on pain of fine. As so often in Tudor

England, national legislation followed very tardily in the wake of local practice. A seven-year minimum was required by Parliament after 1563, but it was not long before the first of several York gilds went further and imposed eight (founders 1574). The most rigorous actually required of each apprentice ten, eleven or twelve years, depending on his age (bakers 1589). These were all, of course, minimal figures, which could be, and were, exceeded. Of thirty-five bakers' apprentices enrolled between 1560 and 1570, nearly half (fifteen) were taken on for more than the required seven years, and one for as many as twelve.[35]

Entry to apprenticeship was also frequently restricted. In the fifteenth century some gilds limited masters to one, or two, apprentices at any one time, while a few insisted also that recruits should be free-born Englishmen. The anachronistic objection to villeins disappeared under the Tudors, but one Elizabethan ordinance still insisted that apprentices should not be aliens, or be crooked, lame or half-blind (weavers 1578). The crafts' restrictions on numbers were overcome by a by-law of 1519 that freemen could take as many apprentices, servants and journeymen as they wished, notwithstanding all ordinances to the contrary.[36] And thereafter, for a period of forty years, no new ordinances were approved by the corporation restricting numbers. It is significant that this period, 1520 to 1560, corresponds to the lowest level of York's population and prosperity, and that a rise in both then brought about renewed restrictions. For under Elizabeth the city was beginning to flourish again, and the population probably doubled, aided by an absence of any serious epidemics between 1559 and 1604, while wealth increased also. Her reign saw not only a rise of 17 per cent in the intake of freemen, but a steeper rise of 63 per cent in the proportion of freemen by inheritance, as mortality rates declined. This meant that the freemen would be concerned not only to limit entry to their numbers again, since they still thought in terms of a fixed economic 'cake' to be shared between them, but also to ensure places for the growing number of their sons surviving into adolescence.[37]

The first sign of the new policy was that a number of crafts again legislated to restrict numbers of apprentices to one or two per master, starting in 1572 (plasterers and tilers).[38] Fourteen years later the corporation ordered all crafts to add to their ordinals a new clause, forbidding anyone within five years of setting up as a master to take any apprentice or servant save a freeman or freeman's son.[39] Many ordinals incorporated this at once, while others drawn up later in the century invariably have something on the same lines. A common omnibus clause by the turn of the century would limit a master's apprentices at any one time to two, of whom one must be a 'free-born child', and would forbid him to take any apprentices at all save a free-born child in his first few years as a master.

But it is fair to add that if in these ways the corporation were protectionist, they did strenuously oppose the insistence in the Statute of Artificers (1563) that all apprentices of merchants and certain other crafts in corporate towns should have fathers worth at least £2 a year in land. No doubt this would rule out many of the lesser York freemen, and we may imagine that since enforcement relied on the local J.P.s, who in York's case were the mayor and aldermen, it would not be rigorously enforced. At any rate, every surviving list of instructions by the corporation to their M.P.s, from 1562 until at least 1586, includes a request that York may be exempted from the act, like London and Norwich.[40]

It is unfortunate that we know chiefly about the rules on recruitment of apprentices, and little of the nature of the practical training involved. We do not even know how old they would be, except for one gild's ruling that men must be at least twenty-four when they ended their apprenticeship and became masters (glovers 1585).[41] Bed and board were provided by the master, who taught his craft by practical demonstration and even, with some technical skills, from books.[42] Scrappy evidence suggests that freemen became increasingly literate as the century wore on, and there are hints that basic reading and writing may have been imparted by master craftsmen as much as by schoolmasters. At any event the bond between master and apprentice could be more than economic, especially where there was the further bond of kinship. Alderman Thomas Moseley, who in his youth was apprenticed to his uncle, also an alderman, remembered him with such affection that when he was dying fifty years later he took the most unusual step of asking for burial near his 'late Maister and Uncle', rather than in his own parish church.[43] But against this rare example we must set cases of great hardships, like the boy whose master did not teach him or keep him properly, but beat him 'with tongs off iron and such oder unresonable wepons'.[44]

It is a pity that the ordinals have so little to say on journeymen and servants, especially as many apprentices had to become journeymen rather than masters. It seems certain that journeymen had no say in gild affairs, which were managed wholly by the masters, and there is no evidence for the separate journeymen's associations found in other towns, except possibly in the case of the cordwainers. But for two special categories of workers, women and aliens, we are in slightly better position to understand their roles, owing to the regulations about them found in the ordinals.

The aliens were those we should now call foreigners, and are not to be confused with the 'foreigns' or English-born non-freemen. Several fifteenth-century ordinances barred them from becoming masters, or even apprentices or servants, and in 1532 the corporation forbade Francis Daragon to be a locksmiths' searcher because of his French birth.[45] Yet they allowed the Spaniard Martin Soza, goldsmith, to join the city council in 1546, so they are not likely to have barred him from gild office. One or two crafts' Elizabethan ordinances confirmed earlier anti-alien rules, one of them making it clear that the rule was being confirmed quite deliberately (pinners and wiredrawers 1425–6 and 1592). But on the whole little is heard of regulations against them in Elizabeth's reign, and the gild office was attained by at least one, Anthony Ruyskaert the Dutchman, master of the weavers' gild four or more times in the nineties.[46] And in practice any intolerance towards aliens by other gilds can have been of little importance, for it affected few. There were small groups of French, Dutch and Scots in the city, but they never formed a large minority of the population as they did in Norwich.

The part played by women was more important, though we know little of it. One per cent of all admissions to the freedom were of women, but these were far from being the only ones engaged in trade. Many crafts assumed that their membership would include women as well as men, and some specifically allowed members to be helped by their wives and daughters, though one gild forbade this (weavers 1578). Several allowed widows to keep up their husband's business, and the practice was given general sanction by the corporation in 1529. Henceforth all freemen's widows, unless and until they remarried, could keep up the family businesses and take on new apprentices.[47] Thus it was, for instance, that in 1575 the son of a local village husbandman was bound apprentice to Isabell Straker, a tanner's widow in her sixties, and that two years later she took on a York boy as well.[48] More doubtful was a widow's right to 'transmit' her first husband's craft membership to a second husband, and such cases were usually settled *ad hoc* as they arose.[49] Perhaps most important of all, women, besides running businesses with or in succession to husbands, will have formed a great part of the pool of servant labour, and many perhaps escaped gild supervision altogether. We hear of them only occasionally, as, for instance, in the will of Margaret Sympson, widow, who bequeathed 16*d* arrears of wages to 'Elisabeth my work woman or carder' and a russet gown to 'old Jenet my spynner'.[50]

Compared with their careful regulation of recruitment and membership, most ordinals have little to say about production or working conditions, much of which was taken for granted. All empower the searchers to hunt out faulty goods and workmanship, and most insist on the need for an applicant for membership to demonstrate acceptable work. The aspiring baker, for instance, had to produce for inspection a trial batch of loaves (bakers 1596), and in a few cases there was something like the Continental masterpiece system, the applicant having to make in the presence of the searchers his 'hablyng ware' or 'ablyng pece of work' (weavers 1578, cordwainers 1580). Occasionally, more informative ordinals explain something of the gilds' products or manufacturing processes, and they are not always what we might expect. The girdlers, for example, are usually considered as purely a clothing craft, making girdles or belts, but they seem to have done much miscellaneous metal-working, since all were ordered to join the gild who made 'daggar chapes, purse knoppes, bulyons [metal knobs], book claspes, dawkes, dog colers, girdilles or any othre maner gere or harnesse of laton stele or yren belonging to the said craft' (girdlers 1485). Some ordinances also demarcate work between kindred gilds, or regulate competition among their members to prevent them cutting one another's throats. A charming minstrel's ordinance forbids any member to play anywhere where his brethren are playing 'wherebie they shal be worse thought of' unless sent for (1578). Another gild rules that when one member buys fish at the coast, he must allow any others there to form a partnership and share the purchase (fishers and panniermen 1593).

As a rule, each master and his men worked in a shop in the master's own home, though a few specialized industries had to be carried on in separate premises at the side or rear, tanning in 'barkhouses', for instance, and horn soaking in hornpits. Goods were produced in the shop and also sold there, over lowered boards which, when raised, acted as window shutters. The shop-board area might be protected from the weather by a penthouse or lean-to, a kind of ancestor to the sunblind. In some gilds the masters displayed signs; not only the innholders did so, but also the vintners, who hung out garlands (those 'bushes' which good wine does not need), and the barbers, who each had 'basinges or other signes . . . againste the strete to shewe his arte' (barbers 1592). The corporation's way of withdrawing a man's freedom was to order his shop to be shuttered, and as this was often the only window a craftsman had for working by, it prevented production as well as sales. In 1579 a Scottish tailor was disfranchised for speaking against the Queen; in asking pardon he said he 'beyng desfranchesed may not open his shoppe wyndowes and worke there, but is forced to woorke ells where, within his dwellyng hows, and hath small light to work with all'.[51] But working at night, by candlelight, was common enough to be forbidden or restricted by many gilds, one, for instance, allowing it only before 10 p.m. and after 3 a.m. (cutlers 1477–8).

Most gilds also restricted the amount and location of a man's trading. It was normal to insist that members could neither hawk goods in the streets, nor sell in the city markets (or even sometimes in markets nearby), for the market was the province of the non-freeman, the shop that of the freeman, and neither was to trespass on the other's preserve. The freeman might also be limited to having only one shop, in his dwelling house (bakers 1581), and one gild blocked an obvious loop-hole by forbidding the keeping of one shop in the city and another in the Minster yard (coopers, 1620 confirmation of 1471–2).

The sole aspect of working conditions on which the ordinals dwelt much was Sabbath observance. This was not, of course, a Protestant innovation, and craft rules against work on Sundays and feast days go back to the fourteenth century. Indeed, William Melton had in 1426 preached against vice to such effect that the corporation were persuaded at one and the same time to banish all prostitutes, and to forbid citizens to keep open shop or stall from Saturday night to dawn on Monday.[52] But the Reformation added its own restrictive twist to these attitudes, once the corporation became firmly Protestant during the seventies. A portent was the mayor's imprisonment of all saddlers in 1573 for being in alehouses in time of divine service.[53] Then on 8 July 1580 the corporation called in all craft ordinals and added to each a standard clause forbidding drinking in taverns or alehouses in time of sermons or services. Any lack of enthusiasm was quickly rebuked. A revision of the glovers' ordinances began with a preamble attacking the members' tendency

> to sende one of their Servauntes on the Sabbothe daye (which
> should onelye be spente in spirituall exercyses) to their Shoppes
> their to tende the whole day . . . wheras they learne nothinge,
> but lewde practizes, neclectinge the tyme bothe of divine
> Service and Sermons, wher they shoulde be heringe the worde of
> good taught and preached, therbye to learne their dewtye towards
> god and their Maister . . . (glovers 1585).

The day-to-day preoccupations of the gilds are perhaps best
mirrored in their financial accounts, a few of which survive to add a
little glimpse of their practice to set alongside the theory of the
ordinals. They followed a fairly standard pattern, and receipts fell
into three main categories. Firstly there were payments for admission
by new members ('abling money'), a standard rate being levied from
all, or in some cases the new entrant providing an 'abling dinner' or
breakfast for all the members instead. Secondly there were members'
annual payments, often a regular sum for general running expenses
and also a levy of 'pageant money', which until the seventies went to
maintain the gilds' religious plays, and thereafter continued to be levied
as a supplement to general income. Finally fines were levied on members:
those of the bakers, for instance, were taken for a number of
offences including baking or selling on Sundays, giving short weight,
disobeying the searchers, and being absent from gild meetings or
brawling at them. More interestingly, these same bakers' accounts cast
a little light on their relations with other gilds. They levied pageant
money not only on their own members but on lesser unorganized
crafts (the water-carriers and sand-carriers) who had no play of their
own, and they raised fines for demarcation infringements, such as
twopence from Peter Harfurth, innkeeper, 'for baking his bread for his
guests' instead of buying it from a free baker.[54]

Gilds' expenditure was more varied. Before the Corpus Christi
plays were stopped around 1570, much was spent by each gild on
keeping up its 'pageant' (movable stage) and costumes, and on paying
actors. Other types of expense included payments at members'
weddings and funerals, the provision of food, drink, and music at gild
feasts, payments for rent at St Anthony's Hall and to the poor there,
and having craft offenders haled before the mayor's court. Occasional
payments were also made to members who fell on hard times, the bakers

in 1599–1600 paying 12*d* by general consent to Robert Waunopp 'in respect of his poverty'.[55]

So far, little evidence has been adduced of the conflicts among craftsmen which Unwin and Kramer have shown to be so common, and which formed a counterpart to the litigation of that quarrelsome age. It may therefore be a useful corrective to look in a little more detail at one gild, the cordwainers or shoemakers, which provides the only York examples known of age conflict and class conflict within the gild, as well as the most spectacular case of a struggle between gilds.

In about 1430 the cordwainers had forbidden their wage-earners (*servientes stipendiarii*) to rebel against their gild ordinances or to form illegal confederacies. The reason given was that some of them had been meeting in a friary to concert plans against the masters. When these rules were revised in 1580, it was reiterated that 'no servant shall make any confederacie or ordynance emong theym selfes', but this may have been simply a repetition of the old rule and not a reaction to a current situation. It is significant, however, that it was the shoemakers, together with the tailors, who provide most of the known cases of separate journeymen's organizations in Tudor towns, and it is certain that the York cordwainers' servants had their own social organization, whether or not they had an economic association any longer. They maintained a Gild of St Augustine quite distinct from their masters' gild, whereas all other known cases of the fraternities run by York craft gilds seem to have been united bodies for both masters and servants.[56]

The masters themselves were not a homogeneous body. At a gild meeting in 1602 some of the 'yonger' members complained that recent ordinances (requiring approval by the mayor and searchers before strangers could be set on work) were 'made onlye against theme being yong men'.[57] After the meeting sixteen or twenty members went about organizing the younger masters to get the ordinances changed, until the searchers arranged for the ringleaders to be imprisoned by the corporation. Next year one of the seven was again in trouble with his searchers, and retaliated by suing one of them before the Council in the North. The corporation fined him, and another young master, for various offences, including setting unlicensed journeymen on work. However, they also ordered some concessions to be made over issues which the young men had complained of. The searchers' accounts were to be made available to all cordwainers, and the several feasts held by the gild, 'wherby they wast and consume a great parte of ther stock', were to be reduced to one a year.[58] There is no reason to believe that this case of friction between seniors and juniors was unique, though neither need it have been usual throughout the period. The reign of Elizabeth was for York a period of great population growth and unusual freedom from epidemics, and this relatively healthy situation meant a large increase in the number of freemen's children growing up to inherit freedom of the city. The combination of a growing number of masters, and a shrinking number of places made vacant by death, may have created tensions in 1602 for which there was no need a half century earlier.

In their relations with the cobblers, the cordwainers also provide a good example of tensions between crafts. Kramer has shown that gilds working in the same field tended to clash if they did not solve the problem by amalgamation, and that this was usually a matter of jealousy between equals, rather than, as Unwin thought, a case of empire-building by powerful crafts over weaker ones. On the whole the York struggles bear out her argument, but there are exceptions, like the carpenters' attempt to establish a kind of hegemony over the other woodworkers. Another was the relationship between cord-wainers and cobblers, who were always poaching on each other's territory. All the York evidence is that the cordwainers were for ever trying to dominate the poorer cobblers, but that the cobblers, as in other Tudor and Stuart towns, were able gradually to assert their in-dependence.[59] In the early Tudor period there is no evidence for a cobblers' gild, the few cobbler freemen being either unorganized or under the supervision of the cordwainers, but a cobblers' gild did later come into being, probably by 1579 and certainly by 1623. Yet well into the eighteenth century the cordwainers kept up a fruitless struggle to revive their domination, instead of collaborating with them as the gild system was increasingly challenged and flouted by their common enemies. Towards 1780 a cordwainer was still reminding his confrères how they had been

> continually plagued with that Sett of People call'd Coblers . . .
> And I doubt not but our Successors will be the Same as long as
> there is a Body of them in being. The only way I know of to
> keep those Antagonists a little humble is to visit Em in
> Searching of them as oft as you can which will let them know we

are their Masters so farr, which is out of their power to return the faviour.[60]

Finally, the cordwainers afford an example of antagonism of a social rather than an economic kind. The bitterest clashes between gilds occurred over precedence in processions, by which great store was set, rather than over demarcation disputes. There was a loosely established ranking of gilds by seniority, beginning with the mercers and merchants, and its observance was a matter of passionate and even violent concern, especially before the Reformation, when the corporation had several times to adjudicate on precedence before rioting developed. The bitterest clashes, over the relative positions of cordwainers and weavers in the annual Corpus Christi procession, flared up year after year. When, in 1490, the corporation took the drastic step of disfranchising all the cordwainers, feelings ran high. The cordwainers tried to gain support from the bowyers and the tailors, telling the latter that 'thai shold be the next craft that shold be in like troble', and a priest was reported as saying that the cordwainers would be aided by three or four hundred other craftsmen and that 'if thai might get a capitan to set thame apon werk they shold strike ther adversaries down'. The dispute was finally ended by arbitration of the Abbot of St Mary's at the King's command, in 1493, after the corporation had been assured that no infringement of their jurisdiction was intended.[61]

The craft gilds, as this dispute reminds us, were kept on a fairly tight rein by the city corporation. Most gilds did compose their own ordinances, but they could not be enforced until ratified by the city, as the affair of the textwriters illustrates. In 1487–8 this gild drew up ordinances, one of them barring any priest with a salary of seven marks ($£4$ 13s 4d) or more from practising their craft. Not until 1492 did the gild ask for them to be copied into the city registers, and when this was done the corporation made the proviso that Sir William Insklyff, priest, might finish the mass book and coucher which he was then writing. It was doubtless Insklyff's activities which led the gild to seek registration, presumably to avoid the charge that the ordinances were not otherwise binding.[62]

The corporation's supremacy was clearly expressed by the building crafts' searchers in 1552 asking (unsuccessfully) for higher wage rates to keep pace with inflation. They told the mayor, 'ye ar the head searcher of all occupacions wythin this said cittie for your yere and sworne to be upreyghtte and rather to meanteane the poor craffttes men than to undoo and begger theme'.[63] The odd title of 'head searcher' refers to the fact that since 1519 punishment of craft offenders had been taken out of the hands of gild searchers and reserved to the mayor and aldermen.[64] That such oversight could be necessary was demonstrated in 1547, when two of the tapiters' searchers sold their coverlets unsearched, and several others, including a gild warden, were selling coverlets of faulty workmanship.[65] *Quis custodiet ipsos custodes?* The corporation clearly had no doubt about the answer.

The city fathers also reserved the right to adjudicate disputes between gilds, some of them the demarcation type familiar to us today. In 1505 the labourers complained that the carpenters 'wold not suffre theym to . . . mayke a bede, a shelffe, a forme, a stole, naile a burde, a dore, a yate, a wyndowe', and the corporation made a qualified ruling in the labourers' favour.[66]

But there was a more positive side to civic control than checking quarrels and abuses. The corporation aimed also to benefit the consumer by keeping up standards of production and by encouraging competition and introducing new crafts, and it would be false to regard them as concerned merely with maintaining a fossilized *status quo* among the gilds. Between 1600 and 1620 men of thirteen occupations were given civic freedom free or at reduced rates, or other privileges, because their skills were scarce or altogether lacking in York.[67] This happened less in the sixteenth century, but instead there had been several attempts at sponsored competition to keep the gilds on their toes. In 1506 the corporation secretly distributed yarn to several York weavers and walkers and to two rural ones, presumably to see who did the best work. The result is not known, but evidence does survive of action taken against the bakers, who were often accused of abusing their monopoly position. For most of the forties and fifties the corporation allowed competition by a rival group of 'bolle bakers', some countryfolk and some members of other city crafts baking part-time. When the free bakers' monopoly was at last restored, it was only on condition of selling bread at the lower rates which their rivals had used.[68]

The relationship between corporation and gilds was not wholly one-sided, for the crafts in turn had a part to play in civic affairs. In most English towns 'the crafts had no political functions, being merely economic organs, strictly subservient to the governing body of the town', but York was one of a group of northern exceptions to the rule.[69] In the later middle ages the York crafts had a share in the election of the mayor, the city's supreme executive officer, though the actual procedure was varied from time to time by the King; and in 1504 the crafts tried to share also in electing the two sheriffs. It was a disturbed period in which the permanent city council, dominated by a mercantile oligarchy, were often at odds with the manufacturing craftsmen, who wanted a greater share in government. Matters came to a head in 1516–17, when elections for two aldermen sparked off a series of riots lasting more than a year. The King's response was to try to bring peace by giving the crafts a formal but limited share in a wide area of city government. Two representatives each from thirteen named major crafts, and one each from fifteen minor crafts, were to form a common council of forty-one members, who were to meet *ad hoc* when summoned by the corporation for advice and consent on important issues. The forty-one were not, however, directly chosen by the crafts, but instead, each major and minor gild made four and two nominations respectively, from whom the corporation chose half. Nor was their council free of mercantile influence, for five of the thirteen major 'crafts' were sections of the merchants' and draper-tailor unions. Besides their occasional advisory functions, the forty-one, joined by the twenty-eight senior searchers of the same crafts, formed a council of sixty-nine for election purposes. They met every year for elections of mayor and sheriffs, and when necessary also for elections of aldermen, in each case choosing nominees from among whom the corporation made a final choice.[70]

Thus reconstituted, the common council played a useful if limited part in city government until 1632. On several occasions the council put forward coherent programmes of reforms which the corporation accepted in whole or in part. They were especially active on matters close to the hearts and purses of ordinary freemen like market tolls and enclosures of city commons, though here they did not always get their way. Relations were normally amicable, except for a short period in the 1560s when Miles Cooke became so much a regular spokesman for the common council as to be called their 'chief'. In 1563 he tried to dictate reforms to the corporation, who finally accepted them after pointing out that the commons' only right course was to petition. Two years later the corporation dismissed Cooke and installed as chief a colleague who seems to have been more compliant.

It would be over-simplifying to picture these clashes as merchants against craftsmen, especially as the mercantile gilds occupied ten seats out of forty-one, and both Cooke and his replacement were merchants. Rather was it probably a struggle between the richest merchants on the one hand, and the middling merchants and craftsmen on the other. The little known of Cooke suggests that he should be placed in the same tradition as London's John of Northampton, or Coventry's Laurence Saunders.[71]

What most aroused the commons' ire in 1563 was indeed a just cause for complaint. The royal letters patent of 1517 had named the twenty-eight constituent crafts of the council, and this was unfortunate since crafts' importance fluctuated, while some died out altogether. In 1554 the city M.P.s tried to get the charter amended, but without any success; and though the corporation agreed to Cooke's demand in 1563 that changes be made in the lists, nothing came of it. After all, it was not in the city's power to do anything without the Queen's agreement. In consequence, by 1579 the situation was most unsatisfactory. Not only were some gilds which had risen in importance still ranked as 'minor' ones with only one representative, like the innholders, and vice versa, but the ironmongers, masons and armourers were without their allotted representatives, at least two of the three gilds being probably extinct.[72] It may have been this rigidity in the constitution, rather than any antipathy to gilds as such, that led to the replacement of gilds by wards on the common council after 1632.

The gilds having now been considered in their primary economic role, it remains to explore more briefly their other activities, for the gilds, or their associated fraternities where these existed, were also much concerned with festivities, mutual aid and religious observance. It is significant that in 1530 the corporation put first in their list of craft activities that 'sum one of the seid occupacons agreyth first that they wyll have an obytt and a masse of *requiem* to be said or songe within one of the Frears . . . and all men of the occupacon to be and offer at the saide masse . . . and sum other occupacon agreyth lykewyse to fynd a lyght before a saynt'.[73]

There survives an indenture of 1487 between the carpenters' gild and the Augustinian friars, who covenanted to perform twice-yearly trentals (30 masses) for all deceased brothers and sisters of the Fraternity of the Resurrection maintained by the carpenters, and a trental for every worthy brother after his death, on payment of 5s a trental.[74] Some earlier ordinances tell us more of this fraternity, which had been long established. It was a distinct and self-financing body, under its own four keepers, to which members of the parent gild were not compelled to belong. It organized its members to bear torches in the civic Corpus Christi procession, and it enforced compulsory attendance at the two yearly obit services and at the funerals of all members. Fourpence a week was to be paid for life to members unable to work through blindness or poverty, and the fraternity undertook to put unemployed brothers in touch with those in need of workmen, who had to take them in preference to non-members (carpenters 1482).

The devotional side of these activities ceased when the friaries and chantries were dissolved, though some forms of Catholic observance lingered for a while longer.[75] Furthermore, the two largest craft gilds were in serious danger of losing their halls at the Reformation. The merchants' hall belonged to their Fraternity of the Holy Trinity, and incorporated a hospital and chapel as well as an assembly hall. Similarly, the tailors' hall was named from their Fraternity of St John the Baptist, and adjoined almshouses maintained by that brotherhood. In the end the two gilds retained their halls, but it was a near thing; in 1587 they felt it prudent to 'present' them before a government enquiry into lands supposed to be concealed from the royal confiscations.[76] The hospitals of the merchants and tailors also escaped suppression, as did a third in Fishergate owned by the cordwainers, though the weavers' hospital in North Street is not heard of after 1557.[77] These were the only four Tudor gilds known to have their own hospitals, though other crafts also helped with poor relief by regular payments to the city poor.

Alongside devotion and charity went pageantry and feasting. The fraternities took part in various civic and religious processions, especially the major one on Corpus Christi morrow, in which every craft bore torches behind the great jewelled casket containing a consecrated Host. On Corpus Christi Day itself was performed the famous cycle of forty-eight miracle plays illustrating cosmic history from the Creation to the Last Judgment. Each play was the responsibility of one or more crafts, sometimes allocated very appropriately (the fishers and mariners performed the Flood), and the final spectacular Doomsday was staged by the wealthy merchants. These plays must have provided much of the citizens' religious instruction, as well as entertainment, until their suppression in the seventies.[78] Finally, the fraternities—

which seem to have included not only the craftsmen but also their wives—had a convivial side of feasting and merry-making. The merchants, for instance, held an annual venison feast, and the tailors a feast with wine and music on their patronal festival of St John the Baptist, which they kept up after the Reformation. What other junketings there may have been we do not know, apart from a cryptic reference to five saddlers imprisoned for horseplay at their craft meetings—'caryeng of a guttor . . . upon the serchers wyffs un-decently'.[79]

Implicit in this study of the way the gilds worked have been questions of wider significance: were they still effective and useful bodies, and if so why, and for how long? It is reasonably certain from the surviving evidence, not all of which could be explored in a study of this length, that the system was fairly effective and by no means in decay. That is to say, in spite of evasions there was a reasonably firm enforcement of the freemen's monopoly of trading and shopkeeping, and within that monopoly, of the smaller monopolies of the individual gilds. This pattern, which can be borne out in other Tudor cities, is worth stressing, since the belief dies hard that the gild system was essentially medieval, and something of an anachronism in the expanding economy of Tudor and Stuart England.

Dr Kramer sees the early modern period as one of amalgamations both among the trading and handicraft gilds, but for different reasons. The mercantile gilds united after the disintegration of the gild merchant, in order to succeed to its trading rights, though in some towns the haberdashers and drapers remained apart from these unions and formed their own. Among the handicrafts, however, amalgamations were an accompaniment of the decay of the gild system, unions taking place initially because the subdivisions of labour had become excessively minute, but later in an increasingly vain attempt to set up a common front against outside competition.

How far does the York evidence accord with Dr Kramer's views? The gild merchant there must have vanished by 1272, as she herself shows, but there is no trace of a mercers' gild succeeding it until the later fourteenth century. And a reverse process can be seen to the idea of a gradual amalgamation of traders, for it was in the sixteenth century that the haberdashers seceded from the York merchants to form their own gild.[80] More importantly, the handicrafts do not accord at all with her correlation of amalgamations and gild decline. Instead of a one-way process of unification after the fifteenth century, York exhibits a diverse pattern of creation and disappearance, separation and amalgamation. New gilds continued to be formed in the seventeenth and even the eighteenth century, balancing the disappearance of others, and the total number remained remarkably constant: fifty-seven in 1415, over fifty in 1485, perhaps sixty-four in 1579, and between fifty and sixty under the Stuarts.[81] Collapse did not come until later still, and from the fourteenth to the eighteenth centuries the gild structure reveals little basic change.[82]

This is not to deny that the system could be modified when economic conditions changed, either by the gilds themselves out of self-interest, or by the corporation if the gilds failed to act. The changing conditions for recruitment of apprentices illustrates this well. During the period of peak prosperity between about 1350 and 1450, many gilds instituted restrictions on the number each master might take, but from 1459 onwards several modified their rules (saddlers etc.). As the recession neared its worst, the corporation stepped in in 1519 to remove all limitations on numbers, and they began to be imposed again only in the sixties and seventies, as economic recovery was under way. But of any wider changes than this during the Tudor period, apart from those consequential on the Reformation, there is no sign.

What, then, does the long survival of York's gilds indicate? The hard-headed businessmen who composed the corporation are not likely to have perpetuated a system which was a brake on the city's prosperity, and the revival of York's fortunes between 1550 and 1650, when the gild structure remained intact, suggests that it was no such hindrance. Admittedly, the town gilds 'did not lead to the capitalism of the Industrial Revolution' and 'were not adaptable to the new conditions', but that did not matter until industrialization became a real issue, which at York was not before the coming of the railways.[83] It could be argued that York was an example, not of an urban gild structure keeping away industry, but of one able to survive intact precisely because there was so little industry there to conflict with it.

Notes

1 C. Gross, *The Gild Merchant* (Oxford, 1890), I, 173.
2 There is little general in print for the period after 1509, though three

satisfactory studies of individual gilds cover the century: M. Sellers, ed.,
The York Mercers and Merchant Adventurers 1356–1917 (Surtees Soc.
CXXIX, 1918); B. Johnson, *The Acts and Ordinances of the Company of
Merchant Taylors in the City of York* (1949); L. P. Wenham, 'Hornpot
Lane and the Horners of York', *Yorks Philosophical Soc. Annual Report*,
1964, 25–56.

3 S. Kramer, *The English Craft Gilds* (New York, 1927), pp. 1–100.

4 J. N. Bartlett, 'The Expansion and Decline of York in the Later Middle
Ages', *Ec.H.R.*, 2nd ser. XII (1959–60), 17–33; D. M. Palliser, 'York
Under the Tudors', in A. M. Everitt, ed., *Urban Studies* (forthcoming).

5 A. Raine, ed., *York Civic Records* (Yorks. Arch. Soc., Record Series,
8 vols., 1939–53), VIII, 17.

6 J. N. Bartlett, 'Some Aspects of the Economy of York in the Later
Middle Ages, 1300–1550' (unpublished Ph.D. thesis, University of
London, 1958), pp. 203–5. I am grateful to Dr Bartlett for permission to
use and quote from this thesis.

7 *York Civic Records*, VIII, 82.

8 Here and subsequently, references to gild ordinances are given only
by name of gild and date in the body of the text. Many of the ordinances,
especially before *c.* 1530, are printed in the works cited in notes 2 and 5,
and in M. Sellers, ed., *York Memorandum Book* (Surtees Soc., CXX,
CXXV, 1912–15). Most others are unprinted, and in two main collections, the York City Archives at York Public Library (classes B
and E) and the York Minster Library archives (class Y1). The bakers'
records are in the B.M. (Add. MSS 33, 852–4 and 34, 604–5).

9 Some groups, e.g. notaries and bellfounders, seem to have had no gild.

10 J. M. Lambert, *Two Thousand Years of Gild Life* (Hull, 1891), pp. 376–85.

11 Johnson, *Merchant Taylors in York*, p. 140.

12 G. Unwin, *Industrial Organization in the Sixteenth and Seventeenth
Centuries* (1904), pp. 103–25. His English evidence is mostly drawn
from London, which was *sui generis*.

13 *York Civic Records*, VIII, 9, 10.

14 Grocers and apothecaries were certainly members later: *York Mercers*,
p. xliii; F. Drake, *Eboracum* (1736), p. 224. The Tudor documents in
York Mercers refer only to mercers and merchants, but different descriptions of the same men in the freemen's register show that mercer,
merchant, grocer, spicer and apothecary were already interchangeable.

15 Haberdashers admitted as freemen numbered 34 in the first decade o ime
sixteenth century, and 33 in the two last decades, but only 7 between
1510 and 1580. During that period most were probably admitted as
merchants.

16 These and other statistics of freemen admissions are drawn from F.
Collins, ed., *Register of the Freemen of the City of York* (Surtees Soc.

XCVI, CII, 1897 & 1900). An analysis of freemen admissions will appear in my forthcoming book on Tudor York.

17 Drake, *Eboracum*, p. 224.

18 SP 1/236, fol. 59v.

19 *York Mercers*, pp. lviii, lix, 164, 165.

20 *Ibid.*, pp. liv, lv, 162, 163.

21 *York Civic Records*, VI, 63–5.

22 Entrants rose from 142 between 1551 and 1575, to 199 between 1576 and 1600, and to 235 between 1601 and 1625: Johnson, *Merchant Taylors*, table opposite p. 114.

23 *York Civic Records*, VI, 17. It is not quite clear if the number of weavers intended is ten or fourteen.

24 Last cardmaker admitted to freedom in 1556–7, last fuller in 1572–3, and last shearman in 1584–5, though one more admitted jointly as shearman and fuller in 1586–7: *Register of Freemen*, I, 276, II, 13, 25, 27.

25 No cappers were made free after 1573–4, whereas admissions of hatters became numerous at just that period. However, hatters themselves vanish from the register after 1591–2, when feltmakers abruptly start. (None occur in the register before 1590, but nineteen were admitted in the nineties.) As the new gild of 1591 was formed of haberdashers, feltmakers and cappers, the hatters had probably renamed themselves feltmakers.

26 L. A. Clarkson, 'The Leather Crafts in Tudor and Stuart England', *Agric. Hist. Rev.*, XIV (1966), 32, 33, 38.

27 The butchers had their own hall and included some wealthy members, but did not provide a single mayor or alderman.

28 Admissions of innholders to freedom held steady at nearly one a year until 1560, rising to two a year between 1560 and 1580 and three a year between 1580 and 1600. In 1596 64 innholders were licensed by the corporation: T. P. Cooper, *Some Old York Inns* (n.p., n.d.), pp. 20–9.

29 D. M. Palliser, 'Some Aspects of the Social and Economic History of York in the Sixteenth Century' (unpublished D.Phil. thesis, University of Oxford, 1968), pp. 332–94.

30 In 1596 all of York's 103 tipplers, and 78 of the 83 brewers, had other occupations: Cooper, *Some Old York Inns*, pp. 20–9.

31 *York Civic Records*, IV, 184. The footnote to this useful document is inaccurate; it was clearly the statement of customs sent by York to Beverley 1530. See *ibid.*, III, 129.

32 BM, Add. MS. 34, 605, fol. 24v.

33 York City Archives, B.32, fol. 314r.

34 *York Civic Records*, II, 86.

35 BM, Add. MS. 33, 852, fols 29, 30.

36 *York Civic Records*, III, 68.

37 For evidence of increasing population and prosperity, see Palliser, 'Social and Economic History of York', pp. 26–34, 60–3, 91–4, 350, 397–404.

38 Also the minstrels in 1561, but their restriction was rescinded in 1578.

39 *York Civic Records*, VIII, 111.

40 Cf. Exeter's similar attempt: *Report and Transactions of the Devonshire Association*, XLIV (1912), 213.

41 Was this typical at York? Boys could be fully trained by sixteen, though poor children could be bound by statute until twenty-four: T. H. Marshall, 'Capitalism and the Decline of the English Gilds', *Cambridge Historical Journal*, III (1929–31), 32, 33.

42 E.g. J. Raine, ed., *Testamenta Eboracensia, IV* (Surtees Soc. LIII, 1869), 217.

43 York Probate Registry, Wills, XXXVIII, fol. 238.

44 C. 1/324/12.

45 York City Archives, B.11, fol. 129v.

46 *Ibid.*, E.56, pp. 33, 43, 46, 52.

47 *York Civic Records*, III, 126, 127.

48 York City Archives, D.12.

49 E.g. *York Civic Records*, IV, 72.

50 York Dean and Chapter Archives, Wills, II, fol. 208r.

51 *York Civic Records*, VIII, 14.

52 *York Memorandum Book*, II, 158–9.

53 *York Civic Records*, VII, 75.

54 BM, Add. MS. 33, 852 and 34, 604, *passim*.

55 BM, Add. MS. 34, 604, fol. 49v.

56 The evidence is in previously unnoticed bequests by Alice Clerk, 1506, to the York cordwainers' Gild of St Mary, and to the Gild of St Augustine founded by the servants of the same craft: York Probate Registry, Wills, VI, fol. 221.

57 The seven named ringleaders had all become masters since 1588, and one as recently as 1601–2. They will have been aged between about twenty and thirty-five.

58 York City Archives, B.32, fols 194v., 218, 284v., 294r., 301v. I owe these references to Miss B. M. Wilson.

59 Unwin, *Industrial Organization*, pp. 63, 64.

60 York Dean and Chapter Archives, Y I d i, unpaginated.

61 *York Civic Records*, II, 56–8, 70, 71, 74, 89, 90, 93, 97–100. Sylvia Thrupp, in *Cambridge Economic History of Europe*, III (Cambridge 1963), 244, strangely misunderstands the 1490 episode, describing it as a case of 'shoemakers . . . angered at standards set for them by the cordwainers in 1490, a year of high costs'.

62 *York Civic Records*, II, 78–80.

63 York City Archives, E.40, No. 73.
64 *York Civic Records*, III, 69.
65 *Ibid.*, IV, 151, 165.
66 *Ibid.*, III, 15.
67 B. M. Wilson, 'The Corporation of York 1580–1660' (unpublished M.Phil. thesis, University of York, 1967), p. 128. I am grateful to Miss Wilson for permission to use and quote from this thesis.
68 *York Civic Records*, V, 166, 167, 178, 179; VI, 1.
69 The others being Carlisle, Durham, Morpeth and Newcastle: Gross, *Gild Merchant*, I, 111–13.
70 *VCH York*, pp. 78, 80–4, 137–9.
71 Palliser, 'Social and Econ. Hist. of York', pp. 151–4. Cooke, like Saunders, was by no means poor. As early as 1546 he was a little wealthier than the poorest alderman.
72 Drake, *Eboracum*, p. 207; *York Civic Records*, VIII, 9, 10.
73 *York Civic Records*, IV, 184.
74 *Ibid.*, III, 186, 187.
75 The bakers' gild made yearly payments until 1567–8 for 'offering days' at St Anthony's Hall.
76 *York Civic Records*, VIII, 137, 138.
77 York Dean and Chapter Archives, Wills, III, fol. 44, is the latest reference known to me.
78 Literature on the plays is too extensive to quote. The text is in L. T. Smith, ed., *York Plays* (Oxford, 1885).
79 *York Civic Records*, VII, 75.
80 Confirmation that haberdashers before 1591 were part of the merchants' gild can be found in men listed under both categories; e.g. Simon Vicars, *Register of Freemen*, I, 224.
81 *VCH York*, pp. 91, 169.
82 The evidence of most surviving gild records is for a collapse in the eighteenth century, or occasionally even later. The innholders' records cease only in 1824.
83 Marshall, 'Capitalism and the Decline of the English Gilds', p. 33.

4

The migrant in Kentish towns
1580–1640[1]

Peter Clark

'Our county,' William Lambarde, Crown lawyer and local historian, complained to quarter sessions in April 1593, is 'overspread not only with unpunished swarms of idle rogues and of counterfeit soldiers but also with numbers of poor and weak but unpitied servitors.' Migration was a major urban phenomenon in the late sixteenth and early seventeenth centuries; this is clear from the most cursory reading of town archives. In 1568 the town of Sandwich in East Kent denounced 'sundry vagrant and stout vagabonds [that] do now very much resort to this town'. The decade of the 1590s, years of severe social distress, exposed every town in Kent to the worst strains of migrational pressure but the problem tramped its way into the seventeenth century. 'Many of the poorer sort,' the mayor and jurats of Maidstone declared in 1608, 'either of their own desire or being for their idle and disordered life driven out of other places do come to inhabit and settle themselves in this town.'[2] The poor migrant was a tattered spectre riding the dreams of town magistrates for much of this period. But the vagrant was only part of the migrant problem, for Kentish towns were also besieged in this period by more respectable immigrants, traders who competed with established inhabitants, and gentlemen who threatened to overawe corporations from the safety of town houses lodged in liberties.[3] Poor and respectable immigrants confronted towns in Kent with a massive, dual problem in the sixty years or so before 1640.

The existence of physical mobility in this period has been recognized for some time, but attempts at quantification and analysis have been isolated and limited in scope. E. E. Rich, in an article, 'The Population of Elizabethan England', relied on the evidence of muster-rolls and concludes: 'Any quantitative assessment of this mobile element is impossible on the data available.' P. Laslett and J. Harrison in their seminal analysis of the Clayworth and Cogenhoe listings of population prove the high rate of mobility but their source is rare and localized, and again we cannot penetrate the demographic veil to ask not only how many people in a community were migrants but who they were and where they came from. The only attempt to discover the geographical pattern of migration in this period has been by J. Cornwall. Using statements made by witnesses in some ecclesiastical courts in Sussex he has shown that only one in four of his sample remained tied to one parish for life, that the great majority of migrants moved only once and that most moves involved a distance no greater than twenty miles. However, Cornwall's sample is small, while the time span and the catchment area for witnesses are both large. The sample is also almost entirely rural in bias.[4] Indeed, the phenomenon of urban migration has been altogether neglected, apart from some analysis of the growth of London, a demographic monster in its own right.[5] For provincial towns our knowledge is limited to the work of P. Styles, itself primarily concerned with administrative counter-action, and that of E. J. Buckatzsch, mostly interested in the period after 1640.[6] But the study of physical mobility in England suffers from an analytical leukaemia not confined to the period of the sixteenth and seventeenth centuries. The work of J. C. Russell, J. A. Raftis and S. Thrupp for the later Middle Ages illuminates brilliantly but too briefly.[7] Our understanding of the impact of the Settlement legislation of 1662 and after depends largely on the light shed by R. A. Pelham, and it is only with the apocalyptic rise of the new industrial towns of the eighteenth century that we have more description of the overall problem, although with the same grinding poverty of analysis.[8]

In this paper we shall examine a sample of Kentish biographies for the period 1580 to 1640, then attempt to describe an outline of the structure of urban migration in Kent, and finally try to assess the impact of this migration on urban society in Kent during the two or three generations before the English Revolution.

The most important source for migration in England before 1640 is the ecclesiastical court deposition book. Witnesses in civil suits, before giving evidence, described their movements since birth with place and time of residence; they also declared their age and occupation at the same time. The registrars of the two courts for Canterbury diocese, the archdeaconry and consistory courts—having a jurisdiction over East and Mid-Kent—copied out these statements with great thoroughness from the 1580s. The deposition books for the Canterbury courts are preserved in two, massive series, the first at the Cathedral Library, Canterbury, and the second in the County Archives Office, Maidstone. Starting with the deposition year 1585 biographical statements in the Canterbury series have been transcribed on to index cards. These transcripts continue up to 1628 when the pre-1640 series at Canterbury disappears. For the years 1628 to 1640 we have used statements in the Maidstone series. Of the many thousand biographies entombed in the deposition books we have selected those made by inhabitants of the towns of Canterbury, Maidstone and Faversham at the time of deposition, and also, for the period 1585 to 1627, the biographies of people who had previously lived in one of our three towns but who now lived elsewhere in Canterbury diocese.[9]

Cornwall, in the study mentioned earlier, dwells on the defects of the deposition biography and these need some explanation. Two possible sources of weakness exist, the first in the deponent and the second in the clerk recording the statement. In the former case deliberate dishonesty can generally be discounted as a factor since it was rare for a deponent to be a principal to the suit in which he testified. Biographical statements were less likely to be false than incomplete through bad memory and the common pre-industrial contempt for numbers; certainly there was some incompleteness. As for the quality of the records, the archives of Canterbury diocese were preserved generally with care in this period—the prestige of the courts attracting a large number of able men to serve as court officials. Although the quality of the record might vary to some extent from clerk to clerk, all in all the deposition books appear to have been kept well throughout the period under discussion.[10]

Having said this we must exclude from our analysis, wholly or partially, statements made by certain groups of deponents. Firstly there was a handful of knights and esquires whose social magnificence denied them the opportunity of providing more than the barest personal biography. More biographical half-men were the clergy—for a less lustrous version of the same reason. Both groups have to be excluded wholly, together with a small number of aliens born on the Continent whose migrational peculiarities would distort our figures.

Other problem people include married and widowed women who depended on the status of their husbands or late husbands in the community, and so offer a curtailed biography. Because of their importance as a group we have made use of their statements to help answer certain questions but throughout we have distinguished them from spinsters who provide complete biographies.[11]

Another important question is whether our sample represents an adequate cross-section of urban society in Kent during this period. As far as any three towns can reflect the cross-currents of this society, the towns of Canterbury, Faversham and Maidstone are a good collective gauge. Canterbury in East Kent with a population by 1640 of about 6,000 was an ancient centre with a decaying economy; Faversham was a North Kent port sharing the same important roadway, the Watling Street, but with a population somewhat over 1,000 and for much of this period quite prosperous through trade; and Maidstone straddling the River Medway in Mid-Kent was a growing social centre with a population edging towards 2,000.[12] How representative is the sample of the people who lived within these towns? Overall, we have a sample of about 7 per cent of the total population of these towns in the period under examination, but what about occupational representation? Our statements arise from law suits which include both the polite violence of a clash over church pews and the crude slander in a parish alehouse. Most sectors of society appear in random fashion although there was some bias towards the respectable man and against the younger (as now, the beggar or the infant was not a very useful witness to have in court). In a society which still treated women traditionally as of semi-dependent status there was also some bias against female witnesses. In categorizing the occupations of male deponents from our three towns together the breakdown is as shown opposite.[13]

Overall we can see unfolded a line-drawing of urban society, if one somewhat distorted by the number of gentry.[14]

Our last problem concerns the constant nature of the sample. Because of the bunching of cases the number of statements varies considerably from year to year, but over a series of five-year periods we can establish a reasonably uniform average level of depositions. Equally important, there was no radical alteration of the mean age of deponents in the period under consideration.[15]

Nobody could claim that our source aspires to demographic certainty. The most serious imperfections have already been pointed out

TABLE 1 *Male occupations*

	Number	Percentage (n = 858)
1 Gentry	182	21·2
2 Professional (excluding clergy)	44	5·1
3 Clothing trades	98	11·4
4 Leather trades	20	2·3
5 Food and drink	93	10·8
6 Textile industry	53	6·2
7 Household goods	25	2·9
8 Distributive	56	6·5
9 Building trades	59	6·9
10 Rural : yeoman	60	7·0
11 Rural : husbandman	27	3·2
12 Rural : labourer	22	2·6
13 Rural : misc.	17	2·0
14 Service industries	22	2·6
15 Servants	45	5·2
16 Miscellaneous	17	2·0
17 Unspecified occupation	18	2·1

and less important ones will be mentioned in their appropriate place. But for the present it remains our most valuable source for the study of migration in the pre-census period.[16]

First then our sample. Excluding the statements of persons in the groups mentioned earlier and also a number of duplicate statements, we have a sample of 1,173 biographies of people resident in our towns when they came to depose (see Table 2).

We also have a group of deponents in the period 1585 to 1628 who had resided at some time in one of the three towns and who now lived elsewhere in Canterbury diocese. There are here forty-nine men who had previously lived at Canterbury, twenty-one at Faversham and forty-eight at Maidstone.

The most obvious question to consider concerns the overall rate of mobility. Of the Canterbury men who deposed, 9·6 per cent were born in Canterbury and had not moved at all; 11·9 per cent were born in Canterbury but had made at least one move within the city since then; 7 per cent were born in Canterbury but refer to a move afterwards which is not specified; and finally amongst those born within the city, 2 per cent of all deponents say that they had left the city but then returned there. Of the Canterbury male deponents 41 per cent

TABLE 2   *Number of persons living at time of deposition*

	in Canterbury	in Faversham	in Maidstone	Total
Males	643	92	123	
Married/widowed women	211	20	20	
Spinsters	56	4	4	
	910	116	147	1,173

were born, allegedly outside the city but within Kent and another 28·5 per cent were born outside the county. The migrational pattern among the male deponents from Faversham and Maidstone was similar. At Faversham, of our sample of ninety-two, only 7·6 per cent say they were born there and had not moved since, 8·8 per cent who were also Faversham-born mention a move whose nature is not specified and then their return, and a further 2·8 per cent mention an emigration from their town of birth (which is specified) and then their return. In all 61·2 per cent were born outside the town but within the county, and 19·6 per cent were born outside the county. Amongst the male deponents from Maidstone 23·5 per cent said they had lived there all their previous lifetime, a further 10·5 per cent refer to an unspecified migration and return, and 4·2 per cent to a specified move out and back; 43·9 per cent claim to have been born outside the town but within Kent and 17·9 per cent to have been born outside the county. Despite the bias of our source towards established status, migration in all three towns appears to have been the rigorous rule.

At Canterbury fewer than one in ten of the male deponents do not mention a significant move in their life and seven in ten claim to have been born outside the city. Indeed about three out of ten allege they were born outside Kent, countering the argument that migration, like gavelkind or patriarchalism, was a peculiarly Kentish phenomenon. The Faversham sample reveals a similar if less acute migrational pattern, for while Canterbury and Faversham shared the important Watling Street communication, Canterbury had a stronger, quasi-metropolitan pull. Maidstone, less favourably placed in the road network, had a more static population, although even here about six in ten of the deponents were born outside the town; thus the rate of mobility was high but its exact velocity varied according to urban location.

The pattern of female mobility was similar. Of our 211 married women and widows at Canterbury who deposed, 35·1 per cent were born there, 45·5 per cent were born outside Canterbury but within Kent and a further 19·4 per cent were born outside the county. Amongst the smaller sum of the same group who deposed from Faversham, numbering 20 in all, 15 were born outside Faversham but within Kent and 4 came from counties other than Kent. A similar group of 20 at Maidstone produced 10 immigrants from the county and 4 from outside the county. Strict comparison of these figures with the analysis of the movement of male deponents is not possible, because in the case of married and widowed women their movements since birth have been excluded. Yet this exclusion is only significant in that it exaggerates the number of immobiles amongst the female deponents. The 56 spinsters who deposed from Canterbury are more comparable to the male deponents: 50 per cent were born outside Canterbury (but within Kent) while only another 7·1 per cent were born outside the county. In general the mobility rate amongst women approached 60 per cent but there tended to be less long-distance migration than in the case of men.

In a consideration of the frequency of moves, we are undoubtedly faced with a war of numerical attrition waged by the incompleteness of statements and the under-registration of moves. The urban immigrant when he or she came to depose mentioned the one move known probably to his or her fellow witnesses; but the chance of under-registration of any previous move mounts sharply. Even so, we can say of the male migrants to Canterbury among our deponents, that about two in nine (131 of 582) made more than one move in their previous lifetime (including moves within city walls). At Faversham one in four of its immigrants (23 of 85) had moved more than once before they deposed, a similar ratio. But at Maidstone only one in six of its male immigrants (15 in 91) had moved more than once in their previous life, suggesting a more static picture. In our sample of deponents the most mobile man was a Canterbury leather worker who refers to having made eight moves in his life before coming to depose, but mention of six is not uncommon.

As we should expect, the majority of migrants appear to have been under thirty years of age when they came into our three towns. Partly this was a reflection of the life-cycle of the migrant and partly a physical pre-condition of the rigours of travel.[17] In the case of the age-composition of the Kentish male immigrants there also appears to have been a connexion with the employment opportunities most open to young men especially in the form of apprenticeships. Almost 24 per cent

TABLE 3   *Ages of male migrants on entry into Canterbury*

	10 and under	*11–20*	*21–30*	*31–40*	*41 and over*
County-born (%)	4·7	23·9	28·6	23·6	19·2
Extra-county born (%)	2·3	15·0	35·8	25·5	21·4

amongst these migrants entering Canterbury had come between the ages of eleven and twenty—when most apprentices were indentured. Amongst the extra-county immigrants into Canterbury only 15 per cent arrived at this stage of their life. In this group by far the greatest incidence of mobility occurred between the ages of twenty-one and thirty, but it is also true to say that the long-distance migrant entering Canterbury was in general somewhat older than his Kentish counterpart.

Where did our urban immigrant come from? What sort of distances had people travelled before they entered one of these three towns? Short of running a pedometer along all the known hedgerows of sixteenth-century England there can be no convincing answer to the second question. Migrants, at least those moving a long distance, tended to move where possible across country. Partly for this reason, and partly for the absence of any better, human method of calculation migrational distances have been measured as the crow flies. Of course a number of migrants probably travelled by water and not overland and they present an insoluble problem, unless we exclude the suspects from our analysis—a serious step since we have little proof. The most we can say is that their numbers were probably not very large. Those moving across estuaries present less of a problem as there were numerous trans-estuary ferries and we can make numerical adjustment.[18] A final problem is presented by about a dozen deponents who mention as their place of birth or residence a village or hamlet we have been unable to locate. Here distances have been estimated from the

TABLE 4   *Mileage travelled by male migrants between birth-place in Kent and entry into the three towns*

| | *(the number of migrants expressed as %age of total for town)* | | |
	Canterbury	Faversham	Maidstone
less than 1	1·1	7·0	—
1 to 5	15·2	22·8	28·2
6 to 10	30·0	24·6	41·3
11 to 15	27·4	15·8	15·2
16 to 20	7·5	12·3	8·7
21 to 30	14·3	10·5	2·2
31 to 40	1·5	3·5	2·2
over 41	3·0	3·5	2·2

county town of their shire. In considering these distances moved by migrants we should think of them primarily as notional rather than real with a strong element of under-registration.

Before discussing immigration into our three towns we must mention inter-parish migration within Canterbury by people born there. Its importance should not be exaggerated, for Canterbury still had fifteen parishes in 1640 and these were often small—to leave one parish and enter another might quite often involve travelling only a few yards. In this intra-city migration we can distinguish two trends. Firstly, the poor inhabitant (or his offspring) of an outer parish like St Paul or St Mary Northgate moved to one of the more prosperous inner parishes to be appointed or work in the business of a great merchant or lawyer living in a three-storeyed mansion of St George's or St Andrew's parish. In the opposite direction came young men and women, leaving service, and turning to the outer parishes to set up home or business. In this sort of migration, motives are more important than distance and here our biographical statements are of no help.

Quantification is more valuable when we look at the distances involved in immigration by persons born in the county (see Table 4). For Maidstone and Faversham the urban pull was strongest in a radius of up to eleven miles from the town, while for Canterbury more immigrants came from a radius of between eleven and fifteen miles than from the immediate one of five miles.[19] With a total population four or five times that of Maidstone and Faversham and a wider market impact, Canterbury extended its siren appeal almost as twice as far as the other two towns. There were strong immigrant thrusts from the Isle of Thanet (significantly without its own market town) and from the small, increasingly disafforested and enclosed woodland villages of the North Downs (to its west) and Barham Down (to its south), but immigrants also came from the Weald and Mid-Kent.[20] Although the catchment area is wider for Canterbury than the other two towns the general impression is still one of localized impact. For Faversham the net was primarily effective over the small Downland villages to the south and the fruit and grain areas to the west; it probably suffered in its intake from the proximity of Canterbury. At Maidstone the pattern of local immigration was more complex, stretching north and south-west (up and down the Medway valley), and east and west (along the scarpland south of the town—occasionally slipping south into the Weald which lay beyond).

For Kentish immigrants tramping or riding into our three towns the journey was short and familiar but migrants from outside the county stumbled into a hostile unknown. Where did they come from? In our sample of deponents we have the county of birth of 223 men and 53 women (wives, widows and spinsters) born outside Kent.

Most obvious is the group of northern counties, Yorkshire, Lancashire and Cheshire, who send in all forty immigrants. They were pushed out by the notorious poverty and backwardness of much of the Highland Zone—the spawn of an economic disequilibrium in relation to the Lowland areas of England. Significantly few claim to have been born in the largest centres of settlement and there was an extra contingent of five from the bleak hills of Cumberland.[21] Out of the Lowland

TABLE 5   *County or place of origin of deponents (n = 276)*

	in Canterbury	*Male in* Faversham	*in* Maidstone	*Female in* all towns	*Total for county* (No.) (%)	
Beds.	2		1	1	4	1·45
Berks.	10	1		4	15	5·43
Bucks.	3		1		4	1·45
Cambs.	8			2	10	3·62
Cheshire	6		1	1	8	2·89
Cornwall	1				1	0·36
Cumberland	4			1	5	1·81
Derbs.	1			1	2	0·73
Devon	5		1	1	7	2·53
Dorset	5				5	1·81
Essex	10	1	1		12	4·35
Glos.	4	1		1	6	2·17
Hants	4	2		4	10	3·62
Herefords.	2	1		1	4	1·45
Herts.	4				4	1·45
Hunts.	1				1	0·36
Lancs.	5	3	1	2	11	3·99
Leics.	4				4	1·45
Lincs.	4	1	2		7	2·53
London	9	2	1	7	19	6·88
Middlesex	3			1	4	1·45
Norfolk	5			2	7	2·53
Northants.	6	1		2	9	3·26
Northumb.	2		1		3	1·09
Notts.	2				2	0·73
Oxon.	10			1	11	3·99
Rutland	2			1	3	1·09
Salop	4				4	1·45
Somerset	11		1		12	4·35
Staffs.	2				2	0·73
Suffolk	7	1		5	13	4·71
Surrey	1			2	3	1·09
Sussex	9	1	8	8	26	9·42
Warwicks.	3				3	1·09
Wilts.	4	1				1·81
Worcs.				3	3	1·09
Yorks.	17		2	2	21	7·61
Wales	2	2				1·45
Calais	1			1	2	0·73

Zone counties there came three phalanxes of migrants. The first stretched through Essex and Suffolk into Cambridgeshire and Norfolk sending forty-two migrants. Some undoubtedly came by land through London but others were shipped by ferry from Tilbury to Gravesend or took cockboat from the small havens of the East Anglian coast. Secondly there came a large group from the counties of the Thames Valley— Berkshire, Buckinghamshire and Oxfordshire exported thirty-one migrants to our three towns and the pattern here may have extended into the border counties with Wales. The third phalanx tramped along the South coast. Sussex sent twenty-six migrants, the largest contingent from any one county, as one would expect; not only was Sussex an adjoining county but there were strong economic links with Kent formalized by the ancient confederation of the Cinque Ports. But the strong migrational movement extended beyond Sussex into Hampshire and perhaps Dorset, Somerset and Devon. These five counties together pushed sixty migrants into our three towns. As in the case of the travellers from East Anglia sea-transport was quite important. From our sample the role of London appears more limited than we might have expected, considering both its population size (by 1600 approaching a quarter of a million) and its proximity. Less than 7 per cent of our extra-county migrants were born there, with the addition of one or two from the adjoining suburbs in Surrey and Middlesex. The explanation may well be found in the nature of its population expansion in the sixteenth century which depended less on natural reproduction than on massive immigration, a demographic imbalance that the high London mobility rate and the excessive poverty of many immigrants did nothing, probably, to rectify.[22]

Turning from volume and extent of migration to variations in migrational patterns caused by occupational differences our figures must be tentative. Not only is there the problem of measuring distances, but also that of an imprecision of occupational styles in this period, which is compounded by occupational groupings with their own rate of arbitrariness. Nevertheless, it seems probable that self-styled gentlemen and labourers stand at opposite ends of a social lift-shaft, and the grocer or mercer or draper together were usually more respectable members of urban society than the husbandman or servant.[23]

The average mileages for Faversham and Maidstone are difficult to interpret. Partly this reflects the smallness of our samples and partly the imprecision of the urban pull of the small town. The migrational

structure from the Canterbury sample is clearer. Here the more prosperous groups such as gentry, yeomen and those engaged in distributive trades seem less likely to have moved long distances from their
birth place. Conversely amongst servants long-distance migration

TABLE 6   *Average mileage moved since birth by immigrants (male*
deponents) according to occupational grouping

	From Canterbury	From Faversham	From Maidstone
1 Gentry	38·2	30·0	28·2
2 Professional	85·2	112·5	75·3
3 Clothing trades	65·4	72·8	34·1
4 Leather trades	104·0		167·5
5 Food and drink	70·8	35·1	92·1
6 Textile industry	52·1	10·5	63·5
7 Household goods	90·6	16·5	23·5
8 Distributive	34·2	9·6	37·0
9 Building trades	90·8	17·8	36·0
10 Rural : yeoman	36·1	44·3	22·0
11 Rural : husbandman	72·4	15·0	24·4
12 Rural : labourer	68·6		
13 Rural : misc.	115·9	112·5	
14 Service industr.	58·5	57·0	10·3
15 Servants	108·3		102·0
16 Miscellaneous	78·5		
17 Unspecified	100·6		

appears to have been much more common.[24] On average the Canterbury servant had travelled almost three times the distance of the
Canterbury gentleman after leaving his place of birth. Other groups
travelling long distances include leather workers, dominated especially
by the poor, and those engaged in the small industries of making
household goods. The poorer rural groups coming into Canterbury,
husbandmen, labourers and the miscellany of gardeners, woodcutters

and the like, also showed a bias towards long-distance migration. Although our path is beset by the sinister traps of statistical high-waymen there appears to be an overall correlation of short-distance movement with prosperous occupational groupings and vice versa—

TABLE 7   *Migration from outside Kent: Canterbury men*

Occupational groupings (as Table 6)	Total no. of incomers	Incomers from outside Kent No.	(%)
1	90	25	27·8
2	27	16	59·3
3	56	20	35·7
4	8	5	62·5
5	53	24	45·3
6	20	7	35·0
7	14	7	50·0
8	24	6	25·0
9	24	14	58·3
10	41	10	24·4
11	17	7	41·2
12	16	5	31·3
13	9	6	66·7
14	8	3	37·5
15	28	18	64·3
16	12	8	66·7
17	13	7	53·8

professional migrants proving the logical exception. Our Maidstone and Faversham figures tend to confirm this picture.

Less susceptible to distortion is a comparison, again by occupational groupings, of the chances of male migrants having come from outside the county—although here only Canterbury provides a viable sample (see Table 7).[25]

Upper social groupings again show a bias against long-distance migration. An immigrant servant in Canterbury was almost three times as likely to have come from outside the county than the gentleman immigrant. More than six out of ten of Canterbury immigrants working in the poorer leather trades came from outside the county. Only about one in four of immigrant yeomen and members of the distributive trades had had a similar experience.

TABLE 8 *Urban/rural contacts before entry*

Men : Places of birth and residence	Rural (%)	Urban (%)
Kentish immigrants		
to Canterbury	80·1	19·9
Faversham	70·2	29·8
Maidstone	68·8	31·2
Extra-county immigrants		
to Canterbury	56·0	44·0
Faversham	53·8	46·2
Maidstone	53·0	47·0
Widows/married women : Places of birth only		
Kentish immigrants		
to Canterbury	81·4	18·6
Faversham	60·0	40·0
Maidstone	70·0	30·0
Extra-county immigrants		
to Canterbury	48·8	51·2

This identification of more prosperous social groupings with a lower rate of mobility, and vice versa, gains support from an analysis by occupational groupings of Canterbury migrants who moved more than once. Amongst the yeomanry and distributive trades only one in ten of the migrants had moved more than once before they came to depose, while for servants and leather workers the chances of having moved more than once were as high as one in two or three. An exception to this pattern centres on our group of gentry where the possibility of having moved more than once in their previous lifetime was about one in five. Here frequency of movement may have been accelerated by the push of social mobility.

Our earlier analysis of the geographical origin of immigrants—by county or mileage—masked an important distinction, that between rural and urban experience. Of course, only London, Norwich and perhaps one or two other cities in this period afforded an *urban environment* in any meaningfully modern sense, but it does appear that settlements of a thousand or so inhabitants had an urban identity in the eyes both of town and country men, as well as being the foci of trade and communication: the distinction has some substance.[26] Here the urban/rural distinction is based on listings published by John Adams in his *Index Villaris* of 1680.[27] We can see that the experience of the Kentish immigrants before entry into one of our three towns was primarily rural—despite the large number of urban settlements in the country (see Table 8).

This generalization appears to be true for all three towns and is common for both men and married or widowed women. Long-distance migration, on the other hand, was more tied to an urban experience. While only one in three or four of the contacts of Kentish immigrants were urban, in the case of extra-county immigrants the ratio was nearer one in two. It may be that long-distance migrants tended to give as their place of birth or residence somewhere known to the officials of the ecclesiastical court such as a market town rather than a nearby hamlet (something it is impossible to prove one way or the other). Or perhaps the original migration from obscure village to neighbouring town was eclipsed by the second, urban experience. This latter possibility, at least, does not seriously counter our argument that long-distance migrants tended to be pre-occupied with towns, moving from urban centre to urban centre, perhaps the offspring of parents themselves migrants from the countryside into the town.

What happened to immigrants when they came to town? Where, if anywhere, did they go afterwards? Of the urban life of the migrant our biographical statements proffer little information and when we consider this problem later we must rely on other sources. Our second question is no less important. Emigration must have been running at a high level—even allowing for the demographic toll on immigrants of bad housing, malnutrition and endemic disease, as well as a fall-out of permanent squatters who swelled the urban population. Although our deposition statements do not tell what percentage of immigrants actually moved on from our urban centres, we can glimpse a little of post-urban migrational structure from the depositions of former inhabitants of our towns who now lived elsewhere in Canterbury diocese. Excluding as it must the later experience of long-distance migrants and being restricted to depositions made from 1585 to 1628 our source is a flickering candle of information. In a sample of ninety-eight emigrants, sixty-three were born in one of the three towns. Bearing in mind that the sample is defined by the limits of Canterbury diocese emigration from the three towns was not surprisingly local in direction, but more significant the distance pattern of local emigration was similar to that of local immigration. Emigrants tended to take up residence no more than fifteen miles or so from Canterbury and rather less from Maidstone or Faversham. Within this radius their choice of settlement had a clear urban orientation. Of the places of residence mentioned by these urban emigrants after they left their town of birth approximately 40 per cent were urban. In this group there was at least some persistent urban attraction for the migrant, although we should be careful of dogmatism with a sample whose migrational span has been castrated by diocesan boundaries. A less unnatural group includes people who migrated into one of our three towns and then left to live elsewhere in Canterbury diocese—twenty-five were born in Kent and ten were born outside the county. The Kentish-born migrants obey the pattern of local migration; almost all immigration was from a radius of less than sixteen miles and once settled in one of our towns they stayed for some time, the average being about five years; when they emigrated they moved in the usual radius of sixteen miles showing a high rural preference (only 24 per cent of their places of residence, excluding their principal stop-over in one of the three towns, were urban). There is little evidence amongst this group that their urban residence seriously affected their subsequent migrational activity. The migrational experience of the non-Kentish emigrants was rather different, revealing a much shorter period of residence in one of our towns and a stronger bias towards staying in towns, more than 50 per cent of their residential experience being found there. In conclusion, there can be only a partial answer to our earlier question: what happened to migrants once they left our towns? If they were local immigrants they migrated back perhaps to their home village within a limited radius of the town. If the migrant had come a longer distance his emigration tended to be towards an urban centre and almost certainly beyond the narrow radius of the local migrant.

By definition, he then almost always disappears from the sight of our source.

One would need to indulge in a high level of simple-mindedness to believe the numbers we have derived from ecclesiastical court statements alone prove very much. However, they do suggest an outline structure of urban mobility whose validity can be tested by reference to other sources. This outline structure can best be seen to describe a series of pyramids, the smaller the pyramid the more acute its form. The span from apex to base represents the sliding-scale of the social structure and the horizontal cross-section migrational distances. The base of each urban pyramid overlaps the next and the larger the size of town the greater the pyramid. Thus at the base of the social pyramid we discover long-distance, urban to urban movement, but as we haul our way to the apex of the social hierarchy we find migrational activity which is not only predominantly short-distance but more restricted to a rural experience. The inadequacies of this model are obvious.[28] Geometrical representations of social phenomena are never very plausible and the migrational pyramid is no exception. Even so, in stressing the essential continuity and overlapping of migrational forms it serves as a useful counterweight in the following discussion where the tendency may be to over-emphasize differences between types of migrational activity, to exaggerate apex and base, to the exclusion of migrational mass.

Persons in the more prosperous occupational groupings, as we saw earlier, at least in Canterbury and probably elsewhere, were often born in the countryside not far away. Where the town was small like Faversham or Maidstone local migration may well have been very local indeed. In the case of a larger urban centre like Canterbury the attraction was more extensive. Another characteristic was probably a low frequency of moves, often no more than one in a lifetime. The driving force behind this form of migrational activity was social mobility—it was, primarily, aspiring or *betterment migration*.

The age-composition of our Kentish migrants into Canterbury suggested that local migration was often effected by an apprenticeship agreement. Certainly there appears to be a strong correlation between the radius of town apprenticeship agreements with countryfolk and the circle of local migration. At Maidstone of the apprenticeship agreements enrolled from 1567 to 1599 over 70 per cent of the incomers came from a radius of up to eleven miles. At Faversham from 1592 to 1642 61 per cent of all agreements with incomers involved the same distance.[29] Sometimes the townsman would be known personally to the parents of the immigrant apprentice. When John Sabine, a draper living at Davington, wanted to apprentice his son Avery in 1597 he chose as his son's master John Rose, an alderman draper of Canterbury eight miles away—a man with whom he had large-scale financial dealings. Kinship played an important role in *betterment migration*. An apprentice coming into a strange town would often find as his surety an uncle or perhaps another relative.[30] Deprived of the support of kinship even the respectable incomer might well be forced into vagrancy. Alice Morrice, who was born at Borden (about ten miles from Maidstone) in the late 1580s, went at the age of ten or twelve as a servant to her uncle Robert Nyn, but later he 'refusing to receive her she has since been vagrant'. In this case the initial migrational slide was greased by money left in her father's will. Bolstered by kinship the respectable immigrant with or without apprenticeship stood a reasonable chance of urban success. Take for example the Claggett brothers: William, son of a West Malling gentleman, followed his elder brother, George, to Canterbury; George may have been apprenticed as a hatter but his brother bought his freedom. Together they groped their way up the social and civic backpassage and held office as mayor and sheriff of Canterbury, respectively.[31]

The importance of the extended family relationship in *betterment migration* is clear but the nature of this relationship is difficult to determine. Patriarchalism is not an entirely satisfactory description— often the brothers of the mother appear the most active members of the kinship group.[32] Better, perhaps, to stress the existence of a two-tiered kinship system—firstly immediate kin living in a limited radius and playing an important role in local migration, and secondly, the much looser collection of 'cousins' in almost unknown degrees of affinity. We need not share the suspicious mind of a Walmer man who declared in 1618 that Mr Broome and a young woman called each other cousins, although 'if there be any affinity between them it is very far off and not within scarce 20 degrees', for the gentry of Kent, we are told, were themselves overwhelmed by a tidal wave of cousin-age.[33] This extensive kin relationship was less significant in the machinery of local migration. Indeed it was never co-ordinated in any meaningful sense except amongst the greatest gentry where it was indistinguishable from political patriarchalism, which has a rather different significance. To conclude, kinship as a factor in local migration may have been supplemented by a more shadowy phenomenon: the godparent. Godparents were often kin but usually of the distant strain. How far godparentage was intended to confirm their ties with the more immediate kinship group is open to speculation but godparents appear to have played some part in migration. Thomas Harman, a gentleman living near the town of Dartford in North Kent in the 1560s, described one vagrant who claimed he was visiting a man 'not only my uncle but also my god-father', and when the mother of Humphrey Horton of Hernhill remarried in the 1590s the boy 'was put forth to his godfather Butcher', probably at Hythe.[34]

Respectability was the ultimate sanction of this form of migration. There was the respectability of rigging civic gilds, of the aldermanic bench and the mayor's posey, and the supreme distinction attained by the most successful, although sometimes delayed for two or more generations, derived from wiping one's fingers clean of the sweet stickiness of urban cash and returning as a landed gentleman to the countryside. Simon Linch, who came from the Weald of Kent to Sandwich (there was a strong clothing contact) using 'much a great trade of merchandises', became jurat and mayor but then retired to Elmestone a few miles into the country to live 'like a great gentleman' with great wealth and lands. Although Linch was exceptional in completing in one generation this salmon-like cycle of the successful migrant family, in other respects he is more typical: he preserved strong connexions with his Wealden origins and was involved in the establishment of a grammar school at Cranbrook.[35] This residual contact with one's place of origin was a characteristic of *betterment migration* as a whole. William Reade, a merchant who moved from Folkestone to Canterbury, 'did not altogether leave Folkestone but at times repaired thither and continued and lay there'. Kinship brought responsibility as well as opportunity. The urban immigrant was expected to look after the education as well as employment of his rural kinsman coming to town.[36] In his prosperity he might be expected to subsidize his rural kin at least as far as extending long-term credit. Rural indebtedness may have played a major role in the maintenance of kinship connexions with the town.[37]

We can only speculate how much physical contact there was between the urban migrant and his original family group. A prosperous gentleman like the very mobile Thomas Godfrey, in addition to Christmas festivities, held large-scale dinners at which almost all his 'children and grandchildren were together' from different parts of the county. For ordinary folk Christmas, together with the numerous christenings, weddings and funeral wakes inflicted by a fragile demographic structure, offered plentiful opportunities for re-dedicating family ties in feasting, drinking, dancing and the striving of folk games.[38] A common figure was the town harvester returning the often short distance to his native village every summer. Such a man was Thomas Burrell, a husbandman who lived in the parish of St Mary Northgate in 1598. He said that before he came to Canterbury he had dwelt for twenty years at Sarre about eight miles away and in the subsequent thirty years he had lived at Canterbury 'he had for the most part every year harvested' at Sarre. When Edna Young went out with two other Canterbury women to harvest one Bartholomew-tide it was significant she chose to work at Milton, a village adjoining that from which she had migrated originally.[39] By harvesting in his native area the townsman fulfilled his kin obligations, preserved family viability and strengthened his own economic position before the oncoming urban winter. Thus the many-stranded relationships of the immediate kinship group were if anything enhanced by local migration.[40]

Betterment migration was not compelled by necessity but encouraged by the hope of social and economic improvement. It tended to be regular and short-distance. Publicity was a strong element whether in drawing up the apprenticeship indenture by a notary before witnesses or enrolling the deed in the presence of the mayor or swearing the freeman's oath or being entertained by one's neighbours when one returned.[41] It was not, of course, a new phenomenon. A rural variant of this sort of migration appears to have been strong in fifteenth-century East Anglian villages, and peasant migration into the towns of the Canterbury region during the same period had some of the characteristics described earlier—including the preservation of strong rural ties.[42] The 1563 Statute of Artificers sought to confirm its bias in favour of the offspring of rural respectability.[43] As an urban phenomenon it may have grown in the sixteenth century; somewhat paradoxically, for although Maidstone and Faversham share some prosperity for part of the period before 1640 the general trend of urban society in Kent was towards contraction of basic industries. However, the self-perpetuating, convector nature of *betterment migration* was not regulated strictly by the dial of industrial reality. Industrial contraction was masked by the growth of internal trade and the development of the social function of towns. The rural migrant, more-over, was heavily impressed by traditional reports of gold-lined, urban gutters—and the possible reality of higher wage-rates.[44] Lastly, not only was it increasingly necessary for the successful merchants, even if there were fewer of them, to return to the countryside for social reasons, but the expansion of internal trade with all its concomitants of improved communications and enlarged contacts, and the extra element of necessity reared by population expansion among the younger sons of prosperous men, increased the pool of betterment migrants on their way to town.

So far discussion has been limited to the heights of our migrational pyramid, but towards its base we find a rather different pattern of mobility—one already touched upon in the first part of this paper. We can call this resultant or *subsistence migration*. The poorer migrant, from our earlier analysis, tended to cover greater distances and move more often than the more prosperous *betterment migrant*. He was somewhat older and had a stronger urban orientation. Other sources confirm the reality of this pattern. A good example is that of George Starr aged 24 who left Canterbury on 14 January 1609. That night he lay at Westgate Court, just outside the walls, and next day walked the twenty odd miles to Rochester and stayed 'at what house he cannot tell'. On 16 January he travelled to Sittingbourne and the next day came to Perry Court, a few miles off, where he stayed three nights. He then lay at a barn near Faversham, moved back to Perry Court and so on to Canterbury. On 28 January, he tramped to Faversham —in all he had travelled about sixty miles in a fortnight. Enforced migration was a disease endemic among most poor people. Thomas Gilbert of Canterbury described how in 1602 'he being a poor man is driven to seek his work abroad and has for some time laboured for his living' in Canterbury, while Nicholas Lawrence, then in Thanet, complained, 'he is a poor labouring man and is sometime in one place and sometime in another'.[45]

The most common time for the poorer migrant to tramp was from June until October. Propelled by the dying days of the last harvest year, the hope of harvest work somewhere on the way, and the comparative usability of the roads, he would keep going until the hiring fair and its fag-end, the mop fair, failed to find him work and the autumn turned sour. Then the only recourse would be to scrape a meagre living from the woodlands where if all else failed the squatter could dig for roots or eat nuts and berries.[46] Otherwise he could stare out the winter clinging to the shackland excrescences of urban society. The subsistence migrant moved often erratically, usually secretively. The function of kinship ties as a roller for *subsistence migration* is more confused. It may have played some part in getting the poorer man moving but it never dominated this kind of migration in the way it did the *betterment* sort. John Ayling who left the service of the Salisbury postmaster in May 1609 used his brother's house in Sussex as a stop-over on his way to the Kent town of New Romney but otherwise relied heavily on victualling houses.[47] Immediate kinship was usually localized, and the subsistence migrant moving outside his home locality had at best to depend, for the most part, on the much looser extended kinship grouping with its more limited set of responsibilities. To some extent, the bonds of community consciousness may have supplemented, for the long distance migrant, the fragile links of the extended kinship group. For instance, when Richard Sawyer travelled from Wiltshire into Kent in 1602 he came, he said, with his countryman, Clerk of Sandwich, who had been buying horses in his home county, and they appear to have travelled about Sandwich together for some time afterwards. But the extent and strength of the 'country' connexion is difficult to define.[48]

Barns and victualling houses were the principal links in the chain of long-distance migration. Richard Caffinch explained he had 'sometimes to go up and down the country to get work and had often lain in a barn as many honest poor men have occasion likewise sometimes to do'. Before Edmund Wells, a runaway apprentice, came into the town of New Romney 'some nights he lay in the fields and some nights in barns'. Harman described several barns about London as the 'chief houses' for the professional vagabond, and for poorer migrants in Kent certain barns appear to have been important stop-over places. Preston barn near Faversham and the barn of the dissolved priory of Dover were used by migrants moving up and down the Watling Street. Barns of course were death traps and the migrant in foul weather tried to hide in the darker corners of dwelling-houses.[49]

For all but the totally destitute the victualling or tippling house represented the other important refuge of the subsistence migrant. Although in strict legality prohibited from lodging travellers, these houses provided migrants with accommodation on a large scale. The victualling house was not only an important stop-over for the migrant *en route* but served as a door of entry for the would-be urban settler.[50] A far cry from the spacious, silk-furnished, faintly fantastical inns and taverns that dominated the principal street of every large town (where the host might be a city magnate and the patrons country gentry or rich bourgeoisie), the victualling house (often unlicensed) was a dwelling-house where the householder usually engaged in tippling as a by-employment.[51] Tipplers were poor people without much social standing—at Sandwich in 1607 it was said, 'the greatest number of those persons are very poor'. Lawrence Grant and his wife who ran a tippling house in St Mary Northgate, Canterbury, 'live idly and will not work' and 'accustomably lodge beggars and vagabonds'. Most were located on the edge of town in bylanes or courts or the suburbs; at Faversham the greatest concentration was in the slum area of West and Tanner Streets—significantly, on the London side of town.[52]

All social statistics derived from criminal records depend heavily on the fluctuating effectiveness of the enforcing agency. This is especially true for inns and alehouses. The number of licensed houses perches precariously on the top of an unlicensed iceberg. In times of acute distress the numbers of unlicensed tipplers fined by town magistrates rose steeply but we cannot be certain that this reflects more a response to increased migrational activity than the determination of town governments to suppress any sort of response; probably both. If we concentrate our attention on licensed houses, Canterbury had twenty-two alehouses in 1577 but by 1596 the number was about forty-two. Rochester doubled its number of licensed victuallers between 1607 and 1635.[53]

The tippling house was a substitute for the kinship tie and the respectable channels of access into urban society. The poor migrant made his first urban contacts there and possibly learnt of employment —a rudimentary alternative to the hiring fair of established society.[54] Victuallers served as sureties for a stranger needing to make a bond, as well as acting as pawnbrokers. Tippling houses were the focus of popular entertainment—gaming, cockfighting, dancing and the sweet oblivion of drunkenness. Watered drink, short measure and poxy women were all there in plenty but tippling houses also preserved in the face of mounting magisterial hostility the relics of communal life.[55] The so-called morris dancers who skipped up and down outside the house of the Puritan mayor of Canterbury on May Day 1589 had their city centre at the 'George' in St George's parish, and in the clothing township of Benenden in the Weald Randall Gregory kept the feast 'commonly known as Coxcombes fair' at his drinking house.[56]

Tipplers were in constant conflict with the regular order of society.

Their presence in large, unlicensed multitudes was an affront to magistracy, their opening in time of divine service was an insult to Church and Puritan minister, their very existence the source of the paranoiac fears that beset the upper classes in the late sixteenth and early seventeenth centuries. They were right. Tippling houses had a traditional function as foci of an older community consciousness, but a new radicalism was to be found in their appeal to the mounting numbers of young people and migrant poor. Occasionally we are able to peer into the dim, dirty light under the low-beamed ceiling and distinguish the customers of a tippling house. On the evening of 29 July 1606 in the 'George', an unlicensed house at New Romney, Samuel Wood the host, aged 36, held a supper. The eldest man there was John Hunt, aged 39 and town serjeant, but the other guests were younger and much less respectable: a migrant baker had come from Rolvenden, two journeymen shoemakers, one aged 27, from nearby, and three youths who were servants in New Romney; another guest was John Neale, a butcher of Fulham, aged about 30, who had been looking for service 'but not finding any caused him to seek for work in haying'. Later they were joined by John Harvey, a rippier nicknamed 'Jack with the pouch', who was about the age of Neale. Alehouses were primarily a masculine preserve and poor men, especially in times of distress, went there for alcoholic release—leaving their family and kin, it was said, to destitution. A classic example was that of Jane, wife of Nicholas Saffrey of Dover, who complained her husband beat her about the face and arms so that she was bloody 'for no other cause than her asking him for money to provide for bread for her and her children'. When she went to call him out of an unlicensed alehouse he threatened to knock her over and the same week he pawned his tools to another victualler. 'Her husband,' she continued, 'is a common frequenter of alehouses and spends most part of the money he gets there that she and her children do want at home.' The wife of Robert Kirby, also of Dover, complained that she was several times turned away from an alehouse although she knew her husband was there. The common alehouse stood as a constant repudiation of the kinship hegemony and respectable hierarchy of urban society.[57]

The suburb was the near-paradise of the immigrant squatter in the big town. Here he or she might sleep under a hedgerow or on the street by a house door or next a church porch or in an alley-shed called a penthouse or even in an empty tenement as a squatter.[58] If the immigrant had a few pennies he or she might hire a room for the infamous penny rents. Partitioning houses became common in order to exploit the pressure for cheap accommodation. At Sandwich in 1578 the governing body prohibited inhabitants from subdividing houses and offering rooms to newcomers.[59] The immigrants lived chiefly on alms and perhaps the odd job of running messages, for which there was often a hopeful ring around the door of the rich man. Grace Goodacke and Margaret Bassocke were widows dwelling in the slum area of St Alphege parish in Canterbury for a year in 1562 and went abroad from door to door in the wealthier parts of the city. 'Mother Bassocke of extreme necessity goes from door to door begging with her pot in her hand for drink with also a basket for her meat and sometimes uses her lap or apron instead of the basket.' Poor immigrants slept saturated in squalor: two immigrant paviours, brothers, hired a house in St Mildreds, Canterbury, and lived there with their mother; they slept all together in the same bed 'having but one pair of sheets' and no 'coverlet or blanket to lay upon them other than their own clothes', and being but 'very poor folk' they spent all they could get 'to the common relief'. They denied committing incest with their mother aged 60.[60] The migrant labourer dwelling in the suburbs would have been hard pressed to find a straw bed and a pot for cooking, as well as the clothes he wore.[61] Not surprisingly, the Canterbury suburbs saw the greatest concentration of squatters and misery mixed with a high incidence of criminals and a lower than average size of household.[62]

Subsistence migration appears to have been largely a new phenomenon in sixteenth-century Kent. There is very little evidence for substantial numbers of migrant paupers in fifteenth-century urban society.[63] By the 1540s it is beginning to get under way but the real surge was in the reign of Elizabeth.[64] Local factors may have accelerated its development in Kent, including the steady disafforestation of the Weald and perhaps the Downlands, depopulation in Sheppey and Romney Marsh, in both cases probably the consequence of intensive farming, and the later contraction of the Wealden iron industry. The maritime physiognomy of the county with its growing coastal traffic and naval establishments may have encouraged movement both within and to the county.[65] But the original sin was not peculiarly Kentish as the large number of non-Kentish immigrants in our earlier analysis testify. William Harrison, whose *Description of England* (1577) was dedicated to the Kentish magnate William, Lord Cobham, explained that vagrancy was caused either through other men's occasion or through their own default. By the former he meant agricultural exploitation and by the latter that leisure-preference of part of a pre-urbanized populace which radical Protestants condemned as vice. More important, doubtless, was another factor he touches on: 'the great increase of people in these days'. Sixteenth-century England saw a large-scale increase in population, followed by an inadequate increase in agricultural and industrial production, a land shortage and massive unemployment. It was an economy with depressingly few 'intervening opportunities' for the migrant once he was on the road. Occasionally we can glimpse the actual processes of *subsistence migration*. Humfrey Gibbons, a labourer, was questioned at New Romney in September 1596. He said he had been married at Godmersham near Canterbury ten years before and then dwelt at Chilham for three or four years—'all this time he kept a carriage'. During the 1590s, a time of escalating economic crisis, Gibbons suffered a fall (perhaps he lost his wife about this time for she is no longer mentioned) and had to move again, this time into West Kent, to Farleigh, where he worked for three years 'by the day'. Then he appears to have recovered enough to farm a small-holding at Sutton Valence, having six or seven acres in his occupation, whereof he sowed two-and-a-half acres with oats, one acre with peas and the rest with summer fallow. But three-and-a-half acres was a meagre defence against the dreadful harvest of 1596 which precipitated his migration from countryside to New Romney; in the week before he arrived we find him borrowing money from a butcher to pay towards his rent. His choice of New Romney was possibly determined by the fact that he had worked in the vicinity earlier in the year as a harvest labourer.[66]

The poorer migrant tended to move on his or her own and was thereby more flexible, more able to move far at short notice to secure employment. Katherine Knight of Hythe said she lived apart from her family 'for want of means . . . each making shift for their own employment'. In times of prolonged crisis, however, wife joined husband and the whole family sometimes came out on to the road, the young and the elderly being carried pick-a-back.[67] This happened in the 1590s, in the 1620s and probably in the 1630s.[68] Only stark poverty can explain the migration of Mary Wilson, a widow, with her four small children from Wendon in Essex into the towns of North Kent or of Henry Holsted, his wife Mary, and their children from Hatfield in Hertfordshire in 1638. *Chain migration*, where the idea of taking to the road swept an impoverished area, led several families to travel together. For instance, two families comprising twelve members, almost all children, tramped from Malvern in Worcestershire into the Kentish Weald in the 1630s. This band was led by two Amazons, Katherine Constable and Mary Washington, the latter giving birth on the road to her youngest daughter, Elizabeth, who was only six weeks old when the party was stopped and sent back to Malvern.[69]

In the depths of distress *subsistence migration* might involve the whole family, but in general the typical poor migrant travelled very much on his own, eschewing the multiplex relationships of kin-oriented society. This picture conflicts radically with that of sixteenth-century commentators who emphasize the secret society of vagrancy —the companies and recognized leaders, the hierarchy of roguery, the upright men, swaddlers, dells and doxes, and the language of rogues called 'pelting speech'. Such a substratum of organized roguery certainly existed; Silvester Fittell, arrested in August 1596, described how he met a 'certain company' at Coventry while going to Ireland from Kent where he had just escaped arrest for theft. The five together 'determined to make booty in Kent' and there entered gentlemen's houses, Fittell adding, 'there were 14 or 15 of the company and that they were about Rye and the Weald'. Another knot of Canterbury men were said, 'to trade themselves yearly to deceive the common people deceitfully with their imagination in places both far and wide', including Sevenoaks, Hythe, Sandwich and Gravesend.[70] London gangs, dumbers and professional cripples armed with sores, often self-inflicted, swarmed into towns with crude counterfeit passports.[71] David Jones, a Somerset rogue, confessed the seal to his passport 'was carved in wood and put to a writing in parchment at 'Bawton on the Bush' in Oxfordshire, 'by a scholar of Oxford'. Daniel Cheseman in 1597 declared himself to be 'called the Lord of Rogues'.[72] But commentators almost certainly exaggerated the importance of professional roguery. The vast numbers ascribed to their companies were the figment of a febrile imagination. Their language and possibly organization may have owed a little to the gypsy bands who appear prominently in the 1540s as Egyptians. But it is significant that the advent of professional roguery coincided with the same economic crisis for the lower classes which spawned *subsistence migration*. The poor migrant driven by necessity too easily turned occasional criminal—few honest poor could have survived. The 'wild rogue' who told Thomas Harman, 'he was a beggar by inheritance—his grandfather was a beggar, his father was one and he must needs be one by good inheritance', over-stated his case but the chances of the child of a subsistence migrant dragging the same path, perhaps into professional roguery, were terrifyingly good.[73]

Although there was considerable overall mobility in this period, our final question must be, why towns in particular were besieged with large numbers of *subsistence migrants*. As we have seen, this type of migrant was much less preoccupied with the future than escaping the past. In the balance of 'push' and 'pull' factors the former were the harsh reality. His hopes of securing urban employment were glossed by traditional accounts of prosperity there, fostered perhaps by somewhat higher wage-rates in towns. Less mythical than golden gutters were rumours of cheap bread and remnants of food cadged from town markets. The authorities were terrified by the threat to public order concentrated in towns, and channelled grain supplies there.[74] Towns organized relief on a large, sophisticated scale. Grain stocks, work-stocks, hospitals and charitable funds supplemented relief authorized by Elizabethan legislation. Thus by 1600 Canterbury and its suburbs had more than twenty relief funds of different sorts. Schemes devised principally for indigenous poor became counter-productive and attracted the subsistence migrant tramping the countryside. Relying desperately on civic charity parents brought their children into Canterbury and abandoned them. Finally, the urban complex with the confused judicial wasteland that encircled it vitiated strict administrative control. Squatters had a good chance of escaping detection for some time. Moreover, it offered the refuge of anonymity and freedom from prying village pressures. Pregnant servant girls from country areas often came; so Mary Mount walked clumsily to Canterbury from Thanet in 1580.[75]

To summarize, we can say that there were within the migrational pyramid two fundamental patterns of urban mobility in the late sixteenth and early seventeenth centuries in Kent. The first was essentially formalized, short-distance, primarily of rural origin and socially respectable. The second was nomadic, long-distance, with a strong element of urban experience, and overshadowed by the tramping curse of necessity. Already we have seen, however, that this proposition needs serious modification. Within the mass of *subsistence migration* there was a hard core of professional roguery, more organized and structured although in other respects obeying the same pattern as the subsistence migrant. Indeed we must go further and argue that there were certain particular groups of migrants who stand outside these patterns and others who appear as migrational hermaphrodites, combining characteristics of both.

Some of these other migrational types belonged equally to medieval society. Thus the preferment hunting parson or curate combining the long-distance movement of the subsistence migrant with the usually regular contacts of the betterment migrant. The growth of Puritanism, the reorganization of the Catholic Church, and an increasing surplus of jobless graduates greased the run of this professional mobility. Puritanism certainly played a part in the movement of Thomas Wilson, a Cumberland man, who left Cambridge after graduating and held livings at Chawswood and Capel in Surrey, Farlington near Portsmouth, Teddington near London, as well as preaching in Cumberland, before coming to Otham and so Maidstone in Kent.[76] The foreign beggar also owed something to the past, to the medieval pilgrim. We hear of a Knight of Hungary, or of a poor minister's wife from out of the Palatinate country, or of the 4s most properly dispensed to 'a man that came out of the Land of Babylon'.[77] Other sixteenth-century migrants appear as transmuted images of medieval types. The anabaptist saint wandering the countryside without a hat on his head evangelizing, or the recusant gentleman travelling in disguise from place to place were not new migrational phenomena—except in their secularity.[78]

If the itinerant craftsman or specialist had also been a medieval figure the expansion of this kind of professional migration in the sixteenth century in response to the needs of an increasingly sophisticated social and economic order had a new, radical importance—both in numbers and impact. The growth of internal trade entailed a major increase in the numbers of pedlars, chapmen and other itinerant retailers with their own trade routes across counties. In 1566 Sir Thomas Cotton complained of 'a superfluous number of badgers or kidders who buy within this shire divers thousand quarters of grain yearly of the farmers at great prices'. The Kentish grain trade was geared to London and the capital probably marked the limit of the corn-buyer's migrational experience, but the trade of the cattle-drover extended much further into the Western counties and Wales. It grew steadily in the sixteenth century because of increased agricultural specialization and by 1600 the driving trail into Kent from the Marches was well established. In 1592, for instance, Francis Johnson who was born at Oswestry but lived in Canterbury took messages into Wales when he went to Shrewsbury fair to buy cattle.[79]

Increased agricultural specialization stimulated professional migration of this sort. It also demanded large supplies of seasonal labour during the summer months. We saw earlier how betterment migrants returned home to harvest and this may well have been a traditional practice. By the early seventeenth century long-distance harvest migration appears on a growing scale. In 1588 John Dray of Stowting near Romney Marsh travelled forty miles or so to and from Thanet for the harvest. John Ireland came from Essex to the Milton area in 1600 by way of London and in the 1590s three migrants claimed, 'they came all three out of London to seek harvest work' in Kent.[80] Although the London and Essex influx may have been the most important group of harvesters coming south to gather an early harvest before the summer moved north, we have at least one harvester who claimed to have come from Yorkshire 'to seek harvest work'. As Quarter Sessions complained in 1631, 'the country [is] now much pestered with harvesters'.[81]

Another new group of migrants were the progeny of Tudor administrative sophistication. The vast scale of impressment, shipment and desertion in the Elizabethan wars from 1585 to 1603 and the Stuart expeditions of the 1620s gave a massive injection of starving soldiery to *subsistence migration*. Soldiers appear as common marauders, raiding churches and breaking into houses, tramping the road in small, tattered gangs. When there was a show of military discipline they were even more frightening—a band of eighteen soldiers marching from Hertfordshire to Gravesend in the 1590s descended on the town of Brentwood in military array, their banner carried before, and proceeded to terrify the town. The soldier confirmed the reality of long-distance migration, merging as he often did into the ruck of subsistence misery.[82]

Migrants in Kent during this period were almost always English. There were settlements of Dutch and French refugees at Sandwich, Canterbury and Maidstone from the early part of Elizabeth's reign and smaller groups at Dover and Faversham, mainly in the seventeenth century, but once landed they were not especially mobile. Later migration in England was to be dominated by the Scots and to a much greater extent the Irish. Scottish immigration into Kent, mostly by sea down the east coast, was of long standing in the sixteenth century and persists through this period, encouraged by the collier trade and the demand of Continental armies for mercenaries.[83] Of the Irish, Thomas Harman complained in the 1560s, but Irish immigration on any scale does not appear until after the military and natural devastations of the last years of the century. Many Irish made their way through Kent to the Continent—some to join a Catholic seminary and others to fight for the Archduke. At Deal in 1623 seven or eight score Irishmen wanting to sail for Flanders were forced to eat grass and roots because their shipping was delayed and they had no money.[84] For the Southern counties the principal port of entry into England was Bristol, and through Bristol in the 1630s poured a tide of starving Irish driven by the dreadful harvests of the late 1620s. From the 1630s we can probably date the scourge of subsistence emigration amongst the Irish peasantry.[85]

Another new phenomenon in sixteenth-century Kent—and England—was social migration. A house in London, a coach-ride to the Spa, or at least a summer in the county town, was demanded by every gentleman's wife as a social *sine qua non*. Both Maidstone and Canterbury had their cluster of town houses for the country gentry who would come up for quarter sessions, assizes, county elections and the odd meeting of the Commissioners for Sewers. Canterbury made a few pretensions to being a spa town and had a number of well-known doctors. John Norwood, a Thanet gentleman, spent the autumn of 1614 there to recover from sickness and a vicar of Seasalter protested his parish was so unhealthy that he had to stay in Canterbury to recover.[86] Tourism again became popular and Canterbury once more the object of gawking praise. There was also a rush down Watling Street through Canterbury to see the Continent.[87]

The professional migrant with his regular contacts and long-distance moves, the seasonal worker with fewer contacts and less regular moves, the deserting soldier pressed out of his parish and now roaming a strange countryside, the starving Irishman, the secretive Papist and the status-struck migrating gentleman do not fit into any obvious pattern within our migrational pyramid. More properly these groups are represented by its external faces or facets. Not only did their increase in this period complete the picture of a society on the move but they helped accelerate the mobility of our two major groups of migrants. The expansion of alehouses owed much to the demands of professional and social migrants. Both may also have led to a gradual improvement in roads and communications. In Kent the post appears well organized from the mid-sixteenth century and wagons and coaches were increasingly in evidence by 1640.[88] In 1617 'the waggoner's coach' carried an Irish recusant from Gravesend to Dover and poorer migrants may have cadged lifts. Complaints about the quality of main roads protest too often and too much to be totally convincing. The main problem was undoubtedly the huge burden of new traffic they had to carry. Anyway many migrants travelled along more accessible by-ways and some on board coastal shipping—the last a consequence of the growth of local trade.[89]

Seasonal and professional migration served to bridge the gap of ignorance for the long-distance migrant beyond the help of his kin, and without the contacts of the local migrant. Harvest migration may often have led to permanent resettlement. John Ireland left his wife in London when he came out of Essex to harvest in North Kent; the following spring he got a house and brought his wife down to live with him near Sittingbourne. John Sabin who lived near Faversham used to drive cattle from Wales and once brought with him a Newport boy whom he apprenticed in the neighbourhood. Isaac Hancock who drove cattle from Worcestershire into Kent settled at Fordwich.[90] In our analysis of ecclesiastical court statements two of our three main lines of long-distance migration coincided with the routes of professional or seasonal migrants—of drovers through the Thames valley into the west, and of harvesters from East Anglia.

To conclude this analysis of migrational structure we must relate the two major patterns of mobility to each other and try to put them in perspective. *Betterment migration*, with its stress on the ebb and flow from countryside to neighbouring town and back, was not new in the sixteenth century. It was important in the fifteenth century and may well have been a constant feature of rural-urban relations in traditional, pre-industrial society. However, during the sixteenth century increased social mobility may have accentuated this kind of migration. *Subsistence migration*, with its tendency to greater distance, urban to urban movement, was largely a sixteenth-century phenomenon. It followed the downward path of wage-rates and the leaps and bounds of food prices, themselves symptomatic of the growing surge of population. Although coming in waves its tidal stain rose steadily into the early seventeenth century. Already by 1640 long-distance migration may have begun to be less common. Partly this reflected incipient declining demographic pressure, partly the impact of accumulating settlement restrictions, and partly the diversion of subsistence migrants to the New World. Even so, for most of the period 1580 to 1640, we see a conjuncture of traditional migrational activity (if somewhat accentuated) with a new pattern of geographical mobility. This coincidence created an immigration crisis of severe proportions for Kentish towns.[91]

In the final section of this paper we must consider, briefly, the consequences for Kentish towns of the immigration crisis discussed above. The most obvious was probably demographic. Most towns, despite uncertain or contracting economies, appear to have experienced a considerable growth in population in this period—at least part of which was caused by immigration. It is impossible to establish the rate of growth and it would be dangerous in any case to see a close correlation of population expansion and migrant influx. Although Faversham may well have had 200 immigrants in the difficult years from 1592 to 1595 these same years saw, apparently, an exceptional number of deaths caused by plague mounting on economic distress.[92] Even so, town populations did grow with the help of immigration. Henry Clement of Deal believed, in 1620, 'there are twice so many houses and more than twice so many inhabitants more now' than thirty years before, and this he blamed on incomers.[93] There are similar signs in other towns—at least into the 1620s.[94] However, overall urban expansion of population masked disproportionate growth in certain social sectors—especially among the poorest sort. The fragile ladder of the urban hierarchy saw its lower rungs engulfed in bottomless poverty.

Although probably fewer in numbers than poor immigrants the influx of respectable migrants attracted a cumulative wealth of restriction. In January 1583 the corporation of Canterbury sought to clamp down on the numbers of freemen being admitted complaining of 'the daily decaying of the inhabitants of this city'. At Rochester the fines for foreigners and freemen were hiked up at a pitch of ferocity fired by panic from the depths of the civic psychosis. Similar attempts to discourage respectable immigrant traders occur at Maidstone in 1604, 1614 and 1626.[95] In response to civic restriction there was considerable evasion of town controls. At Canterbury the fines on foreigners cease as a series in the 1590s and elsewhere, at Faversham, Milton and Maidstone, there are reports of immigrant traders and craftsmen competing with freemen on a large scale.[96] In 1598 the Faversham shoemakers complained that immigrants setting up business deprived them of work and 'if our science decay then we may go beg and steal'. At Maidstone in the 1620s there was determined opposition by strangers to paying fines for freedom.[97]

Not surprisingly, the attack on urban oligarchies in Kent in the early seventeenth century was often led by respectable newcomers. Faversham is a good example. An attempt between 1610 and 1619 to reorganize the guild structure and create a general gild under the effective control of the Mayor and Jurats was overthrown in 1619 by three men—Boys Ower and Thomas Napleton, yeomen, and Edward Hales, a gentleman. Ower had arrived in Faversham about 1612 coming from nearby Ospringe, Napleton had moved to Faversham from Bettshanger in 1611, and Hales came from Chilham some time after 1603. A frontal attack on mayoral control at Faversham, in 1617, was led by Thomas Bixe who had lived in Faversham for about ten years.[98] Outside the enchanted circle of civic power from which he was excluded the respectable immigrant wavered with a gnawing sense of political frustration. The years before 1640 saw the steady disintegration of the customary fabric of the political community in Kentish towns.

Another major field of impact was administration. The urban problem of the poor became overwhelmingly the problem of the immigrant poor and as a problem it came to preoccupy urban concern. An apocalyptic future was envisaged by Sandwich in 1578, seeing many migrants coming there:

> besides their poverty burdened with great numbers of children,
> for whom God calling away the parents charity requires and the
> bonds of nature compel each good person to provide. . . .[so] that
> whole heaps of such poor with their families will intrude and
> bring themselves into this town and so far pester the same with
> such poverty as men in ability shall want wherewith to help them.

There was a frenetic endeavour to exclude or expel poor immigrants. In 1572 Canterbury appointed beadles to arrest beggars and twelve years later the Faversham overseers were ordered to draw up a list of those to be expelled. In the 1590s there was a rash of prohibitions and purges in almost every town in Kent. The early seventeenth century, significantly, saw the reorganization of the Maidstone gilds on a ward basis—their principal duty being to exclude poor immigrants.[99] Everywhere the administrative restrictions on poor migrants foreshadowed the Settlement legislation of 1662.

Despite this rattling skeleton of prohibition migrants still managed (albeit with growing difficulty) to throng the streets of town and city, worsening the problem of indigenous poverty. At Canterbury there was an early attempt to distinguish between native and migrant, the former wearing scutcheons, but this practice soon broke down. The neighbourliness of alms-giving had to give way under immigrant pressure to the compulsory rate. Houses of Correction (called at Canterbury, the 'Harlot's Harbour'), work stocks and the like were established at considerable expense in most towns. In the 1630s Faversham shipped some of its poor to Virginia. For all these efforts many towns appear to be in severe difficulties by the 1620s. The parish of Holy Cross in Canterbury complained, they were so 'overpressed by the multitude of poor people thither resorting . . . that now they are not of sufficient ability to give the aged and lame such relief . . . as they are bound to do'.[100] Indeed the parochial system of poor relief at Canterbury disintegrated as parish followed parish in claiming it was unable to relieve its poor. Determined attempts by city magistrates to force the machinery of relief into action led to much resentment.[101] The poor migrant helped to erode civic neighbourliness, cast doubts on the administrative credibility of the political oligarchy, disrupted town finances and so, perhaps, accentuated the economic troubles of declining urban centres.

Excluded from the political and social arena the poor migrant gravitated to the alehouse, the polar opposite of the aldermanic bench and the gild, the antithesis of ordered, respectable society.[102] But this was more voting with one's feet than taking an active role in politics. There was only political desperation in the words of Richard Evans, a Canterbury squatter: 'I am an Englishman and must dwell somewhere.' Occasionally, of course, we hear the migrant labourer raise the pathetic shout of sedition. It was a poor migrant who declared at New Romney that, 'he would make the highest the lowest' and that 'he would cause all Kent to be plucked out by the ears'. It was another migrant who declared at Canterbury in 1596 that the Queen, like all the maids in England, was not a virgin. The suburbs of the large city filled with squatters sometimes poured out their resentment in riots —as in the Canterbury grain riot of 1596.[103] But although immigrant distress occasionally served as a spark for political crisis, high mobility discouraged a strong political cross-current among the poor. The new-comer was a man of questionable status, whether parson or pauper, so leadership had to come from outside, perhaps from a frustrated betterment migrant who had secured a leading place in the street community.[104] Such a man was Roger Fennold or Vennoll, a lawyer's clerk, who had been born in Battle, Sussex, but had lived in Canterbury for twenty years, and who organized the Canterbury riot of 1596. At the crucial moment he fled the city. Leadership from other social groupings was too easily paralysed by the actual spectre of poverty on the march.[105]

Immigration in Kent played an important role in the decay of the urban identity and the erosion of community consciousness—without precipitating political revolution. But what was the impact of the town on the migrant? As we have seen, the betterment migrant was fixed in a formalized relationship of town and countryside, a relationship which was not very susceptible to major change. The long-distance migrant was, perhaps, more open to the urban impact but even here it would be dangerous to overstress the radical effect of the urban experience, outside the influence of London and the very largest urban centres. More important was the move itself. The erosion of kinship and the family ties may well have been one of the more important consequences of long-distance migration, feminine emancipation possibly one of the most startling manifestations of this development. Women tended to prefer short-distance migration, but good numbers tramped long distances across the countryside from town to town, playing a hand in petty trade and fending for themselves. In 1635 'three travelling women' came to Dover; one was a Southwark widow who sold small wares to keep them alive, another was her sister-in-law from Wrexham and the third the widow's servant girl from Lydd in Kent; the widow had buried a male child at Lydd a few days before.[106]

Based as it is on limited evidence for some of the Kentish towns, migration in the late sixteenth and early seventeenth centuries appears to have had a determinant role in urban society, affecting not only the demographic landscape but the political superstructure and the fabric of community consciousness. But perhaps the most important conclusion of this study concerns demographic technique. Mobility in the Kentish condition is not only large-scale but volatile—fluctuating from place to place and from year to year. There is a need for both a topography and chronology of migrational activity. Consequently, problems are raised for other demographic techniques. Can we still continue to employ aggregative analysis, with all its already undoubted drawbacks, for a meaningful study of population, even less of urban population? The churchwarden who did not know the names of communicants, 'by reason there are many servants and others that do go out and come into the parish before the year be expired', was probably even more hard-pressed to ensure that the demographic droppings (births, marriages and deaths) of these migrant creatures—living in a half-world of their own—were recorded in the parish register.[107] The demographer uncertain of the extent of mobility for which to make statistical adjustment is in a precarious position. Similarly there are problems for demographic exercises based on family reconstitution. Some have already been noted elsewhere.[108] The most obvious is that fully reconstituted families are likely to be the least mobile, or, in other words, the reconstruction of mobile families can only be partial because of the inconstant quality of parish records overall. But on the evidence of this paper we must add two further points. Firstly, the family immobile over more than one generation is in this period exceptional and likely to have peculiar social and demographic characteristics. Secondly, even if we accept that partial reconstitution can capture the demographic structure of the local migrant there remains outside its net the long-distance mobile, the most dynamic demographic phenomenon in the years before 1640. The whole problem of migration needs urgent and extensive examination.

Notes

1 For valuable comments on an earlier draft of this paper I am grateful to Mr C. S. L. Davies, Dr A. Macintyre and Mr P. J. Waller. The evidence for general comments on towns in Kent made in this paper will be found in P. A. Clark, *Kentish Urban Society* (to be published).

2 C. Read, ed., *William Lambarde and Local Government. His 'Ephemeris' and Twenty-Nine Charges to Juries and Commissions* (New York, 1962), p. 114; Kent AO, Sa/AC 5, fol. 6; Maidstone Museum (hereafter cited as MM), Town Archives, Burghmote Book B, fol. 15.

3 For instance: Canterbury Cathedral Library (hereafter cited as CCL), City MSS, AC 3, fol. 310; MM, Burghmote Book B, fol. 162 and Miscellaneous Papers 10/33.

4 Rich, *Ec.H.R.*, 2nd series, II (1949–50), 262; Laslett and Harrison, 'Clayworth and Cogenhoe', *Historical Essays 1600–1750 Presented to David Ogg* (ed. H. E. Bell and E. L. Ollard, 1963), chap. vii; Cornwall, 'Evidence of Population Mobility in the Seventeenth Century', *B.I.H.R.*, XL (1967), 143–52.

5 L. Stone, 'Social Mobility in England 1500–1700', *P. & P.*, no. 33 (1966), 30; E. A. Wrigley, 'A Simple Model of London's Importance in

Changing English Society and Economy 1650–1750', *P. & P.*, no. 37 (1967), esp. 45–55; E. G. Ashby, 'Some Aspects of Parochial Life in the City of London from 1429–1529' (unpublished M.A. thesis, University of London, 1950), p. 486.

6 Styles, 'The Evolution of the Law of Settlement,' *Univ. Birmingham Hist. J.*, IX (1963), 33–63; Buckatzsch, 'Places of Origin of a Group of Immigrants into Sheffield 1624–1799', *Ec.H.R.*, 2nd series, II (1949–50), 303–6.

7 J. C. Russell, *British Medieval Population* (Albuquerque, 1948), p. 314 *et seq.*; Raftis, *Tenure and Mobility* (Toronto, 1964), esp. p. 136 *et seq.*; Thrupp, *The Merchant Class of Medieval London* (Chicago, 1948), p. 206 *et seq.*

8 R. A. Pelham, 'The Immigrant Population of Birmingham 1686–1726', *Trans. Birmingham Archaeolog. Soc.*, LXI (1940), 45–80; A. Redford, *Labour Migration in England 1800–1850* (1926), *passim*. The only attempt at synthesis for the early modern period is by Buckatzsch, 'The Constancy of Local Populations and Migration in England before 1800', *Population Studies*, V (1951–2), 62–9.

9 A few stray volumes are at Lambeth Palace Library (series VC III/I) but these have been ignored for the purposes of this study. The Canterbury series used here is CCL, X, 11, 1–16, 19; the transcripts were the work of F. W. Tyler and W. P. Blore in the 1930s—they are excellent, especially for place names. The Maidstone series is Kent AO, PRC 39/39–52. The division of the original, single series of deposition books came in the nineteenth century with the separation of probate from other papers of the diocesan courts: the deposition books do not distinguish one class of business from another and were broken up in random fashion. From the year 1628 almost all the volumes are at Kent AO.

10 There are some problems in testing the accuracy of statements. Omissions are by definition almost beyond discovery. However, by comparing statements made at different times, and by using lists of freemen and parish registers, it would seem there was no considerable margin of error. For instance, Ralph Grove deposing in 1602 said he was born at Henley-on-Thames forty years before and had come to St Mary Northgate, Canterbury, about 1582. In fact, he was christened at Henley a year or so before 1562 but he was certainly a servant of John Boys, who lived in St Mary Northgate, by 1582. (CCL, X. 11, 8, fol. 24; Bodl. MS. Top Oxon c. 525; J. M. Cowper, *The Roll of the Freemen of the City of Canterbury* (Canterbury, 1903); CCL, X, 10, 20, fol. 204.) Court officials included the offspring of Archbishops Cranmer and Parker and the local historian William Somner. The deposition books used here appear to have been kept more carefully than those of the Sussex courts

(now at the East Sussex Record Office, Chichester) (*ex inform.* Mr P. Wilkinson).

11 In a few cases one detail, usually occupation, is omitted in the statement. Where possible this has been rectified from other sources, otherwise the lacuna is noted at an appropriate place.

12 C. W. Chalklin, *Seventeenth Century Kent* (1965), pp. 24, 30–1, for some suggested population figures.

13 The kernel of craft and trade groupings was derived from W. G. Hoskins, *Provincial England* (1963), p. 94.

14 The large number in group 1 is partly explained by an overlap with the most prosperous merchants among the distributive trades, especially in Canterbury where their success was consecrated with civic office which carried gentle status. For a comment on the value of this occupational analysis *vide* note 23.

15 There was a constant but slight fall in the mean age of deponents during the period.

16 Other possible sources for migrational analysis include muster rolls, apprenticeship records and censuses. The last are probably the most reliable but least informative; muster rolls are probably the least trustworthy of Elizabethan administrative records; and apprenticeship registrations are not only limited in scope but less reliable than they first appear—here they are used only to supplement or confirm conclusions from other sources.

17 Of course the age-composition of the population was weighted towards the young, but the incidence of migration in the most active years (11 to 30) was greater than we should expect from the overall age-structure (Laslett, *The World We Have Lost* (1965), p. 103).

18 Five miles was added to distances travelled by migrants crossing the Thames below Gravesend ferry.

19 There was a similar pattern among the Canterbury women (the only town for which there is a significant sample): over 50 per cent came from a radius of from six to fifteen miles.

20 St Ch 8/194/4; Kent AO, PRC 39/9, fol. 18v.

21 J. Thirsk, ed., *The Agrarian History of England and Wales*, IV (Cambridge, 1967), pp. 9–10, 20, 610; E. Kerridge, *The Agricultural Revolution* (1967), p. 159 *et seq.*; of poor immigrants in Norwich in the early 1570s one-sixth had come from the north (J. F. Pound, 'An Elizabethan Census of the Poor', *Univ. Birmingham Hist. J.*, IX (1962), 139).

22 Wrigley, *op. cit.*, 46, 49. The number of native inhabitants of our towns who spent part of their life there and then came home is also quite small. This may be a reflection of London's power as a springboard to send migrants even further from their native counties.

23 The table of occupational groupings used here is by no means ideal as

an indicator of urban wealth and status. One could possibly devise a more sensitive scheme resting on an analysis of inventorial wealth but this might well cause more problems than it solved.

24 On the mobility of servants: Laslett and Harrison, *op. cit.*, p. 179.

25 Canterbury-born emigrants since returned are included in this sample.

26 Wrigley, *op. cit.*, 50 *et seq.* For examples of the urban image of the provincial town: CCL, X, 1, 11, fol. 133; M. V. Jones, 'The Political History of the Parliamentary Boroughs of Kent' (unpublished Ph.D. thesis, University of London, 1967), p. 18 and note 3.

27 Adams lists cities, towns and substantial market towns in capital letters. For a comment on the value of his list *vide* D. V. Glass, 'Two Papers on Gregory King', in D. V. Glass and D. E. C. Eversley, eds, *Population in History* (1965), pp. 186–8.

28 Other general models of migration are discussed in J. A. Jackson, ed., *Migration* (Cambridge, 1969), chaps iv, v.

29 MM, Burghmote Book A, and Miscellaneous Papers 2/1; Kent AO, Fa/RA 3.

30 Cowper, *op. cit.*, p. 228; Kent AO, PRC 10/20, fol. 18–19v.; Kent AO, Fa/RA 3 *passim* for the kin ties of apprentices; also Dover, Corporation MSS, Minute Book Mary and Elizabeth (reversed), fol. 34 *et seq.*

31 Kent AO, QM/SB 899; CCL, Miscellaneous MSS, History of the Claggett Family: George was mayor in 1609, 1622 and 1632, William was sheriff in 1623.

32 Laslett, *op. cit.*, p. 21. Mr Laslett is not very explicit in his definition of 'patriarchalism'.

33 Kent AO, PRC 39/34, fol. 69; A. M. Everitt, *The Community of Kent and the Great Rebellion 1640–60* (Leicester, 1966), pp. 47–8.

34 T. Harman, *A Caveat or Warening for Common Cursetors* (ed. F. J. Furnivall, New Shakespeare Soc., 1880), p. 38; Kent AO, NR/JQf. 1/2.

35 CCL, X, 10, 15, fol. 121–8v.; W. Tarbutt, *The Annals of Cranbrook Church* (Cranbrook, 1870–5), part iv, pp. 3–4.

36 Kent AO: PRC 39/34, fol. 152v.; U 1044/Fl, p. 17. For a good example of the kinship role in education: Kent AO, PRC 39/1, fol. 6.

37 E.g. Henry Aldey who had migrated to Canterbury from Wingham forty years before was owed money at his death by John Churchman of Wingham, a relative (Kent AO, PRC 39/11, fol. 57; PRC 10/20, fol. 1). The importance of rural indebtedness in nineteenth-century Ireland is described by C. M. Arensberg, *The Irish Countryman* (New York, 1950), pp. 172–4. To some extent successful local migrants with strong kin ties were self-defining. The less successful or poorer local migrant was unable to fulfil, socially or economically, his role in the rural-urban relationship. Thus he became less respectable and further diminished his chance of urban success.

38 BM, Lansdowne MS. 235, fol. 8v. Probate accounts of administrators reveal the considerable scale of kin (and neighbourly) entertainment possible at funerals: e.g. Kent AO: PRC 20/2, fol. 27v.; PRC 20/1, fol. 154v. Seventeenth-century Irish funeral wakes are described by S. O. Suilleabhain, *Irish Wake Amusements* (Cork, 1967), p. 13 *et seq.*

39 CCL, X, 6, 7, fol. 257v.; X, 11, 3, fol. 28.

40 For a significant parallel in a Central African context *vide* J. C. Mitchell, 'The Concept and Use of Social Networks', in J. C. Mitchell, ed., *Social Networks in Urban Situations* (Manchester, 1969), p. 28.

41 Kent AO, PRC 39/17, fol. 87v.

42 Raftis, *op. cit.*, p. 153 *et seq.*; I owe the latter information to Mr Andrew Butcher.

43 R. H. Tawney and E. Power, eds, *Tudor Economic Documents* (1935), I, 339.

44 The urban/rural wage differential is very difficult to establish but the Canterbury regulations of 1594 show markedly higher wages than those proclaimed for the county in 1589; this may or may not reflect higher prices: P. L. Hughes and J. F. Larkin, eds, *Tudor Royal Proclamations*, III (1969), pp. 36–8, 138–41. The confusion of contemporaries is exemplified by the difference between Harrison who contrasted urban prosperity with rural indigence (1577), and Hitchcock who emphasized the poverty of townsfolk (1580). (W. Harrison, *Description of England* (ed. F. J. Furnivall, New Shakespeare Soc., 1877), part i, pp. 259, 216 n. 1.)

45 Kent AO, Fa/JQs 46; CCL, X, 4, 4, part i, fol. 129v.; Lambeth Palace Library, VC III/1/4, fol. 24.

46 J. Thirsk, *op. cit.*, p. 435; Harrison, *op. cit.*, part i, p. 213, stresses the seasonal nature of woodland squatting.

47 Kent AO, NR/JQ, f. 1/2. In some cases the subsistence migrant even before going on the tramp may have not been a full member of an effective kinship group, and this was a factor in his or her migration (*vide*, Jackson, *op. cit.*, p. 114).

48 Kent AO, NR/JQp 1/18.

49 Kent AO, PRC 39/42, fol. 180v.; NR/JQp 1/32; Harman, *op. cit.*, p. 77; Kent AO, Fa/JQ e. 11; Dover, Minute Book James I etc., fol. 165; Kent AO, NR/JQp 1/42.

50 The role of the rural alehouse can be seen from a list of customers at the small Harrietsham establishments in 1631: most came from a radius of eight miles but at least two were from more distant Sheppey; two of the four houses may have catered especially for travellers (CCL, X, 6, 4, fol. 195). For the similar function of the urban beer bar in Kisenyi, Kampala *vide*, A. W. Southall, 'Kinship, Friendship and the Network of

Relations in Kisenyi', in A. W. Southall, ed., *Social Change in Modern Africa* (Oxford, 1961), p. 227.

51 A. M. Everitt, 'Social Mobility in Early Modern England', *P. & P.*, no. 33, 69–70; Kent AO, QM/SB 905; Sa/ZB 3/14.

52 At Sandwich in the 1590s the average period of trading for victuallers was half that of others engaged in the food and drink business (Kent AO, Sa/ZB 3/14); Sa/AC 6, fol. 356v.; CCL, City MSS, JQ 1556; Dover, Minute Book James I etc., fol. 169; CCL, JQ 1611; Kent AO, Fa/JV 60 *et seq.*

53 E.g. CCL, JQ 1620's; SP 12/118/31; CCL, JQ 1596; Rochester City MSS, Ro/JQb 1, 2.

54 There is not much evidence that house signs had any special significance for migrants in this period as they did later, although we should expect Scotsmen to have congregated at the 'St Andrews Cross' kept by the Scot Andrew Davy at Dover (J. B. Jones, *Annals of Dover* (Dover, 1916), pp. 415–17).

55 Kent AO, Fa/JQr 1/4, 6; Dover, Minute Book 1630–59, fol. 79, 83v.; Kent AO, Sa/AC 5, fol. 108v.; CCL: JQ 1626; X, 11, 19, fol. 143.

56 The morris dancers stayed and dressed there; one of them had heard it said, 'that it was never a merry England since men were to go with license' (CCL, JQ 1589); MM, Additional Sessions Papers (1599).

57 Kent AO, NR/JQ f. 1/1, 2; Sa/AC 6, fols 72v.–3; Dover, Minute Book 1630–59, fols 79, 114v.

58 CCL, JQ, 1631; Dover, Minute Book James I etc., fol. 77v.; CCL X, 2, 7, part ii, fol. 126; Kent AO, Fa/JQs 19, 20; St Ch 7/4/10.

59 Kent AO, PRC 39/36, fol. 112v.; PRC 39/20, fol. 33; Sa/AC 5, fol. 122.

60 Kent AO, Fa/JV 46; PRC 39/15, fols 91–2v.; CCL, X, 10, 8, fols 181v., 186; CCL, X, 1, 11, fol. 107; X, 10, 8, fol. 173. Sandwich ascribed its visitation by plague in 1610 to overcrowding caused by immigrants (Kent AO, Sa/AC7, fol. 10).

61 E.g. inventory of a poorer immigrant, John Webbe of St Peter's, Canterbury (Kent AO, PRC 39/40, fol. 58; PRC 10/67, fol. 316).

62 Criminals: based on a survey of extant judicial records; household size: see a discussion of some Elizabethan censuses in P. A. Clark, *Religion, Politics and Society in Kent 1500–1640* (in preparation). Slums also saw a large number of unmarried couples among immigrants (Dover, Minute Book James I etc. (reversed), fol. 37).

63 For Kent *ex inform.* Mr A. Butcher; Raftis, *op. cit.*, p. 172.

64 E.g. BM, Egerton MS 2093, fol. 137 *et seq.* But in the round-up of vagabonds in Kent in 1571 the numbers were still not large (SP 12/80/43, 53).

65 SP 12/93/37; SP 12/75/40; SP 16/312/60; Chalklin, *op. cit.*, p. 131; the Rochester apprenticeship registrations (Rochester, Ro/JA 1/1) which

include many for Chatham dockyard give a good indication of the attraction of naval establishments.

66 Harrison, *op. cit.*, p. 215; Jackson, *op. cit.*, p. 32; Kent AO, NR/JQ f. 1/2 (exam. H. Gibbons).

67 Lambeth Palace Library, VC III/I/22, fol. 233 (see CCL, X, 8, 10, fol. 181v. for another instance of marital separation in pursuit of work); Dover, Minute Book James I etc., fols 189v.–190; Minute Book 1630–59, fol. 86.

68 The presentments for vagrancy at Ightham leet court during the Elizabethan period are usually of single persons, but during the worst period of famine 1593–8 many of those presented were married couples (E. Harrison, 'The Court Rolls . . . of Ightham', *Archaeologia Cantiana*, XLIX (1938), 14–18). In the 1630s, as far as the returns by justices to Assizes are any guide, 1637 with its rapidly deteriorating harvest situation had the highest ratio of multiple groups of migrants (travelling together) to single migrants in the post 1634 period (see the returns for Kent in SP 16).

69 SP 16/393/76; SP 16/314/77.

70 Harrison, *op. cit.*, p. 218; F. Aydelotte, *Elizabethan Rogues and Vagabonds* (reprinted 1967), pp. 26–8; Kent AO, QM/SB 116; CCL, JQ 1568.

71 CCL, JQ, 1600; Kent AO, Sa/AC 6, fol. 239v.; Sa/AC 5, fol. 44; Sa/AC 6, fols 196v.–7.

72 Kent AO, Sa/AC 5, fol. 43v.–4; QM/SB 228.

73 *APC*, II, pp. 448, 452; CCL, F/A 13, fol. 205; Harrison, *op. cit.*, pp. 218, 42.

74 Jackson, *op. cit.*, pp. 65–7; above, note 50; e.g. Rochester, Stafford RO, D. 593, S/4/17; Dover: Dover Minute Book James I etc. (reversed), fol. 70.

75 CCL, F/A 21, fol. 31; Richard Evans and his wife who entered Canterbury in 1601 lived as squatters in an empty house in the suburb of St Martin's for ten days before being discovered (St Ch 7/4/10; CCL, X, 1, 16, fol. 89v. (also X, 2, 10, fol. 86).

76 G. S[winock], *Life and Death of Mr. Thomas Wilson* (1672), pp. 1–8; for an example of the extraordinary mobility of papistical curates, *vide* Kent AO, PRC 39/14, fols 162v.–163. The very mobile schoolmasters were, of course, chrysalid parsons.

77 Kent AO, Fa/ACI, fol. 200; Fa/FAc 62; CCL, F/A 16, fol. 284v.

78 Kent AO, PRC 39/13, fols 159v.–160; J. H. Pollen, ed., 'The Memoirs of Father Robert Persons', *Miscellanea II* (Catholic Record Society, 1906), p. 23. There is also a certain timelessness about the case of a Faversham man who fled the town on a paternity charge, or of a London scrivener who left for Dover, doubtless on his way to sunnier

climes, taking with him £5,000 or so of his clients' money (CCL, X, 5, 6, part i, fol. 60; SP 14/182/13).

79 Everitt, *P. & P.*, no. 33, 68–9; BM, Lansdowne MS. 8, fols 169–v.; Kent AO, QM/SB 1302; PRC 39/14, fol. 177v. For the large volume of driving along Watling Street in the 1620s *vide* Rochester, Ro/ACl, p. 76 *et seq.*

80 Kent AO, PRC 39/13, fol. 22v.; CCL, X, 9, 3, fol. 164; Kent AO, QM/SB 275. Conversely, Kentish harvesters probably followed the harvest north into Essex (PRO, Assizes 35/11/4: I owe this reference to Mr J. Sharpe).

81 Kent AO, NR/JQp 1/35; Q/SOW 1, fol. 32.

82 BM, Addit. MS. 29625, fol. 7; Kent AO, NR/JQ f. 1/2 (exam. H. Moore); QM/SB 145; SP 12/154/10; Stafford RO, D. 593 S/4/35/5.

83 By the 1630s members of the Maidstone congregation were almost indistinguishable from their native counterparts (SP 16/286/85). BM, Egerton MS. 2093, fol. 40–v.; Kent AO, Fa/ACl, fol. 200.

84 Harman, *op. cit.*, p. 82; E. Melling, *Kentish Sources: the Poor* (Maidstone, 1964), p. 19; SP 14/170/4; SP 14/143/73.

85 Kent AO, Fa/FAc 56; H. R. Plomer, ed., *Churchwardens Accounts, Strood* (Kent Records, 1927), pp. 179, 184. Robert Cluett, a shoemaker, and his wife married in Youghal about 1632; 'they made no dinner but what victuals they had' they ate together, and so were compelled to leave Ireland and come to Devon; from there they travelled to London, Strood, Canterbury and Dover (Dover, Minute Book 1630–59, fol. 87v.).

86 Everitt, *The Community of Kent*, p. 21; MM, Misc. Papers 10/33; Jones, *op. cit.*, p. 15; A. Hussey, 'Visitations of the Archdeacon of Canterbury', *Archaeologia Cantiana*, XXVI (1904), 28; Lambeth Palace Library, VC III/I/22, fol. 254.

87 BM, Harleian MS. 1026, fol. 32; L. G. Wickham Legg, ed., 'Relation of a Short Survey of the Western Counties (1635)', *Camden Miscellany XVI* (Camden Society, 1936), 11–20; J. W. Stoye, *English Travellers Abroad 1604–1667* (1952), *passim*.

88 Everitt, *P. & P.*, no. 33, 69; J. Crofts, *Packhorse, Wagon and Post* (1967), pp. 7, 65, 123, 125; by 1598 there were regular wagons to London from Canterbury using alehouses as lading places (St Ch 8/12/3).

89 SP 14/94/54 (1); for the role of carriers bringing children to London: BM, Lansdowne MS. 169, fol. 132; Rochester, Ro/JQb 1 (exam. A. Benet). There is no satisfactory discussion of the impact of the 1555 legislation on road maintenance, but see F. G. Emmison in *Essex Review*, LXII (1955), 15–25, 211–34 for a fine piece of academic fence sitting.

90 CCL, X, 9, 3, fol. 164; Kent AO, PRC 39/15, fols 89, 91–2v.; QM/SB 1302.

91 A rough comparison of deposition statements made before and after 1628 suggests some decline of long-distance migration in the later period.

92 Chalklin, *op. cit.*, pp. 30–1; Kent AO, Fa/JV 44 (a list of incoming (?) heads of households); CCL, Bishop's Transcripts, Faversham.

93 CCL, X, 11, 13, fol. 301v.; 'divers small cottages' were erected towards the castle about this time (SP 16/166/30).

94 E.g. Dover, Minute Book James I etc. (reversed), fol. 61.

95 CCL, AC/3, fol. 56; Rochester, Customal, fols. 55, 74, 74v.; Ro/ACl, pp. 93–5; MM, Burghmote Book B, fols. 2, 32v., 93.

96 The Intrantes fines cease after 1597–8 (CCL, F/A 20, fol. 250v.). There is no evidence that foreigners were being taxed in other ways. Kent AO, QM/SB 516.

97 Kent AO, Fa/JV 48; *Maidstone Records* (Maidstone, 1926), p. 84.

98 SP 14/111/128–9; Ower: Kent AO, PRC 39/32, fol. 211v.; Napleton: CCL, X, 11, 13, fol. 78v.; Hales: X, 11, 19, fol. 183v.; SP 14/93/14(1); Bixe: X, 11, 15, fol. 133. Earlier Napleton may have defended poor commoners' rights in the neighbouring forest of Faversham Blean, later he certainly denounced the king (St Ch 8/194/4; BM, Egerton MS. 2584, fol. 279v.). Ower became an active parliamentarian. The Faversham oligarchy was breaking up under this pressure by the 1620s, and there were similar developments at Sandwich, Canterbury and possibly Dover.

99 Kent AO, Sa/AC 5, fol. 122; CCL, AC/2, fol. 258v.; Kent AO, Fa/AC3, fol. 14; NR/JQ f. 1/2; Sa/AC6, fol. 245v.; MM, Burghmote Book A, fol. 62; *Maidstone Records*, p. 80.

100 CCL: F/A15, fol. 75v.; AC/3, fol. 180; Kent AO, Fa/AC 4, fol. 5; QM/SB 1269.

101 CCL, JQ/01, *passim* and JQ 1626, 1634; JQ 1632.

102 For a parallel politico-social tension in the former Stanleyville (Belgian Congo) between the establishment 'club' and the immigrant drinking house, see V. G. Pons, 'Two Small Groups in Avenue 21', *Social Change in Modern Africa*, pp. 206–15.

103 St Ch. 7/4/10; Kent AO, NR/JQ f. 1/2 (exam. J. Church); CCL, JQ 1596 (exam. Th. Batchelor); this disturbance is analysed in Clark, *Religion, Politics and Society in Kent* (in preparation).

104 For examples of distrust of the newcomer: Kent AO, PRC 39/13, fol. 19v.; CCL, X, 10, 7, fol. 43.

105 The almost pathological hatred of Quakerism in the 1650s grew from its propagation by, and appeal to, poor migrants (especially in the north); from the fear of militant, banded migrancy.

106 K. V. Thomas, 'Women and the Civil War Sects', in T. Aston, ed.,

Crisis in Europe (1965), pp. 317–40, discusses the impact of religious radicalism on the role of the woman; Dover, Minute Book 1630–59, fol. 57v.

107 CCL, X, 5, 6, part i, fol. 9v.; for criticism of aggregative analysis see M. W. Flinn, 'Population in History', *Ec.H.R.*, 2nd series, XX (1967), 141–2.

108 E. A. Wrigley, 'Family Reconstitution', in E. A. Wrigley, ed., *An Introduction to English Historical Demography* (1966), esp. pp. 147–9.

5

Poverty and politics in Salisbury
1597–1666

Paul Slack

> You Inhabitants of Salisbury . . . amongst you . . . I am
> assured . . . that there are many who (with religious piety, open
> hands and relenting hearts) doe acknowledge that your goods are
> but lent in trust unto you, and doe patiently beare the over-
> burthensome relieving of many hundreds of poore wretches
> which (were it not for your charity) would perish in your streets.
> John Taylor, *A Discovery by Sea from London to Salisbury* (1623)[1]

The intellectual and social origins of changing attitudes towards
poverty in the sixteenth and seventeenth centuries continue to arouse
debate and controversy. Was the transition from individual and ecclesiastical relief of the needy by alms and 'hospitality' to increasingly
complex regulation of the poor by statute, by-law and penal institution, the 'new medicine for poverty' in Tawney's phrase, prompted
by Protestantism, or Puritanism, or humanism? Or was it the product
of changing social circumstances?[2] Some recent studies of particular
towns in the sixteenth century have illuminated the municipal origins
of many poor law concepts in both Protestant and Catholic countries.[3]
An analysis of the problem in Salisbury in the first half of the seventeenth century shows the stresses to which urban communities continued to be subjected, and the exceptional way in which one Puritan
oligarchy reacted.

Like the rulers of Venice in the 1520s and Lyon in the 1530s, of Ipswich
in the 1550s and Norwich in 1570, the aldermen of this small cathedral

city in the third decade of the seventeenth century originated an ambitious if short-lived scheme for the relief of the poor. It was a programme which involved the close regulation of the life of the town by the 'godly magistrates' in the cause of charity and good order. But their action, like all attempts at social welfare, was limited and shaped by their definition of the problem: who were the poor?

It was a commonplace of Tudor and Stuart social theory, embodied in legislation and sanctified in sermon literature, that the problem of the poor comprised two distinct fields: the disciplining of the able-bodied rogues who wandered the countryside as vagrants, and the relief of those unable to work, the elderly, the chronic sick, and young children in large families. According to one Elizabethan preacher, the first group was to be excluded from the term 'poor' altogether: 'As for our rogues and vagabonds, I exclude them out of the role and number of poore men, commended by the spirit of God, . . . who because they do not labour they should not eate.' By the poor he meant 'an artificer or handicraftesman, labouring diligently . . . to maintayne his familie', and 'the poore of our almes houses, . . . and other such impotent persons'. The same distinction was expressed more bluntly by another writer in 1654: 'Of Poor there are two sorts: Gods poor and the Devils: impotent poor, and impudent poor: the poor upon whom we should exercise our beneficence is the honest labourer and the poor householder: . . . or the blinde and maimed, the aged and decrepit, the weak widowe or young orphans: which are either past their labour or not yet come unto it.'[4] This conventional distinction was formalized in the Elizabethan Poor Law. The vagrant 'impudent' poor were whipped and sent back to their place of settlement, where they were to be compelled to work in the house of correction. The impotent poor were relieved either from the poor rates or in almshouses, or, if they were children, were bound out as poor apprentices to local masters. The pious hope was that there would be few 'honest labourers' in need of relief from public funds.[5]

Like other local authorities, the corporation of Salisbury adopted this traditional classification when dealing with the poor. Those supported from the poor rate or given part of the charitable doles were the obviously deserving: 'Widow Baker [aged] 72 years', 'John Stainesmore, lame and blind', or 'Twoe Children of William Thringe deceased'. When the town took censuses of its poor, it concentrated on such exceptional cases. In 1625 a 'booke of the veiwe and provision for settinge the poore on worke' pinpointed them.[6] The record listed those who were impotent and in need of relief, those poor children who were bound out as apprentices, and others who were in future to be 'set on work' by masters in the town. There were 263 individuals in these three categories, 4 per cent of the 6,500 inhabitants of Salisbury.[7] These were the irreducible minimum of the poor, those whose

TABLE 9 *Status of poor and vagrants in Salisbury*

	Husbands and wives	Widows, spinsters*	Widowers, bachelors	Children	Total	Children per household where children present
1625 listing:						
Set on work	10	18	5	108	141	
Impotent	18	42	17	4	81	
Apprentices					41	
1635 listings:						
St Edmund's and St Thomas's	58	68	9	115	250	3·03
St Martin's almspeople	6	29	1	29	65	2·64
St Martin's other poor	210	48	21	251	530	2·26
Vagrants						
1598–1638	86	171	343	51	651	

* Includes wives deserted by their husbands

need was conspicuous, and they fell into well-defined groups. Two-thirds of those set on work were under the age of fifteen; a similar proportion of the impotent were aged sixty or more; and only a third of the adults were men (Tables 9 and 10). Respectable poverty was the prerogative of women, children and the old.

The 'impudent' poor, rogues and vagabonds, were an even more conspicuous group. Between 1598 and 1638, a register was compiled of over 600 vagrants whipped out of Salisbury.[8] Typical among them were 'John Sellevand an Ireshman . . . taken wandringe and begging, disordering hym[self] beinge associated with the hangman', a man 'taken dronnke, not able to yeld any accompte of his ydle course of lyffe', and Anne Harris 'wandring . . . with William Gill who she sayth was her husband, he sayd she is his Sister'. Sixteen other couples were 'living lewdly together, being unmarried'. The conclusion was inevitable: as Richard Younge put it, vagabonds 'be generally given

TABLE 10 *Ages of poor in Salisbury*

Age	Set on work	1625 listing		1635 listing St Edmund's and St Thomas's
		Impotent	Apprentices	
Under 1	0	0	0	2
1–4	1	0	0	21
5–9	48	1	1	21
10–14	43	0	19	28
15–19	8	1	11	9
20–9	3	2	1	5
30–9	4	0	0	13
40–9	7	2	0	26
50–9	7	4	0	14
60–9	3	15	0	32
70 and over	2	42	0	45
Unknown	15	14	9	34*
Total	141	81	41	250

* Includes 22 'young children' whose precise ages are not given

to horrible uncleanness, they have not particular wives, neither do they range themselves into Families: but consort together as beasts'.[9] More prosaically, although the record does not state the ages of those punished, it is clear that they were sharply distinguished from the respectable native poor: less than 8 per cent were children and over half appear to have been single men wandering alone (Table 9). The able-bodied, and especially the male, adult who had no apparent means of subsistence was a vagrant if he could not prove his settlement in Salisbury.[10] The two classes of poor singled out by the authorities were both distinct in sex and age structure and treated in different ways.

The governors of Salisbury drew into their nets of relief and punishment the two groups defined for them by contemporary theory and prejudice. But there were other poor who could not be fitted so easily into this simple categorization. The old and young were clearly in need of aid, but what of the able unemployed or the underemployed? Those who drew up the list of 1625 were unable to classify seven married couples and three widows with their forty-five children, who 'wanted stock' with which to work, and they scribbled their names at the bottom of the page. Similarly, the exclusion of individual conspicuous rogues from the town was a simple enough procedure, but too large an influx of more respectable tradesmen, potentially 'diligent in their callings', but looking for work and accompanied by their families, might be as great a threat to Salisbury's prosperity. Hence the plethora of informal methods to prevent their settlement to which the town resorted increasingly from the 1580s onwards: the taking of recognizances, measures against inmates, simple orders to strangers 'to depart the town', and elastic interpretation of the vagrancy laws themselves.[11]

In addition, the number of the deserving poor was always liable to be suddenly increased. It needed only a protracted illness, a food crisis, or the death of a parent to push a family from self-supporting poverty to destitution. The 'diligent Bee or painefull Labourer', wrote one observer, might 'for want of necessary reliefe toward his over great family and charge of children, specially in time of sicknesse, or in old age, or in times of dearth . . . pine away and perish.'[12] Unemployment or falling real wages might force a family to the same end. From the 1590s onwards temporary crisis and prolonged economic depression made these possibilities a reality for increasing numbers of the inhabitants of Salisbury, and demonstrated the impossibility of dealing with the poor by the conventional classification and the simple administrative machinery which followed from it.

At the very end of the sixteenth century bad harvests brought dearth to Salisbury as to other towns. As food prices soared to unprecedented heights,[13] malnutrition and disease were the result among the poorer sections of the population. They were reflected in a sharp rise in the number of burials and a fall in registered baptisms in each of the three parishes. In St Edmund's 230 people were buried in 1597, more than twice the usual number, and of these 78 were specifically described as 'paupers'. In the same parish 'conceptions' fell from an annual average of 89 to 62. Although this was not a serious 'crisis of subsistence' of the classic Continental type, the figures suggest widespread distress.[14] The poor petitioned the bishop for relief, and in order to 'pacyfie the great outcry of the poore' the corporation had to enlist the aid of the Privy Council to free imported grain retained in Southampton when on its way to Salisbury. The customary measures were taken to limit malting and control the market in an attempt to prevent 'the impoverishment of the poorer sorte of people.'[15]

Besides aggravating the condition of the domestic poor, dearth and high prices also brought a huge influx of vagabonds into the town in search of relief. No less than 96 of the 651 vagrants expelled from Salisbury between 1598 and 1638 were whipped out in the first year, and the number apprehended was only the tip of the iceberg. Moreover, these were not the permanent wanderers, the 'lusty rogues' commonly whipped in later years. They were distinguished from later vagrants by the predominance of single women among them (49 adult women as against 37 men) and by the short distances which they had moved. Over 40 per cent of the 96 had come from within twenty miles of Salisbury compared with only 12 per cent of the vagrants whipped in the next forty years. In these crisis years dearth propelled the rural poor of Wiltshire into the town.

Within five years an epidemic brought an even greater blow. Bubonic plague had already been a visitor in 1564 and 1579, and at the end of 1603 the disease pursued the King in his flight from London, sweeping through the town in the following year. In the whole year 1604, 1,144 people were buried in the three parishes and the Close, more than five times the usual number and probably about a sixth of the total population.[16] As usual when urban governments tried to control the disease, the households of the infected were isolated, and since the plague was particularly concentrated in the poorer areas of the town, this involved the public relief of those in quarantine. The result was an unprecedented financial burden. In the year from May 1604 to May 1605 the town spent £589 9*s* 5*d* on relief for the inhabitants of infected houses and in payments to watchmen at their doors, a sum three times the amount usually distributed to the poor from the poor rate, and double the normal annual income of the corporation itself.[17]

At the height of the epidemic, in September, 132 households were receiving relief at a total cost of £27 per week. Several were supported for weeks on end. 'Martin's house' in St Edmund's parish received weekly sums varying from 2s to 5s 3d for almost as long as the accounts lasted, forty-nine weeks in all, and several houses were shut up for more than twenty weeks. These were not the households with most deaths in them but those with infrequent cases of suspected plague. Where mortality was highest, payments for relief lasted only until the family was wiped out. The household of John Silvester, joiner, of St Martin's parish, received 8d a day for two weeks after 11 November 1604; but by 28 November John, his wife Alice, and four of his children were dead, and payments ceased. In contrast, only two burials were recorded in St Martin's parish register from 'Ashley's house' which was maintained for twenty-two weeks in all. It was morbidity rather than mortality which aggravated the problem of the poor.

Over the whole year 411 different households were supported. Since the average number of individuals in each house, where recorded, was slightly over three, 1,300 different individuals probably received some form of relief during the epidemic, one-fifth of the population of the town. But the sick were not the only additional burden on the poor rates. The flight from the town of those who could afford to leave and the ensuing disruption of trade caused unemployment and distress: as the county quarter sessions reported, 'great numbers of poore people who onely live and mayntayne themselves by weaving of wollen clothe and spynning . . . and other manuall trades and occupations now are putt of from their saide worke by the clothiers and others their workmasters'.[18]

The end of the disease brought no lasting recovery. The population may have been temporarily reduced, and hence also the number of the poor. Certainly, expenditure from the poor rate fell for a time from an average of £155 per annum from 1600 to 1603 to £126 from 1605 to 1612.[19] But there was also an influx of vagrants as the immediate aftermath of the epidemic, partially revealed in an increase in the number of those whipped from the town. The dead poor were replaced by immigrants.

As the population recovered, unemployment, especially among the casual workers in the declining broadcloth industry, grew worse: on

top of temporary crisis, the poverty problem was aggravated by industrial depression. Even before the incorporation of the town in 1612
the clothworkers were proclaiming that they were 'greatlie impoverished', and there was more vociferous discontent during the dearth
years 1613 and 1614. In 1616 the council wrote to the Lord Lieutenant
complaining of poverty and the decay of trade, while poor weavers
petitioned the corporation for help. The clothiers reacted by exploiting their employees, whose real wages fell rapidly as prices rose.
They did not venture into the manufacture of new products, serges
or medleys, which proved the salvation of the textile industry elsewhere in the county.[20] Rather, like other towns in these conditions,
Salisbury was already changing from a major industrial community
to a town whose economy depended on its position as a social centre
and stopping-place for travellers—a shift which inevitably reduced
the demand for labour.[21]

It was in the 1620s that all three causes of poverty, depression, dearth
and finally disease, combined to produce critical distress in Salisbury.
Bad harvests followed a glut in the early years of the decade, there
were food riots in the county, and further unemployment and falling
wages in the textile industry as the effects of the Thirty Years War
made themselves felt.[22] By 1623 John Taylor could describe Salisbury
as 'so much overcharged with poore, as having in three Parishes neere
3,000 besides decayed men a great many, . . . the poore being like
Pharaoh's leane Kine, even ready to eat up the fat ones'. The governors
of the town agreed that nearly half the population was impoverished.
In 1625 the council wrote to the Attorney-General that there were
2,700 poor. In the following year in 'A Declaration of the present
estate of the City of Salisbury, upon an exact veiwe thereof taken',
presented to the town's High Steward, the Earl of Pembroke, they
said that there were 1,290 households in the city (suggesting a total
population of 6,500) and almost 3,000 poor people: a great part of
these were impotent and relieved by alms, and more 'must be relyeved
by the City if they happen to be sick but one week'. The town was
totally unable to sustain a burden of this kind for it had 'no staple
trade in it, and is so decaied and poore'.[23]

These statements were doubtless exaggerated, but a further outbreak of plague in 1627 brought them closer to reality. In terms of
actual mortality, the epidemic was not as serious as that of 1604.
There were 470 burials in this year, representing less than 8 per cent
of the population.[24] But the plague caused an even greater immediate

increase in the number of the poor. John Ivie, Mayor of Salisbury in 1627, described some of the reasons in a later pamphlet: 'as many persons of the City that had any friends in the Countrey that would receive them . . . did fly as if it were out of an house on fire', so that 'there was none left to comfort the Poor in so great a misery'. Moreover, the isolation of an infected town added food shortage to the scourge of disease: 'our Markets being gone to Wilton, the Artificers did want supply of corn for their use'.[25] Early in the epidemic the council wrote to the county Justices that only twenty-seven houses were infected, but that 2,674 people were being supported at a weekly cost of £75. At the height of the outbreak there were said to be 2,900 on relief and eighty-eight households shut up. The necessity of relieving almost half the population of the town, foreseen in the letter to Pembroke of the previous year, was apparently realized.[26]

As in 1604 the epidemic had the welcome effect of removing some paupers, although not so many since mortality was less. Some of the poor listed in the census of 1625 died during the plague, like Richard Lowe, a joiner of St Thomas's parish, his wife and four of his six children. But there were more families whose poverty was increased by the plague. Sarah Biby and her two children were included in a listing of the poor in St Edmund's parish in 1635; her husband seems to have died in the epidemic. The 'Widow Braxston' and her son in the same record may be the widow and orphan of Richard Braxton who was buried in 1627.[27]

Just as the epidemic brought some families to destitution by removing a wage-earner, so it might compel the expenditure of the small savings or capital of others. In 1629 petitions from poor tradesmen for money from the loan funds which the corporation had at its disposal referred to the plague as a cause of their poverty. One man had spent 'the better portion of his stocke in the tyme of the last sickness'. A clothworker asked for a loan because his trade was hindered by 'the late sickness within this Cittye as by meanes of stay of Traffique and Commerce with France'. The very fact that mortality was slight in 1627 and yet combined with as serious a disruption of economic activity as the outbreak of 1604 aggravated its impact on poverty. In 1628 weekly payments to the poor jumped to a total of £308, double their level after the previous epidemic.[28]

By the early 1630s there were more complaints than ever about the scale of poverty in the town. The weavers were 'impoverished' in 1630, in 1631 the war with France was said to have produced 'a great dampe and deadnes' in the clothing industry, and 'the poorer sorte of people' who depended on spinning for their living were faced with low wages and unemployment. In 1635 poor weavers and clothworkers were petitioning for licences as victuallers and tipplers because, as one of them put it, 'for certain yeres last past the trade of Clothinge is much decayed in this City . . . by meanes whereof your petitioner and many other of his trade have wanted and do often want employment'.[29] The depression of the 1620s combined with an outbreak of plague had set the seal on the poverty of Salisbury. It brought to destitution some of the self-supporting poor. The needy poor, 'God's poor', now included many more than the merely impotent.

The increase in the size of the poverty problem and the growing recognition of its wider character are partially revealed in the censuses of the poor which survive for the town in this period. The listing of 1625 has already been mentioned. There were two others of equal significance: a list of those receiving relief in the parishes of St Edmund and St Thomas, which divides them into families, and gives ages, occupations, and wages if any; and a listing of the poor in St Martin's parish which records only heads of families and the numbers of their children, but which includes many more than those on relief.[30] Although the two records are undated, the names of the heads of household in the first and of the almspeople in the second correspond almost exactly with the names of the poor in the only surviving rate-book for the town, compiled early in 1635. They were perhaps the imperfect product of an injunction given to the overseers in that year that they should 'examyne everye howse in their Devision what persons are there, howe many children, of what ages, and howe they are ymployed to get their lyvinges'.[31] The censuses may therefore be tentatively dated 1635. Information from both is summarized in Tables 9 and 10.

The list of March 1625 contained 4 per cent of the population of the town. This was a small proportion and the enumerators, as we have seen, were still looking for the obviously needy—the old, and young children of poor families. They included 'Goodwife Hoskins', who 'now lyeth in Childbed, hath 4 Children. Her husband was prest for a souldier; [she] wanteth reliefe'; and a widow with six children who 'keepeth them all at worke and desireth some stock to ymploy them'. But the main purpose of the record was to provide for the employment

of those begging children, who were in most towns 'as the Cater-
pillars, Frogs, Grasshoppers and Lice of Egipt . . . the plagues of
this your common welth'.[32] Of the 141 individuals set to work, 92
were definitely under the age of fifteen and a further 8 were described
as 'children'. Twelve of them were employed by their parents, but
most were to be lodged as well as set to work in the houses of their
masters. Poor children between the ages of five and fourteen were to
follow the common practice and be put out to service. While the town
rid itself of young beggars, their employers gained free labour: for
one year they had both the profit from their work and 6d a week from
the workhouse fund for their maintenance. Although the listing included 33 adults who had to be found work, therefore, it was primarily a blueprint for the future employment of children. Hence it
did not reveal the full extent of poverty in the town.

The listings of 1635 are a more objective record of those who in
fact received alms. The census of the poor in St Edmund's and St
Thomas's parishes in that year contained 250 individuals. Of these 115
were children, and only 25 of them were said to be employed—all
of them in the occupations of the poor such as bonelacemaking, card-
ing and spinning. Five other children, like some of the poor in Norwich, were 'at schoole'.[33] Of the adults, the majority were over the
age of sixty. Joan Lyntch, aged eighty-two, received 6d a week relief
because, as the record succinctly put it, her 'labour done'. Once again
the problem of the poor was seen to be mainly one of numbers of
unemployed children and of the old and impotent. Widow Bagges,
aged seventy-five, 'lame in her handes', was allowed 1s a week relief;
Melior Jones aged fifty was 'sometymes distracted', while his daughter
was 'crocke backed'. Three wives with children deserted by their
husbands were other obvious cases for relief.

But this census also recorded twenty-nine households headed by
married couples, twenty of them with children: complete families who
needed relief. Sometimes the head of the household was unemployed,
like John Nuby, who 'wanted worke', and had a wife and five children,
two of them sick, to support. Others were merely underpaid and their
wages had to be supplemented from the parochial rate. In some households the children had small earnings but the parents none. All were
destitute.

The table opposite summarizes the income of the poor in so far as
it may be assessed for the majority of the families in this census.
Income per head, in spite of poor relief, was obviously tiny at a time

TABLE II   *St Edmund's and St Thomas's poor*

	Married couples	Families headed by: Widows/Spinsters/ Single men	Total
No. of families	27	74	101
No. of individuals	118	114	232
Total weekly earnings	41s 3d	34s 0½d	75s 3½d
Total weekly poor rate	20s 2d	51s 2d	71s 4d
Total income	61s 5d	85s 2½d	146s 7½d
Income per head per week (approx.)	6d	9d	7½d

when the wages of labourers and apprentices in the town were set at 10d a day and when even those people in the town's almshouses were allowed 1s a week maintenance.[34] It can scarcely have been enough for subsistence, and poor relief itself was of only supplementary help. There appears also to have been some discrimination in the distribution of relief between those in broken families, or lonely widows and old men, and complete impoverished households: between the traditional poor and the 'new' unemployed or underpaid poor. To take specific examples: William Hall earned 1s 8d a week plus 'his diet', but he had a wife and six children aged from two months to fourteen years; one child earned 1s 1d a week making bonelace, another was at school. He was allowed only 8d a week relief, bringing the total family income to 3s 5d. In contrast, Widow Smith and her three children, earning 2s 9d weekly between them, received 2s a week in additional relief. The town was still more generous in granting aid to the 'deserving' poor than to those whose only qualification was an economic one—unemployment or underemployment.

This attitude was understandable. Once those other than the traditionally 'impotent' were included among the poor, there was no limit to their numbers. This is apparent from the listing of St Martin's parish, the third parish in the town, in 1635. The enumerators seem to have gone through the streets recording the heads of all poor families and the number of their children and then marking off those who were receiving alms. Out of 207 separate households listed, only 33 were relieved from the poor rate. Yet the rest were equally poor; many of them occur in a list of those receiving wheat or money in a charitable distribution in the same year.[35] The only apparent difference between the two groups was one of social rather than purely economic status. Of the 33 families receiving alms, 29 were headed by widows or spinsters. But out of the 174 other poor families only 48 had women at their heads: the others were married couples or single men (Table 9).[36] The deserving poor, especially those in broken families, were again singled out as meriting relief. Apart from aid from various charitable doles, the rest were expected to fend for themselves.

Taking the lists of those receiving alms in the three parishes together, the number of poor on relief amounted to slightly less than 5 per cent of the population, not unlike the proportion elsewhere in the sixteenth century.[37] But the total who might be considered poor was far greater, up to a third of the inhabitants in St Martin's parish:

TABLE 12[38]

	Population in 1630s	Almspeople in 1635		Total poor in 1635	
		No.	% of pop.	No.	% of pop.
St Edmund's	2,521	167	6·6		
St Thomas's	2,561	83	3·2		
St Martin's	1,785	65	3·6	595	33·3
Total	6,867	315	4·6		

Different censuses might thus reveal different classes and different numbers of poor in urban communities. The poor might be narrowly or broadly defined. A census concentrating on those receiving relief would include a high proportion of elderly people, and a large number of households with widowed or unmarried heads, usually women. But a more comprehensive survey, including 'honest labourers and poor householders' as well as the exceptional cases of the very poor, would contain more people of middle age and more married couples. A comparison of the Salisbury listings with those drawn up in other towns in the Elizabethan period illustrates this.

The Norwich census of 1570 is the most comprehensive known to survive, listing more than a quarter of the English population of that town. Another census of the poor for part of Ipswich in 1597 is almost equally full; though similar in form to that of St Edmund's and St Thomas's, Salisbury in 1635, it lists many more than those on relief. In both cases the proportion of the poor aged sixty and over was low: 13·8 per cent in Norwich and 14·6 per cent in Ipswich. Though not so low as among the population of Ealing in 1599 (6·1 per cent) or as the figure Gregory King suggested for the country as a whole (10·7 per cent), it was still much less than the 30·8 per cent in St Edmund's and St Thomas's, Salisbury. Conversely, in both Ipswich and Norwich large numbers of the poor were middle-aged. Again, a high proportion of the adult poor in both towns—over 50 per cent—were still married; the figure was only 16·6 per cent among the almspeople in St Martin's parish, Salisbury.[39] Figures for the mean size of household show similar differences: the more destitute and deserving the poor, the smaller the average household. The mean was 2·0 among the almspeople of St Martin's in 1635, though 3·0 among the other poor listed; it was 2·3 for the almspeople in St Edmund's and St Thomas's in the same year; but it was over 3·0 among the poor listed in Ipswich in 1597.[40] Here was a whole range of poverty.

Within this spectrum, the poor who normally received alms were a readily distinguishable group of exceptional cases; but the 'poor' generally shaded much more easily into the population as a whole, and when they began to be included among those on relief, there seemed no clear limit to the size of the problem. The evidence of the censuses suggests that this process had already begun in the parish of St Edmund, though not in St Martin's. In the former those on relief included several married couples, representing the unemployed and underpaid families already described, and these account for the higher proportion of the population receiving the dole there than in St Martin's (Tables 9 and 12). In one parish, at least, the overseers were already broadening their concept of those who required alms. The problem of poverty was recognized to be no longer one of relieving a few old women, orphan children, or sick persons, those 'divine poor', who might be regarded as a permanent and acceptable part of a structured society; it had become a problem of larger numbers of people, apparently threatening the whole social order.

For it was not only the spectre of a boundless number of poor in need of relief and the expense this would involve which forced itself on the attention of the magistrates and council: the poor as a whole made up a police problem of growing magnitude. They congregated in particular parts of the town, in alehouses outside the gates which were also the haunts of strangers and vagrants. When in 1629 the corporation tried to obtain the extension of its liberties to include the suburban villages of Fisherton, Milford and East Harnham, it was because their independence was the cause of 'great disorders and Many Inconveniences . . . to the Cittie in Innes, Alehouses, Poore people, and in Trades'.[41] The poor ventured into the heart of the town or the cathedral Close to beg but lived crowded in the slums of the suburbs where the plague had its most pronounced effect. They were represented not only by names in a census or by children 'lyke to perishe and dye in the streates with cold', but also by drunkenness and disorder. John Ivie described the unregulated state of the poor, swarming 'about the City, Close and Countrey, [with] no restraint, whereby Bastardie is much increast, to the great grief of the inhabitants, who complain of their great charge to maintain that, which doth so much dishonour God'.[42] The clear distinction between the 'impudent' and able vagrant poor and the respectable but 'impotent' poor of the town had disappeared in conditions of low wages and unemployment, of high food prices and epidemic disease. Rogues and strangers 'of evil conversation' might still be expelled from Salisbury, but the native poor, as their numbers rose, were themselves disorderly as well as increasingly able.

As the scale and nature of the poverty problem changed, the conventional means of dealing with it became even more clearly inadequate than conventional categories and distinctions. The continuing importance of private charity in the field of poor relief needs no reiteration;[43] but in towns, at least, its significance must not be exaggerated. By 1620 there were five sets of almshouses in Salisbury, providing refuge for forty-seven people, the council filling the places at two of them. In addition, there were several charitable funds established by private benefactors to provide loans for poor tradesmen, or doles of food, clothing and money for the destitute. For example, by Edward Rodes's will of 1611, 1s was to be distributed to forty poor people every Easter; other bequests had provided money for clothing for up to 100 poor people every year; and a gift of land by Dorothy Wotton in 1608 produced £4 per annum for the 'truly poor, aged and impotent'. By 1640 a little under £1,000 should have been available to the council for loans to poor tradesmen, and an annual income of about £100 for general poor relief.[44] Separately, the three parishes had small charitable endowments of their own: St Martin's was able in the 1630s to distribute £7 10s yearly to individual poor and pay out £1 13s 4d for binding poor apprentices. Some of the trade companies, like the Tailors, similarly upheld a community responsibility towards their own poor by distributing corn or making small payments or loans to them.[45]

But these funds were scarcely sufficient to meet the problem. Almshouses catered for a few carefully selected, deserving poor;[46] the various doles though representing publicly a neighbourly responsibility for the unfortunate were open to the criticism of 'indiscriminate' charity; and the revolving loan funds, potentially the most useful for the 'new' poor of Salisbury, those who 'wanted stock with which to work', were like the rest open to constant abuse. In 1597 the corporation complained to the Privy Council that it was unable to obtain some of these gifts from the executors. But it was itself partly at fault. A Chancery inquisition of 1599 revealed that bequests for the poor with a total capital value of £938 were not being used for the intended purposes; some of these were in the hands of the Chamber. One notable example was the rent from a recent gift of land in London by Joan Popley, intended to set the poor on work. Ivie alleged that even when such funds were used for the poor, they did not always go to the most deserving cases: when money was left 'to be given to poor householders', he wrote, 'the Mayor sends for all the Church Officers, and when they come in there is brave sport in the dividing of it'; it was as likely to be given to 'drunken lewd fellows' as to the 'honest working poor'.[47] If charitable funds were to be effective, there must be direction, and they must be supplemented by other relief.

The town was therefore thrown back on the statutory machinery of the poor law. The poor rate brought in almost twice the amount available to the town from charitable benefactions for general poor relief; but even this was insufficient. Income scarcely rose between 1600 and 1623, in spite of rising prices. There were fluctuations, receipts falling between 1607 and 1611, but a rate which produced £187 13s 5d in 1601 still raised only £198 19s 4d in 1623. This was clearly not enough to support an increasing number of poor, and attempts to levy additional rates met with strong opposition. That persistent critic, John Ivie, again alleged corruption: householders bribed the overseers not to assess them, and the overseers themselves distributed doles to their friends and relations. Certainly, in 1629 Christopher Horte was presented before the Justices for misuse of 4*s* given to him 'to relyeve Flower Staple and her daughter who were in sickness, and he delyvered to her onley 6*d* and yet caused yt to be published in the parish churche that she was in great want'.[48]

This state of affairs became less acceptable to the governors of the town as the problem increased. But it was only in time of crisis that they tried to find new solutions. In 1599, following the statute of 1598, they centralized poor relief in the town by calling all the churchwardens and overseers of the three parishes to monthly meetings before the Justices of the Peace, where their accounts were examined, strangers, beggars and inmates presented, and where the richest parish, St Thomas's, was made to contribute to the relief of the poorer parishes of St Edmund and St Martin.[49] But in conditions of industrial depression, their concern was particularly directed towards employing the able-bodied poor and apprenticing their children. Already in 1564 after an outbreak of plague, a workhouse had been planned but had come to nothing. Now in the crisis of the 1590s, the council set up a committee to consider the building of a Bridewell 'for the correction of the idle and the setting to worke of the able poor'. This workhouse was established in 1602, with rooms for six men and six women, one for the correction of rogues and another for any who might be sick. Charity was at last brought into play: the workhouse, and all its successors, were financed by the rents from Popley's lands.[50] But the institution of 1602 was only a tiny contribution.

For the next two decades, especially when food prices rose as in 1613, there was a succession of new committees and fresh 'projects for the poor', all with no practical result.[51] But that the problem was larger than almshouses, poor rates and a small house of correction could deal with, was recognized. The title of an anonymous plan 'for setting at worrcke of Idell wandering people and the releyfe of poore impotent and Aged persons', which seems to come from these years, expressed precisely the two conventional categories of the poor; but its content revealed an appreciation of the broader problem which now confronted the town. The author proposed to take a census of

> every householder, ther wiffes children and family, that have
> not some misterie or handicraft . . . but lyve only by spinning and
> carding, . . . to veiwe . . . how much wool shall be necessary

for every house to serve weekly for the . . . mayntenance of their
lyving.
Secondly to take the names . . . of all those persons whoe partly
may live by labour and partlie have nede of releiffe and comfort.
Thirdly, to take the names of the pore aged and impotent.

By force of circumstances, the definition of the poor was thus broadly
extended.[52]

These projects and committees finally bore fruit in the 1620s.
Salisbury produced its unified effort to deal with the whole problem of
poverty and initiated an experiment as original as that of Norwich in
the sixteenth century. In June 1623, when food prices were high and
the depression in the textile industry at its worst, the council put
forward new orders for the poor. The system was to be based on a
revised and enlarged workhouse. As well as rooms for the correction
of the 'lewder and baser sort', it was to provide lodging for poor
children who should be taught a trade and after three years bound out
as apprentices. Even more important, the workhouse was now to be
supplemented and overshadowed by employment in the town. In
1625 all clothiers, spinners and knitters were asked to certify how
many poor they were willing to set to work, and women were engaged
to teach and in some cases to house poor children. The listing of the
poor in 1625 shows the initial realization of these projects, and in 1627
a further forty-seven poor children were set to work in the town, the
workhouse paying the cost of their maintenance for two years. In 1630
the council described how the scheme worked in practice: 'The overseers cause the poore parentes as soone as their Children are capable
of any work to set them abroade to other howses as it were to schoole
to learne to knitt sowe make bonelace buttons pinnes or such like
worke.'[53]

The aim was not to encourage social mobility, of course. The poor
should merely be able to support themselves. The skills taught were
those on the fringes of a declining textile industry, and they would
guarantee the pupils permanent, though respectable poverty (see
Table 13). But the town was at last attacking the basic problem of
unemployment; and this was only the beginning.

Expenditure on the outdoor employment of the poor brought a
financial burden greater than the poor rate could bear. In an attempt
to find new finance, and also to control one aspect of pauper disorder,
the corporation intervened in the one expanding sector of the town's

TABLE 13   *Occupations of the 141 poor set to work in 1625*

Spinning, quilling, spooling	41	Working for a tailor	4
Making bonelace	35	Making pins	3
Knitting	19	Making cards	2
Making hemp	11	Weaving	2
Making buttons	9	Unspecified	15

economy, the drink trade. It was a common complaint that alehouses 'made many beggars', that the poor spent all their relief on drink 'whereby they starve their children'. 'The meanest beggar', wrote John Taylor, with uncommon understanding, 'dares to spend all he hath at the Alehouse . . . for the poore man drinks stifly to drive care away, and hath nothing to lose.' The problem seemed to be aggravated by the concentration of over one hundred licensed inns and alehouses in this assize and quarter sessions town, one for every sixty-five inhabitants. Attempts to reduce their number under direction from the Privy Council failed, partly because of the growing power of the 'drink' interest in the town, but also because those who set up as tipplers and alehouse-keepers were often the poor themselves: 'verie auged and poore people whose labours are past, and have no other meanes of lyvinge'.[54]

The corporation therefore decided to join in the brewing trade rather than attempt to control it by conventional means. Following the example of Dorchester in the previous year, in June 1623 it set up a 'Common Brewhouse' owned and run by the corporation. The profits from this enterprise should be 'for the good and relyeffe of the poore of the workingehouse, and other poore of the Cittye', and after 1625 the brewhouse paid a weekly contribution of £1 to the workhouse. But it was also intended that the profits would eventually make possible a general reduction in the poor rate. This was the hope held out to justify the imposition of an extra rate in 1623 to finance the programme: 'for yf this half rate should cease then all our endeavours already for the workhouse would be whollye frustrate, which would tend to the disgrace of the City'.[55] In fact, the brewhouse made the reputation of the town. The Recorder of Wells wished for a similar institution there when complaining of the increase in poverty in 1635; the Earl of Stamford proposed in the 1630s that Colchester 'or anie like Corporation' might have a 'Common Brewhouse'; and it was the Salisbury institution that the Water Poet fulsomely admired on his visit in 1623.[56]

But it was the third plank in the town's programme for dealing with the poverty problem which was really original—the token system associated with a municipal storehouse founded in 1628. Salisbury, like other towns, had commonly bought grain for the poor in time of dearth, and during the plague epidemic of 1627, the Mayor, Ivie, set up 'three Storehouses in the three Parishes to serve the poor their victuals'. In the following year these were combined into one institution financed by £100 received from the county, the arrears of the plague rate of the previous year. This storehouse supplied all that was necessary for the subsistence of the poor; bread, butter and cheese, beer and fuel. Instead of weekly payments of money from the poor rate, those on relief were to be given tokens which they could exchange for these goods. Thus food and fuel could be provided at cost price and the poor prevented from spending their dole entirely on drink. Cash might be distributed in extraordinary circumstances, but it was hoped that this would be 'very seldom unles it be to suche as cannot governe themselves'.[57] The town had intervened decisively to re-model not only poor relief, but ultimately the poor themselves.

This scheme to relieve and 'govern' the poor involved an immense outlay in time and money: charitable endowments provided some finance, but other funds of the Chamber were drawn on, and the aldermen and councillors made loans and gifts themselves. The first standing committee in Salisbury was that for the brewhouse meeting weekly, and the council minutes for the 1620s are dominated by the business of the poor. The change in the character of poverty had, of course, forced itself on the attention of all the rulers and made them willing, temporarily at least, to tolerate the cost of innovation; but the new solutions were the contribution of a small determined group of aldermen, whom we can identify from their presence on the committees dealing with the three institutions. They included experienced survivors from the 1597 committee on the poor like Matthew Bee and Roger Gauntlett. But the main impetus came from men new to high municipal office in the 1620s: Thomas Squibbe, Mayor in 1623, Henry Sherfield, elected Recorder of the town at the end of that year, and John Ivie, Chamberlain from 1620 to 1624, and Mayor in 1627.

They were supported by Bartholomew Tookye, 'one of the wyse Aldermen of Sarum', as John Nicholas described him, and by some of the younger councillors, like James Abbott and in later years John and Francis Dove.[58]

The most famous of these was Sherfield. He had been elected Recorder in 1623, with the support of the councillors, apparently against the wishes of the old guard in the town, and of its patron the Earl of Pembroke. In the Parliament of 1626 he was a 'violent' opponent of Buckingham, and in 1633 he achieved national notoriety when he was fined in Star Chamber for breaking a stained glass window of St Edmund's Church depicting the Creation. At his trial a sympathetic Chief Justice Richardson could defend him on the grounds that 'he hath done good in that City since I went that circuit; so that there is neither Beggar nor Drunkard to be seen there.'

Though less well known than Sherfield, others in the group were equally Puritan, and those who survived, notably Ivie and the Doves, were the mainstays of the Commonwealth party in Salisbury during the Civil War. Bartholomew Tookye had attacked the morris dances of the tailors on the Sabbath in 1611; Francis Dove 'used some unreverend and offensive speeches' against the perambulation of St Edmund's parish in Rogation week 1634; Matthew Bee was unscrupulous in trying to prevent cases being heard in church courts.[59] The most important of these men owed their cohesion as a group to their association in control of the select vestry of St Edmund's parish. Ivie, Tookye, John Dove and Sherfield were instrumental in obtaining the presentation of the Puritan Peter Thatcher to the benefice in January 1623, even before Sherfield became Recorder, and within the parish they were all 'commonly reputed and taken to be such persons as doe impugne and oppose Episcopall Jurisdiction'.[60]

Their common religious conviction motivated them. John Ivie declared that his aim was 'to advance God's glory and to settle a livelihood for the comfortable living of poor souls'. When Sherfield asked Ivie to become Justice of the Peace in 1628 he prefaced his invitation with the words 'God's time is come'. Peter Thatcher expressed some of the ideals behind the poor scheme in a letter to Sherfield in October 1627: 'I hold myselfe and all men in conscience bound . . . so to promote the good of the place where God hath sett them all that lies in their power.' He welcomed 'God's providence in setting it on foote at such a time', when potential opponents were absent from the town because of the plague, and he hoped that the scheme would be a means 'to reform the drunkennes, idleness, running to the Alehowse . . . which have been and are the bane of our poore in Sarum'.[61]

This Puritan concern for the poor was not so harsh an attitude as it has sometimes been painted. Certainly, as Thatcher's letter indicates, it was partly the product of a revulsion against begging, drunkenness, bastardy and disorder, of that desire for discipline which was a natural and perhaps inevitable reaction to deteriorating social conditions in towns.[62] Poor relief was undoubtedly a means of social control. The Salisbury scheme involved the deterrent of the workhouse, and close regulation of the diet of the poor. It included the prohibition of relief to anyone who did not 'usually frequent his or her parishe Churche at Morning and Evening prayer and at Sermons', and there sit on a bench with '*For the Poore* in great red letters' on it. There was a paternalistic attempt to make sure that the poor 'governed themselves': the churchwardens and overseers were weekly

> to Examyne and see how they have Laboured all the dayes in the
> weeke past and at what wages . . . and how they have bestowed
> the same money. And they are to Councell and direct them
> how to order themselves and weekely or offener to advise and
> encouredge them to followe their Labour, and if they wante
> worke to examyne the reason thereof and to provide them
> worke . . . at lardge if they cann.[63]

As this statement indicates, however, the insistence on work was a response to unemployment, to the broadening of the class of needy poor; and it was not confined to Puritans, though they might carry its practical application to extremes. It was the attitude behind the orthodoxy of the workhouse, that permanent and simple solution to poverty, succinctly expounded by Bacon, who 'commended most houses of relief and correction' where 'the sturdy beggar' was 'buckled to work, and the unable person also not maintained to be idle'. What distinguished Puritan attitudes to the poor was a determined search for ambitious solutions, and in Salisbury, at least, a comparative generosity and openness in the means adopted. The new scheme did not insist on the absolute segregation of all the poor in a workhouse, out of sight so that they might be out of mind, but provided employment in the town. The brewhouse was a permanent reminder that all must contribute to the relief of the unfortunate. Similarly, individual neighbourly charity was not entirely discouraged. The poor were no longer to beg publicly, but collecting boxes were installed at each inn, attended by two 'aged Impotent poore people', who should 'stand by the Boxe in a quiett and still manner and . . . use noe Clamour nor other words of begging but to say thus . . . in a quiet voyse "We pray you for God's sake remember the Poore" '.[64] The storehouse and brewhouse represented a far greater investment in poor relief than had been made before. Indeed, like that other 'Arch-Puritan', Alderman Ignatius Jourdain of Exeter, Ivie and his colleagues might rather be criticized for 'liberality and forwardness in well-doing' than the reverse.[65] Here were the 'godly magistrates' providing relief as well as repression in an attempt to reduce the problem to manageable size.

Of course, one cannot take Ivie's own picture in his pamphlet of the selfless government of himself and his colleagues entirely at its face value. They were a narrow oligarchy, implacable and high-handed in their rule both in St Edmund's parish and in the town as a whole.[66] They were, and they prided themselves on being, an isolated group, set apart from the 'ungodly rabble'. Thatcher's letter was written to encourage Sherfield to resist the 'violent opposition of such turbulent spirits as made their own gayne the only levell of their actions'. Not the least contribution of Puritanism to the Salisbury oligarchs was the self-confidence to rule in spite of all resistance. For the new measures for poor relief aggravated existing divisions within the town and brought a political crisis in its affairs.

The vested interests of the brewers provided the most formidable threat. At least five of them were aldermen in 1623, another two were councillors and they united against the brewhouse scheme. Their leader, Robert Jole, was elected Mayor in November 1623 after promising that he 'wished all prosperity to that good worke', but once in office he proved himself 'the most bedlamest and troublesomest felloe in contending with his brethren'. He did all in his power to wreck the project, locking the door of the council house, for example, in 1624 to prevent a vote on the brewhouse. The institution was finally confirmed by 37 votes to 8, but the rift in the government of the town continued. The brewers tried to obtain a vote dismissing Matthew Bee from his position as Justice of the Peace, and removing Sherfield from the brewhouse committee; their opponents retorted by voting Thomas Hancock, brewer, off the commission of the peace. Finally in September 1626, Jole himself was suspended from the corporation for attacking his colleagues, for being drunk and disorderly while Mayor, and—the last straw—for procuring 'an injunction *quo warranto* to be exhibited in the Kinges Bench touchinge the brewhouse', a challenge to the authority of the corporation itself. An agreement was patched up in 1627, and the common brewhouse remained. But the brewers refused to take any part in its administration and the antagonism aroused in 1624 persisted for a generation.[67]

The strains imposed by the new policy towards the poor also affected the town's relations with outside authorities. At the end of 1625 the council voted that the brewhouse should be confirmed by Act of Parliament, and to further this end elected John Puxton, a senior alderman, and Henry Sherfield as M.P.s. They turned down the nominees of Sir Robert Heath, the Attorney-General, and more significantly and unusually of the Earl of Pembroke, their patron, writing to both that the need to preserve the town from 'utter ruin', apart from the traditional excuse that they must by their Charter elect freemen of the town, made the election of its own citizens inevitable.[68] The need to deal with the poor fortified the aldermen in their resistance to outside interference.

It similarly reinforced the town's opposition to the Dean and Chapter, whose separate jurisdiction over the Close was a persistent cause of controversy. There was continual dispute about the payment of poor rates, the Close arguing that it was bound only to maintain its own poor, who were virtually non-existent, and refusing to pay the weekly contribution of £1 agreed upon when poor relief was centralized in 1599. During the plague of 1604 the Close had to be compelled by the county commission of the peace to contribute to the relief of the town, and payments were again in arrears in the 1630s.[69] But by then the subject of the poor had become a debating point in the larger controversy caused by the Bishop and Chapter's attempt to restore their authority in the government of the town. They alleged that since the Charter of 1612 Salisbury was 'poorer than ever before' and 'worse governed, noe care beinge taken to sett the poore on worke', while before 1612 the Bishop had kept the poor in order. The town argued the exact reverse. While the Close attacked the inexperience and illiteracy of the councillors, the aldermen suspected the canons of allying with the brewers against them: they would obtain 'the admission of Brewers to be Justices or such which may favor them [which] will destroy' the relief of the poor.[70]

Although both sides used arguments to suit their own purpose, the controversy revealed fundamentally different attitudes to the treatment of the poor. The Dean and Chapter adopted the orthodox position that, apart from traditional and private 'hospitality' which they claimed they maintained, poverty should be controlled by means of a penal workhouse and the suppression of alehouses, not by increasing provision for the poor and participating in the drink trade. If the town followed the letter of the poor law, they said in 1631, 'there need not be that trouble which now peradventure they have in following the patterne of Dorchester for a comon brewhowse . . . The monies that were (in pretence) spent for the poore, would have done them more good, if a workhouse and stuffe to sett them on work had byn provided according to the statutes.' The council's scheme for poor relief was only part of its wider radicalism, they argued, and the aldermen had to defend themselves against the charge of 'inconformitie to the state government and of Puritanisme and the like'.[71] At a time when the very liberties of the town were threatened, the aldermen of Salisbury by their poverty programme had isolated themselves. Although the Charter of 1630 confirmed their powers, the threat of clerical interference grew in the following decade.[72]

If the poverty problem brought additional stress to the corporation's relationship with other authorities, the plague epidemic of 1627 revealed the precarious nature of magisterial rule inside the town itself. Ivie and a handful of councillors were deserted by their colleagues. As in 1604, the county sessions were persuaded to levy a rate on neighbouring parishes to help with the relief of Salisbury's poor; but these rates always remained in arrears, and in 1627 were withheld on the excuse that the infected were allowed to wander into the countryside. Ivie was even presented to the county quarter sessions 'for kepeinge of Townsmen in [his] howsse in unseasonable tymes of the night in the tyme of sicknis'. For their part, the Dean and Chapter cut themselves off entirely: 'The great Robins of the Close was so affrighted that they shut up their gates not suffering any to come in.' Ivie presented his own description of the chaos in his pamphlet: 'God being merciful . . . did put into my heart to rule so great a multitude.' He personally arrested rioters, and turned back Welsh soldiers *en route* for the Rhe expedition, who had rifled shops in the town. He appointed bearers and buriers of the dead, who then complained of their low wages and refused to act. When he established a temporary pesthouse within the town until the sick could be isolated outside it, he was opposed by a crowd of citizens led by Matthew Bee, himself formerly to the forefront in efforts to deal with poverty. When he tried to remove the infected to this institution, one woman 'asked me whether I came of a woman or a beast that I should do so bloody an act upon poor people in their condition'. Finally, Widow Biby, later listed among the poor of St Edmund's parish in 1635, 'a base woman . . . being in her Cabbin at the Pesthouse, desiring to do the Devil's work, set the Pesthouse on fire'. Ivie consoled himself with the fact that 'God's judgment' in the shape of the plague had struck down some of the 'great unjust unruly rabble', but his attempts to put his ideals of regulation and provision into practice during a crisis were scarcely a success.[73]

The poor scheme of the 1620s depended too much on close regimentation of the poor and co-operation by private interests in the town to be successful even in the long term. Although the basic structure persisted until the 1640s it was never essentially secure. The most ambitious part of the programme, the storehouse, was also the most fragile.

As an institution it seems to have functioned efficiently. Wheat to the value of about £100 was purchased every year and baked into bread, besides lesser amounts of cheese, butter, fuel and candles, and beer (418 barrels in 1629) came from the brewhouse. Between December 1628 and July 1629 61 quarters of wheat were baked into 1,660 dozen penny loaves; in 1636 1,750 dozen were produced, and all these were distributed to the poor in return for tokens.[74] From the indications in the storehouse book it seems that the total amount of bread and beer provided in this institution would have been sufficient for the complete support of sixty or seventy individuals.[75] This was only a small proportion of those on relief, and indicates again how supplementary public relief was, but by the standards of the time it was a considerable achievement.

But the success of the system depended on economic stability: it was designed to cater only for those poor specifically granted weekly relief at Easter each year, who now received tokens instead of cash. It did not allow for *ad hoc* payments to individual poor, nor for payments to the suddenly sick: these 'extraordinary' expenses were to be provided for from collections at communion or from the poor boxes in the churches and inns of the town. Up to a point the system was workable. But when extraordinary expenses rose quickly and income declined, as happened in 1635 when there was a minor epidemic in Greencroft Street and when payments from the Close were in arrears, the system was strained to its limits. In 1636 additional poor rates had to be raised to pay off the arrears which had built up in the previous year.[76]

It was this sort of fluctuation rather than the corruption of minor officials in the town, as Ivie alleged, which brought the storehouse to an end. Its accounts show that between 1628 and 1631 when Ivie was in charge, the annual expenditure on poor relief fell from £308 17s to £175 19s 7d. This brought the burden on the poor rate down to a level nearer to that of the first two decades of the century. But this success was due less to the virtues of the scheme and its originator than to the fact that the figure for 1628 was inflated by the consequences of the epidemic of 1627: some recovery was inevitable. Similarly, when expenditure climbed again to over £300 in 1637 this was the consequence of rising extraordinary expenses and an increasing number of poor. Ivie himself admitted that by 1636 the poor were 'very much abroad begging again'. When he again took charge of the storehouse in 1637 he was unable to reduce expenditure below £250. In 1640 the storehouse was closed down. Ivie predictably argued that it was 'let down by the great trouble that was raised by some Innkeepers and Alehouses, Bakers and Hucksters and Brewers, and all the loose unruly rabble'.[77] But the real reason was the unwillingness of the council to maintain an expensive institution which had not succeeded in radically reducing the poor rate.

The brewhouse was similarly unsuccessful. As early as 1625 the council complained that its custom was 'less than is convenient to answere the chardge thereof, much lesse to yelde the profit for relyeffe of the poore, as was expected'. In an attempt to break the boycott by the drink interest all inn- and alehouse-keepers were summoned to an Assembly to say how much beer they would buy: 92 attended but the names of only 44 of these occur in the brewhouse accounts and very few were regular customers.[78] Only poor alehouse-keepers like 'Widow Lissenby' or 'Widow Hyde' bought beer regularly, presumably because they feared for their licences more than they feared the disapproval of the private brewers. The vast majority of the 807 customers in its first years were private individuals buying for their households. John Ivie naturally figured prominently, purchasing 100 barrels a year as long as the brewhouse functioned. A more surprising customer, considering the opposition of the Close to the scheme, was Sir Lawrence Hyde, one of the leading gentry there, who bought nearly twice this amount per year at the end of the 1620s.[79] Other gentry fulfilled their charitable obligations in this painless manner.

The brewhouse was in fact working on a large scale. Accounts for 1625–6 show cash receipts from sales of beer amounting to £1,370 in twelve months. In the first six months of 1635 5,700 barrels of beer were brewed, more than 200 barrels per week. By contemporary standards this was a substantial output: a private brewer in the town in the 1660s was said to produce 130 barrels a week.[80] On average between 1625 and 1641 the brewhouse consumed 900 quarters of malt per year, one-seventh of the amount earlier estimated as the consumption of all private brewers in the town.[81]

Some contribution was made to the poor. The £1 a week promised to the workhouse appears to have continued, and the brewhouse delivered regular amounts of beer to the pesthouse for the infected in 1627 and to the storehouse after 1628. There were weekly payments of 12s to the almshouses at Winchester gate, another example of the association of public and private charity. But the profits were never as large as had been hoped, partly because of the original debts of the brewhouse, incurred when it was set up, partly because of the credit it gave its customers. New loans were raised to pay off old ones, but at the outbreak of the Civil War the burden of debt was so great that the institution had ceased to function. In 1646 Bee and Abbott still urged 'that the Brewhouse should be continued' but the council decided to lease it out, and sold its goods to Francis Dove, a brewer as well as a friend of Ivie and husband of Peter Thatcher's widow.[82] The novel features of the poor scheme came to an end.

Even the workhouse, the only part of the structure of the 1620s to survive the Civil War, suffered radical modification. Its most important function of financing the employment of poor children in the town was weakened by the difficulty of finding willing and responsible masters, and when it was again reformed in the later 1630s the plan was less ambitious. By then the political balance in the town had changed. Sherfield died in 1634, and the new Recorder, Robert Hyde, the son of Sir Lawrence and cousin of Clarendon, had no sympathy with his ideals. In 1640 he was accused of opposing the education of poor children, and he was certainly associated with the Dean and Chapter who were now, with the support of the Privy Council, intruding more successfully in the government of the town. The new situation influenced the provision for the poor. In 1638 the workhouse was transferred to larger premises, the Bishop giving half the property, the town purchasing the rest. The gentry of the Close contributed to the project and both Ivie and the brewer Thomas Hancock were governors of it.[83] This was a cause which the conservative critics of the brewhouse in the Close and the council could support, and the new workhouse bore the marks of their co-operation.

The new orders emphasized the disciplining and segregation of the poor. The house was now to contain up to thirty poor children, and there was no longer any mention of their being employed by their parents or masters in the town. On the contrary, they should be 'continually lodged dyetted and kept to work in the said house and not be permitted . . . to resort home to their parents or else to wander up and down the streets'. They were to wear badges bearing the arms of the city and blue caps 'whereby they might be known the children of the workhouse and distinguished from all other children'. Similarly, the idle sent to the workhouse were to be whipped on arrival, and 'to be kept as prisoners and not to have any admitted to come to them'. Though the poor apprenticeship scheme might still rescue children from this institution, this was a workhouse approaching much nearer to its eighteenth-century equivalent than the smaller and less strictly regulated institutions of earlier years. The ambition that outdoor employment and relief might lead to the gradual abolition of all but minimal poverty was tacitly abandoned, to be replaced by this quasi-penal incarceration of the poor.[84]

The ignominious end to the whole of the poor scheme of the 1620s was not due to any lessening of the problem of poverty. The slump in the cloth industry in Salisbury continued, there were outbreaks of plague in 1644 and 1646, and a series of bad harvests, leading to 'great and lamentable complaints and cry of poore people', at the end of the decade. Indeed these crises evoked some of the old responses: pest-houses were built for the infected, and Ivie was even invited to set up a storehouse again 'for the better provision of the poore', though this plan came to nothing.[85] Rather, the end of the experiment was the result partly of its failure in the 1630s, partly of the disorders of civil war and of the rise of new concerns to monopolize the attention of the council. While the ravages of the warring armies in Salisbury made it impossible to raise extra finance for a poverty programme, the money that was available went towards the purchase of the Bishop's and Dean and Chapter lands, a project which now became the major interest of the governors of Salisbury.[86]

As a result, the overthrow of the ecclesiastical establishment and of

Robert Hyde during the Civil War, with the consequent enthronement of the Ivie group in power, brought no lasting revival of the 1620s machinery. Idealism had been tarnished by experience. There is in fact evidence of a harsher attitude among the aldermen who replaced some of Ivie's associates when the corporation was remodelled by the Cromwellian Charter of 1656. William Stephens, the ejected Presbyterian Recorder, wrote to Ivie that his replacement would 'punish sin, suppress alehouses and administer justice with greater courage than I have done'. At the very time when novel projects for the employment of the poor were commonplace among pamphleteers, that imaginative 'political activism' which Puritanism had inspired among the rulers of Salisbury changed its focus. It was the suppression of alehouses which William Stone, the Cromwellian Mayor, urged on the county justices in typically Puritan terms: 'You are postinge to the grave every day; . . . therefore duble and treble your resolutions to bee zealous in a good thinge . . . How dreadfull will a dieinge bed bee to a negligent magistrate.'[87] The appeal expressed precisely the inspiration of the Puritan aldermen of the 1620s; but the purpose was narrower and more restricted than theirs.

When bad harvest recurred and high food prices again hit the poor at the end of the 1650s, there was a half-hearted attempt to resurrect part of the old machinery. John Ivie, now an irascible old man, was called in yet again to revive the storehouse. But the overseers and churchwardens belonged to a new generation and 'wilfully refused to execute' the new orders, allying with Ivie's old antagonist, the brewer and Royalist Maurice Greene, against him. Even Ivie could only balance the accounts by reducing the cash payments to the poor ordered by the Justices. In the end the Mayor had to pay £13 17s 4d to 'severall poore people to Relieve there greate want when Mr. Ivie abated them halfe'. As Ivie characteristically put it, it was not yet 'God's time to do any good in this City'.[88] That time had passed. With the Restoration, he and some of his colleagues lost their places in the government of the town.[89] Those who continued laid down new orders for the workhouse, expelled immigrants, and continued the monthly meetings to oversee the poor rates, but did no more.

The wheel had come full circle. By the 1660s the town was faced with the same problems as in the first two decades of the century. Charitable funds were again being misapplied as they had been during the Interregnum; when plague returned in 1666 there were again arrears in receipt of money from the county; to meet the continuing burden of the poor, the rates were gradually increased, and additional levies were common whenever there was 'sickness in the town'.[90] But simpler and more indirect solutions were now sought. By the 1670s it was the opening up of the River Avon which was pressed as the panacea for Salisbury: trade and industry would revive, and then, wrote one advocate, 'the Magistrates will not need to put in practice any of their former petty ways of relief (as some call'd 'em; but others, Grievances) as their New-Brew-house, and Leather-Tokens, nor be enforc'd to burthen the Inhabitants with more monethly Rates than there be moneths in the year'.[91]

The innovations of the 1620s, therefore, were a temporary achievement, pushed through by a highly motivated group of Puritan aldermen in immediate response to a deterioration in the condition of the poor. They had tried to dragoon the whole community into employing and relieving the poor, to create a 'godly commonwealth' by direction from above. But their programme, like other municipal experiments, failed to reduce the problem to manageable size, and their successors like their opponents were more concerned with the repression and isolation of the poor. The larger number of those on relief became an accepted part of urban society, as the impotent 'divine poor' had once been—a permanent problem for a town council, but not one which monopolized its attention or its finances. Only the workhouse, settlement legislation and the poor rate remained after 1660. The magistrates fell back once again on the statutory machinery and dealt with symptoms rather than with causes. The 'new medicine for poverty' had become a palliative not a cure.

Notes

1 John Taylor, 'A Discovery by Sea from London to Salisbury', in *Works* (Spenser Society, 1869), p. 186.
2 Cf. the discussion in N. Z. Davis, 'Poor Relief, Humanism and Heresy: the Case of Lyon', *Studies in Medieval and Renaissance History*, V (1968), 217–75; C. Hill, 'Puritans and the Poor', *P. & P.*, no. 2 (1952), 32–50; V. Kiernan, 'Puritanism and the Poor, *ibid.*, no. 3, 45–51; C. Hill, *Society and Puritanism in Pre-Revolutionary England* (1964), chap. 7; A. L. Beier, 'Poor Relief in Warwickshire 1630–1660', *P. & P.*, no. 35 (1966), 77–100; E. Chill, 'Religion and Mendicity in Seventeenth-Century France', *International Review of Social History*, VII (1962), 400–25.

3 B. Pullan, 'The Famine in Venice and the New Poor Law, 1527–9', *Bollettino dell'Istituto di Storia della Società e dello Stato Veneziano*, V–VI (1963–4), 141–202; Davis, *op. cit.*; J. Webb, ed., *Poor Relief in Elizabethan Ipswich* (Suffolk Records Soc., IX, 1966), introduction; J. F. Pound, 'An Elizabethan Census of the Poor', *Univ. Birmingham Hist. J.*, VIII (1962), 135–61.

4 Philip Jones, *Certaine Sermons preached of late at Ciceter* (1588), sigs. E6v–E7; Richard Younge, *The Poores Advocate* (1654), chap. XIV, pp. 9–10. This distinction had its roots in canon law: B. Tierney, *Medieval Poor Law* (Berkeley, 1959), pp. 128–32.

5 On the development of the poor law, see E. M. Leonard, *The Early History of English Poor Relief* (1900), and W. K. Jordan, *Philanthropy in England 1480–1660* (1959), chap. 4.

6 Salisbury Municipal Archives (SMA), S162 (fols 25 ff. My own foliation: the folios are not numbered). I am indebted to the Town Clerk of Salisbury for permission to consult the valuable manuscripts in his care. Most of them, though not some of the miscellaneous loose documents drawn on here, have been listed in M. G. Rathbone, ed., *Records of Wiltshire Boroughs before 1836* (Wilts. Arch. and Nat. Hist. Soc., Records Branch, V, 1951), pp. 63–85.

7 In 1597 the population of Salisbury was said to be 7,000: SMA, Add. 40, document 8. The population in the 1620s may have been about 6,500: see note 38. Cf. *VCH Wilts*, VI, 72.

8 The list is in SMA, Z225 (unfoliated). I hope to analyse this record more fully on another occasion.

9 Younge, *op. cit.*, p. 11.

10 It was no easy matter to prove settlement; vagrants returned to Salisbury from elsewhere were often sent back again: e.g. 'Robert Nelson who was sent unto this Cittye from the parish of Hackney . . . supposing the said Nelson to be borne in this Cittye' was returned to Hackney because of an alleged technical error in his passport.

11 SMA, S162 (fols 1, 2); P/125, fols 68v., 75r.; Ledger C, fols 150v., 214v., 221–2. At the monthly meetings of overseers of the poor, strangers too respectable to be classed as vagrants were presented and ordered to leave the town: S162, *passim*. Cf. P. Styles, 'The Evolution of the Law of Settlement', *Univ. Birmingham Hist. J.*, IX (1963), 33–63.

12 Robert Allen, *A Treatise of Christian Beneficence* (1600), sig. A4v.

13 The price of wheat in Salisbury in 1597 was said to have reached 17*s* a bushel, comparable to the famine level elsewhere in England: SMA, Box 1, doc. 2; W. G. Hoskins, 'Harvest Fluctuations and English Economic History 1480–1619', *Agric. Hist. Rev.*, XII (1964), 38.

14 The parish registers of St Edmund's are deposited at the Salisbury Diocesan Record Office (DRO). Those of St Martin's and St Thomas's

are still in the parish churches: I am grateful to the incumbents for permission to consult them. The full figures for 'conceptions' (calculated by subtracting nine months from the date of baptism) and burials are as follows (all years are January to December):

	St Edmund's	St Thomas's	St Martin's	Total
Burials				
1597	230	86	73	389
Average 1588–94	109	47	63	219
'Conceptions'				
1597	62	56	32	150
Average 1588–94	89	76	56	221

For discussion of subsistence crises, see P. Laslett, *The World We Have Lost* (1965), pp. 111–14; E. A. Wrigley, *Population and History* (1969), pp. 66–8, 70. The drawbacks to using parish register material are well known (cf. the discussion in T. H. Hollingsworth, *Historical Demography* (1969), chap. 5), and even with an apparently reliable set like those of the Salisbury parishes the probability of some under-registration must be borne in mind. But they do indicate changes in mortality and pinpoint the crisis years.

15 *APC 1596–7*, pp. 151–2; *APC 1597*, p. 84; SMA, Add. 40, docs 7, 8; Miscellaneous Papers, L(5).

16 The parish register of St Edmund's refers to 'plague' in 1564; *HMC Various IV*, p. 228. In 1604 burials were as follows: St Edmund's 495, St Thomas's 355, St Martin's 281, Close 13, Total 1,144. (The register of the Close is in the vestry of Salisbury Cathedral.)

17 SMA, S161: accounts of 'chardges layd out for the mayntenance of infected houses'.

18 B. H. Cunnington, ed., *Records of the County of Wiltshire* (Devizes, 1932), p. 11.

19 Figures calculated from the monthly poor accounts in SMA, S161. A fall in the average number of baptisms in St Edmund's parish in the decade after the plague is suggestive of a decline in population.

20 Salisbury Dean and Chapter Records (DCR), Press IV, Petitions; SMA, N101, letter to Hertford 1616; Misc. Papers, 07. On depression in the woollen industry, see G. D. Ramsay, *The Wiltshire Woollen Industry in the Sixteenth and Seventeenth Centuries* (1943), esp. chap. 5 and p. 116; *VCH Wilts*, VI, 128, 129; B. E. Supple, *Commercial Crisis and Change in England 1600–1642* (Cambridge, 1959), *passim*.

21 From the list of freemen compiled in 1612, the distributive and drink

trades appear to be of increasing importance in a community once dominated by mercantile and textile interests: SMA, I/252.

22 Ramsay, *op. cit.*, pp. 77–8, 81. On the interrelationship of dearth and industrial depression, see P. Bowden, 'Agricultural Prices, Farm Profits and Rents' in J. Thirsk, ed., *The Agrarian History of England and Wales IV* (Cambridge, 1967), pp. 631–2.

23 Taylor, *op. cit.*, p. 186; SMA, N100, letter of 31 December 1625; N101, letter of 16 January 1626; Box 4, File 'Various 1600–30', doc. 65A. On the vulnerability of a substantial part of the population in time of sickness, cf. the statement in Sheffield in 1615 that 160 households 'are such (though they beg not) as are not able to abide the storme of one fortnights sickness but would be thereby driven to beggary', quoted in S. and B. Webb, *The Old Poor Law* (1927), pp. 82–3.

24 Registered burials in 1627 were as follows: St Edmund's 215, St Thomas's 106, St Martin's 141, Close 8, Total 470. The average annual number for the town from 1631 to 1640 was 199. (The parish register of St Martin's is blank for the plague year and the total has been taken from the transcripts in DRO.) Gross under-registration might account for the apparently low mortality, but other sources suggest the same; e.g. Bishop Davenant commented from the safety of a country residence on low mortality as well as on the reason for flight: 'The number of those who die weekly is not great, but the danger is that ever and anon some new howse is infected', M. Fuller, *The Life, Letters and Writings of John Davenant* (1827), p. 256. On possible variations in the virulence of bubonic plague, see J. F. D. Shrewsbury, *A History of Bubonic Plague in the British Isles* (Cambridge, 1970), p. 5.

25 John Ivie, *A Declaration* (1661), pp. 11–12, 20. The flight of the wealthy from infection may have been more general in a small town like Salisbury than in larger cities. An observer of the Salisbury plague of 1666 noted: 'When [the plague] comes to rage in these little townes, it is more dangerous than in London itselfe because lesse means of avoiding it', SP 29/129/26.

26 *HMC Various I*, p. 97; cf. *HMC Exeter*, p. 176.

27 SMA, Misc. Papers, listing of St Edmund's and St Thomas's poor. For the dating of this document, see above, p. 173.

28 SMA, N100, Petitions to Sessions 1629; Y216.

29 SMA, S162 (fols 192v., 193r.); DRO, Consistory Court, Deposition Book 45, exam. Edward Page, March 1631; SP 16/243/23; SMA, N100 Petitions to Sessions 1635.

30 SMA, S162 (fols 25 ff.); Misc. Papers, listing of St Edmund's and St Thomas's poor; Misc. Papers, M36.

31 SMA, Misc. Papers, O(3); S162 (fol. 227v.), 9 December 1635.

32 John Hooker, writing of the poor in Exeter, quoted in I. Pinchbeck and

M. Hewitt, *Children in English Society I* (1969), p. 127. For the similar employment of children in Norwich, see the comments of Thomas Wilson, in 'The State of England', *Camden Miscellany XVI* (Camden Soc., 3rd Series, LII, 1936), p. 20.

33 Pound, *op. cit.*, p. 140.

34 SMA, I/253, fol. 7r.; *VCH Wilts*, III, 359. Some individuals in the census have not been included in Table 11 because the amount paid to them in poor relief is not recorded. It is probable also that the census underestimates the earnings of those listed. But the income of the poor on relief in Ipswich in 1597 was as small: 6*d* per head per week on average (calculated from J. Webb, *op. cit.*, pp. 119–40).

35 SMA, Misc. Papers, M39. This conclusion is supported by a comparison of the names in the census with those paying the poor rate in St Martin's parish in 1634: Misc. Papers, M38. Only one name occurs in both.

36 In the breakdown of the St Martin's listing in Table 9 the numbers of husbands and wives are maxima. The listing notes the presence of wives with their husbands only when there are no children. It has been assumed, for purposes of comparison, that all men with children also had wives living. This cannot be wholly the case; there were probably one or two widowers with children who had not remarried. Nevertheless, the contrast between the two groups in the census is clear.

37 Davis, *op. cit.*, pp. 274–5, puts the figure at 5 per cent in Lyon, but her attempt to show that the proportion was the same in Exeter and Norwich is unconvincing. If one includes the families of those receiving alms, it was probably slightly less than 5 per cent in Exeter, slightly more in Norwich: W. T. MacCaffrey, *Exeter 1540–1640* (Cambridge, Mass., 1958), pp. 12, 113; Pound, *op. cit.*, p. 144.

38 Almspeople for St Edmund's and St Thomas's are all those listed in the 1635 census; those for St Martin's are those distinguished as such in the 1635 listing, and the total poor for St Martin's are all those listed in 1635, including assumed wives in both cases (see note 36 above). Total populations have been deduced from baptisms in each parish from 1631 to 1640 by multiplying the annual average by 33: a multiple calculated from a comparison of average baptisms from 1692 to 1698 with the 1695 census figure of 6,976 (R. Benson and H. Hatcher, *Old and New Sarum or Salisbury* (1843), p. 822). The results are inevitably tentative but enable some comparison to be made. In 1626 an 'exact veiwe' of the town stated that there were 1,290 households in it: SMA, Box 4, doc. 65A. Using a multiplier of 5·073 persons per household (P. Laslett, 'Size and Structure of the Household in England over Three Centuries', *Population Studies*, XXIII (1969), 210), the total population would then be 6,544. The figures in Table 12 may not be too far from reality.

39 Figures for Norwich have been calculated from information given in

Pound, *op. cit.*; the Ipswich census is printed in J. Webb, *op. cit.*, pp. 119–40. The figures for Ealing and from Gregory King are cited in Laslett, *World We Have Lost*, p. 103. A third, rather more haphazard census of the poor survives for part of Warwick in 1586: Thomas Kemp, ed., *The Book of John Fisher, Town Clerk and Deputy Recorder of Warwick* (Warwick, n.d.), pp. 165–72.

40 Cf. Laslett, *World We Have Lost*, p. 64. The application of the term 'household' to the very poor is somewhat artificial: several of them were inmates; often two unrelated widows might be found living together. In the Salisbury censuses the poor are divided into families, and hence they include many single-person units. In the Ipswich census there are several cases of two apparently unrelated individuals being bracketed together. If those thus joined are counted as one 'household' the mean size of household among the Ipswich poor was 3·4; if they are counted as separate households it was 3·1.

41 SMA, Misc. Papers, bundle concerning charter disputes 1629; on poverty in Fisherton, cf. *VCH Wilts*, VI, 182, 188.

42 SMA, Z225, November 1635; Ivie, *op. cit.*, pp. 10–11. For disorder in Salisbury alehouses, see DRO, Consistory Court, Deposition Book 46, fols 178–82; Book 36, fol. 69v.; and for inns as harbourers of vagrants, cf. PRO, Asz 24/20 fol. 76r.

43 Jordan, *op. cit.*, esp. chap. 5.

44 The information on charities is taken from *House of Commons Papers 1908*, LXXXVI, 370–592, supplemented by references in Benson and Hatcher, *op. cit.*, and the Council Ledgers. Accounts survive for Edward Rodes's charity and the clothing fund: SMA, Y212, Z225. In 1604 charitable funds were drawn on to the tune of £114 to help support the plague-infected: Ledger C, fol. 179v.

45 SMA, SSM II; SSM IV; I/246, fols 17, 60, 163v. But the weavers at least refused to support their poor journeymen when the Corporation urged them to do so: S162 (fols 192v., 193r.).

46 Those admitted to St Nicholas's hospital were over sixty years old, and action was taken both there and at Trinity hospital to prevent the entry of 'burthensome and troublesome' married couples: C. Wordsworth, *The Fifteenth Century Cartulary of St. Nicholas' Hospital Salisbury* (Salisbury, 1902), pp. 227–8, 269; SMA, Ledger C. fol. 408r.

47 *APC 1596–7*, pp. 488–9; PRO C93/1/15; Ivie, *op. cit.*, p. 32. For early use of the loan funds, see Ledger C, fols 57r., 146r., 152r., 202. Aldermen certainly obtained loans for their own clients: cf. the endorsed remarks on N100, Petitions to Sessions 1629.

48 SMA, S161; S162 (fols 203v., 204r.); Ivie, *op. cit.*, pp. 8–9; S162 (fol. 189r.).

49 SMA, S161 and S162 record the proceedings at these meetings. Cf. the

fear in 1770 that St Thomas's, 'the most opulent parish' in the heart of the town, might withdraw from the municipal organization: *A Short State of the Case . . . for a Bill to consolidate the Poor Rates in . . . Salisbury* (1770).

50 Benson and Hatcher, *op. cit.*, p. 283; SMA, Ledger C, fols 155v., 157v., 159v., 169v.; S163 Accounts of the House of Correction 1602–12.

51 SMA, Ledger C, fols 233–4r., 274v., 277r., 283v., 285r.

52 SMA, Misc. Papers, 07.

53 SMA, Ledger C, fols 291r., 312v., 313v., 315r.; N100 Agreement with Philip Veryn; Y211; S178/1, fols 4r., 5v., 6r.; Box 4, doc. 40. The new workhouse had beds for fifteen people, three more than its predecessor: inventories in S163 and S178/1.

54 Wiltshire County Record Office (WRO), Quarter Sessions Roll, Easter 1628, doc. 121; Taylor, *op. cit.*, p. 188; N. J. Williams, ed., *Tradesmen in Early Stuart Wiltshire: A Miscellany* (Wilts. Arch. and Nat. Hist. Soc., Records Branch, XV, 1960), pp. xiii, xv; C. H. Haskins, *The Ancient Trade Guilds and Companies of Salisbury* (Salisbury, 1912), pp. 328–32; N101, letter of 22 November 1608. Ivie put the number of inns and alehouses at over 130: *op. cit.*, p. 19.

55 SMA, Ledger C, fols 291v., 294v., 312r.; S179 Brewhouse Minutes, fol. 3r. On the Dorchester brewhouse, see C. H. Mayo, ed., *The Municipal Records of the Borough of Dorchester* (Exeter, 1908), pp. 525–9. Other towns used profits from the town mills for poor relief: W. T. Baker, ed., *Records of Nottingham V* (1900), p. 131; *VCH Staffs*, VIII, 31.

56 SP 16/194/19; SP 16/332/67 (I owe this reference to Mr P. Clark); Taylor *op. cit.*, p. 186. For another example of Stamford's interest in his own and the poor's profit from brewing, see H. Stocks, ed., *Records of the Borough of Leicester IV* (Cambridge, 1923), p. 286.

57 *VCH Wilts*, VI, 100; Ivie, *op. cit.*, pp. 13, 21, 27: the whole of Ivie's pamphlet is an apologia for the storehouse; SMA, Y216, Storehouse Accounts.

58 SMA, Ledger C, fols 155v., 291v. ff.; SP 16/311/21.

59 SMA, N101, letter of 30 December 1623; SP 16/525/57; *The Proceedings in the Star Chamber against Henry Sherfield Esq.* (1717), p. 52; SP 14/64/66; DRO, Subdean's Court, Churchwardens Presentments, 1634 St Edmund's, and Sentences; SP 16/183/58, testimony of Michael Mackerell.

60 H. J. F. Swayne, ed., *Churchwarden's Accounts of S. Edmund and S. Thomas Sarum* (Salisbury, 1896), p. 173; *VCH Wilts*, VI, 153; C. Hill, *Society and Puritanism*, p. 435; SP 16/183/58, testimony of John Bowen. In his will Thatcher left books, including works of Cartwright, to Ivie's nephew: PCC 112 Evelyn, proved 1641.

61 Ivie, *op. cit.*, sig. A2r., p. 21; SP 16/527/4.

62 Cf. M. Walzer, *The Revolution of the Saints* (1966), chap. 6; G. Strauss, 'Protestant Dogma and City Government in Nuremberg', *P. & P.*, no. 36 (1967), 38–58.

63 Swayne, *op. cit.*, p. 190; SMA, Misc. Papers, 'Orders touchinge the Poore 1623', in bundle concerning charter disputes.

64 S. and B. Webb, *op. cit.*, p. 85; SMA, Misc. Papers, 'Orders touchinge the Poore 1623'.

65 F. Nicolls, *The Life and Death of Mr. Ignatius Jurdain* (2nd edn, 1655), sig. A7r., p. 65. Like Ivie, Jourdain was one of the few magistrates to remain in a town during an outbreak of plague and attempt to govern it: MacCaffrey, *op. cit.*, p. 273. Dorchester also had its 'Puritan Patriarch', John White, 'by whose wisdom . . . all able poor [were] set on work, and impotent maintained': T. Fuller, *The History of the Worthies of England* (1840), III, 25.

66 Cf. criticisms of the magistrates in SP 16/540/93, SP 16/183/58; and Tookye's request to his fellow Justices to expel from the town a man 'whose conversation is not well thought of. If he may be voided the towne, let it be done . . . The Lorde direct you': SMA, Misc. Papers O(2).

67 There is a list of brewers in SMA, I/112; Ledger C, fols 296v., 299r., 309r., 312r., 326v., 329, 330r., 333; S179, 17 January 1625; BM Add. MS. 41057; Haskins, *op. cit.*, pp. 320–4. Some record of the suits between the town and the brewers may be found in PRO, KB 27/1550, Membrane 22; KB 27/1554, Membranes 1, 30. In contrast to the Ivie group at least two of the brewers, Thomas Hancock and Maurice Greene, were suspected of Royalist sympathies during the Civil War: *Lords Journals*, VII, 485.

68 SMA, S179, 16 January 1626; N101, letters of 16 January 1626; Benson and Hatcher, *op. cit.*, pp. 348–9. No statute confirming the brewhouse was in fact passed, but a bill may have been introduced: *Commons Journal*, I, 837.

69 SMA, File of 'papers about contributions by the lay inhabitants of the Close'; N101, letter of 15 January 1610; DCR, Press IV, Letters on Various Subjects, 29 December 1609; SMA, Box 4, doc. 65A; Y216, MS notes by John Ivie; Ledger C, fol. 348r.; WRO, Quarter Sessions Roll, Trinity 1604, doc. 120.

70 DRO, File on disputes between the town and the Bishop, doc. 16; SMA, Box 4, File 2, doc. 40; Misc. Papers, bundle concerning charter disputes.

71 *HMC*, 4th Report, Appendix, pp. 131, 135; DRO, File on disputes between town and Bishop, doc. 16; SMA, Box 4, File 2, doc. 19A.

72 Benson and Hatcher, *op. cit.*, p. 377. The Charter of 1630 is printed *ibid.*, pp. 786–93.

73 WRO, Quarter Sessions Minute Book 1626–31, Trinity 1627–Easter 1628; Quarter Sessions Roll, Hilary 1628, docs 121, 127; SMA, Z236; Ivie, *op. cit., passim.*

74 SMA, Y216, Storehouse Accounts 1628–39; N98 contains other Storehouse Accounts for 1632–3.

75 This estimate is based on a comparison of the amounts of beer and bread
available in the storehouse in 1628 and 1629 with the diet in St Bartholomew's hospital in 1687 and a sixteenth-century estimate of an
individual's grain consumption: J. C. Drummond and A. Wilbraham,
The Englishman's Food (1957), p. 465; N. S. B. Gras, *The Evolution of the
English Corn Market* (Cambridge, Mass., 1915), p. 77n. In cash terms,
beer from the brewhouse was worth about £50 per annum, a useful
addition to the income from the poor rate.

76 SMA, S162 Poor Accounts; Misc. Papers, O(2).

77 SMA, Y216; Ivie, *op. cit.*, pp. 27–9; SMA, Ledger C, fol. 419r. The
volume of storehouse accounts (Y216) was kept by Ivie but the figures
there do not entirely agree with those in his *Declaration*, where he
deliberately exaggerates his case.

78 SMA, Ledger C, fol. 314v.; S179 (fol. 30v.); N101, list of innkeepers
etc. Customers of the brewhouse are recorded in its Debtors Books:
S181/1, 2, 3.

79 SMA, S181/2, fol. 256v. (Widow Hyde); S181/1, fols 59r., 157v., 240v.,
287v., etc., S181/2, fols 114r., 159r., etc. (Ivie); S181/1, fols 69r., 225v.,
302r., 385r., 429v. (Sir L. Hyde). John and Francis Dove, themselves
brewers and yet allies of Ivie, made token purchases of beer only in 1636
when John was Mayor; even then Francis returned his beer shortly
afterwards: S181/2, fol. 247r.

80 SMA, Box 9, doc. 1; S182, S165 Brewing and Tunning Accounts;
Q136b, 11 December 1668. Output by the mid-1630s was as high as in
the brewery with what were hitherto thought to be the earliest accounts,
that of Edmund Halsey at the end of the seventeenth century, and half
that of the huge naval brewhouse at East Smithfield in the same period:
P. Mathias, *The Brewing Industry in England 1700–1830* (Cambridge,
1959), pp. 7–8, 202.

81 SMA, S182, S165: consumption of malt has been calculated from the
figures given week by week for the years 1625, 1627, 1632, 1635, 1637
and 1641. In 1597 all brewers in Salisbury were said to use 120 quarters
of malt a week: Add. 40, doc. 9.

82 SMA, Box 9, doc. 1; S181/1, fols 1–3, 157, 228 etc.; S181/2, fols 131,
302v.; S179, July 1626 *et passim*; Ledger C, fols 394r., 410r., 413v.;
Ledger D, fols 10v., 17r., 19–23; N98, fol. 43v.

83 Benson and Hatcher, *op. cit.*, p. 391; *CSPD 1637*, pp. 1, 4, 78; *CSPD
1638–9*, pp. 122–3, 148; SMA, S157, fols 4–5; Ledger C, fols 400r.,
403v.; PRO, PC 2/48 p. 399.

84 SMA, S153; see S162, *passim*, for tradesmen taking workhouse children
as poor apprentices. For the growing cult of the workhouse in the

later seventeenth century, see C. Wilson, 'The Other Face of Mercantilism', *Trans. Roy. Hist. Soc.*, 5th Series, 9 (1959), 87–101, and for similar developments in France, Chill, *op. cit.*, and P. Deyon, 'A propos du pauperisme au milieu du XVIIe siècle', *Annales E.S.C.*, 22 (1967), 137–53.

85 *HMC Various I*, pp. 112, 116; Haskins, *op. cit.*, p. 187; *HMC*, 4th Report, Appendix, p. 69; PRO, Asz 24/21, fols 58–9r., 104v.–5r.; SP 18/3/15; SMA, Ledger, D, fols 14r., 24, 39, 42v., 43v.

86 SMA, Box 9, doc. 49; Ledger D, fols 28v., 39r., 46–8.

87 Benson and Hatcher, *op. cit.*, p. 438; *HMC Various I*, p. 132. On projects for poor relief in these years, see Jordan, *op. cit.*, pp. 205–15; and on 'political activism', cf. Walzer, *op. cit.*, pp. 306–7, and Beier, *op. cit.*, p. 95.

88 SMA, Ledger D, fols 107v., 108r., 111, 116v., 117r.; N98, 9 November 1659, S162, 1659–60 account; Ivie, *op. cit.*, pp. 1, 11, 29–30.

89 SMA, Ledger D, fol. 134v.; I/253, fol. 36r. Ivie died in 1666. The refusal of the corporation to co-operate in founding the almshouses projected in his will for the 'godly poor' exemplified the change in attitudes: PCC 180 Mico; SMA, Ledger D, fols 137, 150v., 165v.

90 *Ibid.*, fols 21r., 85r., 128r., 153v., 161v.; PROC93/21/23; *HMC Various I*, pp. 148, 149; PRO, Asz 24/22, fol. 142; SMA, E40, fol. 30r.; S162, *passim*; N98, 23 November 1649.

91 R.S., *Avona: or a Transient View of the benefit of making Rivers of this Kingdom Navigable* (1675), pp. 32–3.

6

Politics in Chester during the Civil Wars and the Interregnum 1640–62

A. M. Johnson

The split between royalist and parliamentarian in Chester in 1642 was essentially a split between the most prominent members of the city Assembly and was for most of the principals the expression and out-growth under national labels of the local political struggle in which they had been engaged throughout the early seventeenth century.[1]

Politics in the city were very disturbed in the first forty years of the century and for much of the period the Assembly was deeply divided into opposing factions. The city was often in conflict with the county of Chester and the cathedral as to their respective rights and jurisdictions. There was little religious unrest in the period: Puritanism never attracted more than a small body of support in this cathedral city, though a handful of prominent parliamentarians were Puritans. But the city's relations with the central government were invariably strained and were at times very poor.[2] Chester, however, was one of a small number of urban centres which took the royalist side in 1642 and, at the outset, displayed little of what the royalist Clarendon described as 'that factious humour which possesed most corporations'.[3] Although the port of Chester was relatively depressed, the city occupied an important strategic position. It commanded the road into royalist north Wales, it was the principal port of transportation to Ireland, and it could be readily garrisoned.

The history of the period from 1640 to 1646 in Chester shows that there was no radical break from earlier in the century either in the framework within which politics operated or in the nature of the local struggle. There was, in fact, a high degree of continuity in Chester politics throughout the seventeenth century and the years after 1642 can be seen as the period during which certain of the key issues and rivalries begun earlier in the century worked themselves out. The politics of the period from 1640 to the commission for investigating municipal corporations in 1661–2 demonstrated, just as the preceding part of the century had done, the independent nature of the local governors in their relations with successive central governments and emphasized the continuing alienation of local from central government. In spite of the political changes of these years there existed deep local determination by whichever party was in power to resist outside interference in city affairs.

The conflict which was to prove decisive in Chester in 1642 arose out of the activities of a small group within the Company of Merchants who sought to control the most lucrative areas of external trade by securing certain exclusive grants to itself. Controversy over these grants flared into prominence on occasions during the early seventeenth century although it was, for long periods, submerged and absorbed into more arresting quarrels which tended to dominate politics in Chester up to 1640. Chester became a royalist city because of the manœuvrings of a small group of aldermen who were determined to retain these privileges which derived from the Crown.

When the Crown, in 1581, made a grant to the Chester mere merchants awarding them exclusive rights to the export of calf-skins from Chester controversy immediately ensued and continued until a compromise was agreed in 1589. The mere merchants claimed that it had been granted for their exclusive benefit while the rest of the trading community regarded the grant as having been made for the benefit of the city as a whole.[4] The grant was renewed in 1605 and in 1615 the Privy Council established that it had been awarded to the mere merchants for the benefit of the community.[5] Meanwhile, early in James's reign the city was held no longer exempt from the impost on prise wines brought into Chester, though the authorities were permitted in 1605 to pay a rent for the farm to the farmer of prise wines in the county palatine of Chester. In 1611, Alderman William Gamull and other prominent merchants became sub-farmers of the impost.[6] In February 1624, William Gamull, William Aldersey, Andrew Gamull, and other associates reached an exclusive agreement with the new farmer, Sir Richard Calveley, for the farm of prise wines in the port of Chester on payment of a fee of £650 per annum.[7]

The grant from Calveley had been obtained as the result of secret negotiations with Gamull and his friends who had clearly been acting against the interests of the remainder of their own company, to say nothing of the rest of the trading community. The opponents of Gamull's clandestine activities found a leader in Councillor William Edwards. Edwards, a Puritan, came to Chester as a young man from a modest family in Rhual in nearby Flintshire.[8] He became a freeman of the city in 1615 upon the completion of a seven years' apprenticeship to an ironmonger but began to branch out as a merchant and in 1623 became a common councillor. Gamull was a member of a prominent Chester family with widespread interests in the city. For some time Edwards had been at odds with the merchants, led by Gamull, and he was refused admission to their society, membership of which was essential to engage in foreign trade.

At an Assembly meeting in March 1624 Edwards led an attack on William Gamull and his associates whom he accused of failing in their trust to the city. He accused Gamull of oppression, cruelty, and tyrannical conduct in his secret dealing to secure the exclusive grant from Calveley.[9] Edwards kept up his attack and at an Assembly in July of that year he was ordered to withdraw his allegations and the Aldermanic Bench demanded that he be imprisoned for his foul language.[10] Edwards, however, continued his opposition to the ruling group in the company for the next two years until the Privy Council, towards the end of 1626, ordered the company to admit Edwards. Though they studiously failed to obey the order at this time he appears eventually to have secured membership in 1629.[11]

The feud between the Gamull and Edwards groups came into prominence again in 1629 when Gamull and his close associates secured by devious means a renewal of the grant for exclusive transportation of calf-skins from Chester. Since the last renewal, in 1605, James I had granted to James Maxwell a patent for the transportation of calf-skins from ports in England for which trade Chester was the most important outlet.[12] The city attempted in 1613 to gain exemption from the patent without success[13] and when in 1629 the grant came due for renewal Alderman William Gamull and others of his group were deputed by the Assembly to go to London to negotiate for a new grant on behalf of the city.[14] Instead of doing so they procured a grant from Maxwell for themselves. Edwards and his colleagues drew up a petition to Viscount Savage accusing Gamull of betraying the interests of the rest of the company and of the city. In December

Gamull utterly refused to heed the advice of the Privy Council that he surrender his patents before the mayor of Chester in order to allow the recorder to go to London to re-negotiate the grant on behalf of the city. Edwards and his allies then prepared a swingeing indictment against Gamull for the Privy Council, setting forth the underhand means which he had employed to procure the licence which gave him and his associates a complete monopoly over the valuable calf-skin trade.[15]

The feud between the groups led by Gamull and Edwards smouldered on for some time during the 1630s.[16] Edwards's determined campaigning against the monopolistic activities of the Gamull group appears to have gained him substantial support in the Assembly for he was elected an alderman in June 1631 and attained the mayoralty in 1636–7.

The intense conflict between the Gamull and Edwards groups may have died down in the late 1630s even though negotiations for the grant of transportation of calf-skins began once again in 1640.[17] Details of the negotiations are not known, but it is possible that after the troubles of recent years most of the merchants reached some sort of accommodation with Gamull which went a good way towards satisfying their grievances and those of the many Assembly members who had sympathized with Edwards's campaigning. Edwards and Gamull, however, remained implacable adversaries.

The first clear indication that the long-standing animosity between Alderman William Gamull and Alderman William Edwards was being transmuted into division between royalist and parliamentarian occurred in March 1642. The occasion was the seemingly innocuous attempt by an Irish woman to sell a number of barrels of herrings in Chester. Mayor Thomas Cowper, later a royalist, in his capacity of clerk of the market, and in the company of Recorder Robert Brerewood, Alderman William Gamull, and other aldermen/J.P.s, agreed to let the woman sell the herrings if she would set aside five barrels for the poor of the city. As soon as the bargaining had taken place Alderman William Edwards intervened on the side of the woman and told her to go and sell her fish freely and to take no notice of anyone. He assured her of his support, 'And lett Mr. Maior or any other doe their worst they can.' Mayor Cowper related that Edwards was reproached by William Gamull and Recorder Brerewood

to forbeare his highe and contemptuous words and to shewe
mee more respect in my place. Notwithstanding whereof he
[Edwards] persisted in his highe language often telling mee that
I had abused the Parliamt. And that I had neglectyed the
commission that came from Parliamt. And threwe yt away wth
many other scandalous and abusive words. And these wear
spoken in a very loud craving and contemptuous maner.

Recorder Brerewood and Alderman William Gamull attempted to
utilize the quarter sessions scheduled for the following day to prepare
an indictment against Edwards.

Edwards retaliated by threatening to bring the question of his indictment before Parliament where he had the close friendship of Sir
William Brereton, soon to become a notable parliamentary commander.[18] Mayor Cowper attempted to invoke the support of the
two Chester M.P.s in case Edwards's allegations were brought to the
attention of the Commons, but Francis Gamull (brother of Alderman
William) and Sir Thomas Smith advised an attempt be made to settle
the matter 'at home' because they did not want the affair raised in
Parliament.[19]

Although in March 1642 the political affiliations of some of the
leading members of the Assembly were beginning to harden along
royalist-parliamentarian lines, the prevailing mood in Chester during
the spring and much of the summer was to seek some sort of accommodation. This mood was in evidence when the first real test of
loyalties came in July 1642 with the issue by Parliament of its Commission of Deputy Lieutenancy and the issue by Charles I of his
Commission of Array.[20] The latter brought forth a strong appeal
from a group of citizens for moderation between King and Parliament,[21] though at the end of July, when it was apparent that little less
than a miracle would prevent the outbreak of hostilities, the Gamull
group was able to take advantage of the general indecision and the
constitutional structure of the city quickly and decisively to align
Chester on the royalist side.

Alderman William Edwards last attended an Assembly meeting at
the end of 1641.[22] He probably realized by 1642 that he had little
prospect of gaining much support against the Gamulls on the Aldermanic Bench. In the worsening political situation it seems that most of
those who had sympathized with Edwards in the past, though not
disposed to the royalists, were not prepared to hazard their livelihoods

by joining with Edwards against the Gamulls and openly declaring for the parliamentary cause.

On 8 August, Sir William Brereton and Edwards, possibly hoping to make one final appeal to the wider support which Edwards had enjoyed in recent years, made a bold attempt on behalf of Parliament to stir up the citizens and gain the loyalty of the hundred-strong city militia. The attempt failed and the sheriffs under instructions from the royalist-dominated Aldermanic Bench forced them to leave the city.[23]

The constitutional structure of the city was such that the effective seat of power lay among the members of the Aldermanic Bench and especially among the aldermen/J.P.s or ex-mayors. Domination of the Aldermanic Bench meant control of the Assembly and thus of the city. Because the sheriff-peers and common councilmen occupied a traditionally inferior place in the Assembly and usually acquiesced in aldermanic control, it was not a difficult matter for the royalist-inclined aldermen/J.P.s who commanded a majority on the Aldermanic Bench under the leadership of the Gamull brothers to manoeuvre Chester on to the royalist side.

In August 1642 there were fifteen aldermen/J.P.s on the Bench of twenty-four. The determined group consisted of William Gamull, his brother Francis, M.P., Sir Thomas Smith Kt, the other Chester M.P., Thomas Throppe, who had re-negotiated the grant of calf-skins in 1640, Mayor Thomas Cowper, Richard Dutton, another merchant, and the influential Recorder Robert Brerewood, who, together with the emotional royalist Randle Holme, could dominate the Aldermanic Bench and thus control the city. They were supported by two other aldermen/J.P.s, William, Earl of Derby, and John, Earl Rivers, who rarely attended Assembly meetings but could when they chose exercise their rights as aldermen and bring pressure to bear on the Bench.

The task of the Gamull group was made relatively easy because the attitude of the remaining aldermen, and of nearly all of the sheriff-peers and common councilmen, was to try to keep out of affairs as much as possible and to wait on events. Most of them simply acquiesced in the fact of royalist control of the city. The arrival of the King in Chester on 23 October 1642 consolidated the position and authority of the royalist aldermen. The small number of Assembly members who determined openly to support Parliament rather than acquiesce in the ascendancy of the royalist group left the city for the suburbs by the end of September 1642.

Clarendon was wrong to ascribe Chester's royalism to the initiatives of the Bishop and his son and to imply that there existed widespread support for the royalist cause in Chester.[24] A pamphleteer described the key figures in Chester's royalism with greater accuracy. 'Master Bridgman took upon him the government of the city, which the soft spirited aldermen durst not contradict, but seemed thankfully to accept of his varnished notions. That which emboldened him thereunto was the malignant party which brought him in, which was the Recorder, the two Gamuls and Master Throp.'[25]

Royalism was superficial in Chester outside this group whose interests were so closely linked with those of the Crown. Just how narrow was the base of solid royalist support in Chester was clearly demonstrated in the period of royalist ascendancy from 1642 to 1646. Although the small group led by William and Francis Gamull had been instrumental in ensuring that Chester became a royalist stronghold, effective government of the city was vested throughout the period of royalist control in foreigners or non-Cestrians. This was because the Crown had for years experienced the independent spirit of corporations and had good reason to be distrustful of them. It was important for the Crown to try to provide against any change of heart among the royalist aldermen or against any serious surge of antagonism among the acquiescent sheriff-peers, councilmen, and freemen. The inclusion of the city within the authority of the Cheshire Commission of Array, the conspicuous absence of prominent Cestrians from the Commission,[26] and the appointment of 'foreigners' to the governorship of the city, were seen to be the most effective hedges against those contingencies and the most effective means of keeping Chester under the close control of the royalist high command.

For the first few months of the royalist ascendancy, however, the government of the city was entrusted to a council which sat at the Bishop's Palace. The members of the council 'for managing the government of Chester' were drawn principally from the Commissioners of Array, the most important of whom were Lord Kilmorey, Sir Edward Savage, the Bishop and his son Orlando Bridgeman, though a pamphleteer claimed that Lady Cholmondeley, wife of Robert Viscount Cholmondeley, also on the council, was as influential as anyone.[27]

Early in 1643 Chester received its first royalist governor, Sir Nicholas Byron. As governor he was answerable to none within

Chester but only to the royalist high command which meant in practice Prince Rupert. The presence of a military governor meant that there existed two distinct forms of government in Chester. Although the Assembly meetings, the city courts, and all the trappings of civil government continued to function seemingly undisturbed by the presence of the military, the garrison served as a reminder that the whole framework was under the surveillance of the governor and that co-operation was expected from the city authorities.[28]

The relationship between the civil and military authorities was from the start an uneasy one and jealousies and underlying disagreements conspired to produce a good deal of friction between the two. The royalist aldermen resented what they regarded as their reduced position in Chester's affairs with the presence of a governor in the city. They especially resented their lack of authority to deal with abuses committed by the soldiers who, they alleged, went unpunished by their superiors.[29]

Certain political events during the period of royalist ascendancy served to illustrate the wisdom of the royalist high command in vesting control of the garrison in the hands of foreign governors. The Crown was clearly wary of interpreting the royalism of a small group of aldermen as representative of much more than their own sectional interests. In January 1644, after the capture by parliamentary forces of the governor of Chester, a replacement was required. The circumstances surrounding the appointment of a successor demonstrated the deep-rooted suspicion which prominent royalists entertained of corporations.

The King wrote to Prince Rupert recommending Alderman and Colonel Francis Gamull for appointment as governor of Chester.[30] The King's proposal prompted Lord John Byron, formerly commander of forces in the Cheshire area and recently deputy to Prince Rupert, to write an urgent letter to Rupert in which he drew attention to the unfaithfulness of corporations and of the potential dangers inherent in appointing someone native-born whose loyalties might be more to his own city than to the royalist cause:

> I thought his Majestye had allready had sufficient experience of
> corporations not to intrust them with the command of a place of
> such importance as this is . . . I hope you will be pleased to
> make a stopp of it, the consequences of it beeinge so dangerous,
> that if this bee admitted of, the like will be attempted in all the

corporations in England that are under his Maties obedience
and if one obtaine it the rest will never bee satisfied till they have
Gouernors of theire owne.[31]

Lord Byron's warnings did not pass unheeded. Prince Rupert dis-
regarded the King's recommendation and appointed Byron himself as
governor under his special commission in March 1644.[32]

The mayoral elections of 1644 and 1645 served to endorse Byron's
fears concerning the fickleness of corporations and of the depth of
royalism in Chester.

The procedure for electing a mayor was a long drawn out affair
which went through six stages. At the first stage the aldermen/J.P.s
met in the Inner Pentice and cast their votes for up to half a dozen
candidates. At this meeting two aldermen usually emerged as the
clear favourites of the aldermen/J.P.s. These two invariably continued
to receive the most votes through the different stages of the election
process. At the subsequent stages the electorate was widened to include the aldermen below the chair, the sheriff-peers, and finally, the
councilmen. In most mayoral elections the candidates continued to
receive votes in roughly similar proportions as they had first received
them in the Inner Pentice. At the fifth stage the list of candidates and
the votes received by them up to that time was presented to the general
body of freemen who usually divided the major part of their votes
between the two leading candidates. The names of the two who had
received most votes were then returned before the twenty-four
aldermen who voted for one of them as mayor. It was only at times of
crisis, or of intense political activity, that the freemen, usually deferential to the wishes of the aldermen, were ever moved sufficiently
to assert their voting power to throw out the obvious choices of the
aldermen/J.P.s and elect someone of their own choosing. The elections of October 1644 and October 1645 were such occasions.

Three days before the election of 1644 Lord John Byron, ever suspicious but no less perceptive of the mood of Chester, wrote to
Prince Rupert to warn him of the unpredictability of the Cestrians:
'Your Highness knowes how full this Towne is, of ill affected and
refractory people . . . for many who heretofore were thought loyall,
upon this success of the Rebells are eyther turned newters, or wholly
revolted to them.'[33] In the Inner Pentice the aldermen/J.P.s nomi-
nated six candidates, though the clear favourites were Sir Francis
Gamull, recently knighted by the King for his service in helping to

secure Chester, and Sir Thomas Smith, who, with Gamull, represented Chester in the Long Parliament. Gamull received 14 votes and Smith 8.[34] Two other aldermen, Broster and Walley, received 4 votes and 1 vote respectively. At the fourth stage, when the voters included the sheriff-peers and councilmen, Gamull continued to hold the lead with Smith in second place. Broster had received 12 votes and Walley 7. So far the Assembly had performed its traditional role of endorsing the wishes of the aldermen/J.P.s. But when the freemen were called upon to cast their votes in Common Hall, the situation changed dramatically. The principal nominees of the aldermen/J.P.s were crushingly defeated. Walley and Broster were given by far the greatest number of votes with 319 and 290 respectively. Sir Francis Gamull polled only 123 votes while Sir Thomas Smith gained a derisory 23 votes which was two fewer than he had received at the final stage in the Assembly.

An account by Randle Holme of the proceedings in this dramatic election showed that the royalist aldermen were reluctant to permit the freemen to exercise their rights in a Common Hall because they feared that they would throw out their candidates Gamull and Smith. Wiser heads among the aldermen, however, appreciated that the consequences of denying the freemen their traditional rights might well have been more serious for the prestige and authority of the royalist regime than the rejection of Gamull and Smith. Thus the mayor, urged by Earl Rivers, 'suffered the commons theyr freedom of howse so that most voyces fell on Mr Walley and Mr Broster'. Walley did not want the mayoralty himself, having put his weight behind Broster, but when elected at the final stage by the aldermen in the Inner Hall he accepted it.[35]

In the spring and autumn of 1645, before and just after the next mayoral election, in an attempt to stem the growing expression of anti-royalist feeling in the Assembly, twelve sheriff-peers and councilmen were suspended from its deliberations, most of whom became parliamentary aldermen after the fall of the city in 1646.[36] In October 1645 the antagonism of the freemen towards the royalist aldermen and to Sir Francis Gamull in particular was even more intense than it had been a year before. The aldermen/J.P.s attempted again to secure the election of Sir Francis Gamull as mayor, but relegated Sir Thomas Smith to a low place in their list. Gamull was their clear favourite while their second choice was William Parnell. In this election division appeared even between the aldermen and the councilmen before the candidates went before the freemen in a Common Hall. So intense was the freemen's opposition to Gamull that he failed to receive even a single vote at their hands. The two who received most votes in an unusually low poll were William Parnell with seventy-two and Robert Harvey with sixty-three.[37] When these two went before the aldermen at the concluding stage Harvey was elected mayor by eight votes to two. Harvey refused to serve when elected. Randle Holme related in indignant tones how Harvey 'would not stand beinge chosen but rudly went out of the hall not willinge to do the Kinge or Citty service'. The aldermen then, quite without any constitutional authority, passed over Parnell, who had received more votes from the freemen than Harvey, and prevailed upon a reluctant Charles Walley, the retiring mayor, to stay on for another year.[38]

The mayoral elections of 1644 and 1645 had demonstrated beyond question just how narrow-based and self-interested was Chester's royalism. The emergence of division even within the Assembly between the aldermen and the usually deferential councilmen and the overwhelming opposition of the freemen to the royalist leaders in the Assembly served to emphasize the isolation of the royalist group among the aldermen/J.P.s. The elections handsomely vindicated Lord John Byron's warnings of the danger of putting too much trust in the loyalty of corporations or of overestimating the strength of royalism in Chester.

Chester remained a royalist garrison until the end of the first Civil War not because of any widespread support among its citizens for the royalist cause but because it was kept under strict military control by 'foreign' governors. The city finally surrendered at the beginning of February 1646 following eighteen months of siege. On 3 February, after terms had been agreed between royalist and parliamentary leaders in the area, Lord John Byron left the city and Sir William Brereton, who had commanded the siege, entered Chester to take control of the city on behalf of Parliament.[39]

The parliamentary leaders were soon to discover that Chester would be no less independent nor any less troublesome than it had been to their predecessors. Although the royalists had been replaced, as far as the majority of Cestrians were concerned the system of government which they disliked so much during the royalist ascendancy remained much the same now that the city was in parliamentary hands. The government of the city continued to be divided between civil and military authorities with the civil government ultimately subordinate to the military. 'Foreign' military governors continued to represent outside interference every bit as much as their royalist predecessors. Friction developed on occasions between the Assembly and the governors and poor relations between the Assembly and the central government remained a feature of the period through to the Corporation Act of 1661.

Faced with a good deal of general antipathy,[40] a depressed city, a predominantly royalist Aldermanic Bench, and an Assembly which had co-operated with the royalists, Parliament had little choice in the short run but to keep the city under strict military control. On 6 February 1646 Parliament appointed Colonel Michael Jones as its first governor and made Alderman William Edwards, colonel of a regiment of soldiers in the city.[41] The Assembly was suspended and the Aldermanic Bench was purged of the great majority of its members. Only seven aldermen survived the purge and for eight months Chester's government was carried on by them acting as a committee under the leadership of Sir William Brereton, the Cheshire parliamentary commander.[42]

It took until October 1646 before Parliament considered it was sufficiently in control of affairs in Chester to issue an ordinance making public the purge from the Assembly of its former royalist leaders and certain other officials.[43] This ordinance, however, provided no more than official confirmation of the dismissals which had been effected immediately after the fall of the city in February. It confirmed that the axe had fallen most heavily on the Aldermanic Bench which had been the royalist power base in the city. Seventeen, or 71 per cent, of the 'Twenty-Four' were officially dismissed from the Assembly.

The figures for expulsions from the Assembly served to emphasize the relative lack of influence exerted within it by the sheriff-peers and councilmen, although the great majority had collaborated with the royalist junta. Only one sheriff-peer and six councilmen were singled out for dismissal from the Assembly. These seven men comprised under 7 per cent of the combined total of the two groups.

The ordinance of October 1646 marked the disbandment of the interim committee under Brereton and the resumption by the Assembly of its accustomed place as the focus of government in the city, in contrast to the counties at large where the county committees dominated local government. The seven aldermen who kept their places were Alderman William Edwards, who was appointed mayor by the ordinance, Christopher Blease (mercer), William Sparke (ironmonger), Robert Harvey (glover), William Ince (merchant), Richard Leicester (mercer), and Thomas Aldersey (ironmonger).[44] Only Edwards and Leicester had openly opposed the Crown from before the arrival of the King in Chester in September 1642. Aldersey had emphasized his support for Parliament by absenting himself from the royalist Assembly in March 1643 and leaving the city. The other four, Blease, Ince, Harvey and Sparke, all attended royalist Assemblies fairly regularly and even if not sympathetic to the royalists acquiesced in their regime.[45]

The most urgent problem facing Edwards and his six aldermen was to find new men to fill the vacant places on the Aldermanic Bench. In order to comply with the city's constitution it was theoretically necessary to recruit new members from the ranks of the sheriff-peers and councilmen, the loyalty of the majority of whom was open to question on account of their co-operation with the royalists.

The first Assembly meeting following upon the issue of the Ordinance of October 1646 was held on 22 October when John Wynne, never previously a member of the Assembly, was simultaneously elected a councillor and one of the sheriffs.[46] Robert Sproston, who had been suspended from the royalist Assembly in April 1645, was installed as the other sheriff. The next meeting was held on 17 November at which John Ratcliffe, a Cestrian, was appointed recorder and alderman to replace Robert Brerewood. The same day ten new men were elevated to the Aldermanic Bench:[47] Robert Whitby, Esq., Robert Wright (baker), Calvin Bruen (ironmonger), Edward Bradshawe (mercer), Owen Hughes (merchant), Richard Bradshawe (merchant), John Whittel (tanner), Hugh Leigh (clothier), William Crompton (merchant), and John Johnson (ironmonger). Except for Whitby who was elected directly to the 'Twenty-Four' without first having been a member of the Assembly, all the other nine had been either sheriff-peers or councilmen. All but two of the new aldermen—Bruen and Whittel had left the city before September 1642—had sat fairly regularly in royalist Assemblies. Seven of the nine former Assembly members, however, had been suspended from the Assembly by the royalist junta in their minor purge in the spring and autumn of 1645 the exceptions being Leigh and Johnson.

Even a year after the raising of the siege the Aldermanic Bench remained five short of its full complement of twenty-four members. It took another year, until June 1648, finally to complete the Bench.

Some of Parliament's difficulties stemmed from Chester's wretched misfortune in being visited with a devastating attack of the plague for about six months between June and November 1647 during which just over 2,000 persons died.[48] This attack seriously inhibited the reorganization of the city's government. Parliament suspended the mayoral election of October 1647 and passed an ordinance by which Robert Wright, one of the post-purge aldermen, was appointed mayor, and two others were appointed sheriffs.[49]

In March 1648 another ordinance confirmed that Wright and his two sheriffs should retain their offices until the time of the next mayoral election in the October following.[50] The two sheriffs—William Wright and Richard Minshull—when appointed by Parliament in October 1647 had not been members of the Assembly as by the city's constitution they should have been, and at the next Assembly meeting, 17 March 1648, they were formally elected councillors.[51] Towards the end of that month the city was clearly free of the plague and the Aldermanic Bench could at last be completed. On 24 March Richard Bird (tanner), Thomas Mottershead (merchant) and William Bennet (mercer) were brought on to the Bench while eight new councilmen were elected to the Assembly.[52] Early in May Peter Leigh, one of the few committed parliamentary councillors in 1642, who had been ceremoniously suspended from the Assembly in April 1645, was elected an alderman to complete the Bench. On the same day after many months without a clerk of the Pentice, John Jones was chosen to replace his royalist predecessor.[53]

Now at last over two years after the purge of the Assembly in February 1646 the Aldermanic Bench was restored to its full strength under parliamentary control and the city was once again being served by both of its chief permanent officials. The lesson of these two years of reconstruction of the Aldermanic Bench was that Parliament was obliged to accept the facts of political life in the city, and elevate individuals whose reliability was always in doubt. Only seven of the aldermen on the reconstructed Bench could be considered committed parliamentarians and three of them were aldermen who had survived the purge of February 1646. The rest—except for Robert Whitby, Recorder Ratcliffe, and John Wynne (Recorder of London)—had sat in royalist Assemblies as sheriff-peers or councilmen until at least the autumn of 1645 when seven of them were suspended from the Assembly for having expressed discontent at conditions in the city under the royalist regime. After the fall of the city these men and most of the other new aldermen slid easily from being 'royalist' sheriff-peers and councilmen to become 'parliamentary' aldermen, which was consistent with their inclination to wait on events. The reorganization of the Bench between 1646 and 1648 entailed no devolution, only a shift, in political power in the city, for all the new aldermen elevated to the Bench from the ranks of the sheriff-peers and councillors had been members of the Assembly since at least the 1630s.

The purge of February 1646 presented Parliament with an opportunity to reduce the composition of the Assembly and make it easier for the parliamentary aldermen to control its members by insisting on the strict interpretation of the city's constitution as laid down in the governing charter of 1506. The unconstitutional hybrid class of sheriff-peers was abolished as a separate group within the Assembly. Within a few years of the grant of the charter the practice had evolved that each year two new councillors were elected to replace the two new sheriffs while the two retiring sheriffs resumed their places in the Assembly as sheriff-peers, thus establishing a group in addition to the aldermen and councilmen. From 1646 to 1660 this practice was stopped. In this period the two retiring sheriffs returned to their places in the Assembly as members of the 'Forty', and until the Restoration new councillors were elected only on the occasion of the elevation of one of their number to the Aldermanic Bench or at death. Thus for well over a decade the Assembly returned to its strict charter composition of the 'Twenty-Four' and the 'Forty'.[54]

Outside the Assembly the end of the first Civil War allowed for the election of two new M.P.s for the county of the city of Chester which had been without parliamentary representation since Sir Francis Gamull and Sir Thomas Smith had been disabled from sitting in the House of Commons in January 1644 on account of their royalism.[55] Chester's two Recruiter M.P.s were Alderman William Edwards and Recorder John Ratcliffe.[56] The election of Edwards marked the apogee of his long and consistent career of opposition to his great adversaries the Gamulls and their ruling group, whom, at last, he had convincingly worsted through his commitment to the parliamentary cause.

Chester's early royalism and its strategic position meant that there was always the possibility of an attempt to recover the city for the royalist cause. At the time of the second Civil War, in June 1648, a plot was discovered to betray the Garrison at Chester into the hands of the royalists which proved abortive. Ever since Chester had been erected a 'county of itself' in 1506 the County of Cheshire had been jealous of the independent spirit of the city and relations between the two authorities had never been harmonious. The plot to betray Chester provided Sir William Brereton, M.P., the former parliamentary commander and long-time adversary of the city, with a strong case for reducing the independence of Chester by joining its militia with that of the county and thus bringing it under the control of the county palatine of Cheshire. Chester's M.P.s, Edwards and Ratcliffe, informed the mayor of Brereton's stratagems in this direction, 'Sir William Brereton moved [in the House] that the County and City might be joined in the Militia, and thereby the County would bring the City under their power, but he prevailed not.'[57] This attempt having proved unsuccessful, Brereton then succeeded in securing the service of another M.P. to move in the House that Brereton might be joined with the city militia together with the governor of the city, for if not, he argued, the governor's power would be taken away. This proposal was agreed to and so there were joined with the city militia, Sir William Brereton, the governor, Colonel Duckenfield, and three other non-Cestrians.[58] There were fears for the city's safety after the discovery of the plot and in the face of the advancing Scottish army under Hamilton. Fortunately for Chester the Scottish troops were halted by a massive defeat by Cromwell at Preston.

Among those excluded from Parliament by Colonel Pride in December 1648 were the two Chester M.P.s, William Edwards and Recorder John Ratcliffe.[59] Edwards's dismissal from Parliament also marked his retirement from active participation in Chester politics and the end of his brief ascendancy in the city. Until victory had been achieved by Parliament there existed a close correspondence between his local aspiration and those of the parliamentary cause. Through his firm commitment to Parliament all his local aims had come to fruition. He himself had supplanted the Gamulls in Chester politics and had had the satisfaction of contributing to the downfall of the Gamull family and their group from their position of dominance in the city. By 1648 the struggle which Edwards and the Gamulls had in so many ways represented in 1642 had lost its immediate significance and other more fundamental questions, with which Edwards probably had little sympathy and wanted no part, came to hold the stage. He lived on past the Restoration in 1660 to be formally dismissed from the Assembly for refusing to subscribe to the Corporation Act of 1661, though from the time of his entry to Parliament at the beginning of 1647 with one exception, in December 1649, he never attended Assembly meetings.[60]

The establishment of the Commonwealth following the execution of Charles I early in 1649 did not bring in its wake any great changes in the personnel of politics in Chester, apart from the retirement of Edwards. Nobody was dismissed from the Assembly as a consequence of either internal or external pressures and there were no conspicuous voluntary abstentions from its deliberations after 1649. This was because the political inclinations of most of the aldermen continued to be opportunist. The majority of Chester's 'Commonwealth' Bench were well experienced in the art of running with the tide. They had moved effortlessly from being 'royalist' sheriff-peers and councilmen up to 1646 to become 'parliamentary' aldermen and were now 'Commonwealth' aldermen.

Following the retirement of Edwards and the erection of the Commonwealth, because of the neutralist inclinations of the majority of the aldermen, a small minority of those who came on to the Bench after 1646 and were committed to the governments of the period came to the fore and assumed the leadership of the Bench. For much of the time from 1649 to 1659 the majority of aldermen and nearly all the councilmen found it expedient to acquiesce and co-operate in running the civil government of the city although they owed no particular allegiance to the central government of the day.

The relatively settled nature of national politics brought about for most of the decade after 1649 a fair measure of stability in local politics and it afforded the usually acquiescent majority of aldermen the opportunity to assert themselves on occasions and to encourage a good deal of recalcitrance in the city's relations with the central governments. The minority of aldermen loyal to the central government were able to retain their ascendancy because the majority found it expedient to co-operate with them and because their authority was ultimately assured by the presence of the local garrison.

From early in the life of the Commonwealth the Council of State increasingly interfered in the localities. In the counties at large steps were taken to stem the power of the county committees and to bring them under much closer centralized control.[61] As far as Chester was concerned it was the establishment of the Committee for Corporations, a branch of the Council of State, which marked the beginning of attempts by the governments of the Commonwealth and Protectorate to impose greater control over the large towns and cities of England and Wales.[62] The establishment of the committee reflects the government's recognition of the age-old problem of the independence of corporations and especially the large cities which were 'counties of themselves'. Loyal supporters were often either in a precarious majority or in a minority on town Assemblies, as was the case in Chester, and since corporations were self-governing and traditionally suspicious and independent of outside interference the central government had to attempt to ensure the authority of its committed supporters by endeavouring to enforce the loyalty of the acquiescent majority. The Committee of Corporations was the first attempt to achieve this. Early on its principal weapon was the Oath of Engagement. This was first proposed in October 1649. It applied originally to all M.P.s but in January 1650 its scope was extended to impose the obligation upon all males over eighteen. In February 1649 Parliament had passed an Act prescribing an oath to be taken by all new freemen in corporate towns obliging them to swear allegiance to the Commonwealth which was followed in September by an oath of allegiance to be taken by all officers in cities and corporate towns.[63]

From the beginning of the Commonwealth, however, a number of Chester aldermen asserted themselves in the city to oppose oaths of allegiance to the new regime. Ralph Davenport, clerk of the Pentice, recalled a few years later, that from the outset, and on many occasions afterwards, when he came to administer the oaths he received express instructions not to administer them but to keep to the oath anciently taken by the citizens 'with a variacon from a kingly to Comon Wealth government notwithstanding'.[64]

When the mayor and Assembly were called upon to take the Engagement early in 1650 they were conspicuously tardy in subscribing to it, as Alderman Richard Bradshawe, one of the loyal minority on the Bench, soon to be appointed English Ambassador in Hamburg, explained to President Bradshawe.[65] Two months later, in May 1650, the Council of State ordered the Chester Assembly to replace the mayor for 1649–50, William Crompton, as he had not subscribed to the Engagement, and to hold an election to choose his successor.[66] No notice was taken of this order. The Council of State wrote again just before the mayoral election of October 1650 reminding the mayor that in the elections of city officials for the coming year the Assembly must respect the rules as laid down in the Acts of Parliament and he was instructed to return a list of any in the city who held office contrary to the Act of Engagement.[67]

An account by Randle Holme of the proceedings of the mayoral election of 1650 shows that after nearly a year of aldermanic recalcitrance over the Engagement the Council of State was no longer prepared to suffer the growing assertiveness of the formerly acquiescent aldermanic majority who were wresting the initiative from the minority of government supporters on the Bench. The response of the Council of State was to invoke the support of the soldiers in the garrison to frustrate an attempt by the aldermanic majority to elect their own mayor. Mr Owen Hughes was elected mayor after a close contest after which Captains Whitworth and Smith drew up troops and sent a message to the mayor to warn the aldermen not to confirm Hughes's election. The governor of the garrison then came down to the Pentice attended by soldiers, 'with lyght mazes their muskets laded in affront and threat to the civill govuernment and antient privilidges of the Citty in choyse of their maior; which perceaved and for more peace they elected Mr Richard Leicester against both his and theyr minds he being then at poole his cuntrey howse in Chester'.[68]

The new mayor, Richard Leicester, had been a committed parliamentarian in 1642. He, like William Edwards, appears to have opted out of Chester politics from the end of 1648 until his unexpected 'election' to the mayoralty, though he consistently attended Assembly meetings from October 1650 until his death in 1658. In spite of the warnings implicit in the government's activities in the election of 1650 Leicester was unable to exert much influence on the Aldermanic Bench for the Assembly went on defying the government on the question of the Engagement.[69]

In June 1651 the Council of State wanted to know again whether the mayor and the Assembly members had taken the Engagement. In July, John Whittel, a loyal Commonwealth man, died and the Assembly elected William Wright to fill his place.[70] He had been appointed sheriff by the ordinance of October 1646 and had been appointed captain of a foot company at the time of the royalist attempt on the city in 1648, but he refused to take the Engagement to the Commonwealth. The Council of State thereupon decided to take the matter of Wright's replacement into their own hands. On 13 August the Council's choice was made known to Sir William Brereton, who, on the 15th, informed the Commons that Jonathan Ridge, a draper, who had been prominent in the Chester sequestration committee, a common councillor since the end of 1648, and a militia commissioner, was to be appointed an alderman in place of Wright 'who was turned out by order of Parliament for being a non-engager'; though Parliament tried to appease the city for having abused its most cherished privilege of complete independence to make all internal appointments by adding 'without prejudice, nevertheless, to the Charter of the said Town for the future'.[71]

The response of the Chester aldermen to the Council of State's attack on the Charter liberties of the city of Chester was stubbornly to assert their independence from any external direction in the appointment of a city official. The Assembly simply took no action. Alderman Wright continued in his place and Ridge was not appointed to the Bench.[72] Ridge was not officially elected an alderman until some four years later, in 1655, early in the Protectorate, when he replaced Randle Holme who had died.[73] Wright became mayor in 1655–6.

The generally poor relations which existed between the central government and the corporations, so clearly exemplified in the case of Chester, caused the Council of State increasing concern throughout eighteen months of failure to gain their co-operation through widespread subscription to the Engagement. A sterner line taken towards the corporations from the summer of 1651 was intensified from September 1652 with the extension of the powers of the Committee for Corporations. The towns were now subject to the threat of examination, revision, or removal of their precious charters. In January 1653 Chester's mayor was instructed to take the city charter to London for inspection though the practical outcome appears to have been more than a warning to the intransigent aldermen as to their conduct.[74] The city received an exemplification of its charter in March 1655 at the request of Alderman Bradshawe[75] but it had no effect on the city's constitutional structure.

Strong centralized control over corporations and the counties was an important feature of government policy from 1652 to 1658. A Committee for Municipal Charters—an open reminder to corporations not to challenge the authority of the Protector—was at work in 1656 and probably came into operation soon after the appointment of the major-generals in September 1655,[76] an event which marked the apogee of central government control over the localities during the Interregnum.

During the Protectorate the neutralist-inclined aldermen in Chester resumed their acquiescent posture and co-operated with the minority of hardcore government supporters. The assertiveness displayed by the aldermanic majority in their relations with the Council of State for about eighteen months from the beginning of 1650 to towards the end of 1651 was virtually absent. In the two parliamentary elections Chester dutifully sent to Westminster good Cromwellian M.P.s with the minimum of fuss.[77] With the advent of the major-generals Chester came under the authority of Colonel Charles Worsley who was responsible for the counties of Lancashire, Cheshire and Staffordshire until he died in June 1656 when he was succeeded by Colonel Tobias Bridge. Relations between the city authorities and the major-generals appear to have been free of serious conflict. This was probably because of the acquiescent temper of the city and the diligence of the small group of city commissioners (most of whom were government supporters on the Bench) in effecting their orders.[78]

It was only at Cromwell's death in September 1658 that there began a revival of intense political activity in Chester which within eighteen months led to the city's own version of the Restoration. In the interim period the government's centralizing policy and the political stability brought about by the Protectorate afforded individuals the opportunity to revive their trades and businesses and help restore the fortunes of a long depressed community.

The reality behind the precarious ascendancy of the Cromwellian aldermen on the Bench, obscured for five years during the Protectorate, swiftly became apparent after the death of Cromwell. From late 1658 and throughout 1659 the majority of previously acquiescent aldermen were less and less inclined to co-operate with the minority of Cromwellian aldermen and came increasingly to assert their majority position, so that by the high summer of 1659 they had wrested the initiative from the hard-core government supporters which they attempted to consolidate by means of an armed plot. The majority of the aldermen, however, were not imbued with old time royalist sentiments for without exception they were post-1646 recruits to the Aldermanic Bench. These men were temperamentally neutralist and inclined to wait on events. Their assertiveness at this time—made possible by the removal of the Protector's iron hand—was the expression of their antipathy for the strong centralizing policies of the

Protector combined with the feeling that the end of the Interregnum was not far away.

One early indication of the increasing confidence of the aldermanic majority was their attempt to worst the minority of hard-line Cromwellian aldermen in the election of M.P.s for Richard Cromwell's Parliament which was to meet on 27 January 1659. The election in Chester was a close contest which took the form of a fierce struggle between the Cromwellian aldermen and the majority on the Bench. The moderate aldermanic majority proposed Recorder Ratcliffe and Alderman Edward Bradshawe while the Cromwellian aldermen put forward Alderman Jonathan Ridge and John Griffiths. The Cromwellian aldermen now on the defensive in Chester politics just managed to secure the election of their men. The election took place on 17 January 1659 and an account of the proceedings by Randle Holme III shows that Ridge and Griffiths won the day by appealing to the freemen against the nominees of the majority of the Bench.[79]

The frustration at the defeat of the majority of the aldermen was reflected at the Assembly on 25 January following the election, at which consideration was given to what were described as 'the undue meanes which hath lately been practized in the obtaininge of voices in the late eleccion of twoe cittizens of this cittie to serve in the Parliament for the said citty', and to avoid similar irregularities in the future it was ordered that a certificate of the proceedings should be drawn up in the name of the mayor and citizens and presented to Parliament.[80] The elected members, Ridge and Griffiths, were hard-line Cromwellians. Ridge it was whom Parliament attempted to force upon the Aldermanic Bench in 1651. Griffiths, an apothecary, became a councillor in 1653 and an alderman at the end of the Protectorate in September 1658. He was the commissioner in Chester who was responsible for supplying Secretary Thurloe with information concerning conditions in Chester and the county at large.[81]

Although the Cromwellian minority on the Bench had succeeded in winning the parliamentary election of January 1659 the days of their ascendancy, secured only by the threat of armed force during the Protectorate, were fast running out. By the summer of 1659 the anti-Cromwellian majority on the Bench were in the ascendant and just waiting for a sign to declare themselves against the Protectorate. Events in August 1659 gave them a good opportunity to take control of the city.

At the end of July 1659 an operation to capture Chester as part of a widespread royalist rising was effected under the leadership of Sir George Booth, who, during the night of 2 August, entered Chester and took control of the city, though the Castle into which Governor Thomas Croxton retreated remained uncaptured.[82] Booth and his soldiers remained within the city walls until the end of the third week in August when they were ejected by parliamentary forces under General Lambert. On 24 August Parliament established a Commission composed of four Cheshire committeemen charged with the task of investigating the recent insurrection.[83]

Recorder Ratcliffe, the mayor and several other aldermen were charged with having had secret meetings with Colonel John Booth, son of Sir George, for the delivery of Chester. The evidence submitted by a number of witnesses shows clearly that there had been collusion between a number of the anti-Cromwellian aldermen and Booth, and that Ratcliffe was not wholly responsible for the insurrection as some alleged. Robert Moulson, the crier, who by virtue of his office looked after the keys of the city, related how he was summoned from his bed during the early hours of Tuesday 2 August to attend in the Pentice. There he found Sheriff Heywood and the rest of the watch who ordered him to open the gates of the city which he did 'and before this examinant had opened the last gate Sir Geo. Booth and his confederates had entered the city'.[84] Several witnesses recalled that on the morning of 2 August Booth met with Mayor Gerrard Jones, the recorder, and several aldermen in the Pentice. There Booth made a speech declaring the ground on which he had taken up arms, which became the substance of his 'Declaration' which crier Moulson was ordered to proclaim at the High Cross in the centre of Chester later that morning.[85]

At the meeting between Booth and the aldermen on 2 August Booth proposed to the mayor that three foot companies should be raised 'for the preservation of the city'. Colonel John Booth was being referred to as 'Governor' Booth. While Booth's 'Declaration' was being read at the High Cross, the mayor sent for Aldermen William Wright and John Witter to take charge of two companies of foot. At that time Witter declined to co-operate, though it appears that both their commissions were confirmed at the Assembly a week later on 9 August.[86] On the day of this Assembly it was decided by the mayor and his 'brethren' that a third company of foot should be raised and put under the command of Jonathan Ridge, the Cromwellian M.P. Ridge, in his own evidence to the commissioners, related that when called upon to accept the command he 'utterly denied to accept the post', though pressed several times by the recorder and other aldermen.[87] Randle Holme the younger noted how on 6 August 'Governor' John Booth and all the insurrectionary captains and commanders went into St Werburgh's Church, being Sunday, where Mr Rawson, the minister, preached for Charles King of England.[88]

The commissioners began to investigate the insurrection on 24 August and on the 27th Parliament passed a special Act for Sequestrations to deal with those involved in Booth's Rising.[89] On 1 September the joint Cheshire and Chester committee took charge of dealing with the local insurrectionaries.[90] At the first Assembly meeting after the ejection of Booth from the city, on 8 September, the Cromwellian aldermen temporarily in the ascendant, ordained that because of the great need for money certain sums should be levied on all Assembly members.[91]

The days of the ascendancy of the Cromwellian aldermen were all but numbered by September 1659. They then made one last concerted effort to stave off their almost inevitable removal from power by calling for help from Parliament, the interests of whose members were inextricably linked with the fortunes of their grass-roots political supporters in the localities. In September two petitions issued from the city in the name of the 'well affected citizens of Chester', addressed to the Parliament of the Commonwealth of England. The first urged Parliament to frustrate the aldermanic majority in Chester by ordering a reduction in the size of the Assembly membership:

> That being divers of the aldermen and Common Councilmen
> of the City by their complying with the riseinge party under
> Sir Geo Booth have rendered themselves incapable of bearing any
> office therein, request that for the immediate future with the
> consent of Parliament, the City may be governed by a fewer
> number of Aldermen and Common Councilmen by such persons
> as are mentioned in this annexed list being all men of approved
> faithfullness to the commonwealth. . . .[92]

Some idea of the narrow base of the Commonwealth party in Chester at this time can be gained from the list submitted to Parliament. It was proposed that the Bench should consist of fifteen members and that the Common Council should be composed of eighteen instead of forty members. Of those proposed for the truncated Bench only six were already aldermen: Richard Bradshawe, Edward Bradshawe, Charles

Walley, Jonathan Ridge, M.P., Daniel Greatbach, and John Anderson, while only three were already councilmen: Samuel Bucke, one of the commissioners for investigating the Booth insurrection, Thomas Parnell and Thomas Ashton. Another four, Gilbert Gerrard, Robert Hyde, John Whitworth, and Henry Birkenhead (who had been a lawyer in the Chester Exchequer and staunch parliamentarian in 1642), were all recently appointed sequestrators, and—significantly— non-Cestrians. Only five of those proposed for the new Council were already members of 'The Forty', including John Griffiths the Cromwellian M.P.[93]

The second petition of 17 September submitted in the name of the 'well affected' by the sequestrators asked that until it was convenient to restore the Assembly to its former size the governor of the city should be invested with special powers to deal with the current situation.[94] Two days later, on 19 September, Parliament sequestrated Recorder Ratcliffe and annulled the city charter. Parliament also resolved that the city and county of the city of Chester should no longer be a county of itself, should lose its distinct county status and should 'be laide to the County at large'.[95] The next day Mayor Gerrard Jones and the two sheriffs were called before the sequestrators to see where they stood in view of their unsatisfactory assurances and, for their implied perfidy in recent events, they were discharged from their places.[96]

The measures taken by Parliament and the local sequestrators in September 1659 proved no more than empty gestures for there existed no machinery for implementing them. Relations between the central government and Chester had clearly broken down from the end of 1659. Only one Assembly meeting, on 30 March 1660, was held between Parliament's decision to remove Chester's charter and county status and the first Assembly of the Restoration period in May 1660. At the meeting in March none of the proposals for a reconstituted Assembly were observed either in its structure or in its personnel.[97]

The Chester aldermen sent the city's petition of loyalty to the new monarch Charles II in the first week of May 1660.[98] On 11 May the aldermen began to dismiss from the Assembly those old parliamentarians and particularly those commonwealthmen who could not expect to retain their positions now that the monarchy was restored, but relatively few were in fact dismissed. The first to go were three common councilmen, Robert Denson, John Sproston, and John

Wynne, all of whom were discharged because they were 'not in a capacity to doe the duty to their places'.[99]

The same day a petition from 'many freemen well affected to the Ancient government of ye Citty' asked that 'divers persons disaffected to the ancient government of the City, being members of the Incorporation had endeavoured to overthrow their rights and privileges contrary to their oaths'. They called upon the Assembly to discharge such persons from the Assembly, especially Jonathan Ridge, M.P. After a long debate it was 'unanimously' ordered that Ridge 'should be degraded and discharged from being an Alderman and from being one of the City's counsel'.[100]

During the summer and autumn of 1660 a few aldermen were dismissed while a small number of aldermen, prominent in Chester politics fifteen years or more previously, were restored to their places. In June Thomas Throppe, one of the group which had manoeuvred Chester on to the royalist side in 1642, and Thomas Cowper, the royalist mayor in 1642, were both restored to the Bench.[101] William Drinkwater, a post-1646 alderman, sensing his fate, resigned at the end of September. Richard Broster, a former royalist purged in 1646, returned to the Bench. Calvin Bruen, one of Chester's few prominent Puritans and a post-1646 alderman, resigned in October.[102]

The Restoration in Chester inevitably saw a number of changes in the personnel of local politics but in almost no other aspect of city government did any changes follow upon it. The only change in government was the revival of sheriff-peers proscribed ever since the purge of the Assembly in February 1646.[103] Two other links with the past were a petition from the merchants in November 1660 for a revival of their grant for the exportation of calf-skins[104] which had been annexed by the Gamull group in the early part of the century, and the election in 1661 of Thomas Throppe, one of the Gamull group, to the mayoralty.

From 1642 to 1660 no changes had taken place in the organization and structure of government in Chester except for the temporary proscription of sheriff-peers. Whatever the shade of opinion of the ruling group it had endeavoured, with rare exceptions, to adhere to the city's constitution and effect its civil government as its predecessors had done since the sixteenth century. Although the fall from power of the Gamull group and the purge of 1646 saw a shift in political power in the city, there ensued no real infusion of new men into Chester politics. All the aldermen of the reconstituted Bench had, with one exception, been members of the Assembly since well before 1642 and most of them lived on to continue in their places under the governments of the Commonwealth and Protectorate. After the reconstruction of the Bench in 1648 few opportunities occurred for new members to enter the Assembly, for councillors to proceed to the Bench, or for the ruling minority to reinforce the Bench with government supporters. In the twelve years up to the Restoration only ten vacancies occurred in the Bench—three of them in 1659—two of which were filled by councillors Ridge and Griffiths and two others by councillors Wright and Minshull who were appointed sheriffs by the parliamentary ordinance of October 1646.

Even though the majority of Chester aldermen welcomed the Restoration there ensued a minimum of local recrimination against those who had actively supported the governments of the Commonwealth and Protectorate. A few conspicuous opponents of the restored monarchy had been removed during 1660 but those who continued in office had acquiesced in the governments since 1649 and could be regarded as having condoned the period of usurpation. Throughout England and Wales, as in Chester, there remained large numbers of members of town assemblies about whose loyalty the Restoration government had cause to be suspicious and thus some action against the corporations became inevitable.

The Restoration period also provided the government with the opportunity to try to deal comprehensively with corporations and especially those large towns which enjoyed the status of 'counties of themselves'. The latter had consistently asserted their independence against interference from successive central governments since the sixteenth century. In the twelve months following the Restoration the government used its prerogative to try to establish direct control over certain corporations by the reinstatement of ejected royalists and by the forced surrender of charters. But this policy often met with stout resistance, the towns insisting as fiercely as ever on the retention of their privileges. There were still too many undesirables in corporations for the government's liking and this led to the 'Act for the well Governing and Regulating of Corporations' of December 1661 which required the holders of municipal offices to take the oaths of allegiance and supremacy and the oath of non-resistance to the King, to repudiate the Solemn League and Covenant, and to qualify for office by taking the Sacrament.[105]

The commissioners appointed to investigate the Corporation of Chester and other towns in the county palatine were named on 19 February 1662.[106] They held a meeting in the Inner Pentice at the end of August at which they confirmed in their places eleven aldermen/J.P.s, or ex-mayors, and the two sheriffs. They restored two others to the dignity of aldermen/J.P.s one of whom was Sir Thomas Smith, formerly one of Chester's royalist M.P.s in the Long Parliament. The commissioners dismissed seven aldermen/J.P.s and four aldermen below the Chair, all of whom, with the exception of William Edwards and Recorder Ratcliffe, had been mayors or had been appointed since 1652. Nine sheriff-peers and twelve councillors were dismissed, and again, with the exception of one, all of them had attained their positions since 1652.[107]

The 'Act for the well Governing and Regulating of Corporations' represented an important landmark in relations between the towns and the central government in the seventeenth century, but as Chester was to show in its battles with the government over its charter rights later in the century, its success was slight. The independent attitude and loyalty of the members of the Chester Assembly to their native city continued after the Act, in the tradition of their predecessors, to come before deference to the demands of the central government.

Notes

1 For an important and detailed analysis of a royalist city from 1640 to 1662 which provides a number of interesting parallels—and differences —with Chester, see R. Howell, *Newcastle-upon-Tyne and the Puritan Revolution* (Oxford, 1966).

2 Based upon the contributor's study of the city from *c.* 1500. The point about Puritanism prior to 1642 is reinforced by R. C. Richardson, 'Puritanism in the Diocese of Chester to 1642' (unpublished Ph.D. thesis, University of Manchester, 1969), esp. pp. 20, 291–6.

3 Clarendon, *The History of the Rebellion and Civil Wars begun in the year 1641* (ed. W. D. Macray, Oxford, 1888), II, 470.

4 R. H. Morris, *Chester in the Plantagenet and Tudor Reigns* (Chester, 1893), pp. 463–8, has printed the principal sources relevant to this phase of the dispute. For the importance of Chester as a centre for the leather industry, see D. M. Woodward, 'The Chester Leather Industry, 1558–1625', *Transactions of the Historic Society of Lancashire and Cheshire*, CXIX (1967), 65–111.

5 *APC 1615–1616*, pp. 651–2.

6 BM Harleian MS. 2104, fol. 27r. (Patent, 10 April).

7 *Ibid.*, 2004, fols 45–64.

8 B. E. Howells, ed., *A Calendar of Letters relating to North Wales, 1533–circa 1700* (Cardiff, 1967), pp. 24–6.

9 BM Harleian MS. 2091, fol. 214r.

10 *Ibid.*, and see M. G. Groombridge, ed., *A Calendar of Chester City Council Minutes, 1603–42* (Lancashire and Cheshire Record Society, CVI, 1966), 128.

11 *APC June–September 1626*, p. 356; BM Harleian MS. 2104, fol. 317r.

12 BM Harleian MS. 2004, fols 7–10: copy of the grant.

13 *Ibid.*, 2104, fol. 34r.

14 Groombridge, *Council Minutes 1603–42*, p. 154.

15 BM Harleian MS. 2004, fols 153–4, no date, but *c.* June–July 1629; *ibid.*, 2104, fol. 51r., a declaration by Gamull and associates, 29 Jan. 1630; *ibid.*, fols 129–32, no date, but *c.* Jan. 1630. The accusations are followed by Gamull's answer and a further reply from Edwards.

16 Groombridge, *Council Minutes 1603–42*, pp. 169–70.

17 *Ibid.*, p. 207.

18 The full circumstances of the incident are in a letter from Mayor Cowper to the two Chester M.P.s: Cheshire County Record Office, Chester, DCC 14/94 (12? March 1642). It is noted in *HMC 5th Report*, p. 352a.

19 *Ibid.*, and DCC 14/93 (March 1642), DCC 14/61 (15 March 1642), DCC 14/65 and 66 (19 March 1642). All the letters are noted in *HMC 5th Report*, pp. 350b, 352a.

20 Northampton County RO, Finch-Hatton MS. 133, the Commission of Array for Cheshire and the city of Chester.

21 J. A. Atkinson, ed., *Tracts relating to the Civil War in Cheshire 1641–1659* (Chetham Society, new series, LXV, 1909), p. 47.

22 Edwards's last attendance at an Assembly before 1646 as recorded in the Assembly minutes was 6 October 1641: Chester City RO (CCRO), AF 23/8. The list for 22 October is damaged. The next meeting was 4 March 1642.

23 BM Harleian MS. 2155, fol. 108r., printed in R. H. Morris, 'The Siege of Chester 1643–1646', *Journal of the Chester and North Wales Architectural Archaeological and Historic Society*, new series, XXV (1923), 23.

24 Clarendon, *History of the Rebellion*, II, 469–70.

25 *Tracts relating to the Civil War in Cheshire*, p. 90.

26 Northampton County RO, Finch-Hatton MS. 133.

27 *Tracts relating to the Civil War in Cheshire*, p. 90.

28 The letter from Prince Rupert requiring Chester to receive Wm Legge, Sergeant-Major and General of his Ordinance, as Governor, 19 May 1644, makes this plain: BM Harleian MS. 2133, fol. 30r.

29 *Ibid.*, 2135, fol. 57v.

30 *Ibid.*, fol. 52 (13 February 1644): Francis Gamull, one of the royalist group which had aligned Chester on the side of the Crown, and M.P. for the city, had raised a regiment of Foot 'and with the same had with much faithfulness and resolution, defended the City of Chester, when it was attempted by the Rebells'.

31 BM Additional MS. 18, 981, fol. 53.

32 BM Harleian MS. 2135, fol. 37r.

33 *Cheshire Sheaf*, II (1880–2), 159: printed from the Brereton Correspondence, BM Additional MS. 11, 133.

34 This account of the election of 1644 is based on the voting lists in CCRO AF 27/2, 3, 4 (11, 12 October 1644).

35 BM Harleian MS. 2125, fol. 147.

36 Sheriff-peers: four from 15 April (CCRO, AF 27/10); one from 21 October 1645 (AF 27/15); two from 17 November 1645 (AF 27/16). Common Councillors: three from 15 April; two from 21 October.

37 This account of the election of 1645 is based upon the voting lists in CCRO, AF 27/12, 13, 14 (10, 11 October 1645).

38 BM Harleian MS. 2158, fol. 8r.

39 The most recent account of the siege is: R. H. Dore, *The Civil Wars in Cheshire* (Chester, 1966), pp. 40–58.

40 Sir William Brereton's letter to Speaker Lenthall: *HMC Portland MS*, I, 352, quoted by Morris in *Jour. Chester North Wales Archit. Arch. & Hist. Soc.*, new series, XXV (1923), 198.

41 *Journal of the House of Commons*, IV, 429.

42 BM Harleian MS. 2158, fol. 8r.

43 C. H. Firth and R. S. Rait, eds, *Acts and Ordinances of the Interregnum, 1642–1660* (1911), I, 876–9. This ordinance was copied into the Second Assembly Book, CCRO, AB 2 fols 76–8v.

44 Assembly list of 23 October 1646, CCRO, AF 28/3.

45 Assembly lists, CCRO, AF 24–8.

46 CCRO, AB 2 fols 78v.–9.

47 *Ibid.*, fol. 79v.

48 The plague at its height lasted for 23 weeks from 22 June 1647. The weekly totals in BM Harleian MS. 1929, fol. 36, are printed in *Cheshire Sheaf*, I (1878–9), 183–4. Although in J. P. Earwaker, *The History of the Church and Parish of St. Mary-on-the-Hill Chester* (ed. R. H. Morris, Chester, 1898), pp. 126–7, the population of the city in 1647 is put at 10,000 my own estimate is that it was about 5,000.

49 *Journal of the House of Commons*, V, 337 (20 October 1647).

50 *Ibid.*, p. 448 (9 March 1648). The ordinance was entered into the Second Assembly Book, CCRO, AB 2 fol. 82.

51 CCRO, AB 2 fol. 82v.

52 *Ibid.*

53 *Ibid.*, fols 82v.–84 (6 May).

54 Assembly Lists, CCRO, AF 28–37c. Doubts as to the position of sheriff-peers were expressed on at least four occasions between 1599 and 1606. In September 1606 the Assembly debated whether its composition ought to conform to the literal sense of the charter whereupon it was decided to retain sheriff-peers and, significantly, to give no place to 'innovation' by interpreting the charter literally: Groombridge, *Council Minutes 1603–42*, p. 25. The number of sheriff-peers in the Assembly at any one time—except between 1646 and 1660—fluctuated but from 1550 to 1662 it was usually between ten and twenty. The designation sheriff-peer was revived in the 1650s but only to signify seniority among the councillors.

55 *Journal of the House of Commons*, III, 374.

56 *Cheshire Sheaf*, II (1880–2), 274–5. A full list of Chester M.P.s begins *ibid.*, p. 175.

57 CCRO, ML 2/320 (4 July 1648).

58 *Ibid.*

59 D. Brunton and D. H. Pennington, *Members of the Long Parliament* (1954), p. 210.

60 CCRO, AF 31/4 (19 December).

61 See especially, A. M. Everitt, *The Community of Kent and the Great Rebellion, 1640–1660* (Leicester, 1966).

62 The Committee appears to have been established in January 1649. See B. L. K. Henderson, 'The Commonwealth Charters', *Trans. Royal Hist. Soc.*, 3rd series, XI (1912), 129.

63 Firth and Rait, *Acts and Ordinances of the Interregnum*, II, 2, 242–3.

64 SP 23/263, fol. 119r.

65 *CSPD 1649–50*, pp. 20–1. Bradshawe became a councillor in July 1637 and was among those suspended from the Assembly during 1645. His diplomatic career is discussed briefly in the *Dictionary of National Biography*. A short article which concentrates more on his Chester connexions is in *Cheshire Sheaf*, II (1880–2), 172–3.

66 *CSPD 1650*, p. 137.

67 *Ibid.*, p. 385.

68 BM Harleian MS. 2125, fol. 73v.

69 *CSPD 1651*, p. 31.

70 CCRO, AB 2 fol. 96v.

71 *CSPD 1651*, pp. 325, 329; *Journal of the House of Commons*, VII, 1.

72 This can be seen from CCRO, Second Assembly Book and Assembly Files.

73 CCRO, AB 2 fol. 106v. (2 February).

74 CCRO, ML 3/347 (25 January 1653). The city charters were to be

brought to London by 8 March. Although not recorded in the Assembly Book, it was agreed at the Assembly of 4 February to comply with the order and to entrust the duty to Alderman Edward Bradshawe: CCRO, MF/77.

75 PRO, AO 3/410, records the exemplification of an unspecified patent at the request of Alderman Edward Bradshawe. Henderson (*Trans., Royal Hist. Soc.*, 3rd ser., XI (1912), 156), citing an old PRO reference dates this patent as of March 1654.

76 Henderson, *op. cit.*, p. 131.

77 *Cheshire Sheaf*, II (1880–2), 281, 293, 301.

78 *A Collection of the State Papers of John Thurloe* (ed. Thomas Birch, 1742), IV, 523.

79 BM Harleian MS. 1929, fol. 20v., printed in *Cheshire Sheaf*, L (1955), 1.

80 CCRO, AB 2 fol. 123v.

81 *State Papers of John Thurloe*, III, 216, 223, 226, 273. This point has been made by P. J. Pinckney, 'The Cheshire Election of 1656', *Bulletin of the John Rylands Library*, XLIX (1966–7), 390–1.

82 For the general significance of Booth's Rising, D. Underdown, *Royalist Conspiracy in England, 1649–1660* (Yale, 1960), pp. 254–85. Of more specifically Cheshire interest is, R. N. Dore, 'The Cheshire Rising of 1659: a study of local origins', *Transactions of the Lancashire and Cheshire Antiquarian Society*, LXIX (1959), 42–69.

83 BM Harleian MS. 1929, fol. 22r., printed in *Cheshire Sheaf*, L (1955), 6.

84 SP 23/263, fols 114–15. The proceedings of the investigation into the Chester insurrection are *ibid.*, fols 98–119.

85 *Ibid.*, especially fols 115v.–17r.

86 *Ibid.*, fols 116v.–17r.; CCRO, AB 2 fol. 124v.

87 SP 23/263, fols 113–14; 116v.

88 BM Harleian MS. 1929, fol. 21r., printed in *Cheshire Sheaf*, L (1955), 2.

89 Firth and Rait, *Acts and Ordinances of the Interregnum*, II, 1347.

90 BM Harleian MS. 1929, fol. 22r., printed in *Cheshire Sheaf*, L (1955), 6.

91 CCRO, AB 2 fol. 125.

92 BM Harleian MS. 1929, fols 10–11.

93 *Ibid.*

94 *Ibid.*, fols 26–7.

95 *Ibid.*, fol. 22v., printed in *Cheshire Sheaf*, L (1955), 7; *Journal of the House of Commons*, VII, 780.

96 BM Harleian MS. 1929, fol. 22v., printed in *Cheshire Sheaf*, L (1955), 7.

97 CCRO, AF 37c/4.

98 *CSPD 1660*, p. 4.

99 CCRO, AB 2 fol. 127.

100 *Ibid.*

101 *Ibid.*, fol. 128v.

102 *Ibid.*, fol. 130.
103 CCRO, AF 37c/4 *et seq.*
104 *CSPD 1660–61*, pp. 84–5.
105 For a discussion of the Corporation Act, see J. S. Sacret, 'The Restoration Government and the Municipal Corporations', *E.H.R.*, XLV (1930), 232–59.
106 CCRO, AB 2 fol. 137v.
107 *Ibid.*, fols 134–7.

7

East London housing
in the seventeenth century

M. J. Power

Maps of London in the late seventeenth century show that the urban area extended far beyond the city boundaries. Development outside the City had spread rapidly in all directions, but the suburban sprawl was most striking in the east and west along the banks of the Thames. East London at this time was the area lying east and north-east of the City of London, comprising the parishes of Stepney and Whitechapel, East Smithfield (part of the parish of Aldgate), the liberty of the Minories and the precinct of St Katharine's Hospital. It was bounded on the north by the parishes of Shoreditch and Hackney, on the south by the River Thames and on the east by the small parish of Bromley and the River Lea. Most of the building development in this area had taken place in the seventeenth century in response to a spectacular increase in population.

Precise population figures are unattainable, but the sharp increase in baptisms in the parishes of East London indicates remarkable growth. Baptisms more than doubled in the first three decades of the century, rising from about 600 to 1,400 per annum. During the middle years of the century growth was slower, for by the 1660s the average number of baptisms was little over 1,500 per annum. Rapid growth was resumed in the late seventeenth century when the average number of baptisms rose from about 1,640 per annum in the 1670s to 2,550 per annum in the 1690s. A crude ratio of 36 people for each baptism provides a rough estimate of the total population. In East London the population rose from about 21,000 souls in 1600 to over 91,000 by 1700.[1]

The housing of a population which more than quadrupled in a century raises many questions about the nature of the living conditions in this suburb. What kind of houses were built? Where were they situated and how many were there? How well were they constructed and of what materials? How well did they accommodate the expanding population? None of these questions has yet received adequate attention.[2] The scarcity of relevant records has certainly helped to inhibit investigation. The most useful documents are large-scale maps, surveys of land and houses and title-deeds. Unfortunately, the extant examples of these sources do no more than provide samples of houses, builders and tenants, with no indication of whether the information they yield is typical or exceptional. But even a study based on these limited sources can throw some light into the darker corners of East London housing in the seventeenth century.

At the beginning of this period most of the acreage of East London was enclosed pastureland, and in spite of extensive building throughout the century, this aspect of the area did not change. In 1600 very little development had taken place. A thin line of buildings followed the boundaries of the City of London along Hog lane (or Petticoat lane) and along the street called the Minories which connected Aldgate and the Tower of London. Just east of the Minories and the Tower, little clusters of buildings filled the precincts of the dissolved monasteries of the Minoresses and St Mary Graces (East Smithfield) and the land of St Katharine's Hospital. Converging on this suburban belt were the main roads into London: Bishopsgate street, running south through Shoreditch, Whitechapel street running south-west from Bow through Mile End to Aldgate and two roads running west through the riverside area to Tower Hill, the one, Ratcliff Highway, a direct route from Ratcliff, the other, Wapping Wall, a more circuitous route along the river bank. Each of these roads was flanked by a ribbon of building. Most of this development had taken place in the late sixteenth century.[3]

Urban growth in East London during the seventeenth century took place in two distinct areas. Close by the City, the line of building along Hog lane and the Minories spread, encroaching on Goodman's fields and extending the urban area directly east of the City as far as Whitechapel church, almost half a mile from the City wall; Spitalfields and Mile End New Town, a new urban area, reached almost to Mile End Green, one mile north-east of the City boundary. The riverside provided the second important development area. Building had grown

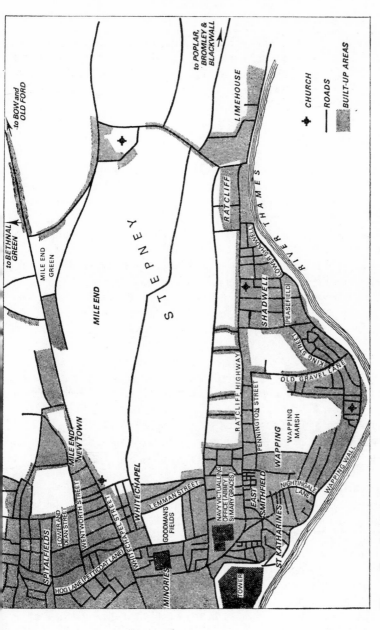

Fig. 1. East London in 1700.

up between Ratcliff Highway and Wapping Wall, creating an uneven
strip almost two miles long by 300 yards to half a mile wide, reaching
to Limehouse. Only one substantial part of this area was still free of
building in 1700, the centre of Wapping marsh which had yet to be
drained. East of Limehouse, a single line of building stretched along
Poplar High street to Blackwall.

It is simple enough to describe the development which took place
between the beginning and end of the seventeenth century. All that is
needed is a comparison of the information supplied in Stow's *Survey
of London* and Morden and Lea's 'Map of London' published in 1598
and 1700 respectively. It is more difficult to establish at what point in
this hundred-year span the changes took place. The documentary
remains of the Privy Council's unsuccessful attempts to prevent
building in the suburbs reveal a rash of building in Wapping during
the late 1620s and 1630s. A schedule of illegal buildings drawn up in
1638 listed 188 houses newly erected there. Significantly, this schedule
mentioned few new buildings in the older urban area nearer the City.[4]
Land for building was evidently more readily available around the undeveloped Wapping marsh than in the inner suburbs, indicating that
the existing building in this area was already quite dense, a point not
made clear in Stow's *Survey*. Shadwell, the hamlet to the east of
Wapping, had a period of rapid growth during the 1630s and 1640s
when nearly 700 houses were built, and thirty years later the hamlet
of Spitalfields was subject to a similar spate of building.[5] A comparison
of William Fairthorne's 'Map of London' of 1658 with William Morgan's map of 1682 shows that most of Spitalfields had been covered
with building in the intervening twenty-four years and that the open
spaces in Wapping and Shadwell north of Ratcliff Highway and east
of Wapping marsh, left untouched by the development of the 1630s
and 1640s, were largely filled in. A further comparison of Morgan's
map with Morden and Lea's map of 1700 shows that building took
place in four areas during the final decades of the century: in Mile
End New Town an extension of the earlier building at Spitalfields,
around Goodman's fields which was now hemmed in with building,
around Wapping marsh and along the road to Bow at Mile End Green.

A study of these three maps shows a striking difference between the
building patterns of the seventeenth century and those of the older
urban areas. Whereas houses in the established districts, such as St
Katharine's, were closely packed together in a seemingly random tangle
of small alleys and courts, from the 1630s development in Wapping,

Plate 1 The whipping of a vagrant (from Holinshed's *Chronicles* 1577)

Plate 2   Houses in Stepney of the late seventeenth century: Nos 134-143 Pennington Street

Shadwell, Ratcliff and Spitalfields proceeded along neat and orderly street patterns, growing ever more regular as time went on. In Pease-field, on the south side of Wapping marsh, where houses were built in the 1630s, the streets were winding and cramped. In Shadwell the streets built in the 1640s ran straight, between Ratcliff Highway and Wapping Wall, the two main roads through the hamlet. Still more regular was the grid-pattern of Spitalfields, laid out in the 1660s and 1670s.

This increasingly orderly development reflects the adoption of a crude form of planning, completely lacking in sixteenth-century building. The development of the Tower bulwark, near St Katharine's precinct, is a good example of haphazard building. Tenants erected houses on the foul laystalls (refuse dumps) and then sublet this rented land to others who built more tenements, all apparently without the knowledge and certainly without the approval of the Gentleman-Porter of the Tower, the owner of the land. In 1587 he instituted pro-ceedings in an attempt to recover the £54 10s 0d per annum which his tenants received as rent for these unauthorized dwellings.[6] Such random building did not entirely disappear in the early seventeenth century. During the summer of 1636 a considerable number of illegal houses were erected in Wapping when the restraining influence of the Justices of the Peace had been removed by their flight from the plague. Some of the houses were reported to have been thrown up overnight probably by squatters, certainly completely unplanned.[7] On the whole, however, landowners tended to organize building on their land by this date. Aaron Williams sublet building plots on land he had leased in Wapping in 1630. He probably laid out the streets first in the same way as the developers of Spitalfields were to do later in the century.[8] Typical of this group was Sir William Wheler of Westbury, who laid out Wheler street and let building plots along it in the 1650s and 1660s.[9] Elsewhere, others followed suit in the 1680s and 1690s. John Pennington laid out Pennington street on the north edge of Wapping marsh, and about the same time Sir William Lemman formed a similar scheme with Lemman street in Goodman's or Lemman's fields, north of Ratcliff Highway.[10]

In spite of the regular streets, the houses were far from stereotyped. As many as half a dozen builders might put up houses in a given street. Since the plots of land in a development were about the same size, houses tended to vary in interior layout and external appearance, but not in the area they covered. In Shadwell in 1650, a single terrace might contain both houses of two and three storeys, each with different numbers and arrangements of rooms, although terraces of uniform houses were also constructed, similar to those shown in the photograph of Pennington street (plate 2).[11] Occasionally the landowner tried to exercise some control over the type of buildings erected on his land. On 28 July 1681 Lady Ivie, owner of part of Wapping marsh, let a plot of land along Old Gravel lane to one Thompson on condition that he was to build houses three storeys high with cellars. William Lemman hoped to prevent jerry-building by declaring in a lease of 28 September 1687 that the lessee was to build houses of the same standard as those already standing in the street.[12] Such examples are exceptional and normally the builder was left to his own devices.

So far we have been referring to built-up areas without trying to determine the numbers of houses involved. The only source which comes near to supplying this information is the hearth tax of 1664, which lists the number of households in each area. Clearly, the number of households does not necessarily equal the number of houses, for more than one household may have lived in a single building, but it is reasonable to suppose that the number of households provides a rough indication of the relative number of houses in each area. As shown in Table 14, the entire East London area contained 14,185 households in 1664. The inner suburban area, comprising Spitalfields, Whitechapel, East Smithfield, St Katharine's and the Minories, contained 5,710 households, the riverside belt from Wapping to Poplar, 7,847 and scattered in the villages of Mile End, Bethnal Green, Bow and Old Ford, outside the urban area, 628. Many households were found along the main roads, but even more lived in the numerous small alleys and yards which flanked them: 892 households in eleven alleys off Whitechapel street, compared with 554 along the street itself, and 729 in twenty-eight alleys in East Smithfield, compared with 510 along the streets. A similar distribution of households existed around Nightingale lane, King street, Green Bank and Wapping Wall. This preponderance of alley dwellers was not invariable. In Ratcliff under 50 per cent of the households lived in alleys, and in Spitalfields, which was developed late in the seventeenth century, the regular street pattern precluded the existence of a warren of alleys and yards.

More important than the total number of households in determining the character of each hamlet must have been their concentration, that is the average number of households per acre. Table 14 shows that St

Katharine's, the precinct next to the Tower of London, contained the heaviest concentration of households at 40·3 per acre. Moving in an anti-clockwise direction around the inner suburban area from the Minories to Spitalfields, this number diminishes from 22·8 to 12. Moving eastward along the riverside from St Katharine's, the average number of households per acre declines from 33·9 in East Smithfield

TABLE 14   *East London households in 1664*[13]

Area	Households	Acreage	Average number of households per acre
Spitalfields	948	79	12·0
Whitechapel	2,482	174	14·7
Minories	114	5	22·8
St Katharine's	927	23	40·3
East Smithfield	1,239	37	33·9
Wapping (Whitechapel), including Wapping Wall	1,927	80	24·1
Wapping (Stepney)	1,549	243	6·4
Shadwell	1,364	99	13·8
Ratcliff	1,121	132	8·5
Limehouse	1,226	265	4·6
Poplar and Blackwall	660	1,490	0·4
Mile End	236	681	0·3
Bethnal Green	217	792	0·3
Bow and Old Ford	175	809	0·2
Total	14,185	4,909	2·9

to 0·4 in Poplar and Blackwall. The only figure which disturbs this pattern is the surprisingly low 6·4 in Wapping (Stepney), in the centre of the riverside chain of development, explained by the presence of Wapping marsh, largely undeveloped in 1664. Outside the urban area in the villages of Mile End, Bethnal Green, Bow and Old Ford the concentration of households is very low, as might be expected in places which were mainly enclosed pasture. The same explanation accounts for the low concentration in Poplar. This pattern of development, resulting in the highest concentration of households and presumably houses in the south-west corner of the suburban area of East London, may be attributed to the dual attractions of the river and the City.

These figures showing the concentration of households within each hamlet obscure important variations in density in different parts of a given hamlet. In Shadwell, for example, fields still accounted for a large part of the hamlet as late as 1682.[14] As a result houses must have been more tightly packed in the remaining portions of the hamlet than the average figure of 13·8 households per acre would suggest. About twelve or thirteen acres of this built-up area containing no large open spaces held 613 buildings in 1650, an average of almost 50 buildings per acre, mostly houses.[15] It seems that housing density in the mid-seventeenth century could be extremely high. Even in the mid-nineteenth century, housing density was only 21 to 27 houses per acre in Whitechapel and a mere 12 houses per acre in Shadwell, of which a large part has since been employed as docks.[16] Today, a housing density of 50 per acre would be considered intolerable without extremely skilful planning and utilization of space. In 1952 the desirable density for two-storied houses was 65 rooms per acre and for three-storied houses 85 rooms per acre.[17] The houses in seventeenth-century Shadwell had an average of almost four rooms each or nearly 200 rooms per acre in the densest part of the hamlet. It would be anachronistic to suggest that the inhabitants of East London thought or worried about the statistics of housing density, but no one could deny that the problems of living 40 households to the acre in St Katharine's must have created tension and stress not felt in the rural surroundings of Bethnal Green. Certainly one of the causes of tension must have been the unrelieved gloom in which many denizens of the crowded streets and alleys passed their days. Separated from their neighbours across the street often by only 15 feet, little sunlight could have penetrated into the rooms of their dwellings, even where these buildings were only two storeys high.[18]

Housing density is only one determinant of the quality of living in an urban environment. It may be that living in the cramped conditions of a seventeenth-century 'Coronation Street' did not affect a man as much as did a leaking roof, damp walls or the ruinous condition of his house. What were East London houses made of? How well were they made and how well did they stand up to the ravages of time? Judging by the few examples which are mentioned in documents, they were commonly built of wood or wood and Flemish wall. Early seventeenth-century schedules of illegal buildings sometimes describe this type of construction. In 1618, for example, 2 new timber tenements in the Minories and 5 in Houndsditch are noted.[19] One great advantage of the use of wood during this period was its local availability. The lessee of the manor of Stepney possessed woodland on the demesne, and trees along the riverside were also used for building.[20] When in September 1699, the Mercers' Company planned to rebuild the house in Ratcliff belonging to the master of St Paul's School, they reserved for it some of the forty trees standing by Ratcliff Highway.[21] Parliamentary surveys provide the best proof that wood and Flemish wall, lath and plaster or other filling were the normal building materials up to the mid-seventeenth century. A survey of houses on Tower wharf in 1651 describes 45 as built of timber, Flemish wall and tile and only 2 of brick and tile.[22] The most comprehensive survey, that of 703 buildings in Shadwell in 1650, mentioned only 61 houses built of brick. Most were probably built of wood and Flemish wall, though this was not specified in the survey, and 45 of the structures described as sheds may have been built entirely of wood.[23] Houses of timber and Flemish wall were also common in East Smithfield and the Tower liberty.[24]

Brick buildings were exceptional in Shadwell in 1650 and probably throughout East London. Those that there were tended to be among the larger houses. Over 25 per cent of the three-storied houses in the hamlet were built of brick in comparison with 10 per cent of the two-storied and 2·5 per cent of the single-storied buildings. Occasionally we find groups of brick buildings along the main roads of Shadwell, Ratcliff Highway and Wapping Wall (or Lower Shadwell). Houses of 'paper' were mentioned in a survey of the manor of Stepney in 1642, a reference to the kind of lath and plaster work noted by Defoe in London, before the fire.[25] His suggestion that these materials 'were very properly call'd paper work' was an apt comment on the quality of this type of construction.[26] Wood went out of fashion with builders in the later seventeenth century. Many bricklayers took building plots on Sir William Wheler's land in Spitalfields in the 1650s and 1660s.[27] When, in August 1661, a proclamation was issued encouraging the use of brick, official approval was given to a change already under way.[28] For once a Stuart government's decree on building was effective. Henceforward a good reason was necessary before construction in wood was permitted. Bridewell Hospital, which owned land in Wapping, claimed that its ruinous tenements there had to be rebuilt with timber because the ground on which they stood was too quaggy to support brick building and a licence was granted on 30 September 1662.[29] After a disastrous fire in 1673, which destroyed these timber buildings, even they were rebuilt with brick.[30]

The occasional mention of ruinous tenements in surveys suggests that they were not originally well built, but the decay of many was due to their age. *The Survey of London* notes that building on the Wheler estate was of poor quality because a house, built about 1656 on ground leased from William Browne, was later described as an 'old ruined messuage', but since this house was probably built of timber it is not surprising that its life should have been only 60 years.[31] Other wooden buildings suffered a similar fate. The wooden tenements of Bridewell Hospital in Wapping were 'decayed and ruinous' in 1662, after a life of less than 100 years.[32]

The custom of the manor of Stepney limited copyhold leases to 31 years, with the result that substantial building was discouraged, but this limitation would not have affected building on the considerable acreage of non-copyhold manorial land or non-manorial land.[33] Whatever the cause, inferior building did take place. John Stow despised the quality of the housing along the riverside and in Whitechapel.[34] It is clear that many poor people lived along the riverside who would probably not have the means to rent or maintain substantial accommodation. A petition to the Council in October 1632 complained of the many new buildings in Ratcliff, Limehouse and other suburbs which were attracting great numbers of poor people and 'loose' immigrants.[35] Another indication of poor quality building was the speed with which some houses were erected. The 200 tenements said to have been erected in Peasefield in Wapping during the plague summer of 1636, some of them by night, must have made poor homes.[36] Although such evidence suggests that inferior building was common individual examples of shoddy workmanship are rare. An exception was provided by the action of the Tilers' and Bricklayers' Company in fining builders for bad work in Mile End New Town in the 1680s and 1690s.[37] It may be that the demand for houses was so great that men were unwilling to complain about the quality of the houses they did obtain and therefore rarely left evidence of their dissatisfaction.

The high density of housing in certain areas raises images of tiny houses packed tightly together. What was the size of the average house? It is impossible to generalize about dimensions, because they are so rarely documented. The width and depth of houses are sometimes noted by parliamentary surveys of the property of the Dean of St Paul's in East London. A survey made in 1649 of a piece of this land on the north side of Whitechapel street describes four tenements held by Eleanor Ireland. All had narrow frontages, three of 11 feet and one of 15 feet 9 inches, but greater depth, two of 26 feet 6 inches and one each of 27 feet 3 inches and 34 feet 6 inches.[38] The Shadwell survey of 1650 describes a terrace of ten tenements, situated on the north side of Ratcliff Highway in Shadwell, which measured 118 feet from east to west and about 60 feet from north to south. If we assume that all the houses in this terrace had an equal frontage, the width of each one was under 12 feet. The depth of the terrace was 60 feet, and no mention is made of any yards which might account for part of this unlikely depth. The dimensions of an entire street in Shadwell, Lime street, show that not all houses were as cavernously deep as the ten tenements along Ratcliff Highway appear. Lime street, with 13 identical dwellings on either side, measured 150 feet from east to west by 60 feet falling to 52 feet, from north to south. Assuming that the street was about 15 feet wide and that the yards behind the houses were about 5 feet long, the houses must have had a frontage of between 11 and 12 feet and a depth of about 15 feet (see Fig. 2). A group of houses with the same dimensions stood nearby to the east.[39]

Although in the Lime street area of Shadwell houses were apparently very small, there were houses which covered a larger area elsewhere in the hamlet. In White Hart lane, in the eastern part of Shadwell, a group of six tenements and a separate yard measured 100 feet by 60 feet, an average frontage of 14 to 15 feet and a depth of 60 feet, including the yards belonging to the houses.[40] Along Lower Shadwell the houses were larger still. A group of seven houses, situated along the north side of the road between Broad Bridge and White Hart lane, had a combined frontage of nearly 200 feet, an average of about 28 feet each, over double the frontage of houses in and near Lime street.[41] On the other side of the street the average width was over 20 feet, with individual frontages ranging from 19 feet in the case of Thomas Ashley's house (see Fig. 2) to 83 feet in the case of the Noah's Ark tavern.[42] The depth of these houses along Lower Shadwell is not given by the survey, but judging by their size as shown on William Morgan's map of 1682, they were all about 30 feet deep.

In contrast the houses of Spitalfields were more uniform in area.

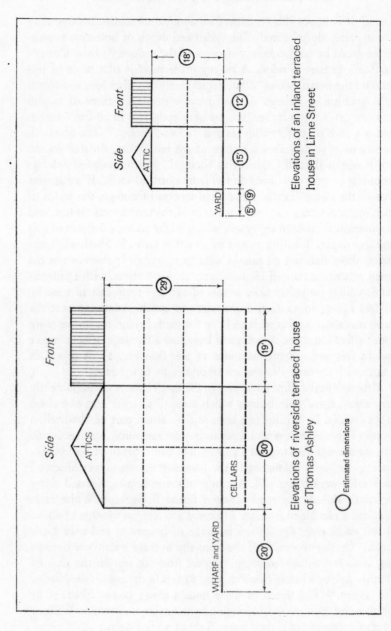

Fig. 2. Two Shadwell houses in 1650

Plots of land with frontages from 10 to 16 feet were granted along Flower and Dean street to various builders in 1656 and 1657 by John Flower and Gowen Dean. Slightly wider plots in the Old Artillery Ground, with frontages from 16 to 20 feet, were sold to builders in the 1680s by John Parsons, Robert Sheffield and Nicholas Barbon.[43] One of the widest houses in the area must have been that owned by John Britton, citizen and joiner of London, with a frontage of 24 feet and a depth of 15 feet.[44] The depth of the other Spitalfields houses was between 15 and 20 feet, again judging by the depth as shown on Morgan's map.

William Morgan's 'Map of London' of 1682 can be used for measuring the depth of buildings but not for their width, for most of the houses are shown in terraces and courts and not individually distinguished. One clue for the measurement of width is the delineation of some yards behind certain terraces, but these are not reliable indications of individual houses. In Spitalfields, the yards shown behind the houses in Flower and Dean street suggest that the houses measured 30 feet wide at least, whereas we know from documentary evidence that they were only about 16 feet wide. On the north side of Lime street, in Shadwell, the map shows four yards, yet we know from the survey of Shadwell that there were thirteen yards there, behind thirteen houses. Evidently the cartographer delineated yards only to show that they existed, not to show how many were there.

The width and depth of a house are sometimes recorded, but never its height. An idea of this third dimension can be gained by discovering how many storeys a house possessed. The most common type was the two-storied house. The four houses of Eleanor Ireland in Whitechapel all had two storeys.[45] A survey of Baylyes place in East Smithfield in 1651 mentioned four two-storied houses and one three-storied house.[46] The survey of Shadwell gives the number of storeys of 701 houses. Of this total 195 had a single storey, 473 had two storeys and 33 had three storeys.[47] The 56 houses on Tower Wharf, surveyed in 1651, ranged in height from a single storey to one exceptional five-storied building, although the most common size was still two storeys.[48] The number of storeys does not indicate the exact height of the houses because there was no standard height for each storey. Using the standards set for the rebuilding of London after the fire, a two-storied house would have been about 18 feet high, a three-storied house 29 feet high and a four-storied house about 37 feet 6 inches high, plus the height of the roof in each case, approximations which probably tend to over-estimate the height of East London houses.[49]

The average house would seem to have been small, a two-storied dwelling with an area of about 200 square feet on the ground floor. A house of this size might have as many as eight rooms, two on each floor and two each in cellar and attic, but most of these houses did not comprise so many rooms.[50] The 4 houses of Eleanor Ireland had between four and six rooms each.[51] The 4 houses in Baylyes Place had between four and seven rooms each; the 1 seven-roomed house was split into two tenements.[52] Over the large area of Shadwell, with a great variety of houses, the number of rooms per house was even smaller. Of the 701 houses analysed, 492 had three rooms or less, 102 had four or five rooms, 102 had between six and ten rooms and 5 had more than ten rooms.[53] Many of the smaller houses had only one room on each floor; 322 of the 473 two-storied Shadwell houses were of this 'one up, one down' type. In contrast the houses on Tower Wharf had substantially more rooms. Of the 56 houses there, only 5 had three rooms or less, 14 had four or five rooms, 29 had between six and ten rooms, and 8 had more than ten rooms.[54] The difference between houses in Shadwell and on Tower Wharf is striking with an average number of rooms per house of about 3·7 and 7·2 respectively. Riverside houses were larger and consequently had more rooms than those inland. Even within Shadwell the same rule applies. The riverside houses in the hamlet had an average of 5·1 rooms, compared with the average of 3·7 for the whole area.

To what use did the typical householder put his small number of rooms? On the ground floor, a single room, perhaps 12 feet wide by 15 feet deep, would serve as a living, dining and cooking room and might also contain a stairway to the room above. On the first floor would be a chamber of approximately the same size, and in the roof a garret both probably used as bedrooms. There might be a cellar which could be used as a storeroom or an additional bedroom. At the back of the house might stand a tiny yard, perhaps five to ten feet deep, and opposite, at the front not 15 feet away, would stand another similar house. Houses of this description were not by any means the worst that existed in seventeenth-century East London, nor did housing conditions necessarily always improve on this standard in the centuries that followed. In Liverpool in 1840, for instance, people commonly lived in three-storied back-to-back dwellings, arranged in tiny courts only nine feet wide, containing only three rooms, each ten and a half feet square.[55] Nevertheless, the average East London house could not have provided very adequate family accommodation.

So far it has been impossible to generalize about the size and shape of the thousands of houses in East London which were not included in the parliamentary surveys. More comprehensive information about the number of rooms in these houses is supplied by the hearth tax of 1664 on the assumption that each hearth mentioned in the enumeration represents one major room in a house. The results of this survey are given in Table 15.[56] The average number of hearths per household in the riverside hamlets varies between 2·6 and 2·9. Near the City there was less uniformity; St Katharine's, East Smithfield and White-chapel averaged from 2·3 to 2·6 hearths per household, but in the Minories and in Spitalfields the average was over 3·0. Higher still were the figures for the country hamlets Mile End and Bow with an average of over 4·0 hearths per household and Old Ford with over 5·0. Here again there was an exception; Bethnal Green had only 2·8 hearths per household. The figures are not consistent enough to allow us to conclude that the average number of hearths per household differed significantly between these groups of hamlets, but in general this figure tended to be lower in urban than in country hamlets.

Although these figures accurately represent the relative position of each hamlet in Table 15, they must be adjusted before they can be used to indicate the average number of rooms per house in a particular hamlet. The average number of rooms per house in Shadwell in 1650 was 3·7. The average number of hearths per household in Shadwell in 1664 was only 2·7. It is possible that some houses were split into tene-ments so that hearths per household would refer to the number in each tenement rather than in each building, but there is evidence to suggest that houses were not commonly divided into tenements. A more likely explanation for the discrepancy is that not all the rooms in a house possessed hearths. Our equation of hearths and rooms is thus likely to underestimate the number of rooms in each house. To convert the number of hearths in Shadwell to rooms a multiplier of about 1·37 is used. Using the same figure for the other averages in Table 15, the average rooms per house in the riverside hamlets would rise to between 3·6 and 4, St Katharine's and Whitechapel to 3·2 or 3·3, Spitalfields and the Minories to 4·4 and the rural hamlets cor-respondingly higher. Urban houses were not quite so small as Table 15 makes them appear.

This table also shows the division of households into chargeable

TABLE 15 *The number of households in East London in 1664 with the number of hearths*

Area	Households	Chargeable	Non-chargeable	Number of hearths	Average no. of hearths per household
Spitalfields	948	521	427	3,062	3·2
Whitechapel	2,482	742	1,740	5,897	2·4
Minories	114	74	40	366	3·2
St Katharine's	927	326	601	2,100	2·3
East Smithfield	1,239	485	754	3,202	2·6
Wapping (Whitechapel)	1,927	899	1,028	5,122	2·7
Wapping (Stepney)	1,549	795	754	4,021	2·6
Shadwell	1,364	761	603	3,816	2·7
Ratcliff	1,121	577	544	3,389	2·9
Limehouse	1,226	864	362	3,164	2·6
Poplar	660	421	239	1,942	2·9
Mile End	236	195	41	1,023	4·3
Bethnal Green	217	104	113	621	2·8
Bow	156	111	45	649	4·2
Old Ford	19	19	—	97	5·1
Totals	14,185	6,894	7,291	38,371	2·7

and non-chargeable groups. The Act of 1662 which introduced the
hearth tax declared that all hearths were to be enumerated, but householders were not to be charged if they did not pay church or poor
rate, lived in a house worth less than £1 per annum, received an
annual income of less than £10, occupied premises with industrial
hearths or stoves or occupied a small charitable institution.[57] Most of
the non-chargeable householders in East London lived in dwellings
with few hearths. Whitechapel, East Smithfield and St Katharine's
had a remarkable preponderance of such dwellings. This area near the
City obviously contained the greatest proportion of small houses and
poor people. Most of the riverside hamlets had fairly equal numbers of
chargeable and non-chargeable households, but in Limehouse and
Poplar and all the inland hamlets, except Bethnal Green, the majority
of chargeable households suggests that houses were larger and the
hamlets more prosperous.

The average numbers of hearths per household varies not only
between hamlets but also within them. If we examine the tax documents for some of the riverside hamlets in which households are
listed by street and yard, one difference is obvious. Households in
streets and lanes had more hearths on average than those in alleys
and yards. In Ratcliff, in the streets households averaged 3·3 hearths,
in the alleys and yards the average was 2·4; in Wapping (Whitechapel)
the averages were 3·4 and 2·5 respectively; in Shadwell the differences
were not so great, 2·9 in the streets against 2·5 in the alleys. There
were other variations within a single hamlet. In Ratcliff, for example,
there were two distinct areas. Around White Horse street and Brook
street the number of hearths averaged between 2 and 2·5 per household, but in the southern part of the hamlet, by the river, the average
was 4. This difference corroborates the evidence of the parliamentary
surveys, reinforcing the conclusion that houses near the river had, on
average, both more hearths and more rooms.

Was multiple occupation common in East London during the
seventeenth century? The evidence suggests that it was the exception
rather than the rule. Occasionally a large house was divided. The
Great Place in Ratcliff, once the home of Sir Henry Colet and later of
Thomas Cromwell, was divided by the Mercers' Company into four
tenements at some time before 1589 and it remained in multiple
occupation until 1695.[58] In 1624 John Cox of Ratcliff was indicted
for dividing a house into seven tenements. In the same year, Richard
Harris, a Whitechapel victualler, was indicted for dividing a house

into three tenements and letting them to married couples.[59] The
Spitalfields messuage of Sir William Wheler was divided into three
tenements and occupied by a silk-throster and his under-tenants in
1665. Nearby in the south-west corner of Spitalfields, stood John
Strype's property, which the antiquarian leased to George Ford, a
dyer, in 1691. Some time between this date and 1723, the three mes-
suages in question were divided into six tenements.[60] The best indication that such division was uncommon in the seventeenth century is
that, of the 768 houses described by the parliamentary surveys, only
4 were noted as containing more than one household. In Baylyes Place
in East Smithfield, a house containing a cellar, a grocer's shop and two
kitchens on the ground floor and three chambers on the first floor
was divided into two tenements.[61] On Tower Wharf a house was
divided into three tenements. On the ground floor, above a cellar,
was a compass-maker's shop, a pulley-maker's shop, two parlours
and two kitchens. On the first floor were six chambers with four
garrets above. This arrangement suggests that the main part of the
house was divided vertically between two tenants and that the third
tenant occupied the four garrets. Two more houses of ten and fourteen rooms were each divided between two households.[62] Although
these tenements contained several rooms apiece, still smaller ones
existed. A number of empty single rooms are mentioned by the hearth
tax in 1664. In Moses alley, Whitechapel, there were six separate
empty rooms belonging to Master Collings, one to Master Barrett
and another to Master May. In the rest of the parish there were seven
empty rooms, in St Katharine's there were eight, in Limehouse thirty-
two, in Ratcliff two and along Wapping Wall and in Shadwell, twenty-
five. Perhaps they were waiting to be let, but there were many more
single rooms in East London which were occupied, for there were
many one-hearth households, especially in Whitechapel. The bed-
sitting room seems to have been as much a necessity in seventeenth-
century London as it is today.

Too few rentals survive to give a comprehensive picture of what the
tenants paid to live in East London houses. Two conclusions about
rents are possible, however: that rent was high in areas near the City
where the demand for housing was high and that rents seem to have
been rising in the first half of the century. A survey of the manor of
Stepney in 1642 reveals a great difference in rent between houses in
Bethnal Green where payments were as low as £2 per annum and
those in Spitalfields as high as £6.[63] Another survey in 1652 shows a

similar discrepancy between rents of about £2 per annum in Bethnal Green and £8 in Wapping nearer the river and the City.[64] Higher still were rents for houses on Tower Wharf. In 1634, fifty-five houses there had an average annual rent of £9 3s 1d. Four years later this average had risen to £10 12s 2d and by 1651 to £16 0s 8d.[65] These high rents reflected both the large size of the houses on the wharf and the desirability of their location. This example also shows the change in average rent which rose £7 in only seventeen years.

The standard of comfort in an East London house is difficult to gauge. We have already established that many of the houses were small and cramped. The inventories of the Commissary Court of London give some indication of the use of the rooms and the nature of their furnishings. Of the relevant inventories drawn up before 1700, fifty-eight list the rooms of the house and describe their contents.[66] In small houses and tenements, the one or two rooms served all purposes. The inventory of the possessions of Samuel Jackman of Stepney mentioned only one room, containing a bed, a chest of drawers, a table and some chairs. John Fernew of Whitechapel inhabited a tenement consisting of two chambers, one containing a bed and kitchen tools and the other tables and chairs, suggesting the odd combination of bedroom and kitchen with a separate living room. John Barrett of Whitechapel possessed a chamber and a garret, the first serving as a bed-sitting room, the second serving as a combined bedroom and kitchen.[67] Most of the tenements described in the inventories were larger than these; forty-two out of fifty-eight describe houses which contained a variety of specialized rooms, chambers, kitchens, parlours and so on. One of the larger houses belonged to Isaac Howe. On the ground floor there was a kitchen, containing grates, spits, a table, cupboards and pewter, a hall with a table, a carpet, twelve leather chairs, cupboards and other minor items, and a shop with quantities of tobacco and sugar and weighing apparatus. On the first floor there were three chambers with beds, chairs, chests of drawers and looking glasses, and on the second floor there were two more chambers similarly furnished.[68] Unfortunately inventories tend to describe more prosperous households. Thus they convey an impression of moderate comfort probably not enjoyed to the same degree by the majority of East London households. Most of the houses described in inventories had adequate provision for heating. Fire-irons were mentioned in chambers and living rooms as well as in kitchens. These establishments were plentifully, if not luxuriously, furnished. There were few carpets, but usually sufficient chairs, tables and beds in living rooms and chambers to suggest that houses were over- rather than under-furnished. In the first chamber of William Hull's house in Whitechapel, there was a bed, two tables and ten chairs, a not uncommon collection.[69]

The number of beds mentioned suggests overcrowding, for they were found not only in garrets, but frequently in living and work rooms as well. In William Hull's house, there were three beds in the kitchen, possibly used by the servants, in addition to three beds in two chambers and a garret. The inventory of the goods of Alan Covell of Stepney mentions two beds in the kitchen, a bed in the hall, and two beds in the two chambers. Occasionally a bed is listed as standing in a workshop within the house, perhaps for the use of an apprentice or lodger. In the workshop of Jordan Brooke of Stepney, citizen and goldsmith, there was a bed, standing beside four looms and a warping frame, and in the house of Richard Alchurch of Whitechapel, another bed was found in the shop beside five looms.[70] Of the fifty-eight inventories, nine mention a workshop and eighteen mention a shop, usually on the ground floor of the house, though occasionally in the garret. Although the trade or craft carried on in these houses was usually confined to one room separated from the living quarters there were exceptions. Cellars and garrets or even chambers were sometimes used as store-rooms for the material used in the craft or trade. John Fitzwilliam of Whitechapel had a shop full of cut glass; in the cellar and in one of the chambers was four hundredweight of lead, probably used in glass manufacture. In another instance, the trade of the occupant dominated the whole house. The inventory of the goods of Mary Yateman of Bethnal Green shows that she was a dealer in coal. In her shed and garden there were 140 sacks of coal, in her garret 65 sacks of dust and 10 sacks of charcoal, and in her two chambers around the beds, a further 16 sacks of coal.[71] Inventories do not supply a complete picture of life and its problems in East London houses. Certain details are not illuminated either in these documents or in any other source. No mention is made of privies, drainage or washing equipment.[72] Neither inventories nor surveys ever describe stairways or where they might have been situated. In smaller houses an internal staircase would have taken up a great deal of space. Ladders may have been used, or perhaps stairways were built behind the houses.[73] Occasionally the phrase 'up one pair of stairs' is used, but only to indicate the division between two storeys.

Did the denizens of East London suffer from overcrowding? According to the Ministry of Housing and Local Government, overcrowding exists where the occupancy rate or average number of persons per room exceeds 1·5.[74] We can make a rough estimate of the number of persons per room in the hamlets of East London by comparing the population in the 1660s with the number of hearths in each hamlet.[75]

TABLE 16 *Population and hearths in East London in the 1660s*

Area	Population	Hearths	Average number of persons per hearth
Spitalfields	1,440	3,062	0·5
Whitechapel	15,804	5,897	2·6
Wapping (Whitechapel)	5,400	5,122	1·1
Wapping (Stepney)	6,804	4,021	1·7
Shadwell	10,800	3,816	2·8
Ratcliff	5,472	3,289	1·7
Limehouse	5,130	3,164	1·6
Poplar	2,106	1,942	1·1
Bethnal Green	414	621	0·7
Mile End	1,026	1,023	1·0
Total	54,396	31,957	1·7

Table 16 indicates overcrowding in Whitechapel and in all the riverside hamlets except Wapping (Whitechapel) and Poplar. These figures do not necessarily reflect actual conditions for they relate to the number of persons per hearth and it has been shown that there were probably about a third more rooms than hearths. If we increase all the hearth figures by this proportion to produce an estimate of the number of rooms, the occupancy rate would fall considerably, to below one person per room in all the hamlets except Limehouse, Ratcliff, Shadwell, Wapping and Whitechapel. Only in two of these, Shadwell and Whitechapel, would the rate be over 1·5 persons per room. It would seem, therefore, that throughout East London generally overcrowding was not a major problem, at least by modern standards. Whitechapel, however, was a housing 'black spot'. Table 15 suggested that Whitechapel houses were among the smallest in the eastern suburban area, Table 16 that they were the most crowded as well.

It is rather surprising that overcrowding is not more evident. The suburbs of London were subject to a rapid influx of immigrants many of whom lacked means to purchase houses, even if builders had been able to erect them sufficiently quickly. One would suppose that the result of this housing shortage would be the renting of tenements or flats, or even rooms by whole families, and that overcrowding would be severe. Occasionally in times of stress such as the plague summer of 1665, we gain a glimpse of this overcrowding. On 9 July an order of the Justices of Middlesex referred to the congested conditions in the suburbs caused by the 'harbouring and placing of inmates and under-sitters in houses and cellars, and by erecting of new buildings, and by dividing and parcelling out the said buildings, and other houses into several petty tenements and inhabitations and pestering and filling the same with inmates and poor indigent and idle and loose persons'.[76] Surveys of housing rarely make any mention of conditions of this kind. Occasionally they refer to inhabited sheds, such as the forty-five recorded in Shadwell, and maps of London show small buildings in the back yards of older and more congested areas which might have been inhabited outhouses, but no similar buildings appear near the neatly terraced houses of Spitalfields and similar areas. Either the evidence of the surveys is deceptive, omitting to mention divided houses and failing to note families living in cellars and outhouses, or the builders and the rapid turnover of tenancies kept pace with the demand for housing. Certainly the first of these suggestions seems the more likely.

From this study of East London we can draw certain conclusions about the nature of suburban housing in the seventeenth century. Houses were built in greater quantity and in increasingly regular patterns. Standards tended to improve as brick replaced wood as the favoured building material. The concentration of houses became less dense as development areas moved further from the City. Although the majority of the new dwellings remained small, they were generally larger than those erected in the sixteenth century close to the City in Whitechapel and St Katharine's and do not appear to have been seriously overcrowded. These improvements provided the background to Strype's complacent description of East London as 'a great town, . . . plenty and wealth the crown of all'.[77]

Notes

1 A crude multiple of 36 was calculated by comparing the average annual baptisms of the 1660s and 1690s with population estimates based on the hearth tax of 1664 and the tax on births, marriages and burials of 1695. The baptism figures are from St Dunstan's Stepney registers, GLCRO P 93/255–9; St Mary Matfelon Whitechapel registers, GLCRO P 93/MRY 1/1–4, 6; St John's Wapping (part of Whitechapel parish, registers commence 1617) registers at St Peter's Church London Docks; St Paul's Shadwell (part of Stepney, made parochial in 1669, registers commence 1670) registers at the church. The hearth tax is at the Middlesex Record Office (MxRO), Hearth Tax 4, and the figures from the tax on births, marriages and burials of 1695 at the PRO, King MS. T64/302. A crude baptism multiple calculated from a population figure of one period is inadequate when applied throughout a century. It is used only to give the roughest idea of the size of the population at two dates, and probably is a misleading guide to the population at the earlier date. However, the considerable increase in population is obvious however inadequate our figures.

2 N. G. Brett-James traced the geographical expansion of London in *The Growth of Stuart London* (1935). But he did not consider building development and housing in East London in detail.

3 J. Stow, *A Survey of London* (ed., C. L. Kingsford, Oxford, 1908), I, 124–7, 129, II, 71–2.

4 SP 16/408/65.

5 George Care claimed in 1684 that in the 1620s he had been one of the first builders in Shadwell; see 'The Lady Ivie's Trial' in T. B. Howell, ed., *State Trials* (1816), X, 608, 615. The 703 buildings in 1650 are described in the Deed of Sale of Shadwell, 22 November 1650, at St Paul's Cathedral Library, press E. drawer 5 (Survey of Shadwell).

6 BM, Lansdowne MS. 52, 27.

7 SP 16/351/78.

8 *CSPD, 1638–39*, p. 259.

9 F. H. W. Sheppeard, ed., *Survey of London, XXVII, Spitalfields and Mile End New Town* (1957), p. 98.

10 Tower Hamlets Library Local Collection (THLLC), Deeds 141, 124.

11 This is true of most of the terraces surveyed in Shadwell in 1650, particularly in the eastern part of the hamlet. Survey of Shadwell, fols 10–20.

12 THLLC, Deeds 102, 124.

13 Household figures, MxRO Hearth Tax 4. Acreage figures, *Parliamentary Papers, Accounts and Papers* (1862), I, 206–7.

14 William Morgan, 'Map of London', 1682.

15 The number of buildings is given by the Survey of Shadwell, the acreage in *State Trials*, X, 563.

16 I am indebted to Dr R. Smith of the University of Birmingham for these figures from the 1851 census.

17 *The Density of Residential Areas* (Ministry of Housing and Local Government, H.M.S.O. 1952), p. 9.

18 After a great fire in Wapping streets and lanes were widened to 20 feet in 1675 (*CSPD, 1673–75*, pp. 588–9).

19 *APC, 1618–19*, p. 245.

20 GLCRO, Survey of Stepney manorial land in Bethnal Green, M 93/158, fols 1, 2, 4, 25, 30.

21 Mercers' Company Acts of Court, 13 December 1649. I am indebted to Miss J. Imray for this reference.

22 E. 317 Middlesex 93.

23 Survey of Shadwell, fols 1–20.

24 E. 317 Middlesex 1 and 91.

25 BM, Additional MS 22253, fols 1–2; *Survey of London XXVII*, p. 238.

26 D. Defoe, *A Tour through the whole island of Great Britain* (Everyman edn. 1962), I, 324–5. I am indebted to Dr D. Palliser for this reference.

27 *Survey of London XXVII*, pp. 98–9.

28 Brett-James, *op. cit.*, p. 296; R. Steele, *Tudor and Stuart Proclamations* (Oxford, 1910), no. 3321.

29 SP 44/8/7.

30 *CSPD, 1673–75*, pp. 588–9.

31 *Survey of London XXVII*, pp. 98–9.

32 SP 44/8/7; Stow, *op. cit.*, II, 70–1.

33 Brett-James, *op. cit.*, p. 109.

34 Stow, *op. cit.*, II, 71–2.

35 *Analytical Index to the Remembrancia* (1878), p. 49.

36 SP 16/351/78.

37 *Survey of London XXVII*, p. 265.

38 St Paul's Cathedral Library, press A, box 25 A, no. 1711.

39 Survey of Shadwell, fols 1, 4, 9.

40 *Ibid.*, fol. 16.

41 *Ibid.*, fol. 14. Tracing this survey on William Morgan's 'Map of London' showed that these houses stood in two back-to-back terraces.

42 *Ibid.*, fols 18, 20.

43 *Survey of London XXVII*, pp. 32–3, 245.

44 Commercial Union Insurance Office, 24, Cornhill, London, Hand in Hand Company Insurance Book 1, policy 611.

45 St Paul's Cathedral Library, press A, box 25 A, no. 1711.

46 E. 317 Middlesex 1.

47 Survey of Shadwell.

48 E. 317 Middlesex 93.

49 *Statutes of the Realm*, 18 & 19 Charles II, c. 8.

50 Of the 701 houses in Shadwell 384 had a garret only, 20 a cellar only and 85 both a cellar and garret.

51 St Paul's Cathedral Library, press A, box 25 A, no. 1711.

52 E. 317 Middlesex 1.

53 Survey of Shadwell.

54 E. 317 Middlesex 93.

55 J. N. Tarn, 'Housing in Liverpool and Glasgow', *The Town Planning Review*, January 1969, 320–1.

56 MxRO, Hearth Tax 4.

57 C. A. F. Meekings, ed., *The Surrey Hearth Tax of 1664* (Surrey Record Soc., XVII, 1940), p. xii.

58 Jean Imray, 'The Mercers' Company and East London: the first two hundred years', *East London Papers*, VI (1963), 91–5.

59 J. C. Jeaffreson, ed., *Middlesex County Records*, II (1887), 182–4.

60 *Survey of London XXVII*, pp. 97, 238.

61 E. 317 Middlesex 1.

62 E. 317 Middlesex 93.

63 BM, Additional MS. 22253, fols 2–12, 15, 16.

64 GLCRO M. 93/157 & 158.

65 SP 16/279/32; SP 16/408/66; E. 317 Middlesex 93.

66 GL MSS 9174/1, 9177/9, 9186/1. More inventories made between 1702 and 1706 are contained in MSS 9177/4, 9177/7, 9177/8.

67 GL MSS 9177/9, 3 January 1699; 9174/1, 17 April 1667, 4 December 1666.

68 *Ibid.*, 22 October 1666.

69 *Ibid.*, 16 April 1667.

70 *Ibid.*, 16 April 1667, 10 February 1667, 4 April 1666.

71 *Ibid.*, 12 July 1667; 9177/9, 8 February 1701.

72 The Survey of Shadwell mentions only a few drains among the many streets it describes, and these were inlets from the river Thames dug to power a water mill at Ratcliff.

73 Margaret Wood, *The English Medieval House* (1965), p. 328.

74 *The Density of Residential Areas* (H.M.S.O. 1952), pp. 4–5.

75 MxRO, Hearth Tax 4. The population of each hamlet was estimated by multiplying the average of the baptisms of 1660 and 1670 by 36 (see note 1), except in three cases. Shadwell people, unlike those from most other

Stepney hamlets, tend to be omitted from the Stepney registers at this period. A population figure for the hamlet was calculated by taking the average baptisms of Shadwell parish in the 1670s, 343 per annum, reducing this to 300 per annum for the previous decade, and multiplying this figure by 36. The Wapping (Whitechapel) register suffers from gaps in 1660. The figure of average annual baptisms in the other years in the decade was calculated and used. Finally the Whitechapel baptism figures for 1660 are much below the average annual baptisms of the decade, and so the average annual figure was used.

76 J. C. Jeaffreson, ed., *Middlesex County Records*, III (1888), 373–5.
77 J. Strype, *Survey of London*, II, iv (1720), 87.

8

A provincial capital
in the late seventeenth century:
The case of Norwich[1]

Penelope Corfield

'As to Norwich, it is a great city and full of people', commented Baskerville in 1681; 'the whole Citty lookes like what it is, a rich thriveing industrious place', Celia Fiennes agreed in 1697; and in 1723 Defoe confirmed that Norwich was 'antient, large, rich and populous'.[2] Not all travellers' tales are true. Yet these comments reflected accurately enough the importance of the city of Norwich in the late seventeenth and early eighteenth centuries. At this time, it was the second city in the kingdom (a position sometimes wrongly ascribed to Bristol) and it had experienced considerable expansion in the course of the seventeenth century, at a rate of growth faster than that of most other provincial cities. Between 1600 and 1700 the population had increased from an estimated 12,000 or 13,000 to an authenticated 30,000.[3] This essay is concerned to chronicle the growth of the city in the latter half of the century and to examine some of the factors which brought this about.

The growth of the city attracts attention for two reasons. In the first place, it was among the comparatively small number of provincial cities that were expanding, in a period which was not one of general urban growth. While there was undoubtedly an increase in the urban population of England and Wales, both in absolute and proportionate terms, much of this increase can be accounted for by the growth of the capital city. London was not only much larger than all other cities, but it was also growing at a faster rate. Indeed, fears were expressed that London would swallow up all England. In the second place, Norwich was among an even smaller number of inland towns that were expanding in this period. By 1700, Norwich was by far the largest inland town in the country, with over twice the population of Birmingham, its nearest rival in this respect.[4] Most of the other leading provincial cities in 1700 were ports. Indeed, the late seventeenth century saw a considerable expansion of overseas trade, to such an extent that the period is sometimes labelled that of 'the Commercial Revolution'. The growth of Norwich suggests that there were other developments in the late seventeenth-century economy which deserve investigation.

Analysis and explanations are alike complicated by the dearth of statistics relating to the demographic and economic history of the city. There are no reliable figures for the size of the urban population before 1693, when the first local enumeration was taken. In this respect Norwich resembles many other towns. With regard to data relating to the economic life of the city Norwich fares rather worse. As an inland town, the city has left no commercial statistics, since inland trade was not subject to any control or fiscal imposition. Furthermore, the official records of the Weavers' Company, which regulated the city's staple industry, were destroyed in the early eighteenth century when formal supervision was ended.[5] Paradoxically, therefore, some of the conditions that assisted in the expansion of the city in the seventeenth century have made it difficult, at a distance of three centuries, to recover evidence for that growth.

The population of the city of Norwich multiplied in the course of the seventeenth century some two-and-a-half times. It is easier to sketch this in outline than to clothe the skeleton. But it seems probable that the growth of the city was not continuous and cumulative throughout the century, but occurred in two discrete periods, in the first three and last three decades of the century. These periods of growth were separated by a population plateau in the mid-century. This is a pattern similar in outline to the growth of the population in the country as a whole, although in both periods of growth the urban population was increasing at a faster rate than that of the rest of the country.

This essay is concerned with the second of these two periods of growth. But in order to establish the size of the city's population by the mid-century plateau, it is necessary to look briefly at the earlier period. That there was an increase in the city's population can be seen from the returns of the city's Bills of Mortality from 1582 to 1646. These show marked increases in the totals of both baptisms and burials in the early years of the seventeenth century. The most rapid growth occurred in the late 1610s and early 1620s. The average annual number of baptisms showed an increase of over 50 per cent between the first and second decades of the century, rising from an average of 478·6 between 1601 and 1610, to an average of 748·9 between 1611 and 1620. In the following decade the average number of baptisms rose again to 836·2. This then fell to the slightly lower figure of 710·6 between 1631 and 1640.[6] Other records indicate a movement of population into the city in the early years of the century. In 1622, the Ordinances for regulating the city's trading companies spoke of the vast increase in numbers of 'foreigners' coming into Norwich.[7]

The Mortality Bills, however, do not so readily yield the size of the total population. There are two problems here. In the first place, there is no means of testing either the accuracy or the consistency of the Bills. The returns were made weekly to the Mayoral Court, and there may well have been errors and omissions in the collection of the material. And the original parish registers, from which the information was culled, were not themselves above reproach as a complete record of the demographic statistics of the city.[8] The second problem consists in the selection of the appropriate birth rate for the city's population at this time. Since there is no evidence to suggest one figure rather than another, the inflation of the number of baptisms to produce the total population can only be a very arbitrary exercise. It has been noted that the increase in the number of baptisms in the early part of the century was so great that, assuming a standard birth rate of 1 in 33, or 30 per 1,000, the population of the city would have reached almost to the total of 30,000 by 1622.[9] Such a total is theoretically feasible, and cannot be disproved given the present state of the evidence. But it is unlikely that the population had reached such a high total by this date. Such an assumption implies a very rapid rate of growth in the early part of the century, followed by a steep decline in the following decades. The population rise can be flattened out by the selection of a higher birth rate. This would be consonant with what is known about the effects of high levels of immigration into a community, which tends to increase the proportion of those in the reproductive age-groups in the population as a whole, and hence pushes up the birth rate.[10] A birth rate of 1 in 25, or 40 per 1,000, would produce the smaller total population of some 20,000 inhabitants in the 1620s.

Certainly any population expansion was halted in the late 1620s and the 1630s, as the result both of renewed outbreaks of plague in 1625–6, 1631 and 1637–8, and of emigration from the city for religious reasons in the 1630s.[11] The average yearly baptismal and burial figures for the decade from 1631 to 1640 were lower than those for the previous decades, and showed, for the first time this century, a preponderance of baptisms over burials, which suggests that there was some emigration.[12] But there is no evidence for any protracted population decline in the middle years of the century. Puritan exiles returned in the 1640s, and some foreign co-religionists also settled in the city in the 1650s.[13] The population of Norwich probably fluctuated therefore around the figure of 20,000 in the mid-seventeenth century.

The evidence for the demographic history of the city in the second half of the century is unfortunately even more scanty than for the earlier period. The Bills of Mortality were still collected (though not without administrative difficulties)[14] but there is a complete hiatus in the records between 1646, when entries in the Mayoral Court Books ceased, and 1707, the date of the earliest surviving local paper, which printed monthly totals. Nor has it proved possible to recover the data on baptisms and burials from the original parish registers. Although many of these registers have survived, the amount of information that can be collected is far from complete, as a result of illegibility and gaps in the records.[15]

Some indices for the growth of the city's population can, however, be devised from fiscal records. Mutilated but legible returns of the inhabitants paying the Hearth Tax in 1662 have survived, although they do not cover the whole city. These returns, for parishes which in 1693 contained 79 per cent of the city's population, listed 1,538 taxpayers, paying for 5,864 hearths, at 3·8 hearths per person. This suggests for the whole city a total of 1,947 taxpayers, paying for 7,423 hearths.[16] Allowance then has to be made for those who were exempted from payment. According to a list of 1671, 61·7 per cent of all householders were exempted.[17] This proportion is very high in comparison with those found in some other cities, but it is not unreasonable in view of the fact that Norwich was a manufacturing city, and that there was some uncertainty about the taxable status of industrial hearths.[18] Assuming an exemption rate of 60 per cent in round figures, the total number of householders was 4,868. With an average household size of 4·2 individuals in Norwich,[19] the total population comes to 20,446 inhabitants. While it is obvious that this calculation is far from exact, it gives some indications of the order of magnitude of the city's population.

A similar calculation can be made for 1671, on the basis of a list of assessments for the same tax. This list is more detailed, in that it contains the names of all householders, including those eventually exempted from payment, but it too is incomplete. The returns survive for parishes which in 1693 contained 76 per cent of the total population. They suggest for the whole city a total of 4,904 householders, with 11,683 hearths, an average of 2·38 hearths per householder.[20] This produces a total population of 20,597 inhabitants, a total not significantly larger than that calculated for 1662. It has, however, been pointed out that the efficacy of the assessments tended to decline over time, as resistance to the tax increased.[21] It may be, therefore, that the figure for 1671 is too low. The evidence of the Compton Census returns, however, also seems to confirm that the population of the city had not reached much above 20,000 by 1676. This census listed 12,562 adult communicants in the city. Assuming that 40 per cent of the population were too young to take communion, this suggests a total of approximately 21,000 inhabitants. But the returns of the Compton Census for the city of Norwich also present problems. Many of the parish totals of Conformists are given in suspiciously rounded numbers. It is also clear that the number of Nonconformists (totalling less than 5 per cent of the whole population) is too low for this traditional Puritan stronghold, but it is not known whether they were counted as Conformists or simply omitted.[22]

These estimates deal in probabilities and not certainties. They do, however, suggest that there was very little population growth in the 1660s, which was a decade of high mortality due to epidemics of plague and smallpox, and that population expansion was not resumed before the 1670s, and possibly not until the end of this decade. The 1670s and 1680s must therefore have seen a return to the sort of growth rate seen at the start of the century, in order to produce the total of 28,881 inhabitants found at the enumeration of the city and county in 1693.[23] This total may be assumed to be reasonably reliable, subject to the inevitable inaccuracies found in all early censuses. It was confirmed by the figures given independently by Gregory King, whose two estimates of 29,332 and 28,546 made in 1695 and 1696 are very similar to the total found by enumeration.[24] On this basis, it seems likely that the population of Norwich had reached a total of 30,000 by 1700.

It is probable that the growth of the city's population was brought about by immigration in this period as in the earlier part of the century, rather than by a 'natural' increase produced by a preponderance of births over deaths. It is difficult to be precise about this, in the absence of relevant statistics. There is a certain amount of circumstantial evidence relating to mortality in the city. Contemporaries showed the preoccupation with death characteristic of an age of high mortality and low expectation of life: indeed Arderon in the eighteenth century considered that the inhabitants of Norwich took an exceptional interest in funerals which were attended by vast crowds.[25] On the other hand, there is a complete dearth of information relating to births and marriages. But, on the basis of this negative evidence, it has been assumed that there were no major changes in either birth or marriage rates in Norwich in this period.

As far as death rates in the city are concerned there was probably no reduction in the prevailing high level of urban mortality. The most significant changes came in the causes of mortality, with the ending of the cycle of plagues in Norwich, culminating in the epidemic of 1665–6. Mortality in this outbreak was heavy: in the twelve months from October 1665 to October 1666, a total of 2,251 plague deaths were reported out of a total of 3,012 reported deaths from all causes. This figure almost certainly underestimates the number of deaths from plague, since registration was especially defective in periods of crisis.[26] The mortality in this epidemic did not in fact constitute as great a proportion of the total population as did the mortality in some of the earlier outbreaks of plague in the city, such as that of 1603.[27] But its effects were none the less very serious. Fear of the contagion kept people from the markets and disrupted supplies of food. Commercial and industrial activities were suspended, causing widespread unemployment. The wealthy began to leave the city, and, to the consternation of a government correspondent, there was also a threat of social subversion from the poor:

> Our city lookes sadley, most of our chefest shopkeepers in the market ar gon and ther shopes shut up. I doe beleve before 10 days come a 4 part of the city will be gone. The pore does much murmur at it and says they will live in beter howses then now they doe, but I hope to God they will be prevented.

The Town Clerk was as frank: 'Wee are in greater feare of the poore than the plague, all our monie beinge gone . . .' As these accounts

268

suggest, the epidemic strained the administrative and financial resources of the city to the utmost,[28] and threatened a complete
breakdown of its economic life.

The disappearance of the plague after this outbreak, however, did
not produce any permanent reduction in the level of mortality in the
city, although it did remove a potent cause of social and economic
instability. The successor to the plague as the major urban killer was
smallpox, which was endemic in cities at this date, while also breaking
out in epidemics of increased intensity from time to time. The incidence
of mortality from smallpox was highest among small children and
survival conferred immunity in the majority of cases, thus producing
the erroneous view that the disease was not contagious.[29] Smallpox
was not therefore a 'panic' disease in the same way that the plague
had been. Specific outbreaks of smallpox were reported in the city
in January 1670, when the Town Clerk noted that 'the smallpox
rageth still, and poverty daily invades us like an armed man', and in
December 1681, when Sir Thomas Browne observed: 'I hardly remember the smallpox so much in Norwich, as it hath been of late and still
continueth.'[30] There may also have been other epidemics, about which
no information has survived. Evidence relating to other diseases is
scarce. Sir Thomas Browne recorded as a general phenomenon an
increase in the incidence of both smallpox and rickets in the late seventeenth century, and a decline in the number of cases of great pox
(syphilis). Throughout this period the incidence of mortality was
highest among the very young. Sir Thomas Browne observed melodi-
ously: 'Nothing is more common with infants than to die on the day
of their nativity, to behold the worldly hours and but the fractions
thereof.'[31]

There is no evidence to suggest that there was any reduction in
levels of mortality through improvements in medical care. The period
was not one which was distinguished by major advances in medical
practice. An extensive range of medical assistance was available in
the city, ranging from doctors, apothecaries and surgeons on the
one hand, to optimistic quacks and vendors of patent medicines on the
other. But it is hardly necessary to point out that there is no automatic
correlation between the number of practitioners and the efficacy of
medical care. Without more detailed information than is available
(or is ever likely to be available), there is no means of estimating the
value of their labours.

Nor does the evidence suggest that there was any radical reduction of mortality through improvements in standards of public health and living conditions. Indeed, it is probable that the growth of the city in itself tended to worsen living conditions in the city centre, and thus to increase levels of mortality. At this date the city's population was concentrated within the medieval city walls, which were still standing. In 1693, 90·5 per cent of all inhabitants lived within the walls. The area thus encircled was, however, the largest of any ancient city centre. As Defoe remarked, the walls seemed to have been laid out with prospects of future expansion in mind. The overall density of population in the city and county of Norwich was 6·68 inhabitants per statute acre in 1693.[32] But this figure conceals many variations. There were fields and pastures within the walls, which, with the flower gardens of the artisans, gave the city a rural air. This was frequently commented upon by visitors. Fuller, for example, described the city as:

> Either a city in an orchard or an orchard in a city, so equally
> are houses and trees blended in it, so that the pleasures of the
> country and the populousness of the city meet here together.[33]

But there were also pockets of densely built-up areas, especially in the low-lying parishes alongside the river in Wymer and Coslany Wards, where the population was crammed into houses in a maze of courtyards and alleyways. There was in this period a certain amount of rebuilding of the city's housing stock, which may have tended to improve living conditions, as the old houses of wood and plasterwork were replaced by brick buildings.[34] But the improvements brought about by this means were probably not of very great significance, and the basic layout of the city was hardly altered at all.

The streets and public places seem to have been reasonably well maintained by the standards of the day. Such at least was the verdict of Celia Fiennes who wrote in 1697 in her characteristically breathless manner: 'The streetes are all well pitch'd with small stones and very clean and many very broad streetes.'[35] But cleanliness lies in the eye of the beholder. There is certainly no evidence to suggest that the Corporation was doing any more than keeping pace with the problem, and that without any spectacular efficiency. The accounts of the River and Street Committee, which was responsible for dredging the river and for the general upkeep of the city, did not show any great increase in expenditure in the late seventeenth century.[36] Expenditure is not, of course, a conclusive index to efficiency. But this certainly does not suggest any great increase in the activity of the Committee. The Corporation issued frequent proclamations against the practice of allowing cattle and swine to roam the streets, and reminders to individual householders of their responsibility for the upkeep of the highway abutting upon their property.[37] No doubt individual officials and householders performed their duties reliably, but the system as a whole depended upon exhortation after the deed rather than preventive measures. There seems, therefore, no reason to doubt that the city of Norwich in this period was both noxious and insalubrious.

Growth was therefore brought about by migration of population into the city. The net rate of immigration must have been in the region of some 400 newcomers per annum in the 1670s and 1680s to produce a net increase of 8,000 inhabitants in these twenty years. Gross totals must have been even higher, to take into account the movement of population out of Norwich. But emigration totals are completely irrecoverable. Poll Books from the early eighteenth century list the names of Norwich citizens living outside the city who returned to cast their vote. As might be expected, the largest contingents returned from Yarmouth and London, both cities with which Norwich had close commercial links.[38] But there is no way of estimating what proportion of all emigrants was represented by these figures. On the basis of the estimated immigration figures alone, it seems that the number of 'foreigners' in the city may have constituted as much as one-quarter of the total population in 1700, a proportion which is almost identical with that found in Norwich at the third local enumeration in 1786 when 26 per cent of the population were without a settlement in the city.[39]

Most of the migration in the late seventeenth century probably followed the usual pattern of movement of single individuals or small family units. But there was one instance of group immigration. This was the arrival in the city in the 1680s of a number of Huguenot exiles. According to a near-contemporary source, the Huguenots had been invited to Norwich by Onias Philippo, one of the city's leading manufacturers, who was himself a descendant of the Walloons who came as exiles to the city in Elizabethan times. There is some uncertainty about the number of Huguenots that eventually settled in Norwich. Estimates vary from 'very few' to 'many', which may or may not mean the same thing. At a guess, they numbered some 100 to 200 individuals. Certainly the refugees arrived in sufficient numbers to provoke the indigenous population to riot in 1682 in the fear that the newcomers would undercut wages and cause unemployment. Tensions did not immediately die away. A petition of 1690 from the French weavers of Norwich to the Houses of Parliament complained of harassment by informers who were reporting the newcomers for working without fulfilling the formal apprenticeship requirements.[40] After the initial problems, however, the Huguenot community was integrated without further difficulties, as indeed a century earlier the much larger numbers of Dutch and Walloon refugees had been assimilated into the host community.

The arrival of 'strangers' is easier to identify than movement among the indigenous population. Information is either too particular, such as removal orders against single individuals who had fallen foul of the city authorities; or too general, such as complaints from freemen of the city against competition from 'foreigners'.[41] Complaints and removal orders were most frequent in periods of economic depression. Although they attest to the reality of movement of population into the city, they provide no information about its timing or quantity.

It seems likely that the major sources for immigration were the agricultural counties of Norfolk and Suffolk, since movement of population at this time usually took place over short distances. But as one of the major urban centres, Norwich would also exercise something of a 'pull' outside its immediate hinterland, since migration distances tended to correlate with the size of the city. No complete documentation of removal orders in the late seventeenth century has survived. Eighteenth-century figures provide some evidence. The surviving accounts of the removal of 433 paupers and vagrants, and their families, in the period from 1740 to 1762 demonstrate the importance of the city's rural hinterland as recruitment ground: 40 per cent of these migrants came from East Anglia; another 15 per cent came from east coast and east midland counties, within an approximate hundred-mile radius of the city; 6 per cent came from London and Middlesex; as many as 39 per cent, however, came from the rest of the country, including 33 migrants from Scotland and 16 from Ireland.[42] Beggars and vagrants may have been an exceptionally mobile section of the populace. Analysis of the place of origin of 1,601 apprentices whose indentures were taken out in Norwich in the period from 1710 to 1731 shows a more circumscribed catchment area: 43 per cent of the apprentices were sons of residents of Norwich; 22 per cent came from Norfolk; and 6 per cent came from elsewhere, leaving a further 29 per cent whose place of origin was not recorded.[43] Neither of these sources is exhaustive, but together they confirm the preponderance of short-distance migration, although comparison of the two sources suggests that distance of migration might also vary with the social status of the migrant.

It should be emphasized that the growth of the city was not taking place at the expense of its rural hinterland. The population of Norfolk was probably not growing very fast in the late seventeenth century, and certainly not as fast as the city of Norwich. But in 1700, Norfolk, with a population of over 200,000, still remained among the most densely populated areas in the country.[44] And the growth of Norwich may have stimulated expansion in its immediate vicinity. As Celia Fiennes observed: 'Most of the great towns and cittys have about them little villages as attendants or appendix's.' Certainly when Defoe visited the county, he was impressed with the concentration of population in the central and eastern region of the county:

This side of Norfolk is very populous, and throng'd with great and spacious market-towns, more and larger than in any other part of England so far from London, except Devonshire and the West Riding of Yorkshire; . . . Most of these towns are very populous and large; but that which is most remarkable is, that the whole country round them is so interspers'd with villages and those villages so large, and so full of people, that they are equal to market-towns in other counties: in a word, they render this eastern part of Norfolk exceeding full of inhabitants.[45]

Although the city still maintained the physical attributes of an enclosed and walled community in the late seventeenth century, and Norwich citizens evinced an attitude of suspicion, and even hostility, towards newcomers, it is clear that recruitment was taking place on a considerable scale. In this period, as in most periods of growth, there was progressive weakening of the institutional barriers which attempted to restrict and control entry into the city. Poor law policy acted only as an *ex post facto* system of control, which removed the economically unsuccessful, and it was not administered with any great degree of efficiency. Furthermore, the formal regulations governing admissions to the city's trades and industries were falling into desuetude in the later part of the century and the Corporation was finding it increasingly difficult to enforce the obligation to take out the freedom of the city.[46] The relaxation of such regulations, which were protective in nature, both reflected and contributed to urban growth; on the one hand, the urban economy demanded ready supplies of labour, while, on the other, the administrative problems of enforcing restrictive regulations were accentuated as the city grew in size.

Investigation into the development of the urban economy illuminates the basis of the city's growth. But reconstruction of the pattern of employment in Norwich involves further documentary problems. There is no comprehensive information relating to occupations in the city at this time. The admissions to the freedom provide information relating to a section of the population. But the material contained in the freemen lists is open to two damaging criticisms: it is highly selective, and the selection is not completely consistent even on its own terms.

In theory, all adult males engaged in trade and industry were obliged to take out the freedom within six months of taking up work in the city.[47] The freemen probably accounted for about half the adult male work-force in the late seventeenth century. They excluded servants, apprentices, and casual labourers. They also excluded women and children who constituted at this time a sizeable proportion of the work-force. Furthermore, the information contained in the freemen lists relates only to the major occupation of each individual, and excludes part-time and secondary occupations. And, needless to say, the information concerns legal occupations only, and provides no guide to the numbers of those making their living by crime, although it is quite possible that the growth of the city produced an increase in the criminal population (the larger the city, the better the lurking-places and the better the prey, not to mention the better the chances of escaping detection).

It is also evident that, by this date, many of those who were theoretically qualified for the freedom were evading the expensive honour. This is demonstrated by the frequent proclamations issued on this topic by the Corporation. In 1677 and in 1701, the Corporation also attempted, unsuccessfully, to obtain legislation 'to bring in freemen'.[48] It is therefore possible that some trades and industries were under-registered, and that some of the newer or smaller trades were completely omitted. This seems to have been the case with the small carpet-manufacturing industry, which admitted no freemen in this period.[49] Despite all these inadequacies, however, the freemen admissions do provide a general guide to the range of occupations in the city,

TABLE 17 *Occupational groups in Norwich, 1660–1749: freemen of the city*

	1660–9	1670–9	1680–9	1690–9	1700–9	1710–19	1720–9	1730–9	1740–9	Total
	%	%	%	%	%	%	%	%	%	%
Textiles	41·3	46·8	40·9	37·5	57·6	57·7	64·0	41·7	42·8	49·8
Leather	8·1	9·3	7·0	9·8	8·0	7·4	7·0	8·7	5·9	7·9
Metal	3·1	3·9	2·0	4·2	2·5	4·5	2·3	3·1	4·0	3·2
Building	5·3	6·5	8·3	7·2	5·3	5·9	3·2	6·5	6·4	5·8
Food and drink	10·3	10·4	15·1	16·3	11·1	9·8	7·2	9·1	11·0	10·5
Clothing	18·1	12·8	13·6	11·6	5·7	6·8	4·3	6·9	6·7	8·9
Professions	3·8	3·0	5·1	7·7	5·4	5·8	4·1	6·3	9·1	5·4
Miscellaneous	10·0	7·3	8·0	5·7	4·4	2·1	7·9	17·7	14·1	8·5

Source: See Appendix

and throw some light on the relative importance of the different trades and industries.

The admissions from 1660 to 1749 were dominated by employment in the textile industry (see Table 17 and Appendix, pp. 297–9). By the early eighteenth century, worsted weavers, and others engaged in the various stages involved in the production of worsted stuffs, accounted for over 50 per cent of all admissions. At the same time, the textile industry may have employed almost the same proportion of the total work-force, since the industry was organized on a domestic basis, and the weaver was assisted by his wife and children. Its dominance was confirmed by visual evidence. Defoe commented:

If a stranger was only to ride thro' or view the city of Norwich for a day, he would . . . think there was a town without inhabitants . . .; but on the contrary, if he was to view the city, either on a Sabbath-day, or on any publick occasion, he would wonder where all the people could dwell, the multitude is so great: But the case is this; the inhabitants being all busie at their manufactures, dwell in their garrets at their looms, and in their combing-shops, so they call them, twisting-mills, and other work-houses; almost all the works they are employ'd in, being done within doors.[50]

Norwich therefore manifested a considerable degree of functional specialization as a textile manufacturing centre. This had not always been a feature of the urban economy. The numbers of those employed in both the production and the distribution of textiles in the mid-sixteenth century was considerably lower: in 1525 they constituted approximately 30 per cent of all freemen; by 1569 the proportion had fallen to 21 per cent.[51] The urban population at this time was static or even declining. The revitalization of the textile industry in the 1570s inaugurated a new period of urban expansion, and thereafter, during the seventeenth century, the numbers of freemen admitted in the production of textiles alone (excluding distribution) increased steadily, from 23 per cent in 1600–19, to 58 per cent in 1700–19 (see Table 18). The growing importance of the industry in the city can also be traced through other sources. The changing occupations of the individuals elected to the mayoralty show the emergence of worsted weavers into the urban ruling class in the second half of the century, joining the mercantile élite that had hitherto dominated the city (see Table 19). Of course, 104 mayors do not make an urban élite.

But the trend is instructive. By the end of the century, the wealthiest man in the city, according to Dean Prideaux, was Robert Cooke, a weaver and conventicler, who became sheriff in 1674 and mayor in 1693.[52]

While Norwich continued to function as a market centre and local capital, the labour-intensive textile industry provided the major demand for labour in the city and the growth of the city was linked closely with its specialization as a textile centre. This is not to say,

TABLE 18 *Admissions to the freedom of the city in textiles, 1600–1739*

	% of all Freemen
1600–19	23
1620–39	31
1640–59	37
1660–79	44
1680–99	39
1700–19	58
1720–39	53

Sources: K. J. Allison, 'The Wool Supply and the Worsted Cloth Industry in Norfolk in the Sixteenth and Seventeenth Centuries' (unpublished Ph.D. thesis, University of Leeds, 1955), for figures to 1660 and P. Millican, *The Freemen of Norwich, 1548–1713*, Norwich, 1934, and *The Freemen of Norwich, 1713–1752* (Norfolk Record Society, XXIII, 1952), for figures to 1739.

of course, that each individual coming to the city was impelled by a desire to work at the loom. But there is at least some evidence to suggest that some textile workers were being recruited specifically from other textile centres. Weavers from Taunton and Exeter were found in Norwich in 1674. And some specialized workers were also moving into Norwich: Michael Brown, a silk-dyer newly arrived from London, was advertising his special fats for dyeing blues and greens in Norwich in 1725. There may have been an unofficial network of communication between textile centres, by which information relating to employment opportunities was circulated. Such at least was implied by reports of the migration of weavers between different textile centres in the depression of 1719,[53] and this may well have applied in the late seventeenth century.

* * *

The continued vitality and expansion of the Norwich worsted weaving industry over a period of two-and-a-half centuries is a subject in itself. The Norwich worsted stuffs were among the 'New Draperies' that were successfully introduced to England in the late sixteenth century.[54]

TABLE 19 *Occupations of 104 mayors elected in the period 1600–1699**

Occupation†	1600–19	1620–39	1640–59	1660–79	1680–99‡	Total
Weaver			3	5	7	15
Dyer			1			1
Ironmonger	3	1	2		1	7
Pinman				1	1	2
Butcher	1					1
Baker		1				1
Grocer	5	6	4	5	5	25
Brewer				3		3
Draper	1	2	2	1	1	7
Mercer	2	3	2	1		8
Hosier			3	2		5
Glover		1				1
Skinner		1				1
Merchant	4	1	3	1		9
Goldsmith	1					1
Scrivener	1	2				3
Apothecary	1	1		1		3
Not traced	2	1	3		5	11
Total	21	20	23	20	20	104

Source: B. Cozens-Hardy and E. A. Kent, *The Mayors of Norwich, 1403–1835* (Norwich, 1938).

* In 1602, 1641, 1649 and 1650 the mayor died in office, and a successor was elected. Two individuals became mayor more than once, Sir Thomas Hyrne, ironmonger, in 1604, 1609 and 1616 and John Tolye or Tooley, merchant, in 1638 and 1644. They have been counted anew at each election.

† In cases of multiple occupations, the major occupation only has been counted.

‡ The mayoral year ran from June–June: dates refer to year of inauguration.

Unlike the 'New Draperies' introduced elsewhere in East Anglia, the Norwich industry continued to flourish and develop throughout the seventeenth century. In this, it contrasted with the Colchester bays industry, which was in decline by the end of this period.

Unfortunately there is no way of constructing a satisfactory index to the economic fortunes of the Norwich industry in the late seventeenth century. No figures have survived relating to either the volume of production, or the value of the trade, or the numbers employed in the industry. Isolated estimates can be produced, but these are of dubious validity.[55] Representatives of the Norwich industry calculated in 1719 that £600,000 worth of stuffs from all sources was consumed annually in the kingdom of Great Britain, but this may have been exaggerated for polemical purposes. In the same year, an estimate was made of the numbers employed by the Norwich industry. This combines reality and fantasy. The declared total of 500 master weavers and 8,000 journeymen and apprentices may well have a basis in reality; the additional figure of over 120,000 other workers, including spinsters, combers, dyers, dressers, throwsters and winders, lacks the ring of verisimilitude. The final estimate of over 130,000 workers engaged in the industry is clearly a partisan and unreliable figure.[56] And estimates for individual years, such as these, give no assistance in constructing an index to changes over time. Nor can admissions to the freedom of the city be used as an index to levels of economic activity. By this date, the number of admissions in any one year was regulated by the exigencies of political conflict, rather than by the dictates of economic activity. In the period from 1660 to 1713, the greatest number of admissions occurred in 1678, the year of the Popish Plot scare, and one of intense political conflict within Norwich. In 1704, another year of vigorous electioneering in Norwich, the mayor was said to have admitted 200 freemen of his own political persuasion.[57] To discover what was happening to the Norwich industry in the late seventeenth century, therefore, reference has to be made to literary evidence. This has the involuntary effect of concentrating attention upon the years of crisis within the industry, since bad trade is more conducive to literary output than is prosperity. None the less, the picture that emerges is not one of unrelieved gloom but one of both expansion and change.

It seems clear that by the later part of the century, the Norwich industry was catering mainly for home demand. This was in marked contrast to the industry both in earlier and later times: in the early part of the century, its expansion was based on production for foreign markets; and in the mid-eighteenth century, the industry again successfully moved into overseas markets when faced with competition in the domestic market.[58] The evidence for the importance of the home market in the late seventeenth century is incontrovertible. At the time of the dispute between the Weavers' Company and the alnage officials, the weavers estimated that in 1688 one-quarter of their output had been sold overseas. This estimate, moreover, was produced at a time when it was in the interests of the Norwich industry to claim the maximum importance for their export sales. By contrast, the alnagers reported, at the same time, that no Norwich stuffs were exported.[59] The truth may be presumed to lie somewhere between the two extremes. The Yarmouth Port Books for 1685 show that some Norwich stuffs were exported in this year,[60] but it is impossible to put this in proportionate terms without knowing the total volume of production. But the implication of both of these statements was clearly that a large proportion of the Norwich stuffs was produced for the home market at least by the late 1680s.

The shift to domestic markets probably took place in the middle years of the century. Overseas markets, especially those in Spain, were disrupted in the 1640s and 1650s. This occurred at the same time as an expansion in domestic demand, which provided new outlets for the Norwich stuffs at home. Despite complaints from the city of declining trade with Spain in the late 1650s, the preamble of the Act of 1662 for regulating production of Norwich stuffs noted that the industry 'hath of late times very much increased, and a great variety of new stuffs have been invented'.[61] This wording was in part polite formula, but choice of formulae is in itself of some significance. Expansion of domestic demand in the late seventeenth century was commented upon by numerous contemporary writers, including Sir Josiah Child and Adam Martindale.[62] The flattening out of the prolonged secular rise in prices improved the standard of real wages in the years after 1640 and released purchasing power, especially among the 'middling sort of people'. One of the ramifications of the expansion of domestic demand was an increased demand for good quality textiles, a demand which the Norwich industry was well qualified to meet.

The generic title of 'Norwich stuffs' concealed a considerable range and variety of fabrics. Most were light and brightly coloured textiles. They were made of long-staple wool, which had been combed, spun and dyed in the yarn. Some stuffs were 'mixed' fabrics, composed of worsted yarn and other fibres, such as silk, mohair or linen. After weaving, the material was treated by special finishing processes, which gave the stuffs their characteristic fine and glossy finish.[63] Some coarse cloths were still produced in the city. These included dornix, the linear descendant of the old worsteds produced in Norfolk in medieval times, fearnothing, a hard-wearing cloth worn by sailors, and bewper, used as sailcloth.[64] But the Norwich industry concentrated increasingly upon the 'light' end of the worsted range, while the production of coarse worsted migrated from East Anglia to the West Riding of Yorkshire.[65] The coarser and cheaper worsteds produced in Yorkshire at this date complemented rather than rivalled the output of the Norwich industry.

Norwich stuffs catered for those who wanted fabrics of stylish and attractive design, lighter and more decorative than the heavier serges or bays, but cheaper than the costly imported luxury fabrics worn by the very rich. Stuffs were used for women's and children's apparel, for gentlemen's suits and waistcoats, and as linings for more expensive fabrics. They were also used for furnishings, as curtains, room-hangings, quilts and coverings. Professor Wilson has specified the ideal market for the Norwich bombasine as that of 'the not-too-affluent squire's lady or the tradesman's wife'.[66] This may be termed the semi-fashionable market, since it was neither a luxury market nor a mass market. The hallmark of the Norwich stuffs was their wide range of both styles and prices. Celia Fiennes noted: 'Their pieces are 27 yards in length and their price is from 30 shillings to 3 pound as they are in fineness.' Variations in patterns and styles were used as a means of promoting sales. A chronicler of the city noted in 1711 that the Norwich weavers were famous for their inventiveness, adding happily: 'Gain always sharpens wit and invention, which has never appeared more than in the improvement of this stuff trade.' And Fuller, writing in the 1650s (where he is clearly referring to the home market), described some of the sales techniques used to titillate demand when the market was sluggish. He wrote of the Norwich stuffs:

Expect not that I should reckon up their several names, because daily increasing, and many of them are *binominous*, as which, when they began to tire in sale, are quickened with a new name. [And he explained] A pretty pleasing name, complying with the buyers' fancy, much befriendeth a stuff in the sale thereof.[67]

Some of the range of Norwich stuffs at this time can be seen from contemporary inventories of the stocks of Norwich weavers, which included damasks, russells, satins, tamines, cheyneys, callimancoes, crapes, camblets, jollyboys, druggets and faringdons.[68]

Throughout the seventeenth century, there was a constant flow of innovation in finish and design, though there were no major technical changes. Techniques of dyeing were improved in the course of the century as the range of dye-stuffs increased; and according to a nineteenth-century historian, the French immigrants contributed new expertise.[69] The Huguenots were also responsible for the introduction of the Norwich crape, the one new fabric developed in this period. This was made of worsted, or of mixed worsted and silk, and was a very light and fine material. It was retailed at under twenty-five shillings the piece. When first introduced, the crape had an immediate fashionable success. Defoe recalled in 1704:

> The first effort of the French refugees was our thin black crape,
> a manufacture purely their own, and I refer to the memory of
> persons conversant in trade, how universally it pleased our people.

Its cheapness had however some disadvantages from the point of view of the woman of fashion. Use of crape spread down the social scale to servant-girls and the fabric then became 'a little obsolete' among upper-class women. This whole cycle, as Defoe makes clear, had taken place within twenty years of its introduction.[70] Norwich crape remained one of the more important varieties of the industry's output in the eighteenth century, although it never regained its first popularity. It subsequently captured two useful markets which were not so subject to the vagaries of fashion. These were the markets for mourning wear and for clerical vestments.[71] The history of the reception of the crape illustrates well the nature of the markets for which the Norwich industry catered and the capriciousness of demand.

The Norwich industry therefore depended for its success upon sedulous cultivation of its markets. In particular, the Norwich weavers paid great attention to the importance of rapid communications with the capital city which was the chief mart for Norwich stuffs. Weavers needed topical information about changing tastes and styles, and merchants needed quick distribution to catch the fashion while it was still in vogue. The bulk of the Norwich stuffs were carried to London by road, which was more expensive but faster and more reliable than transit by river and sea.[72] One of the major reasons behind the weavers' opposition to the alnagers in the late 1680s and 1690s was that the alnagers' practice of stopping waggons on the road to search for unsealed stuffs caused delays and uncertainties in the transport of goods. The alnagers also, the weavers alleged, entered merchants' warehouses and cut or confiscated stuffs.[73] The disruption of trade was more serious than the fiscal imposition on the industry. The conflict was finally settled in 1699, when the weavers agreed to pay an annual composition to the alnagers, who in return abandoned their claim to supervision.

Norwich stuffs were import substitutes, and also relied on protection in the home market from foreign rivals. The markets for which the Norwich industry catered were prone to succumb to the lure of prestigious imported textiles. The industry therefore benefited greatly from the ban imposed on French imported goods from 1679 to 1685. This ban was lifted briefly from 1685 to 1688, but thereafter replaced in the form of heavy import duties, which priced the French textiles out of the range of the markets supplied by Norwich stuffs.[74] The Norwich industry did not play much part in obtaining the ban on their French rivals. It did, however, play a leading part in the prolonged war waged by the English textile interests in the late seventeenth and early eighteenth centuries against imported East India calicoes. The calicoes were light, bright, gaily-patterned printed textiles similar in appearance to the Norwich stuffs and with the advantage of being much cheaper. They began to enjoy a fashionable success in the 1690s, to such an extent that a spokesman for the Norwich industry admitted in 1696 that Norwich stuffs were being made 'in imitation of the India goods'. The English textile interests were temporarily successful in 1699 when an Act was passed against the importation of East India calicoes, wrought silks and Bengalls.[75] But the issue was rekindled within two decades, because, through a loophole in the Act, calicoes were being brought into the country in an unfinished state for printing and finishing in England. The fashion revived with alacrity. The Norwich weavers, in conjunction with the silk weavers of London, again took the lead in a campaign for further legislation, which was successful in 1722.[76] The contest showed that the domestic industries could successfully press for, and obtain, legislation to defend their interests. But the incident again demonstrated the volatility of the consuming public, which constituted an inherent instability in the markets for Norwich stuffs.

Within this framework of protection, the Norwich industry was gradually shedding all internal restrictions and supervision. This was in itself a symptom of expansion. As noted, the Norwich weavers had campaigned successfully in the 1690s against the attempt made by the alnagers to seal Norwich stuffs. In the same period the supervision nominally exercised by the Weavers' Company was increasingly being evaded. This was admitted by the Company itself in 1689 when a number of merchants and dealers in Norwich stuffs petitioned Parliament for the office of search to be made effective. The Company's response was to suggest that the number of officials elected annually to search and seal should be increased. But nothing came of this proposal and in 1705 the practice of sealing was ended. This marked the effective demise of the real powers of the Company, although it continued for a time to act as the official spokesman of the industry. By the 1730s it had been replaced by a Committee of Trade.[77] The Weavers' Company had also fought and lost in the 1690s a battle with the woolcombers over their claim to supervise the standard of yarn. This power had been granted to the weavers in 1650 by their Act of Incorporation. In 1693 the woolcombers of Norfolk and Suffolk mounted a campaign against the methods of search used by the weavers. Ironically, their complaints echoed those made by the Norwich weavers themselves against the alnagers, that the searching disrupted trade for no good purpose and that the weavers' power to issue arbitrary fines was unconstitutional. Parliament upheld the woolcombers in a judgment in 1694.[78] By the end of the century, the whole unwieldy apparatus of control had been jettisoned.

With the growing importance of domestic markets in the late seventeenth century came changes in the location of the industry. While the industry had always been closely associated with the city of Norwich, as the name of the stuffs implied, there had also been a considerable number of weavers resident throughout the county of Norfolk, especially in the area to the north and east of Norwich (the ancient centre of the worsted industry in Norfolk from medieval times). The revival of the worsted weaving industry in the late sixteenth century did not at first produce any great locational changes. The Incorporation of the Weavers in 1650 provided for equal numbers of Wardens and Assistants from the county of Norfolk and from the city of Norwich.[79] But in the late seventeenth century there was a growing concentration of the weaving processes in the city of Norwich and its immediate vicinity, though spinning remained a rural occupation. Locational changes are difficult to pinpoint. The evidence of the places of residence of 581 weavers, as shown in wills proved in the Consistory Court at Norwich in the period from 1611 to 1750, confirms the tendency of the industry to concentrate in the city (see Table 20). This evidence is not in itself conclusive, but its findings are suggestive. Clearly what Tsuru has labelled the 'external economies' afforded by an urban location[80] were important for an industry which was highly dependent upon good communications and rapid access to markets. The advantages of concentration outweighed the potential disadvantages of the fact that wage-levels tended to be higher in the town than in the countryside. There is, however, virtually no evidence relating to labour costs at this time. A speaker in the House of Commons stated in 1680 that an English weaver could expect to earn 1s a day,

TABLE 20 *Location of weavers* in Norwich Diocese, 1611–1750*

	Norwich	Norfolk	Suffolk	Total
1611–30	20	35	6	61
1631–50	22	56	9	87
1651–70	13	26	2	41
1671–90	22	13	4	39
1691–1710	63	26	4	93
1711–30	100	65	4	169
1731–50	56	31	4	91
	296	252	33	581

Source: M. A. Farrow and T. F. Barton, eds, *Index of Wills proved in the Consistory Court of Norwich, 1604–1686* (Norfolk Record Society, XXVIII, 1958) and *Index of Wills proved in the Consistory Court of Norwich, 1687–1750* (Norfolk Record Society, XXXIV, 1965).
* Includes all those listed as 'weavers' and 'worsted weavers', but excludes linen-weavers, ribbon-weavers and coarse cloth weavers.

or 6s a week, but there is no means of checking this statement. The success of the Norwich industry at this time argues in itself that labour costs were not prohibitively high. The absence of any labour disputes over piece-work rates also suggests that the industry did not make any attempts to cut costs by cutting wages.[81]

The continued existence of the worsted weaving industry in Norwich was in fact a tribute to the force of tradition or the momentum of inertia. For at first sight, Norwich does not seem to be especially suited to the production of worsteds. The industry drew all its raw materials from outside the county of Norfolk. Worsteds did not use the short staple wool of the Norfolk sheep but drew on wool from

Lincolnshire, Leicestershire and Northamptonshire, which was then transported into Norfolk and Suffolk for spinning. Furthermore, by the late seventeenth century the demand for yarn in the city was beginning to outrun the capacity of the local spinners to provide for it, and yarn was being combed and spun outside the county for the Norwich industry.[82] But both wool and yarn were relatively cheap and easy to transport. The industry also required supplies of coal for the combing, dyeing and finishing processes. The city of Norwich was always sensitive about the cost of fuel, and in 1696, for example, petitioned Parliament that high coal prices were aggravating discontent among the poor. Similarly, the question of Yarmouth harbour dues on coal was a perennial source of conflict between the two cities.[83] But raw material did not in fact constitute a large proportion of production costs, since labour accounted for five-sixths of the total, according to an estimate made by the weavers' representatives in 1719.[84] A plentiful supply of labour was, therefore, an essential requirement of the industry. In the absence of any technological changes in methods of production there was no particular reason for the industry to move, but on the contrary, there was ample reason why the industry should remain in a locality which had the accumulated expertise of a long tradition of weaving. Once the city had reached and passed a certain critical point, and the old regulations and restrictions on the recruitment of labour had been broken down, growth was self-sustaining, prior to the advent of mechanization.

The Norwich industry had, therefore, adapted successfully to meet changing markets and experienced considerable prosperity and expansion in the late seventeenth century. There were years of depression. For example the plague and its aftermath caused considerable disruption in 1666–7. There were complaints of unemployment and the rising cost of poor relief and it was at this time that the Corporation began investigating the possibility of setting up a workhouse in the city (a project that did not achieve fruition until 1712). There was also a recession in the industry in the years from 1674 to 1676. By contrast the 1680s saw a prolonged boom. This probably explains a comment made by one of the witnesses before the House of Lords in 1692–3 who remarked that 'Norwich stuffs were not heard of till within twelve years'. The industry was still vulnerable to competition as the struggle against the East India calicoes made clear. As a result of competition in the home market, coupled with the disruption produced by the recoinage, the industry was reported as being in a depressed state in

1696. And again in December 1699 Dean Prideaux noted that trade was slack, observing lugubriously that Norwich 'now sinks apace'.[85] This comment makes clear that contemporary observers were well aware of the close connexion between the well-being of the city and that of the worsted weaving industry. But despite these intermittent depressions, the industry was in a fundamentally sound position at the end of the century.

The growth of the textile industry did not prevent the city from continuing to perform other functions. Norwich was a centre of commercial and social life. The city was a natural focal point within the county: it was the county town and Cathedral city; it was situated in the heart of the most densely populated area of the county; it was a point of convergence for several roads within the county, which came to cross the Wensum/Yare river complex (avoiding the flat marshy area to the east of the city); and it was well served with communications to London, both overland and via Yarmouth, the city's port, which was itself one of the largest towns in the country.[86] The growth of the industry, by increasing the size of the city, also augmented its importance *vis-à-vis* its hinterland and hence enhanced its role as a centre of distribution and consumption.

Urban growth in itself entailed an increase in the so-called 'maintenance industries' in the city. The term is used to include the occupations of all those who were engaged in supplying essential requirements for the city's population, such as food and drink, clothing and housing. The freemen's admissions show that, as might be expected, those engaged in the provision of food and drink, and of clothing, constituted the major occupational groups after the textile workers (see Table 17, and Appendix). The numbers admitted in the clothing trades show a puzzling decline, both in absolute and proportionate terms, in the late seventeenth century: they fell from 18 per cent of all admissions between 1660 and 1669 to 5·7 per cent between 1700 and 1709. There is no obvious explanation for this. It may be simply that those occupied in these industries were ceasing to take out the freedom of the city. This is substantiated by complaints made in 1675 and 1681 by the freemen drapers and tailors against competition from non-freemen.[87] Or it may also be that these occupations were being increasingly taken over by women, who were ineligible for the freedom. There is evidence for the employment of women in dressmaking and millinery. Among the apprenticeship indentures of the early eighteenth century were those of 113 women, of whom 90 were apprenticed in the clothing trades.[88] But this is a problem to which there is no satisfactory answer. The freemen figures are in any case rather an erratic guide. One industry which was clearly flourishing at this time, although this is not shown in the freemen figures, was beer-brewing. Considerable wealth was made in the brewing of Norwich 'Nog', a heavy dark brew made from local barley. The power of the brewing industry was discovered by the mayor in 1681 when he mounted a campaign against the growing number of alehouses in the city: 'this town swarms with them . . . most of them, 'tis said, bawdy houses too'. He was reported to the central government by Excise officials, as politically suspect.[89] He survived, but the campaign was dropped.

Norwich was an important commercial centre, supplying goods for a wide rural hinterland as well as for its own growing population. At this time people travelled long distances for luxury goods and even for comparatively small and inexpensive purchases.[90] Much of the city's commercial life was centred in the large open market in the heart of the city, celebrated for its size, good order and for the quantity and quality of goods on sale. Baskerville's description conveys a graphic impression:

> A little way off from this Castle . . . is the chief market place of
> this city, and this being the only place where all things are
> brought to be sold for the food of this great city, they not as in
> London allowing markets in several places, make it vastly full
> of provisions, especially on Saturdays, where I saw the greatest
> shambles for butchers' meat I had ever yet seen, and the like
> also for poultry and dairy-meats, which dairy people also bring
> many quarters of veal with their butter and cheese, and I believe
> also in their seasons pork and hog-meats . . . They setting their
> goods in ranges as near as may be one above another, only
> allowing room for single persons to pass between.

He added that the Friday market was an important market for fish. The market regulations stipulated that all meat slaughtered in the early part of the week was to be sold off by Thursday evening, an unusual provision devised to assist the Yarmouth fishing industry. Indeed his informant told him that it was so successful that at times there were no fish to be had in Yarmouth. There were three markets weekly, of which that on Saturday was by far the largest and most important.[91]

The open market was a very flexible and inexpensive form of establishing retail outlets. It was flexible since the number of stalls could be varied to accommodate changes in the volume of trade. Ample room was provided for country tradesmen. Celia Fiennes noted that special stalls were reserved for country butchers opposite their city counterparts. And many country producers traded directly with the consumer without the intervention of middlemen. Farmers' wives and daughters sat with hampers or 'peds' of dairy produce in the 'ped market'. The market was also inexpensive, from the point of view of the salesman. Setting up a stall required no capital outlay, apart from the cost of renting a stall from the Corporation (and payments were often in arrears). In addition the market was free from tolls, with the minor exception of a small herbage toll.[92]

In this period there was also a growing tendency towards the setting up of permanent retail outlets for round-the-week trading. A growing number of shops were being established in Norwich, especially in the area in and around the market-place. One of the main shopping areas was the ancient Cockey Lane, which was renamed in the course of the eighteenth century as 'London Street' in tribute to its quasi-metropolitan splendour.[93] It is impossible to quantify the amount of retail trade carried on, or even to estimate the number of retail outlets there were in existence. Retail trade was not a specialized occupation; the freeman figures, therefore, cannot be used to distinguish the craft producers from the retailers. And there was a considerable amount of casual trading carried on by pedlars and street-sellers, whose numbers cannot even be guessed at. William Arderon, writing in the mid-eighteenth century, listed forty-two different sorts of shops in the city and fifty-seven different street cries.[94] Retail trade in Norwich is much better documented in the eighteenth century when advertisements appeared in the local press. Earlier, shopkeepers relied upon brightly coloured signs, or commissioned the city Bellman to broadcast information about goods for sale.[95] The growing importance of regular retail trade was paralleled by the gradual decline of the thrice yearly fairs, which were ceasing to be of great commercial significance, although retaining their popularity as social occasions.[96]

Norwich was also an important centre of wholesale trade. Two roles can be distinguished here. The city was one of the main distribution points for the export of the agricultural surpluses of the county of Norfolk. In particular Norwich specialized as a market for livestock, especially cattle, and for grain. These markets were attended by London dealers or their agents. Grain was then shipped via Yarmouth, while livestock were walked to town. The cattle which were sold in the Norwich market included the celebrated 'Scottish runts', which wintered in the marshland to the east of the city where they were fattened up and sent in 'great quantities' weekly to the capital.[97] Secondly, Norwich acted as a nodal point for the distribution throughout Norfolk of heavy goods and groceries which were imported into the city by the river and sea route. It is noticeable that the city did not operate as a very important market for its own industry, nor for the raw materials used in the textile production. Woolcombers ordered their supplies of wool in bulk, often at the annual Stourbridge Fair, while Norwich weavers consigned their goods directly to London merchants and dealers. An attempt was made in 1700 to establish a formal Exchange in the city to facilitate commercial transactions, but this experiment was concluded within three years after a petition to the City Assembly that the Exchange was detrimental to the staple industry.[98]

The economic importance of consumption has also been recognized as a factor of significance in the growth of towns. The sixteenth and seventeenth centuries saw the growing urbanization of the social life of the landed gentry. This was particularly encouraged from the early seventeenth century onwards with the invention and popularization of the coach, which meant that a country gentleman could transport his wife and daughters to town.[99] The towns were able to supply luxury goods, professional services and entertainments that were not available in the countryside. London was of course the mecca in this respect. Its dominance in the social world in the late seventeenth century was as great as it had ever been. In the eyes of London society the world outside the city presented a picture of uniform monotony: provincial England was termed generically 'Hampshire'.[100] But such views were exaggerated. Provincial capitals offered a considerable range of services, which, though not on a par with those of London, were sufficient to attract custom to the city. Norwich came into this category: although not newly fashionable like some of the spa towns, it was a recognized centre of social life in the county. Nor was its development as a textile centre any handicap to this function. The staple industry was un-obtrusive to eyes, ears and noses. This was a negative factor of some importance, for a city that was too dirty or smelly could lose its role as a social centre. Bristol's Hotwells failed to achieve any great social success, partly as a result of the smoky, oppressive atmosphere of the town, as well as through the rivalry of nearby Bath.[101]

The city of Norwich had something of its own winter season, a copy in miniature of that of London, with theatres, shows and assemblies. This catered for the middle-rank gentry, the country clergy and prosperous farmers. On the other hand, it failed to attract the county aristocracy, who tended to gravitate to London. As far as can be ascertained from imperfect records, the leading members of Norfolk society did not keep up town houses in Norwich although they might own property in the city. If they kept a town house it was usually in London. It was in this period that the Howard family ceased to keep up their Palace in Norwich, concentrating their attention instead on their property in the Strand. This decision was taken as much out of disenchantment with Norwich as from the lure of London. The Norwich Palace was on an unattractive site, in a densely built-up and industrial area of the city. Baskerville thought it 'seated in a dung-hole place', and Evelyn concurred that it was 'an old wretched building' despite the fact that the Duke was said in 1681 to have recently spent £30,000 on repairs and rebuilding.[102] In the 1690s the property was in a very dilapidated condition, visited but infrequently. The departure of the family was compounded by a quarrel in 1708 between the Duke of Norfolk and the Corporation, which was jealous of ducal preten- sions: the issue was whether the Duke had the right to have himself played into the city with full ceremonial and a procession. The Corporation subsequently leased the Palace and used part of the pre- mises, suitably enough, as the City Workhouse.[103] The departure of their resident nobility must have occasioned the city some loss of custom. Edward Browne's diary gives an account of the great pro- digality with which Christmas was celebrated by Henry Howard in 1663. He entertained 'so lavishly the like hath scarce been seen. They had dancing every night, and gave entertainments to all that would come.' But provincial society did not relish ducal glamour at all costs. When a later Duke of Norfolk visited the city in 1696 his reputation was so bad, that, although he prepared a great ball, no ladies attended for fear of being compromised.[104]

Besides its miniature winter season, the city had a second string to its bow. When the gentry re-dispersed to their country estates in the summer months, they came into the local capital for specific functions

which offered entertainment to relieve the monotony of rural life.
Such a function, for example, was the annual inauguration of the Lord
Mayor of Norwich, which was attended with much ceremonial every
June. Celia Fiennes described the scene:

> All the streete in which this Mayor elect's house is, is very exact
> in beautifying themselves, and hanging up flaggs the collours of
> their Companyes, and dress up pageants and there are plays and
> all sorts of shows that day, in little what is done at the Lord
> Mayor of London show; then they have a great feast with fine
> flaggs and scenes hung out, musick and dancing.[105]

Another important event in the annual calendar was the Summer
Assize week, which was the occasion of many balls, theatres and shows.
Mary Chamberlayne wrote to her half-brother William Windham in
August 1688: 'As to the Assizes, there happened very little remarkable
besides the good company at them, for it was agreed by all, there
never was more: nor so pittyful a High Sheriff to entertain them.'
Among the 'good company' she noted the Lestranges, the Astleys,
the Hobarts, the Earles and the Potts, all leading Norfolk gentry
families.[106] Other functions which brought county society into the city
were meetings of the Norfolk Lieutenancy Committee, the quarter
sessions, the inauguration of a new Bishop (who was attended to his
palace with a retinue of city notables and country gentlemen) and
other special occasions, such as the visit of Charles II to the city
in 1671.[107] These occasions brought a great deal of business into
Norwich and caused at times acute shortage of accommodation. When
the Hobart family leased out Chapelfield House in the 1680s, they
prudently made arrangements for two annual visits to the city: a clause
in the lease allowed them the use of two rooms free of charge twice a
year, each stay to last a maximum of five days and nights.[108] County
elections, which were held in Norwich, also brought in large numbers
of people. In May 1679 Sir Thomas Browne observed country voters
sleeping 'like flocks of sheep' around the cross in the market-place,
and he wrote in February 1681, with the prospects of a contested
election in mind: 'The people delight in it, and say it will be better
for the towne, as causing more concourse of persons, and more money
to be spent in the towne.'[109]

The Corporation itself made some modest attempts to improve
amenities. For example, it was decided in 1710 to present a piece of
plate as a prize for an annual horse race to be held near the city.

Norwich never rivalled Newmarket, but there was a considerable amount of horse-racing carried on in the vicinity, accompanied by much betting and gambling. Attempts were also made, on private initiative, to give Norwich some of the amenities of a spa. Aylsham spa-water, brought fresh every morning to the Black Boy in St Clement's, was advertised in 1710.[110] Other entertainments, both official and unofficial, included prize-fighting, all-in-wrestling (accompanied by kicking with specially sharpened boots), races, cockfighting, throwing at cocks, bear-baiting, nine-pins and 'camping', described as 'a wild and primitive form of football'.[111] The Corporation made strenuous but unsuccessful attempts to control the amount and variety of popular entertainments in the city, fearing that the industrial population would be distracted from its employment. It was empowered to license plays and shows: for example, permission was given in 1665 for Richard Browne to show an eagle, a vulture and two camels for a fortnight; in 1678 for Isaac Cookson to show 'a girl without bones'; and in 1677 for a group of rope-dancers to perform at the Red Lion in St Stephen's.[112] In addition to entertainment, the city also offered to both town and country society a chance to see and be seen. Hence the growing vogue for promenades along the 'Gentlemen's Walk' in the market-place or in the Chapel Fields, where the walk, 'prettily adorned with young trees' and 'loved by beaux and belles', was described in the mid-eighteenth century as the 'Mall of Norwich'.[113]

There was also in this period a growth in the number of professional men in the city (see Appendix). Norwich offered a gamut of services, ranging from sin to repentance. Sin was catered for by the city prostitutes who flourished despite attempts made by the Corporation to close down bawdy houses, although it seems that in this respect Norwich was considered as inferior to Lynn.[114] Repentance in all its guises was catered for by doctors, lawyers and ministers of religion. Professional men catered for an extensive rural as well as urban clientele. The letters of Sir Thomas Browne show that he was consulted professionally by country gentry families.[115] Other professional services available in the city at the end of the century were those of surveyors, architects, teachers, printers, publishers and musicians.[116] The city also functioned as an informal money-market. Numerous loans, mortgages and pecuniary transactions were conducted in the city. The correspondence of gentry families show that city money-lenders (often widows with cash to invest) were important sources of capital. Some of the carriers and waggoners also acted as unofficial bankers and money-lenders.[117] The numerous inns and alehouses in the city exemplified its commercial and social importance. They provided refreshment, accommodation and entertainment. In 1685 the city had 550 beds and stabling room for 930 horses, although in this respect it was outshone by some of the ports and staging-posts. Norwich ranked as eighth among English towns in terms of beds available and fourth for stabling.[118]

It is notable that the churches of Norwich played a very muted role in the city's economic development. Here there was a contrast between the dominant visual impression created by Norwich as a city of churches, and economic reality. The Church of England no doubt attracted some business to the city for the conduct of diocesan administration and for litigation in the Church Courts. But the evidence suggests that neither was of very great significance: there was no very large ecclesiastical bureaucracy and the volume and importance of business in the Church Courts was declining. The many small parish churches in the city were small and poorly endowed, and the standard of ministers was low. They were characterized as 'drones' by the acerbic Prideaux. An attempt was made in 1677 to provide for Anglican ministers in the city through a local rate, but this was firmly resisted by the Corporation.[119] Probably the most important economic influence of the Church of England was the custom generated by the household of the Bishop whose social life and standards of entertainment approximated to those of a country gentleman. The impact of the Church on town life in England contrasts with that of the Catholic Church on the Continent. In Beauvais, the 'ville sonnante', and in eighteenth-century Bayeux, for example, the Catholic Church dominated the urban economy, as employer, consumer and purveyor of poor relief.[120]

The poverty and dejection of the Church of England in Norwich was both product and cause of the strength of Dissent in the city. The Dissenting churches, however, were decentralized in their administration and modest in their building requirements and they did not, therefore, have such direct impact upon the urban economy. In more indirect ways they may have contributed to the growth of trade and industry by the inculcation of a commercial morality. Such at least was the intention of Dr Collinges, one of the leading Presbyterian ministers in the city in the late seventeenth century. In 1675 he produced the *Weaver's Pocket-book, or Weaving Spiritualised*, which was designed to be read by the weaver at the loom, and which demonstrated considerable familiarity with the processes of worsted production. He urged an ethic of hard work (as a sign of salvation, rather than as a means of redemption); he inveighed against the practice of weaving short lengths, which was as bad as deceiving God, for 'Does not the falseness of our hearts prompt us, to come off as cheap with God as we can?' and he counselled obedience to the officials of the Weavers' Company, provided that they were vigilant, active and disinterested in the execution of their office.[121] The effect of writings such as these must obviously remain incalculable. But they provide yet another illustration of the importance of the city as a textile centre, which overlaid its traditional function as a market town and cathedral city.

In its specialization of function in the seventeenth century, the city of Norwich differs from the formal model of the pre-industrial city, which tends to be heterogeneous in function.[122] The case of Norwich shows that, within the context of a pre-industrial economy, a considerable amount of specialization could occur. The expansion of the city and its growing importance as a textile centre were concomitant developments. The textile industry was the leading sector of the urban economy, productive of the greatest demand for labour in the city. 'We want hands to work', announced Thomas Lombe, describing the industry in its heyday.[123] The urban environment also fostered the growth of the industry. The city's economic regulations were revised to accommodate changed economic circumstances, as the restrictions on the recruitment of labour were broken down and supervision of the industry was waived. Contrary to the opinion of some eighteenth-century writers, overly impressed with the growth of new towns, an old incorporated city could provide a sympathetic environment for industrial expansion. Consequently the expansion of domestic demand in the late seventeenth century which stimulated the growth of domestic textile industries also promoted the growth of Norwich.

The expansion of the city was, however, a cumulative process and did not entail the abandonment of its traditional functions. Indeed these were enhanced as the city grew in size and the volume of business attracted to the city increased. Although the textile industry was the main agent of growth, the other aspects of the urban economy flourished in its wake and may have helped the city to weather the intermittent depressions in the staple industry. Like late seventeenth-century Exeter, which in some ways it closely resembled, Norwich was 'full of gentry and good company, and yet full of trade and manufactures also'.[124]

This meant that in both the long and short term, the crucial determinant of the well-being of the city was the worsted weaving industry. In the long term, this can be seen when the erosion of the textile industry in the early nineteenth century produced a fundamental alteration in the status and relative importance of Norwich.[125] The city then fell back upon its traditional function as a market town and commercial centre. In the short term, too, its fortunes fluctuated with those of the industry. A depression in the textile industry upset the whole urban economy, producing a heavy demand for poor relief at the very time when the city was least able to afford it. Problems were intensified when depressions in trade coincided with epidemics which threw greater numbers out of work. Thus to contemporaries the basis of the urban economy seemed very shaky and insecure, although in retrospect the period seems one of successful growth and adaptation.

But despite anxieties about the staple industry, contemporaries were sanguine about the specifically urban problems produced by growth, such as the increased problems of sanitation and housing, supplies of food and water, and maintenance of public order. All these issues confronted the civic authorities at this time but provoked very little public debate. As often happens, people were more concerned with the problems caused by lack of growth than with those consequent upon expansion. And indeed, the growth of Norwich in the late seventeenth century did not cause a breakdown in the administrative and political structure it had inherited from the past: even its physical expansion was almost entirely contained within the old city walls, which remained standing as visible symbols of continuity and urban self-sufficiency. All commentators therefore agreed in lauding unreservedly the city's size and importance. In the eighteenth century its inhabitants were regaled with the story of Johnny Numps, the country bumpkin come to town, who was dazzled by the sophistication and glamour of the big city:[126] the tale would have applied with even more force in the late seventeenth century, when Norwich led the provincial world.

Appendix
Admissions to the freedom of the city, 1660–1749

Occupations	1660–9	1670–9	1680–9	1690–9	1700–9	1710–19	1720–9	1730–9	1740–9	Total
TEXTILES										
Worsted weavers	335	363	212	218	613	564	699	372	242	3,618
Other weavers[a]	17	13	6	3	1	4	29		1	74
Woolcombers	13	18	3	5	10	38	115	55	26	283
Dyers	2	9	6	4	10	12	12	11	3	69
Finishers[b]	3	6	13	10	30	32	25	19	16	154
Total	370	409	240	240	664	650	880	457	288	4,198
LEATHER										
Leather workers	16	4	1	4	7	5	8	10	1	56
Shoemakers	57	77	40	59	84	79	88	84	39	607
Total	73	81	41	63	91	84	96	94	40	663
METAL										
Metal-workers[c]	28	33	12	27	27	49	31	31	22	260
Clockmakers		1			2	2		3	5	13
Total	28	34	12	27	29	51	31	34	27	273

Continued on next page

Appendix
Admissions to the freedom of the city, 1660–1749

Occupations	1660–9	1670–9	1680–9	1690–9	1700–9	1710–19	1720–9	1730–9	1740–9	Total
BUILDING										
Carpenters	25	33	34	27	36	33	26	53	31	298
Masons	22	21	15	18	25	30	15	13	8	167
Others	1	3		1		4	3	5	4	21
Total	48	57	49	46	61	67	44	71	43	486
FOOD AND DRINK										
Butchers	19	18	18	16	28	28	21	15	13	176
Bakers	24	29	37	36	48	38	43	36	27	318
Fishmongers	2	1	7	3	1	1	3	2		20
Grocers	31	22	15	34	30	22	16	22	25	217
Brewers[d]	17	21	12	15	21	21	16	25	9	157
Total	93	91	89	104	128	110	99	100	74	888
CLOTHING[e]										
Drapers	8	6	1	6	6	11	8	11	8	65
Mercers	10	4	7	7	6	6	5	4	6	55
Merchants	12	1	3	1		2	1	2	3	25
Tailors	91	80	63	52	43	44	38	42	16	469
Milliners	1	3	1	1		4				10
Hosiers	23	4	4	2	3	2	1	4		43
Glovers	8	9	1	4	7	5	6	3	8	51
Hatters	10	6		1	1	3		10	4	35

PROFESSIONS[f]									Total
Goldsmiths	3	2		2	1	1	1	1	1	12
Scriveners	9	8		3	4	5	8	2	2	48
Apothecaries	4	3	7	7	8	6	7	7	6	49
Surgeons[g]	18	13	23	37	49	46	39	46	45	316
Attorneys						6	1	13	7	27
Total	34	26	30	49	62	65	56	69	61	452
MISCELLANEOUS AND NOT STATED	90	64	47	37	52	24	110	195	95	714
Total	899	875	588	640	1,153	1,128	1,375	1,096	673	8,427

Source: P. Millican, *The Freemen of Norwich, 1548–1713* (Norwich, 1934), and *The Freemen of Norwich, 1713–1752* (Norfolk Record Society, XXIII, 1952).

Notes to Appendix

Years are given old-style.

a Other weavers include weavers of cloth, dornix, fearnothing, lace, linen, ribbon and silk.

b Finishers include calenderers, hotpressers, sheermen and twisterers.

c Metal-workers include blacksmiths, braziers, cutlers, founders, ironworkers, locksmiths and whitesmiths.

d Brewers include coopers, maltsters, victuallers and wine-coopers.

e Producers, wholesale dealers and retailers of cloths and clothing are all classified together, since the data do not permit further breakdown.

f Professions include all those working in law, medicine, finance and allied occupations.

g Surgeons include barber-surgeons and barbers, since their functions are not clearly differentiated in the data.

Notes

1 I would like to thank Professor F. J. Fisher for his help in reading early drafts of this chapter.

2 For useful brief accounts of the city, see *HMC Portland MSS*, II, 268–70, C. Morris, ed., *The Journeys of Celia Fiennes* (1949), pp. 146–150, and D. Defoe, *A Tour Through the Whole Island of Great Britain* (Everyman ed., 1959), I, 62–5.

3 For estimates of the city's population, see K. J. Allison, 'The Wool Supply and the Worsted Cloth Industry in Norfolk in the Sixteenth and Seventeenth Centuries' (unpublished Ph.D. thesis, University of Leeds, 1955), pp. 604–5, 732–3, and W. Hudson and J. C. Tingey, *The Records of the City of Norwich* (1906–10), II, cxxviii. (Unless stated to the contrary, all figures relate to both the City and County of Norwich, and also include the precincts of the Cathedral, which came under separate jurisdiction.) Norwich was the second city for most of the seventeenth century. J. E. Thorold Rogers, *History of Agriculture and Prices* (Oxford, 1887), V, 120, ranks Norwich as second city in 1641. It was not overtaken by Bristol until the 1720s or 1730s. The population of Bristol in 1700 was about 20,000, according to W. E. Minchinton, 'Bristol: the Metropolis of the West in the Eighteenth Century', *Trans. Roy. Hist. Soc.*, 5th series, IV (1954), 75.

4 C. Gill and A. Briggs, *History of Birmingham* (Oxford, 1952), I, 48, estimate its population at between 10,000 and 15,000 in 1700. The lower of these two figures is probably the more accurate. W. Hutton, *The History of Birmingham* (Birmingham, 6th ed., 1835), p. 77, estimated a population of about 15,000 in 1700. This was based on a list of 2,504 houses in the city, multiplied by an average household size of six. This multiplier is almost certainly too high. P. Laslett, 'Size and Structure of the Household in England over Three Centuries', *Population Studies*, XXIII, no. 2 (1969), 207, 211, suggests an average of 4·75.

5 F. Blomefield, *An Essay towards a Topographical History of the County of Norfolk* (1806), III, 432.

6 Allison, *op. cit.*, p. 607, gives annual figures collated from weekly returns in the Mayoral Court Books.

7 Bodl. MS. G. A. Norfolk, 4º.14: 'Ordinances for crafts ... 19th August 1622'. 'Foreigners' referred to all coming from outside the city.

8 Discussion of the flaws and idiosyncrasies of parish registers is the stock-in-trade of historical demography. For a survey of the problems, see R. Mols, *Introduction à la Démographie Historique des Villes d'Europe du XIVe au XVIIIe siècle* (Louvain, 1954–6), I, 259–90, and D. E. C. Eversley, 'Exploitation of Anglican Parish Registers by Aggregative Analysis', in E. A. Wrigley, ed., *An Introduction to English Historical*

Demography (1966), pp. 45–53. Ideally figures for baptisms and burials should be inflated to allow for under-registration, but selection of an inflation rate is fraught with problems.

9 Allison, *op. cit.*, pp. 604–5, has multiplied by 33 the baptismal figures for every tenth year, producing a population of 13,000 in 1602, 18,000 in 1612, 32,000 in 1622, 21,000 in 1632 and 27,000 in 1642. This exaggerates fluctuations from year to year. Applying the same birth rate to the decennial averages, a lower total population of 27,500 is produced for the decade from 1621 to 1630.

10 See D. E. C. Eversley, 'Population, Economy and Society', in D. V. Glass and D. E. C. Eversley, eds, *Population in History* (1965), p. 53, and M. W. Flinn, *British Population Growth, 1700–1850* (1970), p. 29.

11 Blomefield, *op. cit.*, III, 372–3, 376–7, 379–80; and Allison, *op. cit.*, p. 607. See also N. C. P. Tyack, 'Migration from East Anglia to New England before 1660' (unpublished Ph.D. thesis, University of London, 1951), *passim*.

12 Allison, *op. cit.*, p. 607. The yearly average for the decade from 1631 to 1640 (my calculation) was 710·6 baptisms, compared with 615 burials.

13 A. Jessopp, *Diocesan History of Norwich* (1884), pp. 203–4, and M. James, *Social Problems and Policy during the Puritan Revolution* (re-issue, 1966), p. 186. The Corporation was not backward in publicizing its grievances, but made no mention in this period of any loss of population. For petitions to the central government in 1649 and 1659, see James, *op. cit.*, pp. 50, 76.

14 Norfolk and Norwich Record Office (NNRO) Case 16, Shelf b, Mayoral Court Book (MCB), no. XXIV, 30/6/1669, 23/9/1676.

15 NNRO has a number of registers and microfilms. These can be supplemented by miscellaneous Archdeacon's Transcripts (NNRO, Case 31, Shelves d–e), Bishop's Transcripts (NNRO Norwich Diocesan Archives), and register transcripts in the libraries of the Norfolk and Norwich Archaeological Society and the Society of Genealogists. But there are many lacunae in the material. A pilot study for six selected years produced complete statistics for only nineteen of the thirty-four intra-mural parishes, which contained 57 per cent of the total population at the enumeration of 1693. The figures exclude the records of the French and Dutch Churches in Norwich, and probably under-register the city's Nonconformists. The figures cannot, therefore, be used as a basis from which to extrapolate totals for the whole city.

16 E179/154/701 Schedule of taxable hearths, 1662. The estimated total of hearths corresponds closely with the total of 7,302 given in W. G. Hoskins, *Local History in England* (1959), p. 177.

17 E/179/338 lists certificates of 3,028 people exempted from payment of the Hearth Tax for the whole city from January to April 1671. The

rate of exemption can be calculated by comparison with the estimated total of those assessed in July 1671. The lists are not strictly comparable since they date from different months of the year. But comparison of names shows a considerable degree of compatibility.

18 *Calendar of Treasury Books 1672–5*, p. 627. Lord Treasurer Danby confirmed to the Mayor of Norwich in 1674 that weavers' and dyers' furnaces were exempt, provided that their chimneys had already been paid for. This suggests that exemption was not *ipso facto* a sign of poverty. Exemption rates elsewhere were 41 per cent in Newcastle in 1671, R. Howell, *Newcastle-upon-Tyne and the Puritan Revolution* (Oxford, 1967), pp. 9–10; just under 40 per cent in Exeter in 1671–2, W. G. Hoskins, *Industry, Trade and People in Exeter, 1688–1800* (Manchester, 1935), pp. 115–16; 20·4 per cent in York in 1672, *VCH Yorkshire: The City of York* (1961), p. 164; and 27·4 per cent in Leicester in 1670, *VCH Leicestershire*, IV (1958), p. 156.

19 D. V. Glass, 'Two Papers on Gregory King', in Glass and Eversley, *op. cit.*, p. 177, suggests an average household size of 4·226 for the city of Norwich in 1696. This is confirmed by a partial census for the parish of St Peter Mancroft in 1693/4, which gives a household size of 4·14 for the 255 households of those paying the Poll Tax: NNRO Case 13, Shelf a, 'A Certificate of the Names'. The household figure is inclusive, so that there is no need to add an additional total for servants and apprentices, as some do: see Howell, *op. cit.*, pp. 8–9.

20 NNRO Case 13, Shelf a, 'Norwich City' Assessment Books, nos 1, 3 and 4, dated July 1671 (no. 2 is missing). A covering letter makes it clear that these are Hearth Tax assessments: NNRO Case 7, Shelf k, Papers re Hearth Tax, 1666–96. The average number of hearths per householder in Norwich was very similar to those found elsewhere: in Newcastle, 2·06, Howell, *op. cit.*, p. 9; in Exeter, 2·59, Hoskins, *op. cit.*, p. 115; in York, 3·2, *VCH Yorkshire: The City of York*, p. 163; and in Leicester, 2·4, *VCH Leicestershire*, IV, 159.

21 C. A. F. Meekings, *Dorset Hearth Tax Assessments* (Dorchester, 1951), pp. viii, xi–xii, and L. M. Marshall, 'The Levying of the Hearth Tax, 1662–1688', *E.H.R.*, LI (1936), 628–46.

22 William Salt Library, Stafford: Compton Census Returns for the Diocese of Norwich. Twenty-three of the thirty-four parishes give totals of Conformists in multiples of ten. The age of communion is conventionally taken to be sixteen: see Glass and Eversley, *op. cit.*, p. 212, for the age structure of English society in the late seventeenth century.

23 The origins of the 1693 enumeration are obscure and extensive search has failed to recover any contemporary references to its making. It was first published in 1752, with the civic enumeration of this date. Printed

copies in *Gentleman's Magazine*, Vol. XXII (1752), 437; *Norwich Mercury*, August 22-9, 1752, and Bodl. MS. Gough Maps, 24: 'A Parochial List', s.s. fol. One MS. copy in NNRO Visitation Book, VSM/3.

24 Glass and Eversley, *op. cit.*, pp. 177, 199.

25 BM Add. MS, 27, 966: Arderon Letters and Tracts, 1745-60 (subsequently Arderon), fols 241-3.

26 Blomefield, *op. cit.*, III, 410-11; *CSPD 1666-7*, pp. 188, 393-4; *CSPD 1667-8*, p. 124. See also J. Graunt, *Natural and Political Observations on the Bills of Mortality* (ed. C. H. Hull, Cambridge, 1899), p. 365, for a note on under-registration of deaths. The Norwich graveyards were reported as being seriously overcrowded by 1671: E. S. De Beer, ed., *The Diary of John Evelyn* (1959), p. 563. See also J. T. Krause, 'The Changing Adequacy of English Registration, 1690-1837', in Glass and Eversley, *op. cit.*, p. 384.

27 Blomefield, *op. cit.*, III, 360, reports 3,076 plague deaths in 1603. Allison, *op. cit.*, p. 607, gives a lower figure of 2,682.

28 *CSPD 1665-6*, p. 523. In September 1665, Sir Thomas Browne and his family left the city on the arrival of the plague: S. Wilkin, ed., *Sir Thomas Browne's Works* (1836), I, 111. See also for reactions to the plague, R. H. Hill, ed., *The Correspondence of Thomas Corie* (Norfolk Record Society, XXVII, 1956), p. 20; *CSPD 1665-6*, pp. 223, 472, 497, 498, 523, 530, 551; *CSPD 1666-7*, pp. 53, 101, 119, 141, 161-2, 179, 191; and NNRO Case 16, Shelf b, MCB no. XXIV, 20/6/1666, 9/7/1666, 14/7/1666, 20/7/1666, 15/8/1666, 30/8/1666, 26/10/1666, and 3/11/1666.

29 M. C. Buer, *Health, Wealth and Population in the Early Days of the Industrial Revolution* (re-issue, 1968), p. 181.

30 Hill, *op. cit.*, p. 30; Wilkin, *op. cit.*, I, 321.

31 T. Browne, 'A Letter to a Friend' in Wilkin, *op. cit.*, IV, 41, 44. For figures relating to child mortality in mid-eighteenth-century Norwich, see Arderon, fol. 245. See also for discussion of infant mortality in towns, M. D. George, *London Life in the Eighteenth Century* (1925), pp. 25-6, 406, 408, and J. D. Chambers, 'Population Change in a Provincial Town: Nottingham 1700-1800' in L. S. Pressnell, ed., *Studies in the Industrial Revolution Presented to T. S. Ashton* (1960), pp. 114-15.

32 Defoe, *op. cit.*, I, 63. The 1851 Census Report gives the area of the city and county of Norwich as 4,325 statute acres.

33 T. Fuller, *The Worthies of England* (ed. J. Freeman, 1952), p. 419. See also De Beer, *op. cit.*, p. 562, for Evelyn's comments on 'the flower gardens, which all the inhabitants excell in'. And see T. Cleer's New Map of the City, 1696, reproduced in W. J. C. Moens, ed., *The Walloon*

Church of Norwich: its Registers and History (Huguenot Society of London Publications, I, 1887), frontispiece.

34 Morris, *op. cit.*, p. 149: Celia Fiennes noted that some rich factors owned houses of brick, but thought that otherwise there were very few. By 1728, however, much of the housing stock was built in brick: *A Compleat History of the Famous City of Norwich* (Norwich, 1728), p. 2. At the same time thatched roofs were being replaced by tiles: see NNRO Case 16, Shelf b, MCB No. XXIV, 16/3/1672.

35 Morris, *op. cit.*, p. 147.

36 NNRO Case 19, Shelf b, River and Street Committee Accounts, 1643–1717. Average annual expenditure was £70 15s 2d from 1650 to 1659 and £60 16s 2d from 1690 to 1699.

37 NNRO Case 16, Shelf b, MCB no. XXIII, 18/8/1655, MCB no. XXIV, 14/7/1666, 26/1/1667, MCB no. XXV, 14/12/1687, MCB no. XXVI, 25/8/1703, 17/10/1705. Also see NNRO Case 5, Shelves e–k, Scavengers' Presentments, and Hudson and Tingey, *op. cit.*, II, 388–90, for examples of fines for negligence imposed by the Sheriffs' Tourn of 1676.

38 Norwich, Colman and Rye Libraries of Local History (subsequently NCRL), *An Alphabetical Draft of the Poll ... October 1710* (Norwich, c.1710) lists 150 country voters, of whom 13 came from Yarmouth. *An Alphabetical Draft of the Poll ... February, 1714* (Norwich, 1716) lists 492 country voters, of whom 30 came from Yarmouth and 67 from London.

39 *Norwich Mercury*, 8 and 15 July 1786.

40 For the arrival of the strangers, see Blomefield, *op. cit.*, III, 418, *CSPD 1683 July–September*, p. 363, and *CSPD 1700–2*, pp. 553–4. For estimates of their numbers: Moens, *op. cit.*, p. 108, says 'very few'; J. James, *History of the Worsted Manufacture in England* (1857), p. 166, says 'many'. R. L. Poole, *A History of the Huguenots of the Dispersion* (1880), p. 90, makes it clear that a colony settled in Norwich, but gives no estimate of their numbers. See also NNRO Case 31, Shelf g, 'Actes du Consestoire de l'Église Wallonne de Norwich', which show very little increase of business in the 1680s.

41 For removal orders, see NNRO Case 16, Shelf b, MCB no. XXIV, 11/2/1665, 18/2/1665, and 13/10/1676. For agitation against 'foreign' traders, see *ibid.*, 2/10/1667, 12/1/1676, MCB no. XXV, 13/8/1681, 20/6/1685, and NNRO Case 10, Shelf d, Petition to prohibit non-freemen from trading (n.d. 1690?) with 165 signatures.

42 NNRO Case 15, Shelf c: Orders for Passing Vagrants, 1742–62. For comparison with some sixteenth-century figures, see J. F. Pound, 'An Elizabethan Census of the Poor', *Univ. Birmingham Hist. J.*, VIII (1962), 139.

43 PRO IR/1/41–9, July 1710–September 1731 (hiatus June 1725–October 1728).

44 N. Riches, *The Agricultural Revolution in Norfolk* (2nd ed., 1967), p. 159, puts the population of Norfolk in 1700 as 210,200, quoting *Annals of Agriculture*, XLII, 267; P. Deane and W. A. Cole, *British Economic Growth, 1688–1959* (1962), p. 103, give a population of 242,511 in 1700, using Rickman's estimates. For population densities, see J. N. L. Baker, 'England in the Seventeenth Century' in H. C. Darby, *The Historical Geography of England before 1800* (Cambridge, 1951), p. 524.

45 Morris, *op. cit.*, p. 146; Defoe, *op. cit.*, I, 62.

46 It is always difficult to prove that regulations which were partially administered did not exert much influence. For comments on the efficacy of the Act of Settlement, see P. Styles, 'The Evolution of the Law of Settlement', *Univ. Birmingham Hist. J.*, IX (1963–4), 33–63. For Company regulations, see NNRO Case 16, Shelf b: Trade Bye-laws, 1543–1714. By the early eighteenth century, at least, the Companies had ceased to exercise formal supervision of the standard of goods produced or on sale: see NNRO Case 16, Shelf b, MCB no. XXVI, 21/6/1703, MCB no. XXIX, 19/1/1732. The names of their annually elected officers ceased to be registered in the Mayoral Court Books by the 1720s, with one or two rare exceptions: see MCB nos. XXVIII–XXIX, *passim*. For the concomitant decline of the apprenticeship system, see P. Millican and W. Rising, *Index of the Indentures of Norwich Apprentices* (Norfolk Record Society, XXIX, 1959), pp. xi–xiii. For the freemen, see P. Millican, *The Register of the Freemen of Norwich, 1548–1713* (Norwich, 1934), pp. xi–xx.

47 *Ibid.*, pp. xiv–xv. Admissions to the freedom averaged seventy-five per annum from 1660 to 1699, suggesting a total of approximately 2,500 freemen at any one time.

48 For proclamations on this subject, see NNRO Case 16, Shelf b, MCB no, XXIV, 2/10/1667, MCB no. XXV, 20/6/1685, and Case 16, Shelf c, Assembly Book, 1665–82, 3/5/1675. For attempted legislation, see *ibid.*, 16/3/1677, and Assembly Book no. VII, 24/2/1701. The Corporation was partially successful in 1723, when it obtained an act to qualify textile workers: see Assembly Book no. VIII, 7/1/1723 and *Commons' Journals*, XX, 114.

49 Carpets were made from the 'niles' or refuse of the wool used in the worsted manufacture. For a reference to the industry in Norwich, see *Calendar of Treasury Papers, 1731–4*, p. 57.

50 Defoe, *op. cit.*, I, 63.

51 J. F. Pound, 'The Social and Trade Structure of Norwich, 1525–75', *P. & P.* no. 34 (1966), 55–63. See also A. R. Bridbury, *Economic*

Growth: England in the Later Middle Ages (1962), p. 49, for figures from fifteenth-century Norwich.

52 See B. H. Allen, 'The Administrative and Social Structure of the Norwich Merchant Class, 1485–1660' (unpublished Ph.D. thesis, Harvard University, 1951), *passim*. See also E. M. Thompson, ed., *Letters of Humphrey Prideaux, sometime Dean of Norwich . . . 1674–1722* (Camden Society, New Series, XV, 1875), p. 167.

53 NNRO Case 16, Shelf b, MCB no. XXIV, 13/10/1676, and *Norwich Gazette*, vol. XIX, no. 287, 1725. See also for movement of labour among textile centres in the eighteenth century, PRO CO/388/21, fols 137–40, and E. Hobsbawm *Labouring Men* (1964),, p. 36.

54 See D. C. Coleman, 'An Innovation and its Diffusion: the New Draperies', *Ec.H.R.*, 2nd series, XXII (1969), 417–29.

55 *Magna Britannia et Hibernia, Antiqua et Nova* (1721–30), III, 320, quotes an estimate of 1711 that the annual value of the industry was £100,000, but this seems a suspiciously round figure.

56 PRO CO/388/21, part ii, fols 196,286. Defoe, *op. cit.*, I, 62, quotes a figure of 120,000 employed in the industry, which is clearly derived from these estimates. J. H. Clapham, 'The Transference of the Worsted Industry from Norwich to the West Riding', *Economic Journal*, XX (1910), 196, took Defoe to task for this statement, but Defoe had in fact toned down the estimates given to him.

57 Millican, *op. cit., passim* (my calculation). See also *HMC Portland MSS*, IV, 27. For the same reasons the freemen admissions cannot be taken to be an adequate index to the growth of the city's population.

58 For markets in the early part of the seventeenth century, see C. Wilson, *England's Apprenticeship, 1603–1783* (1965), p. 55, and Allison, *op. cit.*, pp. 542–608. For eighteenth-century markets, see J. K. Edwards, 'The Economic Development of Norwich, 1750–1850, with Special Reference to the Worsted Industry' (unpublished Ph.D. thesis, University of Leeds, 1963), chap. i, *passim*.

59 BM Lansdowne MS. 846, fol. 284 and J. James, *op. cit.*, pp. 172–4.

60 E190/503/18 Yarmouth Port Book, Overseas, Dec. 1684–Dec. 1685: 125,053 lb. of worsted stuffs were exported in this year. I am grateful to Anthony Michell of Corpus Christi College, Cambridge, for this information.

61 M. James, *op. cit.*, p. 76. See also J. James, *op. cit.*, pp. 157–9, for legislation of 13 and 14 Charles II, c. 5 (1662).

62 *Ibid.*, p. 170, quoting Sir Josiah Child: 'Formerly gentlewomen esteemed themselves well clothed in a serge gown, which a chambermaid would now be ashamed to be seen in.' See also Wilson, *op. cit.*, pp. 185–6, and C. Hill, *Reformation to Industrial Revolution* (1967), p. 137.

63 There are no contemporary descriptions of the processes involved in

the production of worsteds. But there was general agreement on their final effect. See Morris, *op. cit.*, p. 149 and *HMC House of Lords MSS 1692–3*, p. 37: it was reported that Norwich stuffs were so light that seals dropped off them. But some white and unfinished stuffs were still produced at this time: see Morris, *op. cit.*, p. 149 and *Commons' Journals*, XII, 74.

64 Millican, *op. cit.*, pp. 55–8 and P. Millican, *The Freemen of Norwich, 1714–52* (Norfolk Record Society, XXIII, 1952), pp. 30–1. For Norwich bewpers, see *CSPD 1664–5*, p. 137.

65 H. Heaton, *The Yorkshire Woollen and Worsted Industries* (2nd ed., Oxford, 1965), pp. 263–9.

66 PRO CO/388/21, part ii, fol. 196; *HMC House of Lords MSS 1696*, pp. 240–3; Wilson, *op. cit.*, pp. 76–7.

67 Morris, *op. cit.*, p. 149; *Magna Britannia, op. cit.*, III, 320; Fuller, *op. cit.*, pp. 419–20.

68 NNRO Case 33, Shelf e, Norwich Archdeaconry Inventories, Bundle III, no. 200 (1674), Bundle IV, no. 69 (1692).

69 J. James, *op. cit.*, p. 166.

70 *Ibid.*, pp. 166–7, quoting D. Defoe, *Review*, 30 December 1704.

71 *Ibid.*, pp. 200–1. See also D. C. Coleman, *Courtaulds. An Economic and Social History* (Oxford, 1969), I, 25.

72 BM Various Tracts 816. m. 14 'Reasons humbly offered . . . why the waggoners ought not to be obliged to carry any certain weight' (n.d.).

73 After the civil war, the alnagers made an unsuccessful attempt to impose the alnage on Norwich stuffs: see PRO PC/2/55 fol. 206, Petition against the alnage (1661). The issue revived again under James II. For petitions against the alnage, see *Commons' Journals*, X, 203, 361, and also *HMC House of Lords MSS 1692–3*, pp. 34–42.

74 J. James, *op. cit.*, pp. 169–72. The Corporation had also petitioned Parliament against the proposal to license the import of Flemish textiles: NNRO Case 16, Shelf b, MCB no. XXIV, 29/5/1674.

75 See J. James, *op. cit.*, pp. 167–8, 178–81, *Commons' Journals*, XI, 437, ff., and *HMC House of Lords MSS 1696*, pp. 240–3. Legislation was passed in 1699 by the Act of 11 and 12 William III, c. 10, 'for more effectively employing the poor'.

76 See J. James, *op. cit.*, pp. 216–19, and N. Rothstein, 'The Calico Campaign of 1719–21', *East London Papers*, VII (1964), 3–21. Also *Commons' Journals*, XIX, 168 ff., and PRO CO/388/21–2.

77 *Commons' Journals*, X, 129 ff. The Norwich Committee of Trade was advertising a competition for cotton weaving in 1736: *Gentleman's Magazine*, VI (1736), 169.

78 The Woolcombers had been incorporated and empowered to maintain standards of combed wool in 1686, see NNRO Case 17, Shelf d. This

seems to have been the prelude to the contest with the weavers: see
CSPD 1700–2, pp. 579–80, 'Case of the Woolcombers', 1693; *CSPD
1663–4*, p. 189, 'Reply of the Norfolk and Norwich weavers' (wrongly
dated ?1663); and BM Tracts 814. m. 14 (124), 'A Brief Reply to the
Weavers' Answer . . .' (wrongly dated ?1718). For the outcome of the
debate, see *Commons' Journals*, XI, 95, and E. Lipson, *Economic
History of England, vol. II: The Age of Mercantilism* (1931), pp. 48–9.

79 Allison, *op. cit.*, pp. 379–80; Blomefield, *op. cit.*, III, 399.

80 S. Tsuru, *Essays on Economic Development* (Tokyo, 1968), pp. 76–92.

81 Labour disputes were frequently symptoms of a declining industry.
For comments on weavers' earnings, see J. James, *op. cit.*, pp. 168,
191–3. For labour disputes in Exeter, see Hoskins, *op. cit.*, pp. 58–61,
and cf. K. H. Burley, 'A Note on a Labour Dispute in Colchester',
B.I.H.R., XXIX (1956), 220–30.

82 Allison, *op. cit.*, pp. 553–4 and Defoe, *op. cit.*, I, 61.

83 For disputes with Yarmouth, see Blomefield, *op. cit.*, III, 412, and
Commons' Journals, XV, 99 ff.

84 PRO CO/388/21, part ii, fol. 286.

85 See NNRO Case 16, Shelf b, MCB no. XXIV, 10/10/1667, 12/1/1676,
30/8/1676; *HMC House of Lords MSS 1692–3*, p. 37; Thompson,
op. cit., pp. 175–6, 181, 193; and M-H. Li, 'The Great Recoinage in
England, 1696–9' (unpublished Ph.D. thesis, University of London,
1940), pp. 206–57.

86 See W. G. East, 'England in the Eighteenth Century', in Darby,
op. cit., p. 498 and R. H. Mason, *History of Norfolk* (1884), p. 433. See
also Pound, *op. cit.*, pp. 49–69, for comparison with sixteenth-century
Norwich.

87 NNRO Case 16, Shelf b, MCB no. XXV, 13/8/1681 and R. H. Hill,
op. cit., pp. 37–8.

88 PRO IR/1/41–9, *passim*.

89 See Thompson, *op. cit.*, p. 120; *CSPD 1680–1*, pp. 631–2; and Wilkin,
op. cit., I, 323. Arderon, fols 232–3, lists 176 alehouses and taverns in
the mid-eighteenth century.

90 D. Davis, *A History of Shopping* (1966), p. 144.

91 *HMC Portland MSS*, II, 269.

92 Morris, *op. cit.*, pp. 147–8; P. Browne, *The History of Norwich* (Norwich,
1814), p. 174. For regulations governing the hours of sale in the
market, see NNRO Case 16, Shelf b, MCB no. XXV, 8/8/1685.

93 J. Kirkpatrick, *The Streets and Lanes of the City of Norwich* (Norwich,
1889), p. 45.

94 Arderon, fols 228–9, 235. See also Davis, *op. cit.*, p. 45.

95 NNRO Case 16, Shelf b, MCB no. XXIV, 31/1/1667.

96 Celia Fiennes (Morris, *op. cit.*, p. 148) noted the 'vaste concourse' of

people at the fairs. See also Browne, *op. cit.*, pp. 244–5, and Hudson and Tingey, *op. cit.*, II, cxxxv–cxli.

97 Defoe, *op. cit.*, I, 64–5, considered that approximately 40,000 cattle passed this way yearly. See also Riches, *op. cit.*, pp. 30–1.

98 Blomefield, *op. cit.*, III, 399, 427, 431.

99 J. Crofts, *Packhorse, Waggon and Post* (1967), pp. 109 ff.

100 See F. J. Fisher, 'The Development of London as a Centre of Conspicuous Consumption', *Trans. Roy. Hist. Soc.*, 4th series, XXX (1948), 37–50. See also G. Etheredge, *The Man of Mode, or Sir Fopling Flutter. A Comedy* (1676), p. 88.

101 See V. Waite, *The Bristol Hotwell* (Local History Pamphlet. no. 1, Bristol, 1960), pp. 3–15.

102 See *HMC Portland MSS*, II, 270, and De Beer, *op. cit.*, pp. 562–3.

103 See L. G. Bolingbroke, 'St John Maddermarket, Norwich', *Norfolk Archaeology*, XX (1921), 221, and E. A. Kent, 'The Houses of the Duke of Norfolk in Norwich', *Norfolk Archaeology*, XXIV (1932), 81–7.

104 'Journal of Edward Browne', in Wilkin, *op. cit.*, I, 44, and Thompson, *op. cit.*, p. 184.

105 Morris, *op. cit.*, p. 149. R. Beatniffe, *Norfolk Tour* (5th ed., Norwich, 1795), pp. 89–90, describes the Guild Day Feast provided by the St George's Company.

106 R. W. Ketton-Cremer, 'Assize Week in Norwich, 1688', *Norfolk Archaeology*, XXIV (1932), 15.

107 See B. Cozens-Hardy, ed., *Norfolk Lieutenancy Journal, 1676–1701* (Norfolk Record Society, XXX, 1961), *passim*. The Commission met three or four times a year, and more frequently in times of emergency. For the visit of the King in 1671, see R. H. Hill, *op. cit.*, pp. 32–6.

108 B. Cozens-Hardy, 'The Norwich Chapel-Field House Estate since 1545', *Norfolk Archaeology*, XXVII (1941), 377–8.

109 Wilkin, *op. cit.*, I, 241, 306.

110 *Norwich Gazette*, 5 August 1710.

111 See R. W. Ketton-Cremer, 'Camping, a forgotten Norfolk Game', *Norfolk Archaeology*, XXIV (1932), 88–92; Arderon, fols 241–3; and Wilkin, *op. cit.*, I, 49, 322.

112 Blomefield, *op. cit.*, III, 409. The Corporation's powers were superseded by those of the Royal Fishing Company from 1665 to 1670: *CSPD 1664–5*, pp. 139, 438; *CSPD 1668–9*, p. 627; and *CSPD 1670*, pp. 39, 71. For shows licensed by the Corporation, see NNRO Case 16, Shelf b, MCB no. XXIV, 5/3/1665, and MCB no. XXV, 1/12/1677, 5/10/1678.

113 W. Honeycomb (pseud.), *The History of Pudica, a Lady of N-rf-lk* (1754), pp. 21–2.

114 NNRO Case 16, Shelf b, MCB no. XXIV, 1/2/1668, and *CSPD*

1681, July–September, pp. 631–2. For reference to the Lynn prostitutes, see V. H. H. Green, *The Universities* (1969), p. 298.

115 For city doctors, see Wilkin, *op. cit.*, I, 371–3, and R. W. Ketton-Cremer, *Felbrigg, the Story of a House* (1962), pp. 44–6. For doctors employed by the Corporation, see NNRO Case 16, Shelf b, MCB no. XXIV, 24/4/1667, and MCB no. XXV, 14/12/1678.

116 For professional services available in the city, see *Norwich Gazette*, *passim*. For teachers in the city, see also H. W. Saunders, *History of Norwich Grammar School* (Norwich, 1932), chap. vii, *passim*. For the first printer in the city, see Blomefield, *op. cit.*, III, 427. For the City Waits, see NNRO Case 16, Shelf b, MCB no. XXV, 2/10/1678, 18/8/1683 and 17/11/1683.

117 W. Rye, ed., *Calendar of Correspondence and Documents relating to the Family of Oliver Le Neve, 1675–1743* (Norwich, 1895), pp. 30–1, 39–40, 104–5, 162. For carriers as money lenders, see C 5/558/58 Southgate v. Crome, 1683.

118 PRO WO/30/48. Bristol led the list both for beds and for stabling.

119 For comments on the poor standard of ministers, see Thompson, *op. cit.*, pp. 148–9, 151, 160–1. For the proposed rate to finance ministers, see Blomefield, *op. cit.*, III, 317, and C. Hill, *Economic Problems of the Church* (Oxford, 1956), p. 288.

120 See P. Goubert, *Beauvais et le Beauvaisis de 1600 à 1730* (Paris, 1960), pp. 233–41, and O. H. Hufton, *Bayeux in the Late Eighteenth Century* (Oxford, 1967), pp. 20–40, 89–91, 100–2.

121 NCRL J. Collinges, *The Weaver's Pocket-book, or Weaving Spiritualised* (1675), *passim*.

122 See G. Sjoberg, *The Pre-Industrial City: Past and Present* (Chicago, 1960), pp. 87–91; and for a critique of Sjoberg, O. C. Cox, 'The Pre-Industrial City Reconsidered' in P. Meadows and E. H. Mizruchi, *Urbanism, Urbanisation and Change: Comparative Perspectives* (Reading, Mass., 1969), pp. 19–28.

123 *HMC House of Lords MSS 1696*, pp. 240–3.

124 See Hoskins, *op. cit.*, *passim* and Defoe, *op. cit.*, I, 222.

125 For discussion of the decline of the Norwich textile industry, see Clapham, *op. cit.*, pp. 195–210; M. F. Lloyd Pritchard, 'The Decline of Norwich', *Ec.H.R.*, 2nd series, III (1951), 371–7; D. C. Coleman, 'Growth and Decay during the Industrial Revolution: the Case of East Anglia', *Scandinavian Ec.H.R.*, X (1962), 115–27; and J. K. Edwards, 'The Decline of the Norwich Textiles Industry', *Yorkshire Bulletin of Economic and Social Research*, XXVI (1964), 31–41.

126 Bodl. Gough Norfolk. 59: 'The Cabinet of Curiosities' (n.d.).

9

London merchants and the crisis
of the 1690s[1]

D. W. Jones

1694 was to prove a significant year in the history of London. For London as a civic entity it marked the passing of the Orphans' Bill which ended a chapter of financial discredit; for the business community as a whole it witnessed the establishment of the Bank of England. Both events possess a certain symbolic significance, for while the former symbolizes the decline of the old 'Medieval' town, the latter presages the emergence of the great institutions of the eighteenth-century 'city'.

The decline of the old 'Medieval' town, while according tolerably well in broad outline with the sociologists' model of urban decay, lacks nevertheless any simple, or indeed any firmly established, chronology of decline. From at least the beginning of the seventeenth century, government by gild and municipality was ceasing increasingly to reflect the economic vitality of the metropolis as a whole. The growth of the suburbs, and the rise of unfree trading and manufacturing within them, diminished the value of both apprenticeship and freedom: more and more of the trade and industry which were nominally the citizens' exclusive right under successive great charters of London were being intercepted by the activity of the unfree trading and manufacturing in the suburbs. Growing urban congestion and the persistent importunity of shopkeepers, pedlars and hucksters drove in time many of the wealthier citizens to seek more salubrious places of residence in Westminster, Covent Garden, Bloomsbury and the outer reaches of Stepney and Islington.

The outflow of wealth led inevitably to the financial decline of the municipality: from the earliest date at which it is possible to observe its finances the city was only maintaining its solvency by utilizing the net balance of incoming Orphans' portions over outgoing interest payments and capital repayments to bridge the persistent current deficit between income and expenditure. By the early 1680s, the burden of accrued interest outstripped the meagre financial resources of the city; default to the orphans ensued.

As hinted above, the chronology of the municipality's economic, as distinct from its financial, decline is more difficult to date precisely. Judging from the rents paid to the city for the lease of the statutory markets, and from the yield of the 'hallage' in the Blackwell Hall cloth markets, the city was still playing a major marketing role at the end of the seventeenth century. Not until the second quarter of the eighteenth century do signs of marked decline in the use of the London cloth markets become apparent. Significantly enough this was also the period of a marked decline in the numbers of young men entering their apprenticeship and taking up the prescribed company and civic freedoms. Nevertheless, decline in these latter two respects did not preclude a dramatic counter-attack on growing laxity in the second half of the eighteenth century: from 1760 to 1790, numbers admitted to the freedom of the city either through apprenticeship or by patrimony all but reattained the levels of the first decades of the century. The city reasserted its authority over what was admittedly a sphere of economic activity whose importance was contracting relative to that of the metropolis as a whole.

In the Twelve Great Livery Companies of the city, which most concern the merchants who are the subjects of this paper, the basis for such a revival had long since disappeared. In the sixteenth century the growing dominance of the wealthy mercantile element inevitably led to a divorce of the government of these companies from the technical and commercial preoccupations of the crafts and trades which had been their original *raison d'être*. The mobility of mercantile capital led increasingly to the diversification of the economic interests of the liverymen. Once the vocational unity of these companies was destroyed they were soon transformed from economic fraternities, closely identified with a particular craft or trade, into wealthy proprietorial fellowships of self-made men.

When, in 1712, the city abandoned by implication any attempt to enforce the freedom upon wholesalers and merchants trading overseas it merely recognized the facts of life. For over a century, traditional civic institutions had been of diminishing relevance for the great merchants of the city. Hence in part, the fascination of the 1690s: during this decade there emerged new institutions, associated with what has been aptly termed the 'Financial Revolution', which were to be centrally relevant to the calculations of the London business community.[2]

Contracting the perspectives a little, we see that here lies but part of the fascination of the 1690s, for the circumstances surrounding the birth of 'Revolution Finance' are no less remarkable than its historical significance. Annuities were sold, lotteries floated, the Bank of England founded and the capital stock of the East India Company much extended at a time of unparalleled strain.[3] Entry into the first major European involvement since the Hundred Years War brought with it for England in general, and London in particular, a host of new problems of unprecedented magnitude. As far as London was concerned, by far the greatest of these was the weekly remittance of large sums abroad to keep both subject troops and those of the allies in the field. London merchants and syndicates were now in fact to participate in that great sphere of wartime business which had employed the resources of the merchant houses of sixteenth- and seventeenth-century Medina del Campo in the *asientos* of the Spanish Kings, which had brought to eminence in the first half of the seventeenth century such individuals as the de Willem brothers and the Marcellis family in the service of Denmark, Barthellemy de Herwarth in the service of France, and the hapless Hans de Witte in that of the Austrian Hapsburgs. What was unique after about 1690 was that such individuals and firms in the service of France as Pierre Gott, Andreas Pells and the Bookseller merchant Pierre Huguetan, all of Amsterdam, the houses of Saladin, Tourton, Guigier, Fatio and Calandrini of Geneva, and Samuel Barnard in Paris, and such court Jews as Samuel Oppenheimer in the service of Vienna, had their counterparts, and found their match, in the mercantile community of London.[4]

The success of the London merchants possesses a relevance far beyond the specialist concern of urban, economic and financial historians, since the issues which lay behind the Nine Years War, overt and covert, were far greater than the usual territorial baubles of continental dynastic disputes. Behind the question of French frontiers which led to war over the Rhenish Bishoprics in 1688, there lurked the intractable problem of the disposal of the Spanish inheritance. The death of the childless Charles—the 'bewitched'—of Spain was an ever present possibility, and mindful of this eventuality, the Confederate powers had designated, by the Grand Alliance Treaty of 1689, the whole of the Spanish inheritance to the Austrian house in the event of Charles's death. Here, Austrian ambition coincided neatly with the fears of the Maritime Powers: a Bourbon assumption of the Spanish throne would see the French influence dominant in the West Indies, in the Philippines, the Iberian Peninsula, in Italy and in the Mediterranean generally, quite apart from a threatening presence in the present Spanish Netherlands.[5]

It is true of course that the fruits of military and diplomatic victories are seldom unequivocal; only Bengal afforded significant commercial gains to Britain as a result of spectacular military, naval and diplomatic victories of the eighteenth century. Adjustments in the balance of power, the bitterness of the defeated, the jealousy of neutrals and the circumspection of erstwhile allies have an uncomfortable habit of turning victories into ashes within a generation. Nevertheless, the significance of survival in the 1690s, and of victory under Marlborough, cannot be whittled away entirely; as in the eighteenth century, they averted what might otherwise have been.

Had England succumbed in the 1690s, Louis would have had a free hand to dispose of the Spanish inheritance unchallenged, and it is reasonable to suppose that he would have done so in a way which would have favoured the growing French penetration of the Spanish colonial markets and consolidated their gains in the Levant; moreover, given the Franco-Portuguese treaty of 1700, he could well have nipped in the bud that important English penetration of the Luso-Brazilian empire, which, together with the growth of manufactured exports to Britain's mainland American colonies, was to prove the most dynamic sector of an otherwise sluggish economy from 1714 to 1740.[6]

When we examine the factors which determined the outcome at Ryswick, we see that economic resilience was far more important than military or naval success. William III was to lose every battle he fought in the Low Countries in the 1690s; the retaking of Namur in 1695 was no Blenheim or Ramillies. To put the issue more specifically, had the Bank of England not been successfully floated in 1694, there would have been no means of finding the funds to keep troops and allies in the field; or yet again, had the currency crisis, with its dislocative effects, come earlier—in 1693 for instance—there could well have been a Stuart Restoration and an abject peace. The importance of economic and financial stability, embracing as it does complex problems of balance of payments equilibrium, budgetary control, and public and private creditworthiness, needs no further elaboration, but it does raise in an acute form the question of how London blundered through.

A *simpliste* answer to this would be that the outcome was in some way defined by the wealth of the city. After all, by 1690 a great period of mercantile achievement was coming to a close. This period had begun with the penetration and eventual dominance of the Mediterranean, with participation and ultimate pre-eminence, for a time, in the North Atlantic fisheries. It continued with the victory of Caribbean sugar and Chesapeake tobacco over the competing Brazilian staples of the Portuguese; and it came to a close with the 'calico' revolution of the last third of the seventeenth century, by which the products of the great Indian textile industry asserted their price and quality superiority in European markets.

The London merchant community of the later seventeenth century was composed, therefore, not only of those merchants who continued to work the long established markets of the European littoral, with an important extension into Central Europe, but also those who had employed their resources in taking Newfoundland cod to the tables of the Catholic South, Sicilian grain to Italy, New England victuals to the Caribbean, slaves from Benin to the West Indian islands and to the tobacco plantations of Virginia and Maryland, and in exchanging Bengali and Gujerati piece-goods, together with those of the Coromandel coast—sometimes against one another, and sometimes in conjunction with cargoes of silver—in exchange for the cotton of Gujerat, the sugar of Bengal, the rubies and sapphires of Pegu, the tin of Siam and the Malay peninsula, and the gold of China and Arakan. Given these achievements in which we see the germ of the English tramp ship, the failure to oust the Dutch from their control of that great intra-European current of trade which linked the forest and grain lands of the north with the vineyards and salt pans of the south, and which made the emergence of their great seaborne herring industry all but inevitable, was largely an irrelevance.[7]

An answer in terms such as these of mercantile wealth, while at least having the merit of going beyond the unspoken whig shibboleth that virtuous politics alone leads to sound finance, remains inadequate on three counts. In the first place, such an answer would verge dangerously close to being a rationalization of our ignorance; we know all too little about the circumstances of the mercantile community, as distinct from the structure of public finance which impinged increasingly upon its affairs.[8] In the second place it omits some key links in the chain of explanation: wealth generated in trade, anymore than the voracious scale of government needs, could not of itself have created 'Revolution Finance'. Resources would in some way, and from different sectors, have to be released from trade and/or saved from current consumption. Of equal importance, financial expedients would have to be evolved which were acceptable to the differing asset preferences of the investing public. In the third place, such an answer is inadequate if only because it abstracts wholly from the grave economic and political crisis of the 1690s.

A casual analysis of the crisis as it pertained to London in particular does little to clarify the question posed above; rather it underlines the miracle of our survival. Its most striking feature, as we have already noted, was the Remittance Burden which quite apart from its magnitude and quite apart from the inexperience of the merchant syndicates which handled it, was shouldered at a time when the silver currency was fundamentally unsound, when French privateering had successfully disrupted precisely those trades which had been the growth points of the 'Commercial Revolution', and when the mercantile community was split from top to bottom over the future of the East India trade.

The following tabulation of the annual remittance burden, taken in conjunction with the facts that total national income was but an estimated £49m and that the total value of English foreign trade during the immediate pre-war years was in the neighbourhood of £12–13m, underlines the magnitude of the burden. Setting aside the strain of the fiscal year 1689–90, when remittances were inflated by substantial repayments on account of the loan of £600,000 made by the States General of the United Provinces to finance William's invasion of England, the real turning point comes in the course of 1692, when England, with the Irish Problem solved for a time, could assume her responsibilities in Europe. Down to 1 April 1692, foreign remittances on government account had averaged between £10,000 and £15,000 per *month*; thereafter they averaged £16,000 per *week*—a rate which rose further at intervals down to 1695. The totals are as in Table 21.

Contemporaries had no illusions as to the problems involved; immediately the estimates for 1693 were presented to the Commons in December 1692, Sir Richard Temple pointed out: 'There is one thing his Majesty takes notice of in his speech to you, which is worthy your

TABLE 21   *The Remittance Burden, 1688–98[9]*

October 1688–September 1689			£169,335
,,	1689–	,, 1690	£795,547
,,	1690–	,, 1691	£610,437
,,	1691–	,, 1692	£716,463
,,	1692–	,, 1693	£1,101,088
,,	1693–	,, 1694	£1,349,152
,,	1694–	,, 1695	£1,698,808
,,	1695–	,, 1696	£902,288
,,	1696–	,, 1697	£732,763
,,	1697–	,, 1698	£512,781

consideration; you are now like to have an army abroad, which of necessity must occasion great payments there; therefore I think it fit to consider how to keep your money at home . . . .'[10] As Temple pertinaciously foresaw, remittances of the magnitude envisaged would lead inevitably to adverse movements on the balance of payments. During such episodes, international debts could only be met by the export of bullion and in this period this normally meant the export of silver. Silver was the relatively undervalued of the two precious metals —gold and silver—and supplies for export on such occasions were forthcoming in response to rising silver bullion prices. Rising silver prices had the dangerous corollary, however, of increasing the endemic incentive to clip the hammered silver coinage through which the bulk of retail transactions were effected.

Out of sheer necessity, tolerance of the clipped coin was long suffering, but a severe attack on the intrinsic content of the hammered coin could, and did, produce a divergence between the actual bullion content of the coin and its nominal face value too great for credence and trust. Nothing came of interesting suggestions made in response to Temple's warnings that such risks could be obviated by simply swapping English treaty obligations to supply men and finance for the military operations in Europe for Dutch obligations to supply ships. In a very real sense, therefore, the strategic outcome was both improbably and problematically poised on a race between the achievements of the battlefield and the inexorable deterioration of the hammered silver coinage. Things came to a head late in 1694 when confidence was lost in the silver coinage, thus triggering off the great crisis which has become known to posterity as the 'Great Recoinage Crisis'.[11]

Given this situation, it was unfortunate that in addition to the growing animus against the city among certain sections of the landed-class, the city itself was divided. Conflict centered over the capital structure of the East India Company: since about 1679, the privileged position of the limited circle of East India equity holders who reaped handsome dividends from an enterprise which was heavily dependent on fixed interest capital had been under attack. By the 1690s the dislocation of foreign commerce had sharpened the issues of the Company's capital structure and of its monopoly rights to the trade. The opposition syndicates desired either admission into the company or entry to the trade in order to employ resources rendered redundant by wartime dislocation of European trade. The fight for the East India trade did not directly affect the war effort in the 1690s, although it caused a serious run on banks in 1701, while the furore aroused by the electioneering of the New Company members in 1700–1 added something to William's difficulties in diverting the concern of the country gentlemen from the purge of war ministers and war profiteers to the realities of the deteriorating situation in Europe. During the war years of the 1690s the attack on the East India Company was more a manifestation and less an aggravation of the strains imposed on London by the war.[12]

It is only in this way that a semblance of coherence can be introduced into this welter of remittances, party heats, trade balances, factions and syndicates. Were there city counterparts to the disaffected lesser Tory gentry in the country at large? More specifically, did the operations of government finance lead to a significant redistribution of business within the city? Do such redistributions explain, on the negative side, the disruptive pressures for extending the East India Company, and on the positive side, help to explain how such flotations as the Bank of England were successfully achieved?

Unapologetically, therefore, this essay concludes a volume on sixteenth- and seventeenth-century urban history by analysing aspects of urban institutions in general, and problems of the mercantile community in particular, which were to be characteristic of the eighteenth century. Where typically the historian of the medieval merchant class would focus on questions of gild monopoly, gild exclusiveness, and municipal control, a historian of the London mercantile community of the later seventeenth century must be concerned with the new world of stocks and shares, and with the increasingly large indirect intervention of the government in the workings of the economy which determined, in as yet unspecified ways, the distribution of prosperity and depression within that community. Taking our cue from the exotic Thomas Pitt, interloper in the East India trade in the 1680s and 1690s, later governor of Madras, and one of the earliest of the Nabobs, we must draw our analogies from the problems which faced his illustrious descendants. The younger Pitt would have recognized the problems facing Lowndes and Godolphin.

It would be as well to cling to the problem of the manner in which the impact of war determined the distribution of prosperity and depression: without such a unifying preoccupation a study of merchants is apt to degenerate into casual genealogical irrelevance or context-less particularity. Merchants present the historian with a problem of approach no less difficult than that posed by the long suffering peasantries of *ancien régime* Europe, or the restive *menu peuple* of the Revolutionary decades. Inarticulate the merchants certainly were not, as their partisan petitions abundantly demonstrate, but the humdrum diurnal round of remittance, discount, brokerage, commission, the perpetual estimation of profit and loss, together with the more spectacular coups of entrepreneurial skill, seldom excited detailed comment. What mercantile diffidence concealed, the destruction of business records compounded. No less than in the histories of peasants and artisans, therefore, the interpretation of mercantile behaviour must depend upon inferences derived from an analysis of action in the context of changing material circumstances.

How can one then define the impact of the Nine Years War upon trade, and how did that impact relate to the experience of different merchant groups within the London mercantile community? The impact of the war was threefold: most obviously it created a demand for naval stores which guaranteed that resources in the Baltic trades— bringing iron from Stockholm and Gothenburg, and hemp, potash and flax from Riga, Narva, Reval and Danzig—were fully employed meeting naval needs. Imports of all these commodities were considerably higher in 1696, for instance, than in the years 1681 and 1685 respectively.[13]

In the second place, and equally obviously, war precipitated the

Caribbean and Levant trades into an uncertain, and ultimately, disastrous period of costly delays, of narrower speculative margins as shipment depended more and more on the arrival and departures of convoys, and less and less on the course of market opportunities, and of outright loss at the hands of both the privateers and the elements. The Levant merchants suffered losses—which were somewhat improbably estimated at £600,000—in 1693 when the combined Brest and Toulon fleets attacked the Dutch and English Turkey fleet off Lagos Bay. The three Turkey ships which had escaped in 1693 and which had sought refuge in Ireland were grounded off Gibraltar in 1694 when they had again sailed out for the Levant. The Turkey merchants who 'had shut up their shops and warehouses from vending any Turkey commodities' on hearing the news could not have foreseen the happier sequel of 1695 when salvage operations were successfully undertaken.[14]

As for the sugar merchants, they put their losses for the period 1694–5 alone as amounting to £664,100—and their estimates here deserve to be taken seriously—while for the whole war period down to 1695 the Royal African Company calculated its corporate losses at £169,890. The privateering attack on English commerce was not directly responsible for all these losses. Difficulty was encountered in providing adequate naval resources for seasonal convoying requirements: optimal seasonal sailing patterns were thus disrupted. In this connexion, the sugar merchants distinguished between the loss of £187,000 worth of cargo in the hurricanes of 1694 'which was occasioned by the detaining our ships here five months after the time prefixed, and so forced to be winter ships which was the loss of them', and the £200,000 worth of losses sustained in the Soundings at the hands of Nesmond in 1695. A similar combination of circumstances brought heavy losses to the East India Company: for 1695 alone, the company put its losses at £1,500,000.[15]

Thirdly, and perhaps less obviously, the remittance burden implies a significant redistribution of trade within the business community. These redistributions follow from the impact such remittances must have on trade if they are to be effected; in this case, capacity has to be created abroad out of which the needs of the army abroad can be met. This capacity is created by a fall in English import purchases—a movement which releases productive resources abroad—and by an increase in English export sales which may be regarded as supplementing foreign capacity. Simultaneously, trade movements which created the desired capacity effects—namely falling imports and rising exports—provide the necessary surplus on the balance of payments out of which the remittance may be financed.[16]

Arcane theory is perhaps best illustrated by reference to actual practice: how were these foreign remittances handled in London? The first move was always the issue of government I.O.U.s—or 'tallies'—to the remittance contractors who were to deliver funds abroad at a pre-fixed rate of exchange. Usually the remittance contractors instructed foreign bankers to make funds available to the army paymasters, and they then proceeded to purchase bills of exchange, which, after acceptance by the drawees abroad, could be cashed to reimburse the bankers. All our detailed information on these operations comes from the Ledgers and Journals of the Bank of England which handled, from 1694 to 1696, all the subsistence payments, the Savoy subsidy and the Cadiz remittances to finance Russell's epoch-making expedition to the Mediterranean in the years 1694-5. Of the subsistence payments, 61 per cent between October 1694 and April 1695 were effected through bills drawn on Antwerp or Amsterdam; the proceeds of these were collected directly from the drawees. A significant proportion of these payments were remitted, however, in bills drawn on the German ports of Hamburg and Bremen (20 per cent), on the Iberian ports of Oporto, Lisbon, Madrid, Cadiz and Seville (18·5 per cent), and on the Mediterranean capitals of Leghorn, Turin, Genoa and Venice (6·5 per cent). These bills were not negotiable unless accepted by the drawees; thus the bank established a network of correspondents in all these commercial centres who, in return for a commission, tendered these bills for acceptance. Once accepted, these agents posted the bills to the Low Countries where they were sold to merchants requiring remittance to any of these latter centres, or to any port where such bills were negotiable.[17]

At one level, therefore, one could regard the whole operation as an interception of foreign credits earned by English export sales which otherwise could have been used to purchase commodity imports and services, to finance capital export, or to effect bullion inflow. 'Exchange interception' was but one level at which the mechanics of transfer were operative. Simultaneously, part of the current tax proceeds was being paid to the remitters, thus cancelling government I.O.U.s. Out of one cycle, therefore, of getting and spending, English nationals had been prevented from consuming and/or investing as much as previously. If we assume, unrealistically for the purposes of exposition that this fall in consumption is focused entirely on imports, then the remittance would be effected entirely out of the ensuing credit balance of maintained exports over reduced imports. It would be indeed as if the Hidden Hand, at the promptings of the English government, was neatly instructing those sectors abroad catering previously for English import needs to switch their productive efforts to the needs of the army in the Low Countries.

Things were certainly not so simple. For one thing, the volume of imports was not sufficiently compressible downwards; for another, the deflation of internal consumption resulted in a fall in the consumption of *both* import and domestic output, and deflation was thus inevitable in England. Inflation was equally inevitable in the Low Countries: here the expenditures of the Paymasters were in effect moving ahead of the contraction and release of resources from those sectors dependent on English import purchases—whether directly or indirectly. Rising prices abroad, falling prices at home, would help to increase export sales and reduce imports; on the other hand the deterioration in the terms of trade would paradoxically increase the strain of effecting transfer in real terms. In the modern world the co-operation of central banks working through monetary and fiscal devices can minimize such effects, but in a seventeenth-century world which lacked such institutions it is difficult to see how the problem of transfer could be surmounted without some bullion outflow in the transferring country. Bullion flows result in monetary contraction and expansion in the transferring and recipient country respectively, thus bringing about the desired balance on the trade account out of which the remittances can be financed.

All the evidence suggests that this was precisely what happened in the 1690s. Against the inactivity of the English mint in the years prior to the Recoinage, the high level of bullion reserves in the Amsterdam Wisselbank stands in marked contrast.[18] Again, the downward drift of sterling exchange indicates the pressure on the English balance of payments (see Table 22); such a movement amounted to an increasing tariff in favour of English exports, as the foreign exchange costs of our exports fell, and that of our imports increased.[19] Exports, at least for a time, were further encouraged by the 'easy money' conditions which obtained exclusively in the export sector. These conditions arose from the fact that the remitters were purchasing from the exporters those future promises to pay in the form of bills of exchange drawn by the latter on their foreign customers, for ready money.

TABLE 22 *London trade during the later seventeenth century**

(1) Year	(2) Wine imports (in Tuns)	(3) Remittances £m.	(4) Sterling Exchange %	(5) Imports £m	(5) Exports £m	(6) Hallage Receipts £
1680	15,415		+1·85	2·77	2·70	1,795
1681	14,679		+1·12	2·31	2·30	1,741
1682	21,153		+0·78	3·42	2·30	2,000
1683	23,737		+2·81	3·24	2·50	2,006
1684	14,270		+0·70	3·44	2·40	1,831
1685	18,506		+1·54	3·16	2·10	1,747
1686	18,112		+2·98	2·87	2·20	1,789
1687	20,471		+3·83	3·52	2·60	1,934
1688	19,176		+1·57	2·70	2·30	1,972
1689	17,058	0·17		2·44	1·60	1,898
1690	7,149	0·80		2·27	2·10	2,081
1691	9,553	0·61	−2·65	3·67	2·20	2,203
1692	14,074	0·72	−2·22	3·08	2·90	2,164
1693	15,704	1·10	−5·20	2·30	2·30	2,028
1694	19,068	1·35	−8·00	2·50	2·40	2,051
1695	11,257	1·70	−17·27	2·40	2·80	1,931
1696	13,878	0·90	−9·16	3·08	2·60	1,824
1697	12,108	0·75	+1·30	2·50	1·90	1,859
1698	12,460	0·57	−0·06	2·35	2·80	2,032
1699	19,445	0·00	+0·10	3·20	2·85	2,327

* Figures throughout are given for fiscal years running from 29 September to 29 September, and *ending in the years shown*. Totals are rounded to the nearest £10,000 as columns 3 and 5, and to the nearest £1 in column 6. Sources for the figures contained under (2) and (5) are found in note 21. The import series under (5) relates to all imports exclusive of wine imports and of all imports from the Atlantic and Caribbean colonies. Imports from the East Indies are included.

Sources for the figures given under (3) are found in note 9.

The percentages set out in (4) show the percentage deviation of sterling above (+) and below (−) the par rate of sterling in terms of Dutch currency. Exchange rate quotations have been averaged; for the source of these quotations, see note 19.

For details of the Hallage receipts see note 2.

Normally, the exporters themselves would have had to carry a higher proportion of these credits, at least in part, until maturation. Since exporters normally found ready buyers of their bills in the remittance contractors, they did not have to wait for their money. Credit re-

TABLE 23 *London cloth exports to Germany, Holland, Flanders and France for 1685–8 and 1694–7*[*]

	1685	1686	1687	1688	1694	1695	1696	1697
Hamburg	6,487	9,604	8,662	7,532	14,313	18,424	11,014	12,084
Bremen	—	28	—	—	3,955	4,947	4,412	1,879
Amsterdam	902	1,684	969	956	3,014	1,263	250	515
Rotterdam	3,606	3,284	1,627	1,880	7,563	16,873	13,391	12,582
Bruges	1,478	759	1,431	2,133	415	3,391	3,416	4,636
'Flanders'	1,848	2,140	1,297	2,694	4,217	6,804	5,085	3,507
Dunkirk	2,000	1,825	2,859	172	—	—	—	—
Caen	47	35	—	—	—	—	—	—
St Vallery	4,968	2,796	2,208	184	—	—	—	—
Dieppe	—	32	—	—	—	—	—	—
Calais	567	1,569	973	124	—	—	—	—
St Malo	55	339	—	—	—	—	—	—
Rouen	195	54	—	—	—	—	—	—
Bordeaux	182	230	—	—	—	—	—	—
Nantes	4	60	—	—	—	—	—	—
Bayon	—	82	32	—	—	—	—	—
'France'	2,523	3,405	4,208	331	—	—	—	—
Total	24,862	27,926	24,266	18,006	33,477	51,702	37,568	35,203

Sources: P.R.O., E. 190/126/1, 136/6, 140/7, 144/1, 149/9, 150/5, 156/5, 159/1.
  * These totals are expressed in notional long cloth equivalents. The port books record the exports of four kinds of old drapery exports, namely: long, short and spanish cloths, and kerseys; use has been made of customs valuations for 1698 to convert all these into long cloth equivalents (see Customs 3/1).

quirements were minimal and this encouraged the small fry of the mercantile community to handle exports.[20]

The statistical evidence of London trade confirms these predicted effects.[21] The level of domestic exports on the one hand, and the total of imports from East India and from Europe, excluding wines, on the other, rose and fell respectively from an estimated average of £2·3 m and £3·1 m in the peace years of the 1680s, to £2·5 m and £2·54 m respectively during the heavy remittance years of 1690 and 1692 to 1698. Wine imports which had averaged 18,250 tuns in the peace years of the 1680s were down to an average of 12,084 tuns during the war years of the 1690s (see Table 22). Figures culled from London port books, and set out in Table 23, show how old drapery exports boomed in the markets of Near Europe which were receiving English transfers: average old drapery sales from 1694 to 1697 were 68 per cent up on the average level of those from 1685 to 1688.[22]

A part of the rise in exports to Germany and the Low Countries was the bilateral counterpart of increasing import purchases from these markets in place of supplies previously obtained from France—trade with which was now prohibited.[23] It is also possible that English exports benefited to some degree from a modest ground swell of economic recovery for which considerable evidence now exists;[24] on the other hand, it is certainly the remittances which explain the greater part of the increase in the sales of the Old Drapery to the markets of Near Europe.

Trade averages not only conceal sectoral changes, they abstract wholly from annual fluctuations, and ignore capital movements which are equally relevant in determining the balance of payments. Both are fascinating in their own right and must await fuller treatment elsewhere; but two things deserve notice. In the first place, with regard to the fluctuations, the export performance was hampered when easy money conditions no longer prevailed in the export sector. The remitters' capacity to purchase bills with ready cash depended upon the liquidity of the government. The government's financial stability on the other hand was being eroded by the revenue shortfall caused by the fall in high yielding imports which was the necessary corollary of transfer. Hence the acute credit crisis of 1693–4; difficulty was experienced in finding cash for the remitters, so recourse had to be made to bills drawn by Richard Hill, the deputy paymaster of the army in Flanders, on Ranelagh, the paymaster general, in London. Hill raised money by selling these promises to pay in the Low Countries; these bills were then held until maturity.[25] While this operation at least had the merit of obtaining foreign accommodation, it had the disadvantage of removing the direct stimulus of easy money in the English export sector. In this context, the establishment of the Bank of England was vital in resolving this impasse; like Godolphin's annuities of the next decade, it had the important effect of broadening the base of public income and shifting it away from a dangerous dependence upon customs revenues which, quite apart from privateering, was bound to contract if remittances were to be effected.

Secondly, the current strain of meeting the foreign exchange bill was eased by income and capital movements into England. The implication of Dr Dickson's work is that foreign holdings in the 'funds' were not large in these years;[26] on the other hand, a detailed analysis of the port books reveals that it was in the 1690s that the handling of London exports was thoroughly cosmopolitanized. It is in these years that one sees the Huguenot refugees of the 1680s, and German, Baltic and Dutch firms which came in in the 1690s, gaining a significant hold over London trade. By 1695, these foreign firms had increased their hold over the Old Drapery exports from under 5 per cent in the 1680s to 32 per cent.[27] Contemporaries attributed this inflow to the removal of the Merchant Adventurers'—or Hamburg Company's— monopoly in 1689.[28] Whatever the explanation, there can be no doubt that such an inflow was an important accession of strength to the London mercantile community and a significant source of foreign exchange. The contract of the East India Company with the Armenians, by which they undertook to handle the company's cloth exports, had similar implications, but on a smaller scale.[29]

It is quite one thing to identify the impact of war upon the different branches of London's trade, and quite another to perceive how it affected the fortunes of different merchant groups. Fortunately, a systematic analysis of port books shows that the mercantile community was highly specialized, and since the great majority of merchants concentrated their trading investments in activities which generally correspond to a specific branch of trade, and diversified in directions related to their specialisms, it is possible to equate the experience of specific trades with the fortunes of particular merchant groups.[30] Outside the Levant trade the composite import/export merchant appears to have been the exception rather than the rule. Evidently, the great majority of the merchants preferred to trade one way, without the preoccupation of either securing returns for exports or of furnishing credits for import purchases by investment in goods. Many of the wealthy London import merchants indirectly financed provincial exports and the exports of many of the London export merchants by purchasing bills from them drawn on foreign customers.

In this way, importers built up supplies of foreign credits for ultimate investment in imports.[31]

Exceptions there were, of course, to these broad rules of specialization. Thus we have three merchants with very large turnovers in 1695–6 who were import/export merchants.[32] These were Benjamin Ayloff, who handled some £18,514 worth of exports, mainly to Baltic markets, in 1695, and who imported hemp, flax, linen, canvas and spruce yarn from the Baltic, which totalled some £13,166 net of customs and freight charges. Sir William Gore concentrated his activities on the markets of Germany and Holland; his exports, re-exports, and imports were all equally impressive in their value. In 1695, his exports, consisting of 369 Spanish cloths, 1,101 short, 389 long cloths, 17,981 lb of serge, totalled £24,000; his re-exports of tobacco and sugar totalled £6,500. In 1696, his linen imports can be valued at £28,872 prime cost. Thus, net of customs and freight Gore's turnover amounted to some £60,000. Our third example of the import/export firm, Meyer and Berenburg, is also drawn from the trades of Near Europe. This firm, the partners of which migrated to London in the later seventeenth century,[33] divided a total turnover of some £30,000 almost equally between imports on the one hand, and exports and re-exports on the other. The sum of £7,247 was invested in cloth exports to Hamburg, together with £1,197 in calfskin exports; a further £2,116 was invested in cloth exports to the Baltic ports, while smaller investments of some £175 each were destined for Spanish and Italian markets. These exports were supplemented by sugar and tobacco re-exports to Hamburg which amounted to some £2,000. Imports were made up entirely of linen imports which, net of customs and freight, amounted to £15,856.

Nor, indeed, were all merchants confined to working the commodities of a particular geographic area. Thus we find Sir Gilbert Heathcote with extensive interests in both the Caribbean sugar trade and in the naval stores trade from the Baltic. His imports in 1696 are distributed thus: 1,099 cwt of hemp from Danzig and Konigsberg; 134 tons of bar iron and 273 cwt of latten wire from Stockholm; 3,317 lb of cinnamon from Rotterdam; 4,866 cwt of muscovado sugar, 1,073 cwt of ginger, 18 tons of fustic, 300 lb of pimento, 53 bags of raw cotton, 14 tons of logwood, and 16,456 lb of indigo from the West Indies. These imports amounted to some £14,300 net of customs and freight. As an exporter he dispatched some £2,000 worth of cloth exports into the Baltic in 1695; he also supplied the miscellaneous needs of the

Jamaica planters, but the profuse character of these exports defies quantification.

These merchants, however, were exceptional. Despite the close interconnexions of the trading world where Russian hides were saleable in the markets of the Mediterranean, where German linens found a ready market in the English colonies and where colonial staples were re-exported to Europe,[34] the affairs of the great majority of the London merchants preponderated into one or other of three categories, namely export, re-export or import. The character of a merchant's geographic interests depended entirely upon which of these functions predominated in his line of business.

If predominantly an exporter, then simply as a reflection of the fact that English cloth, lead, tin and leatherware found a market anywhere in the world where the English merchant was free to trade, such a merchant's connexions were geographically very wide. Increasing wealth led to an extension of the geographic range of his connexions.

Three examples can be given to clothe the rather skeletal conclusions derived from the port books. When Nathaniel Denew, dyer of London, died in 1690 with a modest personal estate valued at £8,595, his connexions were confined wholly to Lisbon, Port Saint Mary, Alicante, Venice and Genoa. Investments in bays, serge and perpetuanoes remained undisposed of in the Iberian ports, while at Venice and Genoa, credits were outstanding in respect of Lisbon sugar exported to the former and Spanish iron to the latter. The proceeds of Denew's operations were returned in bills of exchange or in bullion ('pieces of eight'); there is no indication that Denew dealt in imports.[35]

In contrast with these modest operations, those of the Huguenot immigrant, Simon le Blanc, who died in 1709 with a personalty of £15,029 net of liabilities and desperate debts, provide an apt contrast. The mid-1690s see him handling substantial cloth exports to Poland, Holland, Germany, Spain, Portugal and Italy; of a total turnover of some £44,000, £33,000 was invested in exports to the German and Dutch markets. By the time of his death he had further extended the range of his connexions; apart from investments in the hands of Francis Ancillon at Brussels, David le Blanc, the brothers Vandersprangle and Isaac le Boulenger at Amsterdam, he had substantial dealings with Bernard Sein of Leghorn, Thomas Cook of Constantinople, and with the partners Dunster and Hayes, and Bird and Ratcliff at Aleppo. In keeping with the import/export character of Levant trading, le

Blanc dealt extensively in silk imports; thus we find in his inventory £6,117 7s 11d given as the proceeds of 'Turkey goods sold'.[36]

The same pattern emerges, albeit in a totally different context of plutocracy, from the affairs of Sir Peter Delmé. In the mid-1690s we find him exporting relatively modest consignments of cloth to Spain and Portugal, and importing wool from Bilbao. When he died in 1728, his personalty was valued at £217,212, with no allowance made for the 211 bags of mohair yarn and the 597 bales of silk remaining unsold in his warehouse. These could have been valued at anything between £100,000 and £200,000. Cloth in his warehouse was sold for over £7,000, while large stocks of cloth were either in transit to, or lying unsold at, Amsterdam (£528), Hamburg (£825), Cadiz (£1,768), Lisbon (£27,076), Constantinople (£25,320), Aleppo (£18,225) and Smyrna (£13,517). The range and amounts of debts were equally remarkable: at Cadiz, £395, Lisbon, £50,629, Rio de Janeiro, £509, Tripoli, £27, Smyrna, £1,100, Aleppo, £7,037 and Constantinople, £13,093.[37]

Merchants such as Denew, le Blanc and Delmé were clearly in the minority by the later seventeenth century. The great majority were either specialist importers or re-exporters. For these merchants the range of their connexions was usually confined to the requirements of a specific commodity or to a given trade area. We may surmise that this pattern was the result of the return of factors from the service of their London principals in foreign ports to establish themselves on their own account in London. Thus, for an ever-growing number of London merchants, the circle of their correspondents, the range of their market intelligence, and the character of their commodity expertise were limited, at least in the first instance, by the place of their factoring experience. Specialization was further accentuated by the immigration of the Huguenot merchants, who were themselves specialists in the wine, the silk, or the paper trades. It was always possible to take up any seasonal slack in the employment of resources by utilizing agents who normally played an ancillary role in handling the merchants' specialism. Thus the Baltic merchants could dispatch the odd speculative cargo of cloth or sugar to Hamburg or Amsterdam by using their agents there who normally purchased bills to cover the English trade deficit with the Baltic. Wine and fruit merchants could similarly use agents in Hamburg who normally furnished supplies of barrel staving. Sugar and tobacco merchants often exported cloth to the Mediterranean during the seasonal slack periods in these trades, but in these cases there would appear to be no obvious way in which their specialisms created the requisite circle of mercantile agents.

These generalizations again may be illustrated by the vignettes drawn from probate inventories. Etched deep upon the affairs of the Baltic merchant, Henry Haswell who died in 1689, net worth £8,967, were the credit difficulties of the Baltic trade. Like his fellow Baltic merchant, Henry Phill, Haswell was forced to seek extensive credit from his English suppliers, since he in turn had to meet bills for naval stores in the Baltic promptly and extend long credits both on his cloth sales there and on his sales of naval stores in England; assets of £24,510 had to be set against liabilities totalling £15,603 at the time of his death. His extensive dealings in potash and hemp which necessitated large advances in Danzig and Konigsberg, and which he supplied not only to the Thames basin market but also to Bristol, Liverpool, Lisbon and Seville, were only made possible, in part, by the credit extended to him by clothiers such as Christopher Lethieullier, Paris Slaughter, Robert Foot and James Boddington, and by the shipowners who freighted his imports. Haswell and Phill traded with the least favourable ratio between net worth and liabilities in the London merchant community.[38]

The character of affairs in the German and Central European trades is well illustrated by the business of two merchants, William Willis who died in 1706, net worth £20,747,[39] and Peter Vansittart, the immigrant merchant, who died in the same year worth £119,348 net in personal estate.[40] Willis had advances in the hands of agents in the Saxon linen manufacturing areas to secure the German linen which formed his major line of business; on a smaller scale he exported English cloth in return. Linen cloth imports were also one of Vansittart's specialities, but naturally his business was conducted on a vaster scale; he combined this with extensive sales of spice and dyestuffs the extent of which reached beyond the ports of Danzig, Hamburg, Bremen, and Amsterdam, where he had large accounts, to Vienna, Elverfeld, and Breslau. Small accounts were also outstanding at Leghorn and Lisbon.

To the south the character, and indeed, indirectly, the vicissitudes of the wine trade, are shown by the affairs of Adam Bellamy and John Newton. Both merchants died within a year of one another—in 1697 and 1698 respectively—Bellamy with net assets of £20,238,[41] and Newton with £12,999.[42] Wine was their major commodity, with cloth exports only amounting to a small percentage of their inventories. Bellamy was also active in the related Newfoundland fish trade: thus we find £1,042 invested in a quarter share of the *Rook* and cargo, in respect of which a bill of exchange was entered in his debts as 'item to Mr. Simon Cole by order of Samuel Shepheard being a bill from Newfoundland on Acc^t of the Rookes cargo'. Newton had small interests in the Jamaica trade by which he returned Spanish pieces of eight. Significantly, as we shall see below, both these merchants held large stock holdings in the Bank of England; nor were they untypical of their group in having substantial shares in the *Antelope*, an interloping ship to the East Indies.[43]

Details of specialist importers from the Mediterranean are not available,[44] but a wealth of material exists in the Inventories for the colonial trades in general, and for the tobacco trade in particular. Taken together, the affairs of William Paggen, whose inventory of 1691 gives a net worth of £12,142, that of John Cary who died in 1701 with a net personalty of £22,000, and that of Francis Levett, whose net worth was calculated at £19,331 when he died in 1705, supply a detailed picture of the distribution of tobacco from quay-side to foreign and home consumers.[45]

Paggen's affairs show how tobacco bulk imports—possibly to cope with the heavy burden of duty—were divided into shares which ranged from quarter shares to ones of three-tenths, seven thirty-seconds and three-sixteenths. In respect of each bulk cargo one shareholder paid customs and freight; he was reimbursed in due course by his other partners. Paggen's affairs were consequently a tangle of mutual indebtedness on these accounts of custom and freight: he received payments for customs and freight expended on 1,984 hogsheads of tobacco owned in shares by other tobacco merchants, while Paggen's executors paid out on these accounts £3,487 in respect of 1,320 hogshead imported on his own account and risk.

The orientation of Paggen's business was dominated by the import of tobacco into England and with meeting the tobacco planters' miscellaneous needs; to supply these Paggen invested in small quantities of German linen and French canvas. A smaller component of the business was directed towards the re-export trade in tobacco to Holland; of total proceeds of £6,942 on tobacco sales, £833 were receipts on Dutch sales for which Paggen possessed warehouses in the Isle of Wight to facilitate transhipment without breach of the requirements of the Acts of Trade. In general, however, the bulk of tobacco re-exports were handled by the partnership of John and

Thomas Cary whose affairs are illuminated by the senior partner's inventory of 1701. Figures of tobacco exports for the scarcity year 1695, when 3,894,864 lb were re-exported, show that this firm accounted for 1·3 m lb re-exports to the markets of Holland, Germany and the Baltic.[46]

In London, sales were handled by great wholesale concerns of which the affairs of Francis Levett supply graphic illustration. He traded as a partner in the partnership of 'Sir Richard Levett and Company'— the total net worth of which in 1705 was £36,962. London sales were clearly the most important—in 1705 £10,089 was realized in London sales—but provincial sales were by no means negligible: thus between 1705 and 1708, £2,959 was realized on the partnership account at Gainsborough, £1,139 at Boston, £2,618 at Beverley, £1,712 at Lenton and £767 at Houlden.

Such illuminating detail is not available for the sugar trades, but we do have the inventory of Robert Heysham, one of the great sugar merchants, who died in 1727 with a net personalty of £19,960; this gives an inadequate indication of his true worth for he had extensive landed estates. Port Books of the mid-1690s show that like the tobacco trade, sugar re-exports were a highly specialized business.[47] Joseph Morewood and Stephen Skinner dominated the trade, exporting respectively 11,400 cwt and 10,500 cwt of sugar out of a total re-export of 46,751 cwt.[48]

This pattern of specialization enables us, therefore, to infer the fortunes of different merchant groups from the course of wartime trade. Bringing together the implications of our previous analysis of the impact of war, in which the redistributive impact of remittances was emphasized, we would expect that the resources of the exporters, with their well-dispersed connexions, together with the resources of the merchants of Near Europe, would have been fully employed in handling the remittance-induced export boom. The statistics of foreign trade are dramatically confirmed by the course of the 'Hallage' yield in the London cloth markets; these reached record levels in the 1690s, and were to do so again for much the same reasons during the Spanish Succession War of the next decade.[49] Importers of the staples of Near Europe would have experienced considerable contraction in the volume of their imports but they had the connexions to switch their activities smoothly into exports, the proceeds of which they could sell in part to the remitters. To the north, government needs guaranteed that the resources of the Baltic merchants were fully stretched not only supplying the naval yards, but also in shouldering the strain of lengthening payment dates.

Elsewhere, merchant groups experienced crisis; it is unnecessary to elaborate further the experience of the Levant and sugar merchants but the predicament of the wine merchants deserves further comment. Unlike the former two groups, these merchants experienced acute resource redundancy without the heavy losses which the former suffered. All the circumstantial evidence suggests that wine imports fell in response to falling demand at home; this would appear reasonable given the burden of the Land Tax. There were no large remittances to the Iberian peninsula during the Nine Years War, so falling wine imports cannot be interpreted as the bilateral concomitant of transfer. It is true that the prohibition of French wine imports reduced for a time total wine supplies, but Portuguese and Spanish wine production expanded rapidly, and when peace came, imports into London from these latter sources alone reattained from 1699 to 1701, the record levels of the 1680s.[50] This in itself would suggest that it was English demand conditions which determined import levels. In so far as England purchased less wine from the wine producers, their incomes suffered, and they could purchase less exports. Contraction in this sector was therefore absolute. Of course things were not wholly determined in this simple bilateral manner. Income inflation in the Low Countries must certainly have increased wine consumption there in response to English remittances; exporters of cloth could have continued to find markets for their cloths among the wine producers, therefore, and sold the resulting bills to the remitters who could send them to Amsterdam for negotiation with Dutch merchants who wished to pay for larger wine imports. The fact that the Bank of England was able to finance nearly one-fifth of the Flanders remittances in Iberian bills indicates that something like this multilateral relationship did in fact obtain.

Exports to the wine-producing regions of Europe may not, therefore, have contracted to the degree indicated by the fall in wine imports, but this hardly helped the predicament of the specialist wine importer. At a time of rising insurance and freight charges, volume was falling while prices, regulated by proclamation, appear to have remained stable.[51] The war effort was therefore paid for, in part, at the expense of wine consumption; the wine merchants suffered as a result.

*   *   *

In considering the ways in which the wine merchants responded to this predicament of dead trade one must bear in mind both the availability and acceptability of alternative employments for their funds. So far we have given some precision to Houghton's interpretation of the stock boom of the 1690s that 'trade being obstructed at sea, few that had money were willing it should be idle, and a great many that wanted employments studied how to dispose of their money'; we have defined from which point of the trading compass pressure on investment outlets was most acute. It is just as important to remember, however, that Houghton stressed the 'liquidity' and capital security dimensions of asset appraisal in determining the character of the outcome as much as the role of footloose funds in occasioning it. In order 'that they might be able to command it whensoever they had occasion', he explains, joint stocks were preferred to 'laying out the same in lands, houses or commodities' since the former were 'more easily shifted from hand to hand'.[52] We need, therefore, to examine both the availability and relative desirability of different opportunities within the three major types of investment outlets which presented themselves to prospective investors at the end of the seventeenth century. These were: first, direct investment in real assets—land, property, shipping; second, lending on the security of real assets: here we have bottomry bonds for loans secured on ships, respondentia bonds if secured on the cargo, and mortgages for loans secured on real estate. Finally, there is a diverse category where lending either took the form of a capitalization of future income stream, or was secured either by corporate and private creditworthiness, or by the future taxation receipts of municipal and national government. To the former belong the joint stocks of East India and Royal African Companies and the Bank of England; to the latter the fixed interest dated bonds of private individuals and of corporate bodies such as the great trading companies and the London livery companies, and the tallies of anticipation struck on the proceeds of future tax collection by the government.[53]

Some of these outlets are quickly dealt with: bottomry and respondentia bonds were highly speculative and did not meet the requirement of capital security. In any case, their volume was likely to have contracted with the trade depression. Of the thirty-eight merchants[54] from 1680 to 1735 whose affairs may be closely studied from inventories, only Sir John Fellowes, the slaver whose net worth was put at £239,596 in 1720, held large sums in bottomry.[55] These amounted to £16,450; added to his inventory was the significant rider that: 'I apprehend there may be a considerable Loss on the Adventures ... besides what may happen on the Bottomries, by Insufficiency of the Borrowers, as well as Losses at Sea.' Such risks also diminished the attractions of investment in shipping shares, and explain why ship ownership was spread wide both within and without the mercantile community. Of our sample group of merchants[56] not more than 5 per cent of their non-trade investments, calculated at present values, was held in shipping shares. Here again shipping utilization, and thus shipping income, was probably reduced by the dislocation of overseas commerce although allowance must be made for the extensive ton-nages hired by the government for the Irish campaigns from 1689 to 1691, and for the 'Descents' of 1692 and 1693. Nor would shipping shares, being depreciating assets, and given the high risks of wartime loss during a period of expensive, inadequate and unreliable insurance cover, have provided a suitable investment outlet for merchants seeking capital security.

The availability and desirability of investment opportunities in real estate is more problematical. Until more work has been done syste-matically on the Close Rolls and on the Feet of Fines it is at present difficult to say more than that it would appear improbable that sellers with acceptable propositions were conveniently available in sufficient numbers to solve the problems of the wine merchants. In the light of current teachings on the land market, such propositions would not have been attractive anyway: merchants, it is thought, could obtain greater rates of return on the new innovations of 'Revolution Finance' than on land purchases which now bore the burdens of the land tax. This left the greater landed magnates—who, for reasons of scale and access to external sources of income, were better equipped to weather the economic storms—to expand their estates at the expense of the landholdings both of the lesser gentry and of the peasantry who were less resilient in face of high taxation and fluctuating produce prices.[57]

Since, however, the capital value of land during these war years appears to have been falling both in terms of the number of years' purchase which determined capitalization and possibly in terms of the net yields which were being capitalized, it would be as well to suspend judgment as to whether divergent yields between land and government paper did in fact confront prospective purchasers.[58] In this situation purchasers could have been enticed by the prospects of higher future yields on their current investments: the war could not last for ever and the easing of the rate of the land tax with the return of peace would lead to a corresponding rise in net yield. Possibly the separation of land from mercantile society, which is so frequently dated to the period from 1688 to 1714, came about in fact between 1660 and 1688, when, simultaneously with a marked reduction in the volume of royal land sales, and with a depression in agriculture, the expansion of English overseas trade offered the opportunity for the reinvestment of trade profits. Conceivably, in the subsequent war years, this trend was reversed.

There are other considerations, of course, which could have exercised contradictory influences. On the supply side, the great magnates, for social reasons, may have been prepared to tolerate lower current yields than prospective merchant purchasers and this could have established a floor below which capital values could not fall. Yet again, low capital values could make potential sellers reluctant to sell until better times. On the demand side, merchants caught in mid-career by the vagaries of war may not have been prepared to divert their resources away from trade into land given the degree of supervision demanded by such investments; on the other hand, older merchants could well have hastened their departure from trade into gentility as war telescoped the natural length of their mercantile careers.

The evidence which can be marshalled at present is certainly too limited to resolve these problems, but material contained in inventories, supplemented by individual cases, indicates the continued readiness of merchants to invest in land: there is no obvious indication that land- and stock-holding were in any way exclusive of one another, or that landed investment declined after 1688.[59]

Even more darkness surrounds the question of urban property. In the city of London itself, it is quite clear that a large proportion of property was held in private freehold: at most corporate bodies such as the City Corporation, the great hospitals and the Livery Companies, held 30 per cent of all the houses in the city.[60] It is also clear from Oliver and Mills's survey—inadequate though it must be as the basis of any property map of the Restoration city—that some individuals did own blocs of urban property, although holdings of more than five houses were the exception rather than the rule.[61] The evidence of the inventories suggests that merchants rarely held a large percentage of their non-trade assets in either freehold or leasehold urban property. The only owner of a 'bloc' of urban property in the full meaning of the phrase was John Blunt, and he was not a foreign trade merchant.[62] In the case of freeholds, a high degree of supervision was required to maintain the value of the property: depreciation was rapid, judging from the normal fourteen to fifteen years purchase given for urban property; risk may have been high, from fire in particular. It was estimated that by 1690 only one-tenth of London houses were insured against fire.[63] Leasehold urban property was subject to all these difficulties, with the added disadvantage from the point of view of capital security that such investments were depreciating: with each rent payment the capital value of the lease fell. In the city property market of the later seventeenth century, the capital value of leasehold property must have been low in aggregate because in areas devastated by the Great Fire, long building leases of between forty and sixty years had been granted.[64] It is reasonable to suppose, therefore, that fag-end leases existed in respect of a great deal of London property. All these factors may help to explain why in the affairs of the merchants extracted from the Orphans' Inventories, the present value of urban leasehold property amounts to no more than 6 per cent of their non-trade investments.[65]

Mortgages do not appear to have exercised a greater degree of attraction for the merchant investors in our sample: only 6 per cent of their non-trade assets were in mortgages, while no South Sea Director is given as a mortgage holder. The absence of a comprehensive land register which makes the task of a social historian very difficult also appears to have perplexed investors: other than personal knowledge and common repute it was impossible to determine whether a prospective land or property security was encumbered with previous borrowings. The lamentations and exhortations of the pamphleteers on this score are confirmed by the experiences of some of the merchants in our sample who invested in this form of asset. The executors of John Woolfe, the Russia and Levant merchant, had to obtain a decree in chancery to liquidate £3,818 in respect of a mortgage from Sir William Leman;[66] Peter Vansittart had lent £2,000 on mortgage of which we read in his inventory that 'the intestate [had] expended severall sums of money for the obteyning possession of part of the mortgaged premisses and there being severall suits now depending in the court of chancery by severall persons who claim severall sums of money as chargeable upon the said premisses'.[67] It is true that since the early seventeenth century intermediaries such as scriveners had developed as land agents and mortgage brokers in London,[68] but the bulk of their business, at least in the second half of the seventeenth century, was engaged in expediting mortgage loans between gentle-men. In a sample of mortgages between 1660 and 1740, drawn from the schedules of the National Registry of Archives and—adding new borrowings and assignments—totalling over £1·2 m, the total of mercantile lending on mortgage was exceedingly small; the over-whelming bulk of mortgage borrowing occurred between members of the landed class.[69] This would suggest that, to a considerable extent, the mortgage market was largely independent of supplies of funds originating from the mercantile capital market. Any putative diversion of funds from mortgages into the 'Funds' came about, not through the diversion of mercantile funds, but rather through that of landed savings. Symbolically, the rise of the West End banks of the early eighteenth century institutionalized an informal separation of these capital markets which had long existed.[70]

It was in the stocks and shares of city companies, and in government lending, that the bulk of the overseas merchants' investments was concentrated; such 'paper' securities accounted for nearly 85 per cent of the non-trade, non-freehold, investments of the twenty-eight merchants in our sample.[71] Partly as a result of the relative size of the respective concerns, but also for reasons of asset preference, port-folios were dominated by holdings in the Bank of England, in the East India Company, and later, in the South Sea Company; of the paper investment as defined above, 66·6 per cent belonged to these three corporations. Government paper, including tallies, exchequer bills, annuities, departmental paper and lotteries, accounted for a mere 22·8 per cent of this sample of merchants' investment.[72] Of course, such sampling based on inventories drawn up in both war and peace years is inevitably biased against government paper: the volume of tallies contracted in peacetime, while the volume of private joint stocks was not affected in this way by the chronology of war and peace. Annuities were also self-liquidating and any still picture or cross-section of investment inevitably understates the capital value of funds committed to leases and annuities in comparison with growth stocks.[73]

Despite this difficulty, the validity of the above picture is substanti-ally confirmed by an analysis of exchequer records for the fiscal year 1692–3. The overseas merchants contributed £93,924 on the Land Tax, £45,100 on the Poll Tax, and £65,070 in the Tontine Loan. A mere £12,700 was invested in annuities. The typical pattern was the investment of a few hundred pounds by many individuals spread widely throughout the mercantile community, with some great merchant such as Sir William Gore holding substantial amounts across the whole range of government securities.[74] Small individual amounts held across a wide range of government securities could, of course, add up to considerable totals of merchant holdings in government paper. In 1692–3, this totalled £216,794, but this was still smaller than the £332,550 invested by merchants in the Bank of England in 1694, and substantially smaller than the £562,000 subscribed to the East India loan of 1698.[75]

Par excellence, therefore, Bank and East India stock were the dominant passive investments of the overseas trading merchants; nor is it difficult to perceive the reasons why. Facility of investment was greatly enhanced by the system of 'calls' under which subscriptions were paid in over a period of time by instalments. It was thus possible to undertake investment out of the proceeds of future maturing trade credits rather than from merely such cash balances as were immediately available. This was not the case in exchequer procedures, and it was consequently more difficult to redeploy resources from trade into government paper. From the point of view of capital security, the prospect of future banking and trading profits offered the promise of capital growth, while investors could influence the conduct of business through the General Courts, the Committees and Directorates of these corporations. Above all, stocks were readily saleable to third parties on the embryonic stock market which had emerged in the later seventeenth century.[76] Unlike tallies, whose attractiveness depended upon the particular fortunes of the funds which were earmarked for their redemption and on the serial numbers which determined the holder's place in the queue for repayment, each bloc of stock was as good as another; no lengthy process of verification was necessary prior to transfer. Extensive deals in tallies were usually the preserves of great merchants with government connexions, and with possibly, therefore, a degree of expert knowledge as to the state of the tax funds. They also had the reserves to weather the great crisis periods of short-term government finance, when large discounts emerged on illiquid tallies. Indeed, these great merchants appear to have been purchasers of tallies during crisis years, presumably with a view to pocketing fat gross redemption yields on heavily depreciated tally purchases when eventually the government was able to cancel them at par.[77] Annuities offered an attractive rate of return at 14 per cent, but they were essentially income rather than growth investments; like leases, their capital values fell with each annual repayment. Nor were they readily sold; the historian of the English Financial Revolution has written that 'transfers of annuities resembled in length and complexity a conveyance of land'.[78]

The significance of these asset preferences can be succinctly summarized in the following way: merchants contributed but 5·3 per cent to loans on the Land Tax in 1692–3; yet they accounted for 30 per cent of investments in both the Bank of England and East India subscriptions of 1694 and 1698 respectively. The Bank rapidly assumed the status of a blue-chip investment, as a correspondent amply testifies when he wrote to Thomas Pitt at Madras in 1708 that 'the Bank is at present shaken a little, not having recovered the shock given it by the Scotch invasion; but not only in my own opinion but of all my acquaintance, is thought the surest estate and scarce any money'd man but has a share which he looks upon as his nest egg'.[79]

Within the limits set by mercantile asset preference, it is quite clear that the wine merchants contributed a disproportionate share to the establishment of Revolution Finance. The basis for this conclusion is provided by a comparison of trade shares with investment contributions to the joint stocks of the Bank and the newly established East India Company, and to the miscellaneous Government borrowing of 1692–3. In calculating trade shares use has been made of the statistics of the Inspector General of Imports and Exports for 1698.[80] On the face of it, it would appear to have been more appropriate to have used those for the year 1697 as typical of conditions in the 1690s. This does not prove to be the case however; all the circumstantial evidence suggests that throughout this year England obtained substantial accommodation abroad in respect of remittance payments. The visible trade balance was nowhere near large enough in 1697 to have supplied the foreign exchange to pay subsistence in Flanders. The debts of 1697 were cleared in 1698, and this is why 1698 was a year of high exports and low imports (see Table 22 p. 323). For this reason, 1698 may be regarded as fairly representative of trade shares in the 1690s with the proviso that it may be a little generous to the long-distance trades. Minor adjustments have been made to the figures to remove trade shares which were effected on the corporate account of the Royal Africa Company. For this same reason the East India trade has been excluded from these calculations. The results are set out as follows:

TABLE 24 *Business shares and investment in the Bank of England, the East India Loan and government lending 1692–3*

Trade	% Business	% Investment in Bank of England	% Investment in East India Loan	% Investment in Government Securities
Colonial	17·98	4·7	11·5	16·9
Baltic	8·90	10·2	16·7	4·34
Near Europe	41·33	25·7	22·7	24·63
Iberian Pen.	17·96	30·3	29·7⎫	
Western and			⎬	33·2
Central Med.	8·69	9·7	6·8⎭	
Turkey	5·12	18·4	12·3	20·0

The underlying relationship between resource utilization and investment in the 'Funds' comes out strongly in this tabulation. Merchants of Near Europe, where we have argued trade was booming, made a disproportionately small contribution to Revolution Finance in relation to their share of trade. In the case of the Iberian merchants— that is, mainly the wine merchants—the converse holds very clearly. Of course, this factor of utilization should not be allowed to explain everything. The evidence of assessments shows that the relative wealth level of the Levant merchants was higher, and that of the sugar merchants lower, than the average of the rest of the merchant community.[81] This may well have a great deal to do with the large contributions relative to trade shares made by the former, and the small contribution as measured in this way, made by the latter. It is also important to remember that although utilization was high in the trades of Near Europe, mercantile resources had been significantly supplemented by the inflow of foreign firms.[82] Finally, in respect of the wine merchants, circumstances favoured their contributions to the great flotations of 1694 and 1698: in both cases they must have had the proceeds of the transient recoveries of the wine trades in 1693– 1694 and 1696 available for investment. Even allowing for these considerations, however, the point appears to be well established that a relationship does exist between the depression in the wine trade and the contribution of the wine merchants to 'Revolution Finance'.

It was not until mid-1694, however, that the Bank of England was founded, and the East India Company loan was not floated until 1698 after an arduous campaign against the 'Old' East India Company. What, therefore, had the wine merchants done in the intervening years of dead trade? How prominent were they in the opposition to the old East India Company? Does the evidence exist to establish that interloping itself was a manifestation of the problems of merchants facing contracting wartime markets, in which the wine merchants suffered in particular?

The evidence suggests that from 1690 to 1692, when the wine trade was depressed and when acceptable government paper was not yet on the market, the wine merchants put their money into privateering. Of the fifty-two ships owned by London merchants which were granted letters of marque, and which are subsequently given as having made one or more captures, forty-one belonged to wine merchants and seven to Mediterranean merchants; of the remaining four, two belonged to Turkey merchants, leaving one each owned by the sugar merchants and the exporting merchants. Looking at the record of captures, the dominance of the wine merchants is even more striking: of 197 captures made by London-owned ships and adjudicated in the High Court of Admiralty, 160 were taken by privateers owned by the wine merchants. Where the great majority of London merchants appear to have taken out letters of marque to legalize such lucky bonuses of capture as presented themselves in the course of trade, the wine merchants fitted out full-time privateers; these were usually ships of small burthen. Thus we have, typically, the wine merchants John Degrave, Samuel Lockley, Peter Eaton, Francis Minshull, John Burridge, Samuel Eyre and Thomas Chambers operating the *Elizabeth and Katherine*; she was a 70-tonner, which, under her captain William Young, captured a total of nineteen ships in the month beginning 27 August 1691.[83]

From 1693 to 1695 the problems of the wine merchants eased when the recovery of the wine trade was followed by the diversion of funds into the Bank of England. Late in 1695, however, a new group of merchants, in which wine merchants predominated, emerged into view in opposition to the Old Company. Under the umbrella of the grant of a charter to the Scottish Indies Company—the Darien scheme— and fortified by the resolution of the Commons Committee of January

1694 that trade to the Indies was free unless the newly granted Royal Charter to the Old Company was confirmed by Act of Parliament, this group fitted out interlopers to the East and petitioned Parliament for the establishment of a regulated Company for the Indies trade on the model of the Levant Company.[84]

This group was 'new' in the sense that it was dominated by merchants—and by wine merchants in particular—in a way which had not been the case in the previous interloping episodes between 1679 and 1684 and between 1690 and 1693. In this group is found indeed the characteristic complement of Old East India hands; of the thirty signatories of petitions from this group who can be identified, four belonged to this category.[85] The Company never really solved the problem of controlling its servants in the East; friction was created by the conflicting calls of the Company's business and its servants' private trade ventures in the Eastern coasting trade. Profits of this trade were difficult to remit home; hence the temptation either to repatriate them covertly by the export of prohibited goods to England on the Company's own ships, or to trade with such interlopers as conveniently presented themselves. In addition there was full scope for dishonesty, extortion and double-dealing. Unlike European trades where the existence of price currents gave principals some check on the prices debited them by their agents, there was no such control in the East. Native merchants fared no better. Often they were obliged to pay the Company's servants—particularly the warehouse-keepers—a commission to accept their goods for the Company's account. Such stresses and strains meant that opposition syndicates to the East India Company could always count on finding expert assistance in both London and India.[86]

Nevertheless, with twenty-three petitioners, merchants predominated, and among them the largest single element consisted of ten Londoners who were connected with the wine trade.[87] This would appear to confirm the hypothesis that the parliamentary and interloping attack on the Old Company was connected with the strains of war. This in part must certainly have been true; on the other hand it is important to note that in previous attacks on the Company, while not being as dominant, the wine merchants had always played an important part. Thus of seventy-three interlopers proceeded against in the 1680s, forty-seven can be identified. Of these, thirty were London merchants, of whom eleven were wine merchants.[88] Between 1690 and 1693, of the twenty-seven persons who can be identified as being either members or associates of the opposition syndicate of these years, and aptly characterized by the Company as a 'Combination of Inter-lopers, Malcontents, quondam committeemen, and some Adventurers, that have sold their stocks at high rates, and would fain come in again at low rates, or [would] procure a New Company that they might rule the roost'—nine can be identified as wine merchants.[89] That the wine merchants were prominent in the opposition during the boom years of the wine trade of the 1680s does suggest that part of the reason they opposed the Company was that its charter gave it control of a trade which was a natural outlet for diversifying their activities. With trade credits in Spain and Portugal it was convenient to obtain bullion there and send it to the East. In this respect, one element of their opposition parallels that of the West India merchants to the monopoly of the Royal African Company which again stood in the way of what was for them a natural path of diversification.[90]

Not all the wine merchants, however, who invested in the East India loan in 1698 desired direct participation in the East India trade, while many of the protagonists of a regulated company in 1695–6 led the bid for control of the East India trade in 1698 which secured an essentially passive access to the trade on a joint-stock basis. Nor, in-deed, do protagonists of a regulated Company appear to have traded privately on any significant scale once the New Company was es-tablished.[91] The desire for new passive investment outlets was there-fore crucial, and the consistent feature of the 1690s was the failure of the Old Company to absorb it. At first sight this seems surprising, since the books of the Company would appear to confirm their claim that 'without restraint, cramping, or taking care for Rotations or changes in the East India Company the whole stock . . . is in a kindly, natural, and continual motion'.[92] Thus, in the seven-month period down to November 1693, stock sales totalled £366,822; with turn-over of this order of magnitude, there would appear to be abundant stock available for prospective purchasers. Closer examination reveals, however, that 77·6 per cent of these sales were to parties who had themselves sold stock at some time during this period. The manner in which sales and purchases were often carefully matched by individual holders suggests time-deals of various sorts in which speculation on the future price of stock was covered. Over three-quarters of the turnover in East India stock was accounted for, therefore, by the speculative shifting of stock among *existing* holders. In this the transactions of the jobbers such as Gabriel Glover, Robert Lancashire, Peter Monger and

William Shepheard accounted for a significant share of the total turn-over. Hence the repeated attack on stock-jobbing in East India Stock.[93]

The bitterness of opposition to the Old Company must have been sharpened by the fact that the ownership of its stock, both before and after the extension of its capital which was completed by early 1694, was predominantly non-mercantile. Prior to 1694, not more than 10 per cent of East India equity was held by merchants currently trading overseas in the middle years of the 1690s; even after the extension of the stock, the amount did not exceed 15 per cent. We have seen that in the case of both the Bank of England and the New East India sub-scription, this figure was about 30 per cent. Moreover, the character of the Directorates were even more contrasting. In 1698, only four of the Directors of the Old Company were merchants currently trading overseas; in the New Company Directorate there were nine-teen trading overseas.[94]

Such were the stresses and strains within the City during the 1690s: transfers abroad redistributed income within the mercantile com-munity, and the wine merchants who suffered from these redistribu-tions in particular were disproportionately active in privateering, interloping, parliamentary petitioning against the East India Company, and in investment in the two great joint-stock flotations of the early years of 'Revolution Finance'. To a certain extent, the establishment of the New East India Company in 1698 solved the problem of capital utilization in the city as trade was already recovering strongly. The return of war in 1702 did not bring with it a return of the old pres-sures on the wine merchants, for the opening in 1703 of the Iberian war theatre—so disastrous in all other respects—had the effect of distributing the largesse of remittance-induced export booms more widely within the mercantile community. Stresses and strains, at least of the kind experienced in the city during the 1690s, were prob-ably not generated during the period of the War of the Spanish Succession.

In time, it is hoped to extend the analysis for the whole period of the Wars of the Grand Alliance, that is from 1688 to 1714; for the time being, however, it is hoped that some definition has been given both to the statistical pattern and to the nature of the crisis of the 1690s, and to the fortunes of the London merchants who shouldered a vital part of the burden. Enough has been said above to demonstrate that the typology of the crisis belongs more firmly to Napoleonic than to seventeenth-century parallels. The historian meets common features at every turn. Where in the later seventeenth century the established East India Company was being discomfited by the initiative of its servants in beginning to sway the metaphorical trunks of the Indian pagoda trees, in the later eighteenth century the government was forced to intervene to limit the pillage of the fallen fruit. In the later seventeenth century it was the wine merchants who attacked the Company monopoly—partly, we have supposed, to employ their bullion balances in the Eastern trade and partly to compensate for depression in Europe. In the later eighteenth and early nineteenth centuries it was the manufacturers of Lancashire who led the ultimately successful attack on the Company's exclusive rights to the India trade so that they could dispose more easily of the expanding output of a revolutionized industry when sales prospects in England and Europe were bleak. The transfer burden was a feature common to both periods, and the dynamics engendered by the burden which lay behind the Recoinage Crisis of 1695–6 were exactly analogous to those which led to the suspension of payments, and thus of the convertibility of the pound sterling, in 1797.

In a way, survival until Ryswick was more remarkable than the settlement at Amiens. In the 1690s, no industrial revolution was *en marche* to facilitate the creation of an exchange surplus out of which the remittances could be financed; neither merchant nor administrator had any precedent to guide him in meeting the challenge of a European war. Two factors were decisive in determining the outcome: first, the agricultural revolution of the seventeenth century made England independent of foreign grain supplies—even during the dearth years of the decade; second, the progressiveness of the tax burden aided the maintenance of social stability and cohesion. If this paper is correct in its inferences, the progressiveness of the tax burden reduced wine purchases by reducing the disposable income of the landed-classes. For this reason resources were released from trade in London, and these funds aided the realization of some of the crucial innovations of 'Revolution Finance'. Not inappropriately was the foundation of the staid 'Old Lady of Threadneedle Street' materially assisted by the consequences of an interlude of enforced sobriety.

Notes

1 It is a pleasure to acknowledge my indebtedness to Professor S. H. F. Johnston of the University College of Wales, Aberystwyth, who launched my researches into late seventeenth-century economic and political history, and to Dr G. D. Ramsay, of St Edmund Hall, Oxford, who has supervised the bulk of the actual research work. I am also greatly indebted to Dr P. G. M. Dickson of St Catherine's, Oxford, for copies of his transcripts of lenders on the Land Tax for 1692–3. My wife, Margaret, has assisted me with many of the statistics quoted here, but this is only the least of my debts to her.

2 J. R. Kellett, 'The Causes and Progress of the Financial Decline of the Corporation of London' (unpublished Ph.D. thesis, University of London, 1952), pp. 341–4, and chap. 3; J. R. Kellett, 'The Breakdown of Gild Incorporation and Control over the Handicraft and Retail Trade of London', *Ec.H.R.*, 2nd Series, X (1958), 388–90; W. F. Khal, *The Development of London Livery Companies: an historical essay and a select bibliography* (Cambridge, Mass., 1960), pp. 25–6, 29; V. Pearl, *London and the Outbreak of the Puritan Revolution* (Oxford, 1961), pp. 322–8; N. G. Brett-James, *The Growth of Stuart London* (1935), *passim*; D. V. Glass, 'Socio-Economic Status and Occupations in the City of London at the End of the Seventeenth Century', in A. E. J. Hollaender and W. Kellaway, eds, *Studies in London History presented to P. E. Jones* (1969), p. 385.

I hope myself, shortly, to publish a study on the Hallage receipts in the London cloth markets: the series begins in 1562, and is virtually continuous down to the last decade of the eighteenth century.

3 P. G. M. Dickson, *The Financial Revolution in England, 1688–1756* (1967). This provides an authoritative account; the tables on pages 48, 60, 63 and 68 are particularly useful for quick reference.

4 H. R. Trevor-Roper, *Religion, The Reformation and Social Change* (1967), pp. 7–15; M. Grunwald, *Samuel Oppenheimer und sein Kreis* (Vienna, 1913), *passim*; F. Freiherr von Mensi, *Die Finanzen Osterreich von 1701–1740* (Vienna, 1890), *passim*; H. Lüthy, *La Banque Protestante en France de la revocation de l'Édit de Nantes à la Revolution* (Paris, 1949–61), I, 36–274.

5 J. B. Wolf, *The Emergence of the Great Powers, 1685–1715* (Harper Torchbook ed., New York, 1962), chap. 2; J. B. Wolf, *Louis XIV* (1968), pp. 402–45; S. B. Baxter, *William III* (1966), chaps 16 and 17; R. Hatton, *Europe in the Age of Louis XIV* (1969), pp. 91–116.

6 P. Deyon, 'La Production Manufacturière en France au XVIIᵉ siècle', *XVIIᵉ Siècle*, LXX (1966), 55, 59–60; P. Deyon, 'Variations de la Production textile aux XVIᵉ et XVIIᵉ siècles; Sources et Premiers Resultats',

Annales E.S.C., XVIII (1963), 953–4; P. Deyon, *Amiens, capitale provinciale* (Paris, 1967), pp. 162, 171–2, 537–8; R. Paris, *Histoire du commerce de Marseille*, V (Paris, 1967), pp. 568–9, 600; E. Le Roy Ladurie, *Les Paysans de Languedoc* (Paris, 1966), pp. 645–6; J. Delumeau, *L'Alun de Rome* (Paris, 1963), p. 272; H. E. S. Fisher, 'Anglo-Portuguese Trade, 1600–1770', *Ec.H.R.*, 2nd Series, XVI (1963), 219–33; P. Deane and W. A. Cole, *British Economic Growth, 1688–1959* (Cambridge, 1964), pp. 75–82. Given the greater degree of complementarity between the English and Portuguese economies than was true in the French case, it is doubtful whether France would have reaped comparable gains had the political outcome been different.

7 For a detailed account and a full bibliography, the reader is referred to: W. E. Minchinton, ed., *The Growth of English Overseas Trade in the Seventeenth and Eighteenth Centuries* (1969).

8 As this chapter is being written, a number of articles by Richard Grassby are appearing. These are based on an impressive range of business records, and clearly, the English merchant class in the seventeenth century will soon find its historians. Business records have not survived in sufficient quantity for any decade of the seventeenth century, however, to provide a basis for answering the kind of preoccupations which concern this article. For much illumination on the problem, see: R. Grassby, 'The rate of profit in seventeenth-century England', *E.H.R.*, LXXXIV (1969), pp. 721–51; and 'English merchant capitalism in the late seventeenth century: The Composition of Business Fortunes', *P. & P.*, 46 (1970), pp. 87–107.

9 Calculated from entries in W. A. Shaw, *Calendar of Treasury Books (C.T.B.)*, vols IX–XIII (1931–3); J. Dumont, *Corps Universal Diplomatique du Droit des Gens* (The Hague, 1726–31), VII (ii), VIII (i), *passim*; B.M. Lansdowne MS. 1215, fol. 62; *Commons Journals (C.J.)*, XII, 5–10, 86, 163, 165, 181, 184, 190, 194.

10 Narcissus Luttrell, 'An Abstract of the Debates Orders and Resolutions in The House of Commons . . .' (Luttrell, 'Debates'), Codrington Library, All Souls College, Oxford, MS. 158b, fols 160–1.

11 J. K. Horsefield, *British Monetary Experiments, 1650–1710* (1960); W. A. Shaw, *Calendar of Treasury Books, Introduction to Vols. XI–XVII, 1695–1702* (1934), pp. cvii–cxxviii; W. Letwin, *The Origins of Scientific Economics* (1963), pp. 64–71, 241–50; Luttrell, 'Debates' *loc. cit.*; *HMC House of Lords Manuscripts (H.L.MSS), 1690–1*, pp. 179–183, 205–7, *ibid.*, 1693–5, pp. 510–11; W. Lowndes, *A Report containing an Essay for the Amendment of the Silver Coins* (1695), pp. 42–3, 64–5. The attitude of the Commons was anticipated by Ministers in August 1692: see Sir J. Dalrymple, *Memoirs of Great Britain and Ireland* (1790 edn.), III, 264; *HMC Finch*, IV, 418.

12 *C.J.*, X, 590–1, 705; W. R. Scott, *The Constitution and Finance of English, Scottish and Irish Joint-Stock Companies to 1720* (Cambridge, 1912), II, 140, 151; R. Walcott, 'The East India Interest in the General Election of 1700–1', *E.H.R.*, LXXI (1956), 223–39.

13 S. E. Astrom, *From Cloth to Iron, The Anglo-Baltic Trade in the late seventeenth century* (Helsinki, 1963), pp. 204–9.

14 Narcissus Luttrell, *A Brief Historical Relation of State Affairs* (1877), III, 136–45, 150, 156, 287–8; A. C. Wood, *A History of The Levant Company* (Oxford, 1935, reprinted 1964), pp. 111–12.

15 *H.L.MSS, 1695–97*, pp. 64, 76–80.

16 For a treatment of the transfer problem see J. E. Meade, *The Theory of International Economic Policy* (1962 ed.), I, 87–93, 144–8; F. Machlup; *International Monetary Economics* (1966): see in particular the essay on 'The Transfer Problem: Theme and Four Variations', pp. 374–95, Gottfried Haberler, *A Survey of International Trade Theory* (Princeton, 1961), pp. 30–51.

17 Bank of England, Secretary's Office, Court Minute Book A, esp. fols 75–6, 171, 177–8; *ibid.*, B, fols 13–4; Supplementary Ledger to the General Ledger, vol. I, fols 26–7, 117, 144.

18 J. G. van Dillen, *Mensen en achtergronden, Studies uitgegeven ter gelegenheid van de tachtigste verjaardag van de schrijver* (Groningen, 1964), pp. 382–4, 411–12; Sir J. Craig, *The Mint* (Cambridge, 1953), pp. 416–17.

19 J. G. Posthumus, *Inquiry into the History of Prices in Holland* (Leyden, 1946), I, 593–5; Horsefield, *op. cit.*, pp. 254–5; J. E. Thorold Rogers, *The First Nine Years of the Bank of England* (1887), pp. 165–8.

20 This has been inferred by comparing turnover data collected from the port books with assessment data which indicate comparative wealth. For detailed references, see notes 30 and 81 below. Merchant bill sales to the Bank are found in the sources cited above under note 17.

21 Since between 1672 and 1698 sub-totals of customs collected in London are given for 'domestic exports', 'plantation goods', 'wine and vinegar' and for imports not included in either of these latter categories, it has been possible to apply multipliers to these yield figures to derive estimates for manufactured imports and domestic exports. These estimates provide tolerable substitutes for more comprehensive trade statistics. The multipliers were calculated from PRO Customs 3/1 where customs yield is recorded side by side with trade totals. The yield figures are found in Shaw's introductions to the *C.T.B.*; his figures have been supplemented from PRO AO/756–60, and E/351. It should be remembered that on average roughly £250,000–350,000 p.a. of the import reduction in the 1690s was attributable to the reduction of East India Company imports. Totals of wine imports come from *C.J.*, XVII, 363–5.

22 E 190/126/I; 136/6; 140/7; 144/1; 149/9; 150/5; 156/5; 159/1.

23 *Statutes of the Realm*, 1. Wm. & M. c. 34; 2. Wm. & M. Sess. 2, c. 14; 4. Wm. & M. c. 25.

24 I hope to present the full evidence elsewhere.

25 E.g., *C.T.B.*, XI, 47, 73, 161, 263, 298, 299, 330, 345; XII, 4, 32, 44, 52.

26 Dickson, *op. cit.*, pp. 306, 311; and see E 406/54, fols 73, 81v., 88, 89, 91, 95, 109, 110, 114, 136, 147, 173, 236, 241, 339.

27 Details on the letter of denization and acts of naturalization are found in W. A. Shaw, ed., *Letters of Denization and Acts of Naturalisation for Aliens in England and Ireland, 1603-1700* (Huguenot Society of London Publications, XVIII, 1911). Import port books for the 1680s have been carefully combed to eliminate the possibility that these foreign houses had merely switched their activities out of imports into exports.

28 PRO, CO 388/II/76; Luttrell, 'Debates', MS. 158b, fols 118, 268, 281, 366.

29 India Office Library (I.O.L.), Court Minutes XXXV, fols 133-4; XXXVI, fol. 49; Home Miscellaneous, XXXVI, fols 131-41, 185, 227, 243, 349, 443, 459.

30 This section is based on the compilation of detailed commercial biographies of nearly 2,000 merchants from E 190/158/1, 157/1, 150/1.

31 F. Atkinson, ed., *Some Aspects of the Eighteenth Century Woollen and Worsted trade in Halifax* (Halifax, 1956), pp. xii–xvi, 34, 38, 39-40; Doncaster Museum, Papers of Matthew Frank.

32 See note 30. Quantity data derived from the port books have been multiplied by valuations for 1698 in Customs 3/1-2.

33 See Shaw, *Letters of Denization*, III, 224, for Peter Meyer's naturalization on 24 December 1691, and p. 228 for that of John Henry Berenburg, 4 March 1693.

34 R. Davis, 'English Foreign Trade, 1660-1700', *Ec.H.R.*, 2nd Series, VI (1954), 150-66, 164-6; Astrom, *op. cit.*, p. 175.

35 Corporation of London Record Office (C.L.R.O.), Common Sergeant's Book (C.S.B.), IV, fol. 196v., Inventory Box 25.

36 *Ibid.*, V, fol. 229, box 44.

37 *Ibid.*, VI, fol. 135v., box 50. The same generalizations could be made about the affairs of John Jolliffe: see *ibid.*, IV, fol. 113v., box 21.

38 *Ibid.*, IV, fol. 268, box 29, and V, fol. 18v., box 31; J. M. Price, 'Multilateralism and/or Bilateralism: the Settlement of British Trade Balances with the North, c. 1700', *Ec.H.R.*, 2nd Series, XIV (1961), 254-74; Astrom, *op. cit.*, pp. 77-122. The same pattern emerges from the affairs of Henry Phill: PRO C 111/127.

39 C.S.B. V, fol. 157v., box 40

40 *Ibid.*, fol. 150v., box 40.

41 *Ibid.*, fol. 24, box 32.

42 *Ibid.*, fol. 35v., box 37.

43 See pages 342–5.

44 Such information would have been provided by Nathaniel Herne's inventory but his net share in partnership with Joseph Herne was paid over to the executors *en bloc* with no details given: see C.S.B. IV, fol. 98, box 21.

45 *Ibid.*, fol. 278v., box 29; *ibid.*, V, fol. 185, box 42; *ibid.*, fol. 86v., box 37. See also the inventory of Benjamin Whichcote, *ibid.*, fol. 204v., box 43.

46 E 190/152/1.

47 C.S.B., VI, fol. 114v.

48 E 190/152/1.

49 The hallage averages are £18,707 in the 1680s; £20,914 in the 1690s. This amounts to nearly a 12 per cent increase.

50 H. E. S. Fisher, *op. cit.*, p. 152, n. 5; P. Vilar, *La Catalogne dans L'Espagne moderne* (Paris, 1962), I, 650–3.

51 *H.L.MSS, 1688–90*, no. 134, pp. 250–3; PRO, CO 388/3/fol. 186 provides a graphic account of the problems of the wine trade—even during the years of recovery in 1693 and 1694. Wine prices have been collected from the archives of the Duke of Bedford in the Bedfordshire County Record Office.

52 John Houghton, F.R.S., *A Collection for Improvement of Husbandry and Trade* (1692–1703), 15 June 1694.

53 Dickson, *op. cit.*, offers the most recent and the most authoritative account.

54 These thirty-eight merchants comprise a group of businessmen whose affairs can be studied in depth from inventories in either the Orphans Court in C.L.R.O. or those drawn up of the Directors of the South Sea Company and printed as *Inventories of the Estates of the South Sea Directors of 1720* (1721). It should be noted that when in the text a sample is referred to, then only the affairs of the twenty-eight merchants whose estates are inventorized in the Orphans Court of the City Corporation are concerned.

55 See *Inventories of the Estates*.

56 As explained in note 54 this sample consists of the affairs of thirty-eight merchants whose inventories are found in the City's Orphans Court. Conclusions drawn from such a narrow sample must be treated with some caution; here it has been possible to verify them in many respects by comparison with the results of other analyses pursued in the more comprehensive Exchequer records. Given the state of the evidence, it is inevitable that conclusions emerge not from individual samples which are themselves satisfactory, but from the convergent indications of different sources which may, individually, be less than satisfactory. The total passive investment in our sample amounts to £212,808.

57 H. J. Habakkuk, 'English Landownership 1680–1740', *Ec.H.R.*, X (1940), 1–17; H. J. Habakkuk, 'The English Land Market in the Eighteenth Century', in J. S. Bromley and E. H. Kossmann, eds, *Britain and the Netherlands* (1960), pp. 154–73; H. J. Habakkuk, 'La disparation du paysan anglais', *Annales E.S.C.*, XX (1965), 649–63; F. M. L. Thompson, 'Landownership and Economic Growth in England in the Eighteenth century', in E. L. Jones and S. J. Woolf, eds, *Agrarian Change and Economic Development* (1969), pp. 41–60.

58 The evidence is well summarized in W. A. Speck, 'Conflict in Society', in G. Holmes, ed., *Britain after the Glorious Revolution, 1688–1714* (1969), esp. pp. 138–40, 147; G. Holmes, *British Politics in the Age of Anne* (1967), chap. 5; O. R. F. Davies, 'The Wealth and Influence of John Holles, Duke of Newcastle, 1694–1711', *Renaissance and Modern Studies*, IX (1965), 22–46.

59 Evidence of land-holding is contained in a third of the Orphans Court Inventories used here as our 'sample'. The personalty alone was inventorized, but land-holdings are indirectly indicated by rent payments made after the merchant's death to the executors which in turn they accounted for to the Common Sergeant. Thomas Pitt offers an instructive example of a merchant seeking landed investment and of the difficulties experienced in finding a suitable estate: see Col. Henry Yule, ed., *The Diary of William Hedges, III* (Hakluyt Society, 1889), pp. xcviii, cxii, cxlviii; *HMC Fortescue*, I, 15, 32, 34, 41, 42; PRO C 110/28, Dolben to Pitt, 20 November 1708.

60 C.L.R.O., Cash Account 1/23 fols 75–93v., for City's land-holdings; GL, MSS 5854, 11,571, and 10,127 for the Fishmongers', Grocers', and Bishopric of London property respectively; GL MS. 12,819 and *Parliamentary Papers*, XIX (1840), part I, for Christ's Hospital; GLCRO H 1/ST/E29/6 for St Thomas's; archives of St Bartholomew's Hospital are preserved at the hospital. Access was granted to the records of the following Great Livery Companies preserved at their respective halls: Mercers, Vintners, Skinners, Clothworkers, Haberdashers, Goldsmiths, Merchant Taylors and the Drapers; an estimate was made for the Ironmongers and the Salters on the basis of information in *Parliamentary Papers*, XXXIX (1884). The basis for the total of houses in the city was furnished by: P. Mills and J. Oliver, *The Survey of Building Sites in the City of London after the Great Fire of 1666* (eds, P. E. Jones and T. F. Reddaway, 1962–7), I, ix.

61 Mills and Oliver, *op. cit.*, I, xxxi–xxxii and index. These conclusions are further supported by details of subletting contained in the records of the Goldsmiths' Company, and by the policy registers of the Hand in Hand Insurance Company: see GL, MS. 8674.

62 For John Blunt see *Inventories of the Estates*.

63 De Laune, *The Present State of London* (1690 edn), p. 353; cited by Kellett, 'The Causes and Progress', p. 208, n. 3.

64 P. E. Jones, ed., *The Fire Court*, pp. xvi–xix.

65 Calculated according to the formula for annuities—certain immediate.

66 John Woolfe inventory, C.L.R.O., C.S.B., V, fol. 162, box 41.

67 Vansittart inventory, *loc. cit.*

68 Lawrence Stone, *The Crisis of the Aristocracy, 1558–1641* (Oxford, 1965), pp. 536–8; D. C. Coleman, 'London Scriveners and the Estate Market in the later seventeenth century', *Ec.H.R.*, 2nd series, IV (1951–2), 221–30.

69 Of the total lending represented in the sample, £225,808 can be identified as lent by Londoners. Here the most important categories comprised the overseas trading merchants (£46,048); lawyers and bureaucrats (£76,341); West End gentlemen (£17,543); and widows (£18,421).

70 D. M. Joslin, 'London Private Bankers, 1720–1785', *Ec.H.R.*, 2nd series, VII (1954), 167–86.

71 'Non-freehold' because we have excluded evidence of such land-holdings from the sample. It is impossible to be certain whether rent payments accounted for by the executors relate to a calendar year; given this uncertainty, rent receipts cannot be capitalized with confidence.

72 Annuities, as in the case of leases, are calculated at present values.

73 Some 25 per cent of the assets in the sample relate to merchants who died in peacetime.

74 E 228/1991–2; C.L.R.O. MSS 40/47, 40/57, 40/52, 40/55.

75 Bank of England, Secretary's Office, Subscription Book for Original Stock 1694; I.O.L., Parchment Records, Subscription to Capital 1698.

76 K. G. Davies, 'Joint Stock Investment in later seventeenth century', *Ec.H.R.*, 2nd Series, IV (1952), 283–301; Dickson, *op. cit.*, esp. chaps 18 and 20.

77 Bank of England, Secretary's Office, Bank Stock Alphabet to Subscription of 1697; Original Subscription to Capital 1697.

78 Dickson, *op. cit.*, p. 459.

79 PRO, C 110/28: Dolben to Pitt, 20 October 1708.

80 PRO, Customs 2/1, 3/1–2.

81 Assessments made under 5 Wm and Mary, c. 1: see C.L.R.O., Assessment Boxes 4, 6, 9, 11, 15, 17, 22, 35, 36, 38.

82 See above p. 326.

83 PRO, H.C.A. 30/774; *ibid.*, 26/1–3.

84 For a necessarily covert activity, a surprising amount of hard information can be gleaned about interloping. For the campaign of the mid-1690s the sources used were I.O.L., Despatches to India, IX and X; Original Correspondence, number 6538; India Office Transcripts from Factory Records, XXIII; Letters from Fort St George; Records of Fort St

George; Factory Records, Surat V; Factory Records, Fort St George; Home Miscellaneous, XXXVI; PRO, H.C.A. 26/3, E 190/152/1; PC 2/75; BM Add. MS. 17477, fols 53–6; *CSPD, 1699–1700*, pp. 171, 177; *CSPD, Colonial Series, America and the West Indies, 1699*, nos 247 and 343; *C.J.*, XI, *passim*.

85 *H.L.MSS 1695–97*, pp. 32–3. These petitioners can be classified as follows: unknown—John Albertson, John Baskett, Francis Annesley 'old East India hands'—Edward Littleton, Nicholas Waite, Streynsham Master, Thomas Lucas; Tobacco merchants—Peter Paggen; Mediterranean merchants—Robert Atwood, Edmund Harrison, John Wright; Baltic merchants—William Benson, Nathaniel Gould, Gilbert Heathcote (who also had extensive connexions with the sugar trades), Joseph Martin, Joseph Woolfe and John Cary; Turkey merchant—P. Riaulx; Wine importers—Benjamin Rokeby, Adam Bellamy, Samuel Locke, Samuel Shepheard, Arthur Shallett, Peter Godfrey, Abraham Beake, John Lloyd, John Shipman and Peter Albert. John Fentzell and Richard Harrison, who were in partnership as silk importers, are also associated with the Iberian markets to which they dispatched considerable exports. Strictly non-mercantile were Edward Darell, Richard Chiswell and George White, although the last represented the interests of 'Siamese' White who had been in the Company's service in the East.

86 A wealth of information on these questions is contained in: Col. H. Yule, ed., *The Diary of William Hedges*; Sir R. C. Temple, ed., *The Diaries of Streynsham Master, 1675–1680* (2 vols, Indian Records Series, 1911); Sir C. Fawcett, ed., *The English Factories in India* (New Series, 4 vols, Oxford, 1936–55).

87 See note 85.

88 Based on an analysis of a list of interlopers proceeded against by the Company in I.O.L., Home Miscellaneous, XXIII: Committee of Law Suits.

89 Names in PRO, CO 77/16 and Bodl., Rawlinson MS. C 449. Sources used for the interloping and parliamentary activity of this group are largely identical with those cited in note 84; in addition, Luttrell, 'Debates', and Bodl. Rawlinson MS. C 449 are particularly useful.

90 In relation to the condition of the wine trade in general, and of the Iberian trade in particular during these years, the high levels of wine imports, while fairly indicative of a high degree of utilization, need not be synonymous with prosperity. For some interesting allusions to the difficulties of the wine trade in these years see R. Gravil, 'Trading to Spain and Portugal 1670–1700', *Business History*, X (1968), 78–81; for mounting protectionism in Portugal, see V. N. Godinho, 'Le Portugal; les flottes du sucre et les flottes de l'or', *Annales E.S.C.* (1950), 186–7.

91 PRO CO 388/9/43–6.

92 *C.J.*, X, 705.

93 I.O.L., Court Minutes XXXV, fols 178–98, Turnover of stock 10 March–
25 September 1693; *C.J.*, X, 740; *H.L.MSS, 1695–7*, p. 33.

94 Stock Lists in I.O.L., Home Miscellaneous, vols II and III and Parchment Records; Names of Directors in Court Minutes for Old Company,
and in the Charter of 1698 for the New: see *Charters Granted to the East
India Company from 1601* (1774), pp. 193–4.

Index